Sources of
THE MAKING OF THE WEST

PEOPLES AND CULTURES

Third Edition

Volume II: Since 1500

Sources of
THE MAKING OF THE WEST

PEOPLES AND CULTURES

Third Edition

Volume II: Since 1500

KATHARINE J. LUALDI
University of Southern Maine

BEDFORD/ST. MARTIN'S   Boston ◆ New York

For Bedford/St. Martin's

Publisher for History: Mary V. Dougherty
Director of Development for History: Jane Knetzger
Developmental Editor: Kathryn Abbott
Editorial Assistant: Alix Roy
Senior Production Supervisor: Dennis J. Conroy
Executive Marketing Manager: Jenna Bookin Barry
Project Management: DeMasi Design and Publishing Services
Text Design: Wanda Kossak
Cover Design: Donna Lee Dennison
*Cover Art: Andre Gide and His Friends at the Moorish Coffeehouse of the Universal
     Exhibition of 1900* by Jacques Emile Blanche (1861–1942). Canvas, 1900. Musée
     des Beaux-Arts, Rouen, France. Erich Lessing/Art Resource, NY.
Composition: LinMark Design
Printing and Binding: RR Donnelley & Sons Company

President: Joan E. Feinberg
Editorial Director: Denise B. Wydra
Director of Marketing: Karen Melton Soeltz
Director of Editing, Design, and Production: Marcia Cohen
Manager, Publishing Services: Emily Berleth

Library of Congress Control Number: 2007925246

For information, write: Bedford/St. Martin's, 75 Arlington Street, Boston, MA 02116
(617-399-4000)

ISBN-10: 0-312-46518-1
ISBN-13: 978-0-312-46518-6

Acknowledgments

Preface

Compiled specifically to accompany *The Making of the West: Peoples and Cultures,* Third Edition, *Sources of The Making of the West* is intended to help instructors bring the history of Western civilization to life for their students. The newly expanded collection is organized chapter by chapter to parallel *The Making of the West,* Third Edition, and offers instructors many opportunities to promote classroom discussion of primary documents and their connection to historical analysis and interpretation. This new edition contains more visual sources and at least five written documents per chapter that complement the thematic and chronological framework of the textbook and highlight the intellectual, emotional, and visual landscapes of many different peoples. Thus, the reader helps reveal that the study of history is not fixed but is an ongoing process of evaluation and interpretation.

I selected the sources for *Sources of The Making of the West,* Third Edition, both to reflect historians' changing understanding of Western civilization and to underscore the continued relevance of more conventional written sources. Thus, several new traditional political sources are included in the collection; these are enhanced by documents illuminating not only social and cultural life but also Europe's increasing connection to the world beyond its borders. Women and minorities are often underappreciated for their roles in shaping the course of Western history, and this volume offers both a special place in the selection process. In Chapter 14, for example, students encounter three documents about the Spanish conquest of the Americas. From Bernal Díaz del Castillo (Document 1), they can read of the conquest from the perspective of a soldier in the Spanish army. *Lienzo de Tlaxcala* (Document 2) offers an illustrated view of the conquest from a native perspective. Finally, students encounter an excerpt from the Spaniard Bartolomé de Las Casas (Document 3) calling for the humane treatment of Amerindians.

Of course asking the right questions and finding the right answers is at the heart of the "doing" of history. For this reason, *Sources of The Making of the West,* Third Edition, begins with a revised introduction on how to interpret written and visual primary sources that leads students step by step through the process of historical analysis. A brief overview of what this process entails is followed by an extended discussion of the process at work in the analysis of two sources drawn specifically from this collection. I adopted this integrated approach for the introduction to help students move easily from abstract concepts to concrete examples. As a result, the introduction does not rely on telling students what to do but rather on showing them how to do it for themselves based on the raw data of history.

The inclusion of additional visual primary sources adds an exciting dimension to students' ability to see and interpret the past. These sources visually enrich traditional written documents while challenging students to read the past in new ways. Along with training their minds to analyze texts for meaning, students learn to view images as an equally valuable window into the past. For example, the visual source chosen for Chapter 24 in Volume II (Document 6), which depicts an idealized family featured in a pamphlet of the Eugenics Education Society of London at the turn of the twentieth century, speaks clearly to the philosophy and goals of the eugenics movement in the early 1900s. Similarly, the visual source for Chapter 3 in Volume I (Document 5) provides an overhead view of a Greek house and asks students to analyze the division of domestic space into male and female domains. Throughout the collection, I chose written and nonwritten sources that fit together to elucidate important events and opinions of specific historical eras.

Each source was also selected based on its accessibility and appeal to students. For this reason, when necessary, I have carefully edited documents to speak to specific themes without impairing the documents' overall sense and tone. I have also included documents of varying lengths to increase their utility for both short class exercises and outside writing assignments.

To assist students with their journey into the past, each chapter opens with a summary that situates the sources within the broader historical context and addresses their relationship to one another and to the main themes in the corresponding chapter of *The Making of the West*. An explanatory headnote accompanies each source to provide fundamental background information on the author or artist and the source while highlighting its significance. Revised and expanded discussion questions help students examine key points and issues in greater depth. Finally, each chapter concludes with at least four comparative questions intended to encourage students to see both the harmony and discordance among the sources. Although these editorial features intentionally strengthen the coherence of each chapter as a unit, they also allow instructors to choose sources and questions that best suit their specific goals and methods.

Acknowledgments

Many people deserve thanks for helping to bring this third edition to fruition. First among them are the authors of *The Making of the West*. Many thanks as well to the reviewers who provided valuable insights and suggestions: Megan Armstrong, Mc-Master University; Elizabeth Jane Dennison, University of Alaska–Anchorage; David D. Flaten, Tompkins Cortland Community College; Helen Grady, Springside School; Ginger Guardiola, Colorado State University; David B. Hollander, Iowa State University; John M. Hunt, Ohio State University; Ronald Huch, Eastern Kentucky University; Elizabeth A. Lehfeldt, Cleveland State University; Keith P. Luria, North Carolina State University; John Moser, Ashland University; Johanna Moyer, Miami University–Ohio; Michelle Anne Novak, Houston Community College; Christopher Ohan, American University–Kuwait; Eli Rubin, Western Michigan University; Enrique A. Sanabria, University of New Mexico; David Stone, Kansas State University; Carol Symes, University of Illinois; Laura Talamante, Loyola Marymount University; and Theodore R. Weeks, Southern Illinois University.

I would also like to thank Mary Miller, Diana Magaloni Kerpel, Mack Holt, Anne Thayer, Jeannine Uzzi, and Christine Holden for their editorial assistance. Once again, I also owe thanks to Ashley Waddell for her help in selecting and editing several of the new documents included in Volume II.

Contents

Sources of
THE MAKING OF THE WEST

PEOPLES AND CULTURES

Third Edition

Volume II: Since 1500

Introduction: Working with Historical Sources

The long history of Western Civilization encompasses a broad range of places and cultures. Textbooks provide an essential chronological and thematic framework for understanding the formation of the West as a cultural and geographical entity. Yet the process of historical inquiry extends beyond textbook narratives into the thoughts, words, images, and experiences of people living at the time. Primary sources expose this world so that you can observe, analyze, and interpret the past as it unfolds before you. History is thus not a static collection of facts and dates. Rather, it is an ongoing attempt to make sense of the past and its relationship to the present through the lens of both written and visual primary sources.

Sources of The Making of the West, Third Edition, provides this lens for you, with a wide range of engaging sources — from a Mesopotamian epic to a political cartoon of the Old Regime to firsthand accounts of student revolts. When combined, the sources reflect historians' growing appreciation of the need to examine Western civilization from different conceptual angles — political, social, cultural, economic — and geographic viewpoints. The composite picture that emerges reveals a variety of historical experiences shaping each era from both within and outside of Europe's borders. Furthermore, the documents here demonstrate that the most historically significant of these experiences are not always those of people in formal positions of power. Men and women from all walks of life have also influenced the course of Western history.

The sources in this reader were selected with an eye to their ability not only to capture the multifaceted dimensions of the past but also to ignite your intellectual curiosity. Each written and visual document is a unique product of human endeavor and as such is often colored by the personal concerns, biases, and objectives of the author or artist. Among the most exciting challenges facing you is to sift through these nuances to discover what they reveal about the source and its broader historical context.

Interpreting Written Sources

Understanding a written document and its connection to larger historical issues depends on knowing which questions to ask and how to find the right answers. The following six questions will guide you through this process of discovery. Like

1

a detective, you will begin by piecing together basic facts and then move on to more complex levels of analysis. You should keep these questions in mind every time you read a document, no matter how long or how short.

1. Who wrote this document, when, and where?

The "doing" of history depends on historical records, the existence of which in turn depends on the individuals who composed them in a particular time and place and with specific goals in mind. Therefore before you can begin to understand a document and its significance, you need to determine who wrote it, and when and where it was written. Ultimately, this information will shape your interpretation because the language of documents often reflects the author's social and/or political status as well as the norms of the society in which the author lived.

2. What type of document is this?

Because all genres have their own defining characteristics, identifying the type of document at hand is vital to elucidating its purpose and meaning. For example, in content and organization, an account of a saint's life looks very different from an imperial edict, which in turn looks very different from a trial record. Each document type follows certain rules of composition that shape what authors say and how they say it.

3. Who is the intended audience of the document?

The type or genre of a source often goes hand in hand with the intended audience. For instance, popular songs in the vernacular are designed to reach people across the socioeconomic spectrum whereas papal bulls written in Latin are directed to a tiny, educated and predominantly male elite. Moreover, an author often crafts the style and content of a source to appeal to a particular audience and to enhance the effectiveness of his or her message.

4. What are the main points of this document?

All primary sources contain stories whether in numbers, words, and/or images. Before you can begin to analyze their meanings, you need to have a good command of a document's main points. For this reason, while reading, you should mark words, phrases, and passages that strike you as particularly important to create visual and mental markers that will help you navigate the document. Don't worry about mastering all of the details; you can work through them later, once you have sketched out the basic content.

5. Why was this document written?

The simplicity of this question masks the complexity of the possible answers. Historical records are never created in a vacuum; they were produced for a reason, whether public or private, pragmatic or fanciful. Some sources will state outright why they were created whereas others will not. Yet with or without direct cues, you should look for less obvious signs of the author's intent and strategies for success, as reflected in word choice, for example, or the way in which a point is communicated.

6. What does this document reveal about the particular society and period in question?

This question strikes at the heart of historical analysis and interpretation. In its use of language, its structure, and its biases and assumptions, every source opens a window onto its author and time period. Teasing out its deeper significance will allow you to assess the value of a source and to articulate what it adds to our understanding of the historical context in which it is embedded. Thus, as you begin to analyze a source fully, your own interpretive voice will assume center stage.

As you work through each of these questions, you will progress from identifying the basic content of a document to inferring its broader meanings. At its very heart, the study of primary sources centers on the interplay between "facts" and interpretation. To help you engage in this interplay, let us take a concrete example of a historical document. Read it carefully, guided by the questions outlined above. In this way, you will gain insight into this particular text while training yourself in interpreting written primary sources in general.

1.

Legislating Tolerance

Henry I, *Edict of Nantes* (1598)

The promulgation of the Edict of Nantes in 1598 by King Henry IV (r. 1589–1610) marked the end of the French Wars of Religion by recognizing French Protestants as a legally protected religious minority. Drawing largely on earlier edicts of pacification, the Edict of Nantes *was composed of ninety-two general articles, fifty-six secret articles, and two royal warrants. The two series of articles represented the edict proper and were registered by the highest courts of law in the realm (parlements). The following excerpts from the general articles reveal the triumph of political concerns over religious conformity on the one hand, and the limitations of religious tolerance in early modern France on the other.*

Henry, by the grace of God, King of France, and Navarre, to all present, and to come, greeting. Among the infinite mercies that it has pleased God to bestow upon

---

From English text of "The Edict" as in Edmund Everard, *The Great Pressures and Grievances of the Protestants in France*, London, 1681, appendix 4 in Roland Mousnier, *The Assassination of Henry IV*, trans. Joan Spencer (London: Faber and Faber, 1973), 316–47.

us, that most signal and remarkable is, his having given us power and strength not to yield to the dreadful troubles, confusions, and disorders, which were found at our coming to this kingdom, divided into so many parties and factions, that the most legitimate was almost the least, enabling us with constancy in such manner to oppose the storm, as in the end to surmount it, now reaching a part of safety and repose for this state . . . For the general difference among our good subjects, and the particular evils of the soundest parts of the state, we judged might be easily cured, after the principal cause (the continuation of civil war) was taken away. In which having, by the blessing of God, well and happily succeeded, all hostility and wars through the kingdom being now ceased, we hope that we will succeed equally well in other matters remaining to be settled, and that by this means we shall arrive at the establishment of a good peace, with tranquility and rest. . . . Among our said affairs . . . one of the principal has been the complaints we have received from many of our Catholic provinces and cities, that the exercise of the Catholic religion was not universally re-established, as is provided by edicts or statutes heretofore made for the pacification of the troubles arising from religion; as well as the supplications and remonstrances which have been made to us by our subjects of the Reformed religion, regarding both the non-fulfillment of what has been granted by the said former laws, and that which they desired to be added for the exercise of their religion, the liberty of their consciences and the security of their persons and fortunes; presuming to have just reasons for desiring some enlargement of articles, as not being without great apprehensions, because their ruin has been the principal pretext and original foundation of the late wars, troubles, and commotions. Now not to burden us with too much business at once, as also that the fury of war was not compatible with the establishment of laws, however good they might be, we have hitherto deferred from time to time giving remedy herein. But now that it has pleased God to give us a beginning of enjoying some rest, we think we cannot employ ourself better than to apply to that which may tend to the glory and service of His holy name, and to provide that He may be adored and prayed unto by all our subjects: and if it has not yet pleased Him to permit it to be in one and the same form of religion, that it may at the least be with one and the same intention, and with such rules that may prevent among them all troubles and tumults. . . . For this cause, we have upon the whole judged it necessary to give to all our said subjects one general law, clear, pure, and absolute, by which they shall be regulated in all differences which have heretofore risen among them, or may hereafter rise, wherewith the one and other may be contented, being framed according as the time requires: and having had no other regard in this deliberation than solely the zeal we have to the service of God, praying that He would from this time forward render to all our subjects a durable and established peace. . . . We have by this edict or statute perpetual and irrevocable said, declared, and ordained, saying, declaring, and ordaining;

That the memory of all things passed on the one part and the other, since the beginning of the month of March, 1585 until our coming to the crown, and also during the other preceding troubles, and the occasion of the same, shall remain extinguished and suppressed, as things that had never been. . . .

We prohibit to all our subjects of whatever state and condition they be, to renew the memory thereof, to attack, resent, injure, or provoke one another by reproaches for what is past, under any pretext or cause whatsoever, by disputing, contesting, quarrelling, reviling, or offending by factious words; but to contain themselves, and live peaceably together as brethren, friends, and fellow-citizens, upon penalty for acting to the contrary, to be punished for breakers of peace, and disturbers of the public quiet.

We ordain, that the Catholic religion shall be restored and re-established in all places and quarters of this kingdom and country under our obedience, and where the exercise of the same has been interrupted, to be there again, peaceably and freely exercised without any trouble or impediment. . . .

And not to leave any occasion of trouble and difference among our subjects, we have permitted and do permit to those of the Reformed religion, to live and dwell in all the cities and places of this our kingdom and countries under our obedience, without being inquired after, vexed, molested, or compelled to do any thing in religion, contrary to their conscience. . . .

We permit also to those of the said religion to hold, and continue the exercise of the same in all the cities and places under our obedience, where it was by them established and made public at several different times, in the year 1586, and in 1597.

In like manner the said exercise may be established, and re-established in all the cities and places where it has been established or ought to be by the Statute of Pacification, made in the year 1577 . . .

We prohibit most expressly to all those of the said religion, to hold any exercise of it . . . except in places permitted and granted in the present edict. An also not to exercise the said religion in our court, nor in our territories and countries beyond the mountains, nor in our city of Paris, nor within five leagues of the said city. . . .

We prohibit all preachers, readers, and others who speak in public, to use any words, discourse, or propositions tending to excite the people to sedition; and we enjoin them to contain and comport themselves modestly, and to say nothing which shall not be for the instruction and edification of the listeners, and maintaining the peace and tranquility established by us in our said kingdom. . . .

They [French Protestants] shall also be obliged to keep and observe the festivals of the Catholic Church, and shall not on the same days work, sell, or keep open shop, nor likewise the artisans shall not work out of their shops, in their chambers or houses privately on the said festivals, and other days forbidden, of any trade, the noise whereof may be heard outside by those that pass by, or by the neighbors. . . .

We ordain, that there shall not be made any difference or distinction upon the account of the said religion, in receiving scholars to be instructed in the universities, colleges, or schools, nor of the sick or poor into hospitals, sick houses or public almshouses. . . .

We will and ordain, that all those of the Reformed religion, and others who have followed their party, of whatever state, quality or condition they be, shall be obliged and constrained by all due and reasonable ways, and under the penalties contained in the said edict or statute relating thereunto, to pay tithes to the curates, and other ecclesiastics, and to all others to whom they shall appertain. . . .

To the end to re-unite so much the better the minds and good will of our subjects, as is our intention, and to take away all complaints for the future; we declare all those who make or shall make profession of the said Reformed religion, to be capable of holding and exercising all estates, dignities, offices, and public charges whatsoever. . . .

We declare all sentences, judgments, procedures, seizures, sales, and decrees made and given against those of the Reformed religion, as well living as dead, from the death of the deceased King Henry the Second our most honored Lord and father in law, upon the occasion of the said religion, tumults and troubles since happening, as also the execution of the same judgments and decrees, from henceforward canceled, revoked, and annulled. . . .

Those also of the said religion shall depart and desist henceforward from all practices, negotiations, and intelligences, as well within as without our kingdom; and the said assemblies and councils established within the provinces, shall readily separate, and also all the leagues and associations made or to be made under any pretext, to the prejudice of our present edict, shall be cancelled and annulled, . . . prohibiting most expressly to all our subjects to make henceforth any assessments or levies of money, fortifications, enrollments of men, congregations and assemblies of other than such as are permitted by our present edict, and without arms. . . .

We give in command to the people of our said courts of parlement, chambers of our courts, and courts of our aids, bailiffs, chief-justices, provosts and other of our justices and officers to whom it appertains, and to their lieutenants, that they cause to be read, published, and registered this present edict and ordinance in their courts and jurisdictions, and the same keep punctually, and the contents of the same to cause to be enjoined and used fully and peaceably to all those to whom it shall belong, ceasing and making to cease all troubles and obstructions to the contrary, for such is our pleasure: and in witness hereof we have signed these presents with our own hand; and to the end to make it a thing firm and stable for ever, we have caused to put and endorse our seal to the same. Given at *Nantes* in the month of April in the year of Grace 1598, and of our reign the ninth.

Signed

HENRY

1. Who wrote this document, when, and where?

Many documents will not answer these questions directly; therefore, you will have to look elsewhere for clues. In this case, however, the internal evidence is clear. The author is Henry IV, king of France and Navarre, who issued the document in the French town of Nantes in 1598. Aside from the appearance of his name in the edict, there are other, less explicit, markers of his identity. He uses the first person plural ("we") when referring to himself, a grammatical choice that both signals and accentuates his royal stature.

2. What type of document is this?

In this source, you do not have to look far for an answer to this question. Henry IV describes the document as an "edict," "statute," or "law." These words reveal the public and official nature of the document, echoing their use in our own society today. Even if you do not know exactly what an edict, statute, or law meant in late sixteenth-century terms, the document itself points the way: "we [Henry IV] have upon the whole, judged it necessary to give to all our subjects one general law, clear, pure, and absolute. . . ." Now you know that the document is a body of law issued by King Henry IV in 1598, which helps to explain its formality as well as the predominance of legal language.

3. Who is the intended audience of the document?

The formal and legalistic language of the edict suggest that Henry IV's immediate audience is not the general public but rather some form of political and/or legal body. The final paragraph supports this conclusion. Here Henry IV commands the "people of our said courts of parlement, chambers of our courts, and courts of our aids, bailiffs, chief-justices, provosts, and other of our justices and officers. . ." to read and publish the edict. Reading between the lines, you can detect a mixture of power and dependency in Henry IV's tone. Look carefully at his verb choice throughout the edict: *prohibit, ordain, will, declare, command*. Each of these verbs casts Henry IV as the leader and the audience as his followers. This strategy was essential because the edict would be nothing but empty words without the courts' compliance. Imagine for a moment that Henry IV was not the king of France but rather a soldier writing a letter to his wife or a merchant preparing a contract. In either case, the language chosen would have changed to suit the genre and audience. Thus, identifying the relationship between author and audience can help you to understand both what the document does and does not say.

4. What are the main points of this document?

To answer this question, you should start with the preamble, for it explains why the edict was issued in the first place: to replace the "frightful troubles, confusions, and disorders" in France with "one general law . . . by which they [our subjects] might be regulated in all differences which have heretofore risen among them, or may hereafter rise. . . ." But what differences specifically? Even with no knowledge of the circumstances surrounding the formulation of the edict, you should notice the numerous references to "the Catholic religion" and "the Reformed religion." With this in mind, read the preamble again. Here we learn that

Henry IV had received complaints from Catholic provinces and cities and from Protestants ("our subjects of the Reformed religion") regarding the exercise of their respective religions. Furthermore, as the text continues, since "it has pleased God to give us a beginning of enjoying some rest, we think we cannot employ ourself better than to apply to that which may tend to the glory and service of His holy name, and to provide that He may be adored and prayed unto by all our said subjects, and if it has not yet pleased Him to permit it to be in one and the same form of religion, that it may be at the least with one and the same intention, and with such rules that may prevent among them all troubles and tumults. . . ." Now the details of the document fall into place. Each of the articles addresses specific "rules" governing the legal rights and obligations of French Catholics and Protestants, ranging from where they can worship to where they can work.

5. Why was this document written?

As we have already seen, Henry IV relied on the written word to convey information and, at the same time, to express his "power" and "strength." The legalistic and formal nature of the edict aided him in this effort. Yet as Henry IV knew all too well, the gap between law and action could be large indeed. Thus Henry IV compiled the edict not simply to tell people what to do but to persuade them to do it by delineating the terms of religious coexistence point by point and presenting them as the best safeguard against the return of confusion and disorder. He thereby hoped to restore peace to a country that had been divided by civil war for the previous thirty-six years.

6. What does this document reveal about the particular society and period in question?

Historians have mined the *Edict of Nantes* for insight into various facets of Henry IV's reign and Protestant-Catholic relations at the time. Do not be daunted by such complexity; you should focus instead on what you see as particularly predominant and revealing themes. One of the most striking in the *Edict of Nantes* is the central place of religion in late sixteenth-century society. Our contemporary notion of the separation of church and state had no place in the world of Henry IV and his subjects. As he proclaims in the opening lines, he was king "by the Grace of God" who had given him "virtue" and "strength." Furthermore, you might stop to consider why religious differences were the subject of royal legislation in the first place. Note Henry IV's statement that "if it has not yet pleased Him [God] to permit [Christian worship in France] to be in one and the same form of religion, that it may at the least be with one and the same intention. . . ." What does this suggest about sixteenth-century attitudes toward religious difference and tolerance? You cannot answer this question simply by reading the document in black and white terms; you need to look beyond the words and between the lines to draw out the document's broader meanings.

Interpreting Visual Sources

Historians do not rely on written records alone to reconstruct the past; they also turn to nonwritten sources, which are equally varied and rich. By drawing on archeological evidence, historians have reconstructed the material dimensions of everyday life in centuries long past; others have used church sculpture to explore popular religious beliefs; and the list continues. This book includes a range of visual representations to enliven your view of history while enhancing your interpretive skills. Interpreting a visual document is very much like interpreting a nonvisual one — you begin with six questions similar to the ones you have already applied to the *Edict of Nantes* and move from ascertaining the "facts" of the document to a more complex analysis of the visual document's historical meanings and value.

1. Who created this image, when and where?

Just as with written sources, identifying the artist or creator of an image, and when and where it was produced will provide a foundation for your interpretation. Some visual sources, such as a painting or political cartoon signed by the artist, are more forthcoming in this regard. But if the artist is not known (and even if he or she is), there are other paths of inquiry to pursue. Did someone commission the production of the image? What was the historical context in which the image was produced? Piecing together what you know on these two fronts will allow you to draw some basic conclusions about the image.

2. What type of image is this?

The nature of a visual source shapes its form and content because every genre has its own visual conventions. Take a map as an example. At the most basic level, maps are composites of images created to convey topographical and geographical information about a particular place, whether a town, a region, or a continent. Think about how you use maps in your own life. Sometimes they can be fanciful in their designs but typically they have a practical function — to enable the viewer to get from one place to another or at the very least to get a sense of an area's spatial characteristics. A formal portrait, by contrast, would conform to a different set of conventions and, of equal significance, a different set of viewer expectations and uses.

3. Who are the intended viewers of the image?

As with written sources, identifying the relationship between artist and audience is essential to illuminate fully what the artist is trying to convey. Was the image intended for the general public, such as a photograph published in a newspaper? Or was the intended audience more private? Whether public, private, or somewhere in between, an artist's target audience shapes his or her choice of subject matter, format, and style, which in turn should shape your interpretation of its meaning and significance.

4. What is the central message of the image?

Images convey messages just as powerfully as the written word. The challenge is to learn how to "read" pictorial representations accurately. Since artists use images, color, and space to communicate with their audiences, you must train your eyes to look for visual rather than verbal cues. A good place to start is to note the image's main features, followed by a closer examination of its specific details and their interrelationship.

5. Why was this image produced?

Images are produced for a range of reasons — to convey information, to entertain, or to persuade, to name just a few. Understanding the motivations underlying an image's creation is key to unraveling its meaning (or at least what it was supposed to mean) to people at the time. For example, the impressionist painters of the nineteenth century did not paint simply to paint — their style and subject matter intentionally challenged contemporary artistic norms and conventions. Without knowing this, you cannot appreciate the broader context and impact of impressionist art.

6. What does this image reveal about the society and time period in which it was created?

Answering the first five questions will guide your answer here. Identifying the artist, the type of image, and when, where, and for whom it was produced, allows you to step beyond a literal reading of the image into the historical setting in which it was produced. Although the meaning of an image can transcend its historical context, its point of origin and intended audience cannot. Therein rests an image's broader value as a window onto the past, for it is a product of human activity in a specific time and place, just like written documents.

 Guided by these six questions, you can evaluate visual sources on their own terms and analyze the ways in which they speak to the broader historical context. Once again, let's take an example.

2.
Illustrating a Native Perspective

Lienzo de Tlaxcala (c. 1560)

Like Bernal Díaz, the peoples of central Mexico had a stake in recording the momentous events unfolding around them, for they had long believed that remembering the past was essential to their cultural survival. Traditionally, local peoples used pictoriographic representations to record legends, myths, and historical events. After the Spaniards' arrival, indigenous artists borrowed from this tradition to pro-

duce their own accounts of the conquest, including the image that follows. It is one of a series contained in the Lienzo de Tlaxcala *painted on cloth in the mid-sixteenth century. Apparently, the* Lienzo *was created for the Spanish viceroy to commemorate the alliance of the Tlaxcalans with the Spaniards. The Tlaxcalans were enemies of the Aztecs and after initial resistance to the Spanish invasion decided to join their forces. This particular image depicts two related events. The first is the meeting between the Aztec leader Moctezuma and Hernán Cortés in Tenochtitlán in August 1519. Cortés is accompanied by Doña Marina, his translator and cultural mediator; Moctezuma appears with warriors at his side. Rather than showing Moctezuma in his traditional garb, the artist dressed him in the manner of the Tlaxcalans. Both sit in European-style chairs, a nod to European artistic influence, and a Tlaxcalan headdress is suspended in the air between them. Game and fowl offered to the Spaniards are portrayed at the bottom. Within a week of this meeting, Cortés imprisoned Moctezuma in his own palaces with the Tlaxcalans' help. Moctezuma the prisoner appears in the upper right of the image as an old, weak ruler whose sun has set.*

From Prospero Cahuzortzi, ed., *Lienzo de Tlaxcala* (Mexico City: Libreria Antiquaria G. M. Echaniez, 1939).

1. Who created this image, when and where?

In this case, you will have to rely on the headnote to answer these questions. The image was created by an unknown Tlaxcalan artist in the mid-sixteenth century as part of a pictorial series, the *Lienzo de Tlaxcala*, depicting the Spanish conquest of Aztec Mexico. Although the image commemorates events that took place in 1519, it was produced decades later, when Spanish imperial control was firmly entrenched. Thus the image represents a visual point of contact between Spanish and indigenous traditions in the age of European global expansion. Although knowing the identity of the artist would be ideal, the fact that he was Tlaxcalan is of greater value. The Tlaxcalans had allied themselves with the Spanish and considered the *Lienzo* a way of highlighting their role in the Aztecs' defeat.

2. What type of image is this?

On the one hand, this image fits into a long pictorial tradition among the peoples of central Mexico. Before the conquest, they had no alphabetic script. Instead, they drew on a rich repertoire of images and symbols to preserve legends, myths, and historical events. These images and symbols, which included the stylized warriors shown here, were typically painted into books made of deerskin or a plant-based paper. On the other hand, the image also reveals clear European influences, most noticeably in the type of chair in which both Cortés and Moctezuma sit. Looking at the image again with these dual influences in mind, think about how the pictorial markers allowed both indigenous and Spanish viewers to see something recognizable in an event that marked the destruction of one world and the creation of another.

3. Who are the intended viewers of the image?

As the headnote reveals, the image's creator had a specific audience in mind, a Spanish colonial administrator. You should take this fact into account as you think about the image's meaning and significance. Just because a Tlaxcalan artist created the image does not necessarily mean that it represents an unadulterated native point of view. And just because the image documents two historical events does not necessarily mean that the "facts" are objectively presented.

4. What is the central message of the image?

There are many visual components of this image, each of which you should consider individually and then as part of the picture as a whole. As you already know, the artist combined indigenous and European representational traditions. What does this suggest about the image's message? The merging of these two traditions represents the alliance the Tlaxcalans forged with the Spanish. Looking closer, think about how the two leaders, Cortés and Moctezuma, are represented. Cortés is accompanied by his translator, Doña Marina, a Nahua woman. Originally a slave, she had been given to Cortés after his defeat of the Maya at Potonchan. She became a crucial interpreter and cultural mediator for Cortés in the world of the Mexica. Language appears here as a source of his power as well as his alliance with the Tlaxcalans. Although the Spanish contingent was relatively small, thousands of Tlaxcalan and other native warriors entered Tenochtitlán with them, a show of force not lost on local residents. The artist captures this fact by clothing Moctezuma in Tlaxcalan dress — he had once ruled over them but now he was to be ruled. Soon after this meeting, Moctezuma was imprisoned in his own palaces. The artist captures this event in the upper right where Moctezuma is shown as a prisoner.

5. Why was this image produced?

Examining this image reveals the complexity of this question, regardless of the nature of the source. At first glance, the answer is easy: the image was created to commemorate specific events. Yet given what you know about the setting in which the image was produced, the "why" takes on a deeper meaning. The image does not simply record events; it sets a scene in which multiple meanings are embedded — the chairs, Doña Marina, the warriors — that suggest how the Spanish conquest transformed native culture. The image thus served a dual function — to inform the Spanish of the Tlaxcalans' role in the conquest while affirming Spanish dominance over them.

6. What does this image reveal about the society and time period in which it was created?

Answering this question requires you to step beyond a literal meaning of the image into the historical setting in which it was produced. Here you will uncover multiple layers of the image's broader significance. Consider the artist, for example, and his audience. What does the fact that a native artist created the image for a Spanish audience suggest about the nature of Spanish colonization? Clearly, the Spaniards did not make their presence felt as a colonial power simply by seizing land and treasure; they also reshaped indigenous people's understanding of themselves in both the past and present. That the Tlaxcalans expressed this understanding visually in a historical document lent an air of permanence and legitimacy to Spanish colonization and, equally important, to the Tlaxcalans' contributions to it.

Conclusion

Through your analysis of historical sources, you will not only learn details about the world in which the sources were created but also become an active contributor to our understanding of these details' broader significance. Written documents and pictorial representations don't just "tell" historians what happened; they require historians to step into their own imaginations as they strive to reconstitute the past. In this regard, historians' approach is exactly that described here. They determine the basics of the source — who created it, when, and where — as a springboard for increasingly complex levels of analysis. Each level builds upon the other, just like rungs on a ladder. If you take the time to climb each rung in sequence, you will be able to master the content of a source and to use it to bring history to life. The written and visual primary sources included in *Sources of The Making of the West*, Third Edition, will allow you to participate firsthand in the process of historical inquiry by exploring the people, places, and sights of the past and how they shaped their own world and continue to shape ours today.

Religious Reforms and Global Encounters, 1492–1560

I n the late fifteenth century, Europe stood on the threshold of profound transformations within its borders and beyond. Portuguese fleets had opened up new trade routes extending along the West African coast to Calicut, India, the hub of the spice trade. Their success whet Europeans' appetite for maritime exploration, with Spain ultimately taking the lead. The Spaniards' colonization of the Caribbean was in full gear by 1500, and from there they moved westward into Mexico. The first two documents illuminate aspects of the Spanish conquest of Mexico from both Spanish and native perspectives. As they suggest, European colonization permanently changed the lives of native peoples of the Americas, often with devastating results. The third document reveals that some Europeans openly criticized colonization while at the same time embracing the opportunities it provided to spread Catholic Christianity. Catholicism had long been a unifying force in the West. In the early sixteenth century, however, the religious landscape shifted dramatically. Problems within the Catholic Church combined with the spirit and methods of the Renaissance to usher in the Protestant Reformation, a time of questioning, reform, and revolt. The fourth and fifth documents allow us to see the Reformation through the eyes of two of its leaders, Martin Luther and John Calvin. Together, their ideas helped to shatter the religious unity of Europe forever. As the final document attests, despite the many challenges it faced, Catholicism underwent its own process of change and renewal.

1.
Worlds Collide

Bernal Díaz del Castillo, *The True History of the Conquest of New Spain* (c. 1567)

By the mid-sixteenth century, Spain had built an empire in the Americas that extended from Mexico to Chile. The Spanish crown especially prized Mexico, then called "New

15

Spain," because of the precious metals (gold and silver) found there. Numerous Spanish accounts of the conquest of Mexico have survived, perhaps none more vivid than that of Bernal Díaz del Castillo (1495–1583). Díaz had been in the thick of colonization from an early age, having joined a Spanish expedition to Panama in 1514 and two more to Mexico before meeting up with Hernán Cortés (1485–1547) in Cuba. In 1519, Cortés led a group of fellow adventurers, including Díaz, to the Mexican heartland, which they ultimately brought under Spanish control. By the mid-1550s, Díaz had begun to record his version of events, which he called The True History of the Conquest of New Spain, *to counter what he considered to be "false" histories by people who had not participated in the conquest. Díaz was also sensitive to critics of the colonists' treatment of native peoples. Completed around 1567, the book languished in obscurity until its publication in 1632. In the excerpt that follows, Díaz recounts a key moment in the conquest — the Spaniards' arrival in Tenochtitlán, the Aztec capital, on November 8, 1519. Here Cortés and his men were greeted by the Aztec leader, Moctezuma, with great hospitality. In its close attention to detail, Díaz's description reveals a blend of wonder and disdain underlying Spanish attitudes toward Aztec civilization.*

When Cortés was told that the Great Montezuma was approaching, and he saw him coming, he dismounted from his horse, and when he was near Montezuma, they simultaneously paid great reverence to one another. Montezuma bade him welcome and our Cortés replied through Doña Marina[1] wishing him very good health. And it seems to me that Cortés, through Doña Marina, offered him his right hand, and Montezuma did not wish to take it, but he did give his hand to Cortés and then Cortés brought out a necklace which he had ready at hand, made of glass stones, which I have already said are called Margaritas, which have within them many patterns of diverse colors, these were strung on a cord of gold and with musk so that it should have a sweet scent, and he placed it round the neck of the Great Montezuma and when he had so placed it he was going to embrace him, and those great Princes who accompanied Montezuma held back Cortés by the arm so that he should not embrace him, for they considered it an indignity.

Then Cortés through the mouth of Doña Marina told him that now his heart rejoiced at having seen such a great Prince, and that he took it as a great honor that he had come in person to meet him and had frequently shown him such favor.

Then Montezuma spoke other words of politeness to him, and told two of his nephews who supported his arms, the Lord of Texcoco and the Lord of Coyoacan, to go with us and show us to our quarters, and Montezuma with his other two re-

---

From Bernal Díaz del Castillo, *The True History of the Conquest of New Spain*, vol. 2, trans. Alfred Percival Maudslay (London: The Hakluyt Society, 1910), 41–44, 55–59.

[1]A Nahua slave of a Maya cacique, she was given to Cortés by the Maya after their defeat at Potonchan. Speaking both Nahuatl and Yucatec Maya, she (and the ex-Maya captive Gerónimo de Aguilar) became crucial interpreters for Cortés as he entered the world of the Mexica. She was also the mother of Cortés's illegitimate son, Martín. See Stuart B. Schwartz, ed., *Victors and Vanquished: Spanish and Nahua Views of the Conquest of Mexico* (Boston: Bedford/St. Martin's, 2000), 251. [Schwartz's note.]

lations, the Lord of Cuitlahuac and the Lord of Tacuba who accompanied him, returned to the city, and all those grand companies of Caciques[2] and chieftains who
had come with him returned in his train. . . . Thus space was made for us to enter
the streets of Mexico, without being so much crowded. But who could now count
the multitude of men and women and boys who were in the streets and on the
azoteas, and in canoes on the canals, who had come out to see us. It was indeed
wonderful, and, now that I am writing about it, it all comes before my eyes as
though it had happened but yesterday. Coming to think it over it seems to be a
great mercy that our Lord Jesus Christ was pleased to give us grace and courage to
dare to enter into such a city; and for the many times He has saved me from danger of death, as will be seen later on, I give Him sincere thanks, and in that He has
preserved me to write about it, although I cannot do it as fully as is fitting or the
subject needs. Let us make no words about it, for deeds are the best witnesses to
what I say here and elsewhere.

Let us return to our entry to Mexico. They took us to lodge in some large houses,
where there were apartments for all of us, for they had belonged to the father of the
Great Montezuma, who was named Axayaca, and at that time Montezuma kept there
the great oratories for his idols, and a secret chamber where he kept bars and jewels
of gold, which was the treasure that he had inherited from his father Axayaca, and
he never disturbed it. They took us to lodge in that house, because they called us
Teules, and took us for such, so that we should be with the Idols or Teules which
were kept there. However, for one reason or another, it was there they took us, where
there were great halls and chambers canopied with the cloth of the country for our
Captain, and for every one of us beds of matting with canopies above, and no better bed is given, however great the chief may be, for they are not used. And all these
palaces were [coated] with shining cement and swept and garlanded.

As soon as we arrived and entered into the great court, the Great Montezuma
took our Captain by the hand, for he was there awaiting him, and led him to the
apartment and saloon where he was to lodge, which was very richly adorned according to their usage, and he had at hand a very rich necklace made of golden
crabs, a marvelous piece of work, and Montezuma himself placed it round the neck
of our Captain Cortés, and greatly astonished his [own] Captains by the great honor
that he was bestowing on him. When the necklace had been fastened, Cortés
thanked Montezuma through our interpreters, and Montezuma replied — "Malinche, you and your brethren are in your own house, rest awhile," and then he went
to his palaces which were not far away, and we divided our lodgings by companies,
and placed the artillery pointing in a convenient direction, and the order which we
had to keep was clearly explained to us, and that we were to be much on the alert,
both the cavalry and all of us soldiers. A sumptuous dinner was provided for us according to their use and custom, and we ate it at once. So this was our lucky and
daring entry into the great city of Tenochtitlan, Mexico. . . .

---

[2]A Taino word meaning ruler, brought from the Indies to Mexico by the Spanish and used
to refer to native rulers in Mexico and Latin America in general. See Schwartz, *Victors and
Vanquished*, 254. [Schwartz's note.]

Thanks to our Lord Jesus Christ for it all. . . .

Let us leave this talk and go back to our story of what else happened to us, which I will go on to relate. . . .

The next day Cortés decided to go to Montezuma's palace, and he first sent to find out what he intended doing and to let him know that we were coming. . . .

When Montezuma knew of our coming he advanced to the middle of the hall to receive us, accompanied by many of his nephews, for no other chiefs were permitted to enter or hold communication with Montezuma where he then was, unless it were on important business. Cortés and he paid the greatest reverence to each other and then they took one another by the hand and Montezuma made him sit down on his couch on his right hand, and he also bade all of us to be seated on seats which he ordered to be brought.

Then Cortés began to make an explanation through our interpreters Doña Marina and Aguilar, and said that he and all of us were rested, and that in coming to see and converse with such a great Prince as he was, we had completed the journey and fulfilled the command which our great King and Prince had laid on us. But what he chiefly came to say on behalf of our Lord God had already been brought to his [Montezuma's] knowledge through his ambassadors, Tendile, Pitalpitoque and Quintalbor, at the time when he did us the favor to send the golden sun and moon to the sand dunes; for we told them then that we were Christians and worshipped one true and only God, named Jesus Christ, who suffered death and passion to save us, and we told them that a cross (when they asked us why we worshipped it) was a sign of the other Cross on which our Lord God was crucified for our salvation, and that the death and passion which He suffered was for the salvation of the whole human race, which was lost, and that this our God rose on the third day and is now in heaven, and it is He who made the heavens and the earth, the sea and the sands, and created all the things there are in the world, and He sends the rain and the dew, and nothing happens in the world without His holy will. That we believe in Him and worship Him, but that those whom they look upon as gods are not so, but are devils, which are evil things, and if their looks are bad their deeds are worse, and they could see that they were evil and of little worth, for where we had set up crosses such as those his ambassadors had seen, they dared not appear before them, through fear of them, and that as time went on they would notice this.

The favor he now begged of him was his attention to the words that he now wished to tell him; then explained to him very clearly about the creation of the world, and how we are all brothers, sons of one father, and one mother who were called Adam and Eve, and how such a brother as our great Emperor, grieving for the perdition of so many souls, such as those which their idols were leading to Hell, where they burn in living flames, had sent us, so that after what he [Montezuma] had now heard he would put a stop to it and they would no longer adore these Idols or sacrifice Indian men and women to them, for we were all brethren, nor should they commit sodomy or thefts. He also told them that, in course of time, our Lord and King would send some men who among us lead very holy lives, much better than we do, who will explain to them all about it, for at present we merely came to give them due warning, and so he prayed him to do what he was asked and carry it into effect.

As Montezuma appeared to wish to reply, Cortés broke off his argument, and to all of us who were with him he said: "with this we have done our duty considering it is the first attempt."

Montezuma replied — "Señor Malinche, I have understood your words and arguments very well before now, from what you said to my servants at the sand dunes, this about three Gods and the Cross, and all those things that you have preached in the towns through which you have come. We have not made any answer to it because here throughout all time we have worshipped our own gods, and thought they were good, as no doubt yours are, so do not trouble to speak to us any more about them at present. Regarding the creation of the world, we have held the same belief for ages past, and for this reason we take it for certain that you are those whom our ancestors predicted would come from the direction of the sunrise. . . .

. . . Then Cortés and all of us answered that we thanked him sincerely for such signal good will, and Montezuma said, laughing, for he was very merry in his princely way of speaking: "Malinche, I know very well that these people of Tlaxcala with whom you are such good friends have told you that I am a sort of God or Teul, and that everything in my houses is made of gold and silver and precious stones, I know well enough that you are wise and did not believe it but took it as a joke. Behold now, Señor Malinche, my body is of flesh and bone like yours, my houses and palaces of stone and wood and lime; that I am a great king and inherit the riches of my ancestors is true, but not all the nonsense and lies that they have told you about me, although of course you treated it as a joke, as I did your thunder and lightning."

Cortés answered him, also laughing, and said that opponents and enemies always say evil things, without truth in them, of those whom they hate, and that he well knew that he could not hope to find another Prince more magnificent in these countries, and, that not without reason had he been so vaunted to our Emperor.

While this conversation was going on, Montezuma secretly sent a great Cacique, one of his nephews who was in his company, to order his stewards to bring certain pieces of gold, which it seems must have been put apart to give to Cortés, and ten loads of fine cloth, which he apportioned, the gold and mantles between Cortés and the four captains, and to each of us soldiers he gave two golden necklaces, each necklace being worth ten pesos, and two loads of mantles. The gold that he then gave us was worth in all more than a thousand pesos and he gave it all cheerfully and with the air of a great and valiant prince.

DISCUSSION QUESTIONS

1. How does Díaz describe Tenochtitlán and the Aztec leader Moctezuma? What impressed him in particular? What does he seem to criticize, and why?

2. How does Díaz portray Cortés and his interactions with Moctezuma? What was the role of Donã Marina in their exchanges?

3. In what ways is Díaz's account colored by his own preconceptions and beliefs as a European in a foreign land?

4. Based on this account, what motivated Díaz and other conquistadors? What did the New World have to offer them?

2.
Illustrating a Native Perspective
Lienzo de Tlaxcala (c. 1560)

Like Bernal Díaz, the peoples of central Mexico had a stake in recording the momentous events unfolding around them, for they had long believed that remembering the past was essential to their cultural survival. Traditionally, local peoples used pictoriographic representations to record legends, myths, and historical events. After the

From Prospero Cahuzortzi, ed., *Lienzo de Tlaxcala* (Mexico City: Libreria Antiquaria G. M. Echaniez, 1939).

Spaniards' arrival, indigenous artists borrowed from this tradition to produce their own accounts of the conquest, including the image on page 274. It is one of a series contained in the Lienzo de Tlaxcala *painted on cloth in the mid-sixteenth century. Apparently, the* Lienzo *was created for the Spanish viceroy to commemorate the alliance of the Tlaxcalans with the Spaniards. The Tlaxcalans were enemies of the Aztecs and after initial resistance to the Spanish invasion decided to join their forces. This particular image depicts two related events. The first is the meeting between the Aztec leader Moctezuma and Hernán Cortés in Tenochtitlán in August 1519. Cortés is accompanied by Donā Marina, his translator and cultural mediator; Moctezuma appears with warriors at his side. Rather than showing Moctezuma in his traditional garb, the artist dressed him in the manner of the Tlaxcalans. Both sit in European-style chairs, a nod to European artistic influence, and a Tlaxcalan headdress is suspended in the air between them. Game and fowl offered to the Spaniards are portrayed at the bottom. Within a week of this meeting, Cortés imprisoned Moctezuma in his own palaces with the Tlaxcalans' help. Moctezuma the prisoner appears in the upper right of the image as an old, weak ruler whose sun has set.*

DISCUSSION QUESTIONS

1. In what ways do the artist's depictions of Cortés and Moctezuma differ? In what ways are they the same?

2. Why do you think the artist chose to depict Moctezuma in Tlaxcalan dress? How was this choice related to the artist's audience and the message he sought to convey?

3. What are the possible strengths and weaknesses of using pictures to record and convey information?

3.
Defending Native Humanity
Bartolomé de Las Casas, *In Defense of the Indians* (c. 1548–1550)

Indigenous peoples in the Americas suffered heavily under Spanish colonization. Millions died as the result of war and disease, and many who remained were used as forced labor. The Amerindians' fate did not go unnoticed in Europe, where the ethical and legal basis of their harsh treatment became the subject of significant debate. Charles V, king of Spain and the Holy Roman Emperor, added fuel to the fire. In 1550, he ordered a panel of lawyers and theologians at the University of Valladolid to evaluate the positions of two prominent opposing voices on the issue, Juan Ginés de Sepúlveda (1490– 1573) and Bartolomé de Las Casas (1474–1566). Drawing heavily on Aristotle's notion that hierarchy was natural, Sepúlveda argued that the Spanish had the right

From Bartolomé de Las Casas, *In Defense of the Indians,* trans. Stafford Poole (DeKalb: Northern Illinois University Press, 1974), 41–46.

to enslave Amerindians because they were an inferior and less civilized people. Las Casas, whose response is excerpted below, rejected Sepúlveda's position, based in part on his own experience living in Spanish America. Here he witnessed firsthand the devastating human impact of colonization and was ultimately swayed by the local Dominicans' campaign against the mistreatment of Indians. He joined the order and thereafter was a vocal advocate for Amerindians until his death in 1566. Although the Valladolid panel did not declare a winner, in the end, Las Casas's views did not hold the day in the New World.

As a result of the points we have proved and made clear, the distinction the Philosopher [Aristotle] makes between the two above-mentioned kinds of barbarian is evident. For those he deals with in the first book of the *Politics*, and whom we have just discussed, are barbarians without qualification, in the proper and strict sense of the word, that is, dull witted and lacking in the reasoning powers necessary for self-government. They are without laws, without king, etc. For this reason they are by nature unfitted for rule.

However, he admits, and proves, that the barbarians he deals with in the third book of the same work have a lawful, just, and natural government. Even though they lack the art and use of writing, they are not wanting in the capacity and skill to rule and govern themselves, both publicly and privately. Thus they have kingdoms, communities, and cities that they govern wisely according to their laws and customs. Thus their government is legitimate and natural, even though it has some resemblance to tyranny. From these statements we have no choice but to conclude that the rulers of such nations enjoy the use of reason and that their people and the inhabitants of their provinces do not lack peace and justice. Otherwise they could not be established or preserved as political entities for long. This is made clear by the Philosopher and Augustine. Therefore not all barbarians are irrational or natural slaves or unfit for government. Some barbarians, then, in accord with justice and nature, have kingdoms, royal dignities, jurisdiction, and good laws, and there is among them lawful government.

Now if we shall have shown that among our Indians of the western and southern shores (granting that we call them barbarians and that they are barbarians) there are important kingdoms, large numbers of people who live settled lives in a society, great cities, kings, judges and laws, persons who engage in commerce, buying, selling, lending, and the other contracts of the law of nations, will it not stand proved that the Reverend Doctor Sepúlveda has spoken wrongly and viciously against peoples like these, either out of malice or ignorance of Aristotle's teaching, and, therefore, has falsely and perhaps irreparably slandered them before the entire world? From the fact that the Indians are barbarians it does not necessarily follow that they are incapable of government and have to be ruled by others, except to be taught about the Catholic faith and to be admitted to the holy sacraments. They are not ignorant, inhuman, or bestial. Rather, long before they had heard the word Spaniard they had properly organized states, wisely ordered by excellent laws, religion, and custom. They cultivated friendship and, bound together in common fellowship, lived in populous cities in which they wisely administered the affairs of both peace and war justly and equitably, truly governed by laws that at very many points surpass ours, and could have won the admiration of the sages of Athens. . . .

Now if they are to be subjugated by war because they are ignorant of polished literature, let Sepúlveda hear Trogus Pompey:

> Nor could the Spaniards submit to the yoke of a conquered province until Caesar Augustus, after he had conquered the world, turned his victorious armies against them and organized that barbaric and wild people as a province, once he had led them by law to a more civilized way of life.

Now see how he called the Spanish people barbaric and wild. I would like to hear Sepúlveda, in his cleverness, answer this question: Does he think that the war of the Romans against the Spanish was justified in order to free them from barbarism? And this question also: Did the Spanish wage an unjust war when they vigorously defended themselves against them?

Next, I call the Spaniards who plunder that unhappy people torturers. Do you think that the Romans, once they had subjugated the wild and barbaric peoples of Spain, could with secure right divide all of you among themselves, handing over so many head of both males and females as allotments to individuals? And do you then conclude that the Romans could have stripped your rulers of their authority and consigned all of you, after you had been deprived of your liberty, to wretched labors, especially in searching for gold and silver lodes and mining and refining the metals? And if the Romans finally did that, . . . [would you not judge] that you also have the right to defend your freedom, indeed your very life, by war? Sepúlveda, would you have permitted Saint James to evangelize your own people of Córdoba in that way? For God's sake and man's faith in him, is this the way to impose the yoke of Christ on Christian men? Is this the way to remove wild barbarism from the minds of barbarians? Is it not, rather, to act like thieves, cut-throats, and cruel plunderers and to drive the gentlest of people headlong into despair? The Indian race is not that barbaric, nor are they dull witted or stupid, but they are easy to teach and very talented in learning all the liberal arts, and very ready to accept, honor, and observe the Christian religion and correct their sins (as experience has taught) once priests have introduced them to the sacred mysteries and taught them the word of God. They have been endowed with excellent conduct, and before the coming of the Spaniards, as we have said, they had political states that were well founded on beneficial laws.

Now if Sepúlveda had wanted, as a serious man should, to know the full truth before he sat down to write with his mind corrupted by the lies of tyrants, he should have consulted the honest religious who have lived among those peoples for many years and know their endowments of character and industry, as well as the progress they have made in religion and morality. . . .

From this it is clear that the basis for Sepúlveda's teaching that these people are uncivilized and ignorant is worse than false. Yet even if we were to grant that this race has no keenness of mind or artistic ability, certainly they are not, in consequence, obliged to submit themselves to those who are more intelligent and to adopt their ways, so that, if they refuse, they may be subdued by having war waged against them and be enslaved, as happens today. For men are obliged by the natural law to do many things they cannot be forced to do against their will. We are bound by the natural law to embrace virtue and imitate the uprightness of good men. No one, however, is punished for being bad unless he is guilty of rebellion. Where the Catholic faith has been preached in a Christian manner and as it ought to be, all men are bound by the natural law to accept it, yet no one is forced to accept the faith of Christ. No one is punished because he is sunk in vice, unless he is rebellious or harms the property and persons of others. No one is forced to embrace virtue and show himself as a good man. . . .

. . . Therefore, not even a truly wise man may force an ignorant barbarian to submit to him, especially by yielding his liberty, without doing him an injustice. This the poor Indians suffer, with extreme injustice, against all the laws of God and of men and against the law of nature itself.

DISCUSSION QUESTIONS

1. Why does Las Casas reject Sepúlveda's argument? What is the basis of his reasoning?
2. How does Las Casas depict Amerindian civilization? What attributes does he highlight and why?
3. Why does Las Casas cite the example of Rome's conquest of Spain under Caesar Augustus to support his point?
4. Despite Las Casas's vigorous defense of the Indians, what prejudices and assumptions of his own did he bring to bear in this work?

4.
Scripture and Salvation
Martin Luther, *Freedom of a Christian* (1520)

German monk Martin Luther's attempt to reform the Catholic Church from within developed into a new branch of Christianity known as Protestantism. After his excommunication by Pope Leo X in 1520, Luther published several treatises that attacked church authority, clerical celibacy, and the sacraments while elucidating his evangelical theology. He set forth the guiding principles of his beliefs with particular clarity in Freedom of a Christian. *Although originally written in Latin and addressed to the pope, the tract was soon translated into German and widely circulated among Luther's*

From Martin Luther, *Christian Liberty*, ed. Harold J. Grimm (Philadelphia: Fortress Press, 1957), 6–10.

ever-growing number of followers. In the excerpt that follows, Luther defined what be-came a central tenet of the reform movement: faith in Christ and his promise of sal-vation is all that a Christian needs to be saved from sin.

Many people have considered Christian faith an easy thing, and not a few have given it a place among the virtues. They do this because they have not experienced it and have never tasted the great strength there is in faith. It is impossible to write well about it or to understand what has been written about it unless one has at one time or another experienced the courage which faith gives a man when trials oppress him. But he who has had even a faint taste of it can never write, speak, meditate, or hear enough concerning it. It is a living "spring of water welling up to eternal life," as Christ calls it in John 4 [:14].

As for me, although I have no wealth of faith to boast of and know how scant my supply is, I nevertheless hope that I have attained to a little faith, even though I have been assailed by great and various temptations; and I hope that I can discuss it, if not more elegantly, certainly more to the point, than those literalists and subtile disputants have previously done, who have not even understood what they have written. . . .

First, let us consider the inner man to see how a righteous, free, and pious Christian, that is, a spiritual, new, and inner man, becomes what he is. It is evident that no external thing has any influence in producing Christian righteousness or freedom. . . . It does not help the soul if the body is adorned with the sacred robes of priests or dwells in sacred places or is occupied with sacred duties or prays, fasts, abstains from certain kinds of food, or does any work that can be done by the body and in the body. . . .

One thing, and only one thing, is necessary for Christian life, righteousness, and freedom. That one thing is the most holy Word of God, the gospel of Christ, as Christ says, John 11 [:25], "I am the resurrection and the life; he who believes in me, though he die, yet shall he live"; and John 8 [:36], "So if the Son makes you free, you will be free indeed"; and Matt. 4 [:4], "Man shall not live by bread alone, but by every word that proceeds from the mouth of God." Let us then consider it certain and firmly established that the soul can do without anything except the Word of God and that where the Word of God is missing there is no help at all for the soul. If it has the Word of God it is rich and lacks nothing since it is the Word of life, truth, light, peace, righteousness, salvation, joy, liberty, wisdom, power, grace, glory, and of every incalculable blessing. . . .

You may ask, "What then is the Word of God, and how shall it be used, since there are so many words of God?" I answer: The Apostle explains this in Romans 1. The Word is the gospel of God concerning his Son, who was made flesh, suffered, rose from the dead, and was glorified through the Spirit who sanctifies. To preach Christ means to feed the soul, make it righteous, set it free, and save it, provided it believes the preaching. Faith alone is the saving and efficacious use of the Word of God. . . . Therefore it is clear that, as the soul needs only the Word of God for its life and righteousness, so it is justified by faith alone and not any works. . . .

· When you have learned this you will know that you need Christ, who suffered and rose again for you so that, if you believe in him, you may through this faith become a new man in so far as your sins are forgiven and you are justified by the merits of another, namely, of Christ alone. . . .

Discussion Questions

1. According to Luther, what is faith and where does it come from?

2. How can an individual Christian become a "new man" through such faith?

3. By defining faith alone as essential to salvation, in what ways does Luther undermine basic Catholic teachings?

4. What authority does Luther draw on to defend his point of view? What does this reveal about the basis of his theology?

5.
Reforming Christianity
John Calvin, *Articles Concerning Predestination* (c. 1560)
and
The Necessity of Reforming the Church (1543)

Studying in Paris at the same time as Ignatius of Loyola (1491–1556) in 1533–1534, Frenchman John Calvin (1509–1564) became a convert to the reform movement. Fleeing the dangers of Paris, Calvin settled in Geneva and produced the first edition of his famous treatise, Institutes of the Christian Religion, *in 1536. With Guillaume Farel (1489–1565), he began to implement a program of religious and moral reform. Calvin and Farel soon clashed with the city's leaders, who were unwilling to go along with the radical disciplinary measures they proposed, as the measures would have made the city a virtual theocracy — a state governed by officials in the name of God. Although banished from the city in 1537, Calvin and Farel were invited back in 1540. Calvin then began to build a godly city, making Geneva a haven for reformers and a training ground for preachers. The first excerpt that follows, "Articles Concerning Predestination," was written late in Calvin's life and is one of the simplest explanations of his doctrine. The second excerpt, from "The Necessity of Reforming the Church," addresses the problem of idolatry, especially the cult of the saints.*

Articles Concerning Predestination

Before the first man was created, God in his eternal counsel had determined what he willed to be done with the whole human race.

From *Calvin: Theological Treatises*, vol. 22, trans. Rev. J. K. S. Reid (Philadelphia: The Westminster Press, 1954), 179, 188–91.

In the hidden counsel of God it was determined that Adam should fall from the unimpaired condition of his nature, and by his defection should involve all his posterity in sentence of eternal death.

Upon the same decree depends the distinction between elect and reprobate:[1] as he adopted some for himself for salvation, he destined others for eternal ruin.

While the reprobate are the vessels of the just wrath of God, and the elect vessels of his compassion, the ground of the distinction is to be sought in the pure will of God alone, which is the supreme rule of justice.

While the elect receive the grace of adoption by faith, their election does not depend on faith but is prior in time and order.

As the beginning of faith and perseverance in it arises from the gratuitous election of God, none are truly illuminated with faith, and none granted the spirit of regeneration, except those whom God elects. But it is necessary that the reprobate remain in their blindness or be deprived of such portion of faith as is in them.

While we are elected in Christ, nevertheless that God reckons us among his own is prior in order to his making us members of Christ.

While the will of God is the supreme and primary cause of all things, and God holds the devil and the godless subject to his will, nevertheless God cannot be called the cause of sin, nor the author of evil, nor subject of any guilt. . . .

The Necessity of Reforming the Church

. . . Both sides confess that in the sight of God idolatry is an execrable crime. But when we attack the worship of images, our adversaries immediately take the opposite side, and lend support to the crime which they had with us verbally condemned. . . . For they strenuously defend the veneration of images, though they condemn idolatry. But these ingenious men deny that the honor which they pay to images is worship, as if, when compared with ancient idolatry, it were possible to see any difference. Idolaters pretended that they worshipped the celestial gods, though under corporeal figures which represented them. What else do our adversaries pretend? But is God satisfied with such excuses? Did the prophets on this account cease to rebuke the madness of the Egyptians, when, out of the secret mysteries of their theology, they drew subtle distinctions under which to screen themselves? What too do we suppose the brazen serpent which the Jews worshipped to have been, but something which they honored as a representation of God? . . .

I have not yet adverted to the grosser superstitions, though these cannot be confined to the ignorant, since they are approved by public consent. They adorn their idols now with flowers and chaplets, now with robes, vests, girdles, purses, and frivolities of every kind. They light tapers and burn incense before them, and carry them on their shoulders in solemn state. They assemble from long distances to one statue, though they have similar things at home. Likewise, though in one shrine there may be several images, of the Virgin Mary, or someone else, they pass

---

[1]Reprobates refers to those who were damned. [Ed.]

these by, and one is frequented as if it were more divine. When they pray to the image of Christopher or Barbara, they mutter the Lord's Prayer and the angel's salutation. The fairer or dingier the images are, the greater is their excellence supposed to be. They find new commendation in fabulous miracles. Some they pretend to have spoken, others to have extinguished a fire in the church by trampling on it, others to have moved of their own accord to a new adobe, others to have dropped from heaven. While the whole world teems with these and similar delusions, and the fact is perfectly notorious, we who have brought back the worship of the one God to the rule of his Word, who are blameless in this matter, and have purged our churches, not only of idolatry but of superstition also, are accused of violating the worship of God, because we have discarded the worship of images. . . .

. . . As to the matter of relics, it is almost incredible how impudently the world has been cheated. I can mention three relics of our Savior's circumcision; likewise fourteen nails which are exhibited for the three by which the soldiers cast lots; two inscriptions that were placed over the cross; three blades of the spear by which our Savior's side was pierced, and about five sets of linen clothes which wrapped his body in the tomb. Besides they show all the articles used at the institution of the Lord's Supper, and endless absurdities of this kind. There is no saint of any celebrity of whom two or three bodies are not in existence. I can name the place where a piece of pumice-stone was long held in high veneration as the skull of Peter. Decency will not permit me to mention fouler exhibitions. It is therefore undeservedly that we are blamed for having studied to purify the Church of God from such impurities.

In regard to the worship of God, our adversaries next accuse us, because, in omitting trivialities not only foolish but also tending to hypocrisy, we worship God more simply. . . .

DISCUSSION QUESTIONS

1. Describe the doctrine of predestination according to Calvin. How were the elect and reprobate "chosen"?

2. What potential problems might arise from a person's belief that he or she was predestined to election or damnation?

3. To whom does Calvin compare Catholics in their "worship" of saints and relics, and why?

4. What specific evidence does Calvin provide to undermine the cult of the saints?

6.
Responding to Reformation
St. Ignatius of Loyola, *A New Kind of Catholicism*
(1546, 1549, 1553)

The interests of Ignatius of Loyola (1491–1556), born of a Spanish noble family, centered more on chivalry than religion before his serious injury at the Battle of Pamplona in 1520. While recovering, he experienced a conversion when he began reading the only books available to him, The Golden Legend *(about saints' lives) and the* Life of Christ. *After begging and spending time at the monastery of Montserrat, he began work on* The Spiritual Exercises, *a manual of discernment for the pilgrim journeying to God. After studying at the University of Paris, Ignatius, Francis Xavier (1506–1552), and other friends made vows of chastity and poverty, determining to travel to Jerusalem. When this became impossible, they went to Italy. The Society of Jesus (the Jesuits), founded by Ignatius and his early companions, was officially recognized by Pope Paul III in 1540 as a new order directly under the papacy. Its spirituality would be expressed most prominently in teaching and missionary work. The following letters of Ignatius reveal a new form of Catholic spiritual expression that was active and apostolic in its orientation. It was less a "response" to Protestantism than a model for Catholic life and work. Along with the works of other early Jesuits, it embodied a new spirit that so many had sought but not found in the late medieval church.*

Conduct at Trent: On Helping Others, 1546

Our main aim [to God's greater glory] during this undertaking at Trent is to put into practice (as a group that lives together in one appropriate place) preaching, confessions and readings, teaching children, giving good example, visiting the poor in the hospitals, exhorting those around us, each of us according to the different talents he may happen to have, urging on as many as possible to greater piety and prayer. . . .

In their preaching they should not refer to points of conflict between Protestants and Catholics, but simply exhort all to upright conduct and to ecclesiastical practice, urging everyone to full self knowledge and to greater knowledge and love of their Creator and Lord, with frequent allusions to the Council. At the end of each session, they should (as has been mentioned) lead prayers for the Council.

They should do the same with readings as with sermons, trying their best to influence people with greater love of their Creator and Lord as they explain the meaning of what is read; similarly, they should lead their hearers to pray for the Council. . . .

They should spend some time, as convenient, in the elementary teaching of youngsters, depending on the means and disposition of all involved, and with more or less explanation according to the capacity of the pupils. . . . Let them visit the almshouses once or twice a day, at times that are convenient for the patients' health, hearing confessions and consoling the poor, if possible taking them something, and urging them to the sort of prayers mentioned above for confession. If there are three of ours in Trent, each should visit the poor at least once every four days.

When they are urging people in their dealings with them to go to confession and communion, to say mass frequently, to undertake the Spiritual Exercises and other good works, they should also be urging them to pray for the Council.

It was said that there are advantages in being slow to speak and measured in one's statements when doctrinal definitions are involved. The opposite is true when

From Joseph A. Munitiz and Philip Endean, eds. and trans., *Saint Ignatius of Loyola, Personal Writings: Reminiscences, Spiritual Diary, Select Letters, Including the Text of The Spiritual Exercises* (New York: Penguin Books, 1996), 165, 166, 230, 233–34, 257, 259, 262–63.

one is urging people to look to their spiritual progress. Then one should be eloquent and ready to talk, full of sympathy and affection.

Spreading God's Word in a German University, 1549

The aim that they should have above all before their eyes is that intended by the Supreme Pontiff who has sent them: to help the University of Ingolstadt, and as far as is possible the whole of Germany, in all that concerns purity of faith, obedience to the Church, and firmness and soundness of doctrine and upright living. . . .

They must be very competent in them, and teach solid doctrine without many technical terms (which are unpopular), especially if these are hard to understand. The lectures should be learned yet clear, sustained in argument yet not long-winded, and delivered with attention to style. . . . Besides these academic lectures, it seems opportune on feast days to hold sermons on Bible readings, more calculated to move hearts and form consciences than to produce learned minds. . . . They should make efforts to attract their students into a friendship of spiritual quality, and if possible towards confession and making the Spiritual Exercises, even in the full form, if they seem suitable to join the Society. . . .

On occasion they should give time to works of mercy of a more visible character, such as in hospitals and prisons and helping other kinds of poor; such works arouse a "sweet fragrance" in the Lord. Opportunity may also arise to act as peacemakers in quarrels and to teach basic Christian doctrine to the uneducated. Taking account of local conditions and the persons concerned, prudence will dictate whether they should act themselves or through others.

They should make efforts to make friends with the leaders of their opponents, as also with those who are most influential among the heretics or those who are suspected of it yet seem not absolutely immovable. They must try to bring them back from their error by sensitive skill and signs of love. . . . All must try to have at their finger-tips the main points concerning dogmas of faith that are subjects of controversy with heretics, especially at the time and place when they are present, and with those persons with whom they are dealing. Thus they will be able, whenever opportunity arises, to put forward and defend the Catholic truth, to refute errors and to strengthen the doubtful and wavering, whether by lectures and sermons or in the confessional and in conversations. . . .

It will be helpful to lead people, as far as possible, to open themselves to God's grace, exhorting them to a desire for salvation, to prayer, to alms, and to everything that conduces to receiving grace or increasing it. . . .

Let [the duke] understand also what glory it will mean for him if he is the first to introduce into Germany seminaries in the form of such colleges, to foster sound doctrine and religion.

The Final Word on Obedience, 1553, to the Brothers in Portugal

To form an idea of the exceptional intrinsic value of this obedience in the eyes of God Our Lord, one should weigh both the worth of the noble sacrifice offered, involving the highest human power, and the completeness of the self-offering undertaken, as one strips oneself of self, becoming a "living victim" pleasing to the Divine Majesty. Another indication is the intensity of the difficulty experienced as one conquers self for love of God, opposing the natural human inclination felt by us all to follow our own opinions. . . .

Let us be unpretentious and let us be gentle! God Our Lord will grant the grace to enable you, gently and lovingly, to maintain constantly the offering you have made to Him. . . .

All that has been said does not exclude your bringing before your superiors a contrary opinion that may have occurred to you, once you have prayed about the matter and you feel that it would be proper and in accord with your respect for God to do so. . . . Such is the model on which divine Providence "gently disposes all things," so that the lower via the middle, and the middle via the higher, are led to their final ends. . . . The same can be seen upon the earth with respect to all secular constitutions that are duly established, and with respect to the ecclesiastical hierarchy, which is subordinated to you in virtue of holy obedience to select among the many routes open to you that which will bring you back to Portugal as soon and as safely as possible. So I order you in the name of Christ Our Lord to do this, even if it will be so as to return soon to India. . . . Firstly, you are well aware how important for the upkeep and advancement of Christianity in those lands, as also in Guinea and Brazil, is the good order that the King of Portugal can grant from his kingdom. When a prince of such Christian desires and holy intentions as is the King of Portugal receives information from someone of your experience about the state of affairs in those parts, you can imagine what influence this will have on him to do much more in the service of God Our Lord and for the good of those countries that you will describe to him. . . .

You are also aware how important it is for the good of the Indies that the persons sent there should be suitable for the aim that one is pursuing in those and in other lands. . . . Quite apart from all these reasons, which apply to furthering the good of India, it seems to me that you would fire the King's enthusiasm for the Ethiopian project, which has been planned for so many years without anything effective having been seen. Similarly, with regard to the Congo and Brazil, you could give no small help from Portugal, which you cannot do from India as there are not the same commercial relations. If people in India consider that your presence is important given your post, you can continue to act as superior no less from Portugal than from Japan or China, and probably much better. Just as you have gone away on other occasions for longer periods, do the same now.

DISCUSSION QUESTIONS

1. What does the Catholic life mean to Ignatius?

2. What advice does Ignatius offer about dealing with the problem of heresy?

3. What role will Jesuits play throughout Europe and the rest of the world according to Ignatius's instructions?

4. How does Ignatius think political leaders can be enlisted to support the aims of the reform movement?

COMPARATIVE QUESTIONS

1. How do Díaz, the *Lienzo de Tlaxcala*, and Las Casas portray native peoples? Can you trust these portraits? What do they reveal about the ways in which Europeans and native peoples viewed themselves?

2. According to Las Casas, Amerindians were not "barbarians" because they had many marks of "civilization," including cities and self-sustaining governments. What evidence can you find in Díaz to support this view?

3. What similarities and/or differences do you see among Luther, Calvin, and Ignatius's models of Christian life?

4. How do you think Las Casas might have responded to Ignatius's advice to Jesuit missionaries in Portugal? What does this suggest about the role of Catholic Christianity in European colonization?

Wars of Religion and Clash of Worldviews, 1560–1648

For kings, nobles, and ordinary folk alike, the late sixteenth through mid-seventeenth centuries were a time of turmoil and change, as the following documents illustrate. Religious wars galvanized much of Europe during this period, fueled by both ecclesiastical and lay leaders' attempts to maintain the commonly held idea that political and social stability depended on religious conformity. With the escalation of violence, however, some people came to question, and in some cases openly criticize, conventional views about the basic order of governance. They argued successfully that peace would come only if state interests took precedence over religious ones. Europeans' views of the earth and the heavens also expanded because of the rise of new scientific methods and overseas exploration. At the same time, the lure of traditional beliefs remained strong within communities struggling to make sense of the upheavals occurring around them.

1.
Legislating Tolerance

Henry IV, *Edict of Nantes* (1598)

The promulgation of the Edict of Nantes in 1598 by King Henry IV (r. 1589–1610) marked the end of the French Wars of Religion by recognizing French Protestants as a legally protected religious minority. Drawing largely on earlier edicts of pacification, the Edict of Nantes was composed of ninety-two general articles, fifty-six secret articles, and two royal warrants. The two series of articles represented the edict proper and were

From English text of "The Edict" as in Edmund Everard, *The Great Pressures and Grievances of the Protestants in France*, London, 1681, appendix 4 in Roland Mousnier, *The Assassination of Henry IV*, trans. Joan Spencer (London: Faber and Faber, 1973), 316–47.

registered by the highest courts of law in the realm (parlements). The following excerpts from the general articles reveal the triumph of political concerns over religious conformity on the one hand, and the limitations of religious tolerance in early modern France on the other.

Henry, by the grace of God, King of France, and Navarre, to all present, and to come, greeting. Among the infinite mercies that it has pleased God to bestow upon us, that most signal and remarkable is, his having given us power and strength not to yield to the dreadful troubles, confusions, and disorders, which were found at our coming to this kingdom, divided into so many parties and factions, that the most legitimate was almost the least, enabling us with constancy in such manner to oppose the storm, as in the end to surmount it, now reaching a part of safety and repose for this state . . . For the general difference among our good subjects, and the particular evils of the soundest parts of the state, we judged might be easily cured, after the principal cause (the continuation of civil war) was taken away. In which having, by the blessing of God, well and happily succeeded, all hostility and wars through the kingdom being now ceased, we hope that we will succeed equally well in other matters remaining to be settled, and that by this means we shall arrive at the establishment of a good peace, with tranquility and rest. . . . Among our said affairs . . . one of the principal has been the complaints we have received from many of our Catholic provinces and cities, that the exercise of the Catholic religion was not universally re-established, as is provided by edicts or statutes heretofore made for the pacification of the troubles arising from religion; as well as the supplications and remonstrances which have been made to us by our subjects of the Reformed religion, regarding both the non-fulfillment of what has been granted by the said former laws, and that which they desired to be added for the exercise of their religion, the liberty of their consciences and the security of their persons and fortunes; presuming to have just reasons for desiring some enlargement of articles, as not being without great apprehensions, because their ruin has been the principal pretext and original foundation of the late wars, troubles, and commotions. Now not to burden us with too much business at once, as also that the fury of war was not compatible with the establishment of laws, however good they might be, we have hitherto deferred from time to time giving remedy herein. But now that it has pleased God to give us a beginning of enjoying some rest, we think we cannot employ ourself better than to apply to that which may tend to the glory and service of His holy name, and to provide that He may be adored and prayed unto by all our subjects: and if it has not yet pleased Him to permit it to be in one and the same form of religion, that it may at the least be with one and the same intention, and with such rules that may prevent among them all troubles and tumults. . . . For this cause, we have upon the whole judged it necessary to give to all our said subjects one general law, clear, pure, and absolute, by which they shall be regulated in all differences which have heretofore risen among them, or may hereafter rise, wherewith the one and other may be contented, being framed according as the time requires: and having had no other regard in this deliberation than solely the zeal we have to the service of God, praying that He would from this time forward render to all our subjects a durable and established peace. . . . We have by this edict or statute perpetual and irrevocable said, declared, and ordained, saying, declaring, and ordaining;

That the memory of all things passed on the one part and the other, since the beginning of the month of March 1585 until our coming to the crown, and also during the other preceding troubles, and the occasion of the same, shall remain extinguished and suppressed, as things that had never been. . . .

We prohibit to all our subjects of whatever state and condition they be, to renew the memory thereof, to attack, resent, injure, or provoke one another by reproaches for what is past, under any pretext or cause whatsoever, by disputing, contesting, quarrelling, reviling, or offending by factious words; but to contain themselves, and live peaceably together as brethren, friends, and fellow-citizens, upon penalty for acting to the contrary, to be punished for breakers of peace, and disturbers of the public quiet.

We ordain, that the Catholic religion shall be restored and re-established in all places, and quarters of this kingdom and country under our obedience, and where the exercise of the same has been interrupted, to be there again, peaceably and freely exercised without any trouble or impediment. . . .

And not to leave any occasion of trouble and difference among our subjects, we have permitted and do permit to those of the Reformed religion, to live and dwell in all the cities and places of this our kingdom and countries under our obedience, without being inquired after, vexed, molested, or compelled to do any thing in religion, contrary to their conscience. . . .

We permit also to those of the said religion to hold, and continue the exercise of the same in all the cities and places under our obedience, where it was by them established and made public at several different times, in the year 1586, and in 1597.

In like manner the said exercise may be established, and re-established in all the cities and places where it has been established or ought to be by the Statute of Pacification, made in the year 1577 . . .

We prohibit most expressly to all those of the said religion, to hold any exercise of it . . . except in places permitted and granted in the present edict. As also not to exercise the said religion in our court, nor in our territories and countries beyond the mountains, nor in our city of Paris, nor within five leagues of the said city. . . .

We prohibit all preachers, readers, and others who speak in public, to use any words, discourse, or propositions tending to excite the people to sedition; and we enjoin them to contain and comport themselves modestly, and to say nothing which shall not be for the instruction and edification of the listeners, and maintaining the peace and tranquility established by us in our said kingdom. . . .

They [French Protestants] shall also be obliged to keep and observe the festivals of the Catholic Church, and shall not on the same days work, sell, or keep open shop, nor likewise the artisans shall not work out of their shops, in their chambers or houses privately on the said festivals, and other days forbidden, of any trade, the noise whereof may be heard outside by those that pass by, or by the neighbors. . . .

We ordain, that there shall not be made any difference or distinction upon the account of the said religion, in receiving scholars to be instructed in the universities, colleges, or schools, nor of the sick or poor into hospitals, sick houses or public almshouses. . . .

We will and ordain, that all those of the Reformed religion, and others who have followed their party, of whatever state, quality or condition they be, shall be obliged and constrained by all due and reasonable ways, and under the penalties contained in the said edict or statute relating thereunto, to pay tithes to the curates, and other ecclesiastics, and to all others to whom they shall appertain. . . .

To the end to re-unite so much the better the minds and good will of our subjects, as is our intention, and to take away all complaints for the future; we declare all those who make or shall make profession of the said Reformed religion, to be capable of holding and exercising all estates, dignities, offices, and public charges whatsoever. . . .

We declare all sentences, judgments, procedures, seizures, sales, and decrees made and given against those of the Reformed religion, as well living as dead, from the death of the deceased King Henry the Second our most honored Lord and father in law, upon the occasion of the said religion, tumults and troubles since happening, as also the execution of the same judgments and decrees, from henceforward canceled, revoked, and annulled. . . .

Those also of the said religion shall depart and desist henceforward from all practices, negotiations, and intelligences, as well within or without our kingdom; and the said assemblies and councils established within the provinces, shall readily separate, and also all the leagues and associations made or to be made under any pretext, to the prejudice of our present edict, shall be cancelled and annulled, . . . prohibiting most expressly to all our subjects to make henceforth any assessments or levies of money, fortifications, enrollments of men, congregations and assemblies of other than such as are permitted by our present edict, and without arms. . . .

We give in command to the people of our said courts of parlement, chambers of our courts, and courts of our aids, bailiffs, chief-justices, provosts and other of our justices and officers to whom it appertains, and to their lieutenants, that they cause to be read, published, and registered this present edict and ordinance in their courts and jurisdictions, and the same keep punctually, and the contents of the same to cause to be enjoined and used fully and peaceably to all those to whom it shall belong, ceasing and making to cease all troubles and obstructions to the contrary, for such is our pleasure: and in witness hereof we have signed these presents with our own hand; and to the end to make it a thing firm and stable for ever, we have caused to put and endorse our seal to the same. Given at *Nantes* in the month of April in the year of Grace 1598, and of our reign the ninth.

Signed

HENRY

DISCUSSION QUESTIONS

1. What are the edict's principal objectives?
2. In what ways does the edict balance the demands of both French Catholics and Protestants?
3. What limits does the edict place on Protestants' religious rights?
4. Did Henry IV regard this edict as a permanent solution to the religious divisions in the realm? Why or why not?

2.
Barbarians All

Michel de Montaigne, *Of Cannibals* (1580s)

The Edict of Nantes was a victory not only for Henry IV but also for the politiques, *moderate French Catholics and Calvinists who advocated putting the viability of the state ahead of religious uniformity. Their support of religious toleration emerged in direct response to the violence and futility of civil war. French nobleman Michel de Montaigne (1533–1592) was among the most influential voices of moderation and open-mindedness in war-torn France. Alongside his public life as a lawyer and government official, Montaigne was a prolific writer who invented a new genre in European literature, the essay, as a concise form of expression. An excerpt from one of his best-known essays, "Of Cannibals," follows. Here Montaigne casts his gaze in two directions: at newly colonized peoples in the Americas and at his fellow citizens consumed by religious hatred. In the process, he questions the basis of Europeans' supposed moral and cultural superiority over the "barbarians" of the New World.*

I had with me for a long time a man that had lived ten or twelve years in that order world which has been discovered in our century, in the place where Villegaignon landed, which he called Antarctic France.[1] This discovery of so vast a country seems worthy of consideration. I do not know if I can be sure that in the future there may not be another such discovery made, so many greater men than we having been deceived in this. I am afraid our eyes are bigger than our bellies and that we have more curiosity than capacity. We grasp at all, but catch nothing but wind. . . .

This man that I had was a plain ignorant fellow, which is a condition fit to bear true witness; for your sharp sort of men are much more curious in their observations and notice a great deal more, but they gloss them; and to give the greater weight to their interpretation and make it convincing, they cannot forbear to alter the story a

---

From Michel de Montaigne, *Montaigne: Selected Essays*, ed. Blanchard Bates (New York: Modern Library, 1949), 74, 77–79, 82–84.

[1]Brazil, where he arrived in 1557.

little. They never represent things to you simply as they are, they slant them and mask them according to the aspect they saw in them; and to give authority to their judgment and to attract you to it, they are willing to contribute something there to the matter, lengthening it and amplifying it. We should have a man either of irreproachable veracity, or so simple that he has not wherewithal to contrive and to give a color of truth to false tales, and who has not espoused any cause. Mine was such a one; and, besides that, he has diverse times brought me several seamen and merchants whom he had known on that voyage. I do, therefore, content myself with his information without inquiring what the cosmographers say about it. . . .

Now to return to my subject, I find that there is nothing barbarous and savage in this nation according to what I have been told, except that everyone gives the title of barbarism to everything that is not according to his usage; as, indeed, we have no other criterion of truth and reason than the example and pattern of the opinions and customs of the country wherein we live. There is always the perfect religion, there the perfect government, there the perfect and accomplished usage in all things. They are savages in the same way that we say fruits are wild, which nature produces of herself and by her ordinary course; whereas, in truth, we ought rather to call those wild whose natures we have changed by our artifice and diverted from the common order. In the former, the genuine, most useful, and natural virtues and properties are vigorous and active, which we have degenerated in the latter, and we have only adapted them to the pleasure of our corrupted palate. And yet, for all this, the flavor and delicacy found in various uncultivated fruits of those countries are excellent to our taste, worthy rivals of ours. . . .

These nations then seem to me to be barbarous so far as having received very little fashioning from the human mind and as being still very close to their original simplicity. The laws of Nature govern them still, very little vitiated by ours. . . .

. . . [T]here is no manner of traffic, no knowledge of letters, no science of numbers, no name of magistrate or of political superiority; no use of servitude, riches, or poverty; no contracts, no successions, no dividing of properties, no employments, except those of leisure; no respect of kindred, except for the common bond; no clothing, no agriculture, no metal, no use of wheat or wine. The very words that signify lying, treachery, dissimulation, avarice, envy, detraction, and pardon were never heard of. . . .

They have wars with the nations that live farther inland beyond their mountains, to which they go quite naked and without other arms than their bows and wooden swords pointed at one end like the points of our spears. The obstinacy of their battles is wonderful; they never end without slaughter and bloodshed; for as to running away and fear, they know not what it is. Everyone for a trophy brings home the head of an enemy he has killed and fixes it over the door of his house. After having a long time treated their prisoners well and with all the luxuries they can think of, he to whom the prisoner belongs forms a great assembly of his acquaintances. He ties a rope to one of the arms of the prisoner, by the end of which he holds him some paces away for fear of being struck, and gives to the friend he loves best the other arm to hold in the same manner; and they two, in the presence of all the assembly, dispatch him with their swords. After that they roast him and eat him among them and send some pieces to their absent friends. They do not do this, as some think, for nourishment, . . . but as a representation of an extreme revenge. And its proof is that having observed that the Portuguese, who were in league with their enemies, inflicted another sort of death on them when they captured them, which was to bury them up to the waist, shoot the rest of the body full of arrows, and then hang them; they thought that these people from the other world (as men who had sown the knowledge of a great many vices among their neighbors and were much greater masters in all kind of wickedness than they) did not exercise this sort of revenge without reason, and that it must needs be more painful than theirs, and they began to leave their old way and to follow this. I am not sorry that we should take notice of the barbarous horror of such acts, but I am sorry that, seeing so clearly into their faults, we should be so blind to our own. I conceive there is more barbarity in eating a man alive than in eating him dead, in tearing by tortures and the rack a body that is still full of feeling, in roasting him by degrees, causing him to be bitten and torn by dogs and swine (as we have not only read, but lately seen, not among inveterate enemies, but among neighbors and fellow-citizens, and what is worse, under color of piety and religion), than in roasting and eating him after he is dead. . . .

We may, then, well call these people barbarians in respect to the rules of reason, but not in respect to ourselves, who, in all sorts of barbarity, exceed them. Their warfare is in every way noble and generous and has as much excuse and beauty as this human malady is capable of; it has with them no other foundation than the sole jealousy of valor. Their disputes are not for the conquests of new lands, for they still enjoy that natural abundance that supplies them without labor and trouble with all things necessary in such abundance that they have no need to enlarge their borders. And they are still in that happy stage of desiring only as much as their natural necessities demand; all beyond that is superfluous to them.

DISCUSSION QUESTIONS

1. How does Montaigne describe the Amerindians?

2. How does Amerindian culture compare to that of Europeans? Who is more barbaric and why? Why does Montaigne make such a comparison?

3. What does this essay suggest about the ways in which the colonization of the New World affected European identity and self-understanding?

3.
The Scientific Challenge

Galileo, *Letter to the Grand Duchess Christina* (1615)

Italian-born and educated, Galileo Galilei (1564–1642) was among the most illustrious proponents of the new science in the seventeenth century. Early in his studies, he embraced the theory held by Nicolaus Copernicus (1473–1543) that the sun, not the Earth, was at the center of the universe. Having improved on the newly invented telescope in 1609, Galileo was able to substantiate the heliocentric view through his observations of the moon and planets. Because Galileo's work challenged traditional scientific views, it sparked considerable controversy. In the letter excerpted here, written in 1615 to the Grand Duchess Christina of Tuscany, an important Catholic patron of learning, Galileo defends the validity of his findings while striving to separate matters of religious faith from the study of natural phenomena.

Galileo Galilei to The Most Serene Grand Duchess Mother

Some years ago, as Your Serene Highness well knows, I discovered in the heavens many things that had not been seen before our own age. The novelty of these things, as well as some consequences which followed from them in contradiction to the physical notions commonly held among academic philosophers, stirred up against me no small number of professors — as if I had placed these things in the sky with my own hands in order to upset nature and overturn the sciences. . . .

Well, the passage of time has revealed to everyone the truths that I previously set forth. . . . But some, besides allegiance to their original error, possess I know not what fanciful interest in remaining hostile not so much toward the things in question as toward their discoverer. No longer being able to deny them, these men now take refuge in obstinate silence, but being more than ever exasperated by that which has pacified and quieted other men, they divert their thoughts to other fancies and seek new ways to damage me. . . .

Persisting in their original resolve to destroy me and everything mine by any means they can think of, these men are aware of my views in astronomy and philosophy. They know that as to the arrangement of the parts of the universe, I hold the sun to be situated motionless in the center of the revolution of the celestial orbs while the earth rotates on its axis and revolves about the sun. . . .

Now as to the false aspersions which they so unjustly seek to cast upon me, I have thought it necessary to justify myself in the eyes of all men, whose judgment in matters of religion and of reputation I must hold in great esteem. I shall therefore discourse of the particulars which these men produce to make this opinion detested and to have it condemned not merely as false but as heretical. To this end they make a shield of their hypocritical zeal for religion. They go about invoking the Bible, which they would have minister to their deceitful purposes. Contrary to the sense of the Bible and the intention of the holy Fathers, if I am not mistaken, they would extend such authorities until even in purely physical matters — where faith is not involved — they would have us altogether abandon reason and the evidence of our senses in favor of some biblical passage, though under the surface meaning of its words this passage may contain a different sense. . . .

The reason produced for condemning the opinion that the earth moves and the sun stands still is that in many places in the Bible one may read that the sun moves and the earth stands still. Since the Bible cannot err, it follows as a necessary

From *Discoveries and Opinions of Galileo*, trans. Stillman Drake (New York: Doubleday, 1957), 175–86.

consequence that anyone takes an erroneous and heretical position who maintains that the sun is inherently motionless and the earth movable.

With regard to this argument, I think in the first place that it is very pious to say and prudent to affirm that the holy Bible can never speak untruth — whenever its true meaning is understood. But I believe nobody will deny that it is often very abstruse, and may say things which are quite different from what its bare words signify. Hence in expounding the Bible if one were always to confine oneself to the unadorned grammatical meaning, one might fall into error. Not only contradictions and propositions far from true might thus be made to appear in the Bible, but even grave heresies and follies. Thus it would be necessary to assign to God feet, hands, and eyes, as well as corporeal and human affections, such as anger, repentance, hatred, and sometimes even the forgetting of things past and ignorance of those to come. These propositions uttered by the Holy Ghost were set down in that manner by the sacred scribes in order to accommodate them to the capacities of the common people, who are rude and unlearned. For the sake of those who deserve to be separated from the herd, it is necessary that wise expositors should produce the true senses of such passages, together with the special reasons for which they were set down in these words. This doctrine is so widespread and so definite with all theologians that it would be superfluous to adduce evidence for it.

Hence I think that I may reasonably conclude that whenever the Bible has occasion to speak of any physical conclusion (especially those which are very abstruse and hard to understand), the rule has been observed of avoiding confusion in the minds of the common people which would render them contumacious toward the higher mysteries. Now the Bible, merely to condescend to popular capacity, has not hesitated to obscure some very important pronouncements, attributing to God himself some qualities extremely remote from (and even contrary to) His essence. Who, then, would positively declare that this principle has been set aside, and the Bible has confined itself rigorously to the bare and restricted sense of its words, when speaking but casually of the earth, of water, of the sun, or of any other created thing? Especially in view of the fact that these things in no way concern the primary purpose of the sacred writings, which is the service of God and the salvation of souls — matters infinitely beyond the comprehension of the common people.

This being granted, I think that in discussions of physical problems we ought to begin not from the authority of scriptural passages, but from sense-experiences and necessary demonstrations; for the holy Bible and the phenomena of nature proceed alike from the divine Word, the former as the dictate of the Holy Ghost and the latter as the observant executrix of God's commands. It is necessary for the Bible, in order to be accommodated to the understanding of every man, to speak many things which appear to differ from the absolute truth so far as the bare meaning of the words is concerned. But Nature, on the other hand, is inexorable and immutable; she never transgresses the laws imposed upon her, or cares a whit whether her abstruse reasons and methods of operations are understandable to men. For that reason it appears that nothing physical which sense-experience sets before our eyes, or which necessary demonstrations prove to us, ought to be called in question (much less condemned) upon the testimony of biblical passages which may have some different meaning beneath their words. For the Bible is not chained in every expression to conditions as strict as those which govern all physical effects; nor is God any less excellently revealed in Nature's actions than in the sacred statements of the Bible. . . .

From this I do not mean to infer that we need not have an extraordinary esteem for the passages of holy Scripture. On the contrary, having arrived at any certainties in physics, we ought to utilize these as the most appropriate aids in the true exposition of the Bible and in the investigation of those meanings which are necessarily contained therein, for these must be concordant with demonstrated truths. I should judge that the authority of the Bible was designed to persuade men of those articles and propositions which, surpassing all human reasoning, could not be made credible by science, or by any other means than through the very mouth of the Holy Spirit.

Yet even in those propositions which are not matters of faith, this authority ought to be preferred over that of all human writings which are supported only by bare assertions or probable arguments, and not set forth in a demonstrative way. This I hold to be necessary and proper to the same extent that divine wisdom surpasses all human judgment and conjecture.

But I do not feel obliged to believe that that same God who has endowed us with senses, reason, and intellect has intended to forego their use and by some other means to give us knowledge which we can attain by them. He would not require us to deny sense and reason in physical matters which are set before our eyes and minds by direct experience or necessary demonstrations. This must be especially true in those sciences of which but the faintest trace (and that consisting of conclusions) is to be found in the Bible. Of astronomy, for instance, so little is found that none of the planets except Venus are so much as mentioned, and this only once or twice under the name of "Lucifer." If the sacred scribes had had any intention of teaching people certain arrangements and motions of the heavenly bodies, or had they wished us to derive such knowledge from the Bible, then in my opinion they would not have spoken of these matters so sparingly in comparison with the infinite number of admirable conclusions which are demonstrated in that science. . . .

From these things it follows as a necessary consequence that, since the Holy Ghost did not intend to teach us whether heaven moves or stands still, whether its shape is spherical or like a discus or extended in a plane, nor whether the earth is located at its center or off to one side, then so much the less was it intended to settle for us any other conclusion of the same kind. And the motion or rest of the earth and the sun is so closely linked with the things just named, that without a determination of the one, neither side can be taken in the other matters. Now if the Holy Spirit has purposely neglected to teach us propositions of this sort as irrelevant to the highest goal (that is, to our salvation), how can anyone affirm that it is obligatory to take sides on them, and that one belief is required by faith, while the other side is erroneous? Can an opinion be heretical and yet have no concern with the salvation of souls? Can the Holy Ghost be asserted not to have intended teaching us something that does concern our salvation? I would say here something that was heard from an ecclesiastic of the most eminent degree: "That the intention of the Holy Ghost is to teach us how one goes to heaven, not how heaven goes." . . .

From this it is seen that the interpretation which we impose upon passages of Scripture would be false whenever it disagreed with demonstrated truths. And therefore we should seek the incontrovertible sense of the Bible with the assistance of demonstrated truth, and not in any way try to force the hand of Nature or deny experiences and rigorous proofs in accordance with the mere sound of words that may appeal to our frailty. . . .

To that end they would forbid him the use of reason, divine gift of Providence, and would abuse the just authority of holy Scripture — which, in the general opinion of theologians, can never oppose manifest experiences and necessary demonstrations when rightly understood and applied. If I am correct, it will stand them in no stead to go running to the Bible to cover up their inability to understand (let alone resolve) their opponents' arguments.

DISCUSSION QUESTIONS

1. What do you think Galileo's goal in writing this letter to the Grand Duchess was?

2. What is the basis of the attacks by Galileo's critics?

3. According to Galileo, what role should the Bible play in scientific inquiry?

4. How does this document lend support to historians who have credited Galileo for helping to popularize the principles and methods of the new science?

4.
The Persecution of Witches

The Trial of Suzanne Gaudry (1652)

Even as the new science gained support, most Europeans continued to believe in the supernatural, especially at this time of religious wars, economic decline, and social strife. This belief found violent expression in a wave of witchcraft persecutions across Europe between 1560 and 1640. The following selections from the trial records of Suzanne Gaudry attest to the predominant notion that witches were agents of the devil. Although conducted at a time when the number of witch hunts and persecutions were in decline, her trial attests to the persistence of a deeply felt fear among many people regarding the presence of diabolical forces in everyday life.

At Ronchain, 28 May, 1652. . . . Interrogation of Suzanne Gaudry, prisoner at the court of Rieux. Questioned about her age, her place of origin, her mother and father.

— Said that she is named Suzanne Gaudry, daughter of Jean Gaudry and Marguerite Gerné, both natives of Rieux, but that she is from Esgavans, near Odenarde, where her family had taken refuge because of the wars, that she was born the day that they

From Alan C. Kors and Edward Peters, eds., *Witchcraft in Europe, 1100–1700: A Documentary History* (Philadelphia: University of Pennsylvania Press, 1972), 266–75.

made bonfires for the Peace between France and Spain, without being able otherwise to say her age.

Asked why she has been taken here.

— Answers that it is for the salvation of her soul.

— Says that she was frightened of being taken prisoner for the crime of witchcraft.

Asked for how long she has been in the service of the devil.

— Says that about twenty-five or twenty-six years ago she was his lover, that he called himself Petit-Grignon, that he would wear black breeches, that he gave her the name Magin, that she gave him a pin with which he gave her his mark on the left shoulder, that he had a little flat hat; said also that he had his way with her two or three times only.

Asked how many times she has been at the nocturnal dance.

— Answers that she has been there about a dozen times, having first of all renounced God, Lent, and baptism; that the site of the dance was at the little marsh of Rieux, understanding that there were diverse dances. The first time, she did not recognize anyone there, because she was half blind. The other times, she saw and recognized there Noelle and Pasquette Gerné, Noelle the wife of Nochin Quinchou and the other of Paul Doris, the widow Marie Nourette, not having recognized others because the young people went with the young people and the old people with the old. [. . .]

Interrogated on how and in what way they danced.

— Says that they dance in an ordinary way, that there was a guitarist and some whistlers who appeared to be men she did not know; which lasted about an hour, and then everyone collapsed from exhaustion.

Inquired what happened after the dance.

— Says that they formed a circle, that there was a king with a long black beard dressed in black, with a red hat, who made everyone do his bidding, and that after the dance he made a . . . [the word is missing in the text], and then everyone disappeared. . . .

Questioned if she has abused the Holy Communion.

— Says no, never, and that she has always swallowed it. Then says that her lover asked her for it several times, but that she did not want to give it to him.

After several admonitions were sent to her, she has signed this

Mark

X

Suzanne Gaudry

Second Interrogation, May 29, 1652, in the Presence of the Afore-Mentioned

This prisoner, being brought back into the chamber, was informed about the facts and the charges and asked if what she declared and confessed yesterday is true.

— Answers that if it is in order to put her in prison it is not true; then after having remained silent said that it is true.

Asked what is her lover's name and what name has he given himself.

— Said that his name is Grinniou and that he calls himself Magnin.

Asked where he found her the first time and what he did to her.

— Answers that it was in her lodgings, that he had a hide, little black breeches, and a little flat hat; that he asked her for a pin, which she gave to him, with which he made his mark on her left shoulder. Said also that at the time she took him oil in a bottle and that she had thoughts of love.

Asked how long she has been in subjugation to the devil.

— Says that it has been about twenty-five or twenty-six years, that her lover also then made her renounce God, Lent, and baptism, that he has known her carnally three or four times, and that he has given her satisfaction. And on the subject of his having asked her if she wasn't afraid of having a baby, says that she did not have that thought.

Asked how many times she found herself at the nocturnal dance and carol and who she recognized there.

— Answers that she was there eleven or twelve times, that she went there on foot with her lover, where the third time she saw and recognized Pasquette and Noelle Gerné, and Marie Homitte, to whom she never spoke, for the reason that they did not speak to each other. And that the sabbat took place at the little meadow. . . .

Asked what occurred at the dance and afterwards.

— Says that right after the dance they put themselves in rank and approached the chief figure, who had a long black beard, dressed also in black, with a red hat, at which point they were given some powder, to do with it what they wanted; but that she did not want to take any.

Charged with having taken some and with having used it evilly.

— Says, after having insisted that she did not want to take any, that she took some, and that her lover advised her to do evil with it; but that she did not want to do it.

Asked if, not obeying his orders, she was beaten or threatened by him, and what did she do with this powder.

— Answers that never was she beaten; she invoked the name of the Virgin [and answered] that she threw away the powder that she had, not having wanted to do any evil with it.

Pressed to say what she did with this powder. Did she not fear her lover too much to have thrown it away?

— Says, after having been pressed on this question, that she made the herbs in her garden die at the end of the summer, five to six years ago, by means of the powder, which she threw there because she did not know what to do with it. [. . .]

Charged once more with having performed some malefice with this powder, pressed to tell the truth.

— Answers that she never made any person or beast die; then later said that she made Philippe Cornié's red horse die, about two or three years ago, by means of the

powder, which she placed where he had to pass, in the street close to her home.
Asked why she did that and if she had had any difficulty with him.
— Says that she had had some difficulty with his wife, because her cow had eaten
the leeks.[. . .]

After having been admonished to think of her conscience, was returned to prison
after having signed this

Mark

X

Suzanne Gaudry

Deliberation of the Court of Mons — June 3, 1652

The under-signed advocates of the Court of Mons have seen these interrogations
and answers. They say that the aforementioned Suzanne Gaudry confesses that she
is a witch, that she has given herself to the devil, that she has renounced God, Lent,
and baptism, that she has been marked on the shoulder, that she has cohabited with
him and that she has been to the dances, confessing only to have cast a spell upon
and caused to die a beast of Philippe Cornié; but there is no evidence for this, ex-
cepting a prior statement. For this reason, before going further, it will be necessary
to become acquainted with, to examine and to probe the mark, and to hear Philippe
Cornié on the death of the horse and on when and in what way he died. . . .

Deliberation of the Court of Mons — June 13, 1652

[The Court] has reviewed the current criminal trial of Suzanne Gaudry, and with
it the trial of Antoinette Lescouffre, also a prisoner of the same office.
    It appeared [to the Court] that the office should have the places probed where
the prisoners say that they have received the mark of the devil, and after that, they
must be interrogated and examined seriously on their confessions and denials, this
having to be done, in order to regulate all this definitively. . . .

Deliberation of the Court of Mons — June 22, 1652

The trials of Antoinette Lescouffre and Suzanne Gaudry having been described to
the undersigned, advocates of the Court of Mons, and [the Court] having been told
orally that the peasants taking them to prison had persuaded them to confess in
order to avoid imprisonment, and that they would be let go, by virtue of which it
could appear that the confessions were not so spontaneous:
    They are of the opinion that the office, in its duty, would do well, following
the two preceding resolutions, to have the places of the marks that they have taught
us about probed, and if it is found that these are ordinary marks of the devil, one
can proceed to their examination; then next to the first confessions, and if they

deny [these], one can proceed to the torture, given that they issue from bewitched relatives, that at all times they have been suspect, that they fled to avoid the crime [that is to say, prosecution for the crime of witchcraft], and that by their confessions they have confirmed [their guilt], notwithstanding that they have wanted to revoke [their confessions] and vacillate. . . .

Third Interrogation, June 27, in the Presence of the Afore-Mentioned

This prisoner being led into the chamber, she was examined to know if things were not as she had said and confessed at the beginning of her imprisonment.
— Answers no, and that what she has said was done so by force.
Asked if she did not say to Jean Gradé that she would tell his uncle, the mayor, that he had better be careful . . . and that he was a Frank.
— Said that that is not true.
Pressed to say the truth, that otherwise she would be subjected to torture, having pointed out to her that her aunt was burned for this same subject.
— Answers that she is not a witch.
Interrogated as to how long she has been in subjection to the devil, and pressed that she was to renounce the devil and the one who misled her.
— Says that she is not a witch, that she has nothing to do with the devil thus that she did not want to renounce the devil, saying that he has not misled her, and upon inquisition of having confessed to being present at the carol, she insisted that although she had said that, it is not true, and that she is not a witch.
Charged with having confessed to having made a horse die by means of a powder that the devil had given her.
— Answers that she said it, but because she found herself during the inquisition pressed to say that she must have done some evil deed; and after several admonitions to tell the truth:
   She was placed in the hands of the officer of the *haultes oeuvres* [the officer in charge of torture], throwing herself on her knees, struggling to cry, uttering several exclamations, without being able, nevertheless, she shed a tear. Saying at every moment that she is not a witch.

The Torture

On this same day, being at the place of torture.
   This prisoner, before being strapped down, was admonished to maintain herself in her first confessions and to renounce her lover.
— Said that she denies everything she has said, and that she has no lover. Feeling herself being strapped down, says that she is not a witch, while struggling to cry.
Asked why she fled outside the village of Rieux.
— Says that she cannot say it, that God and the Virgin Mary forbid her to; that she is not a witch. And upon being asked why she confessed to being one, said that she was forced to say it.

Told that she was not forced, that on the contrary she declared herself to be a witch without any threat.

— Says that she confessed it and that she is not a witch, and being a little stretched [on the rack] screams ceaselessly that she is not a witch, invoking the name of Jesus and of Our Lady of Grace, not wanting to say any other thing.

Asked if she did not confess that she had been a witch for twenty-six years.

— Says that she said it, that she retracts it, crying Jésus-Maria, that she is not a witch.

Asked if she did not make Philippe Cornié's horse die, as she confessed.

— Answers no, crying Jésus-Maria, that she is not a witch.

The mark having been probed by the officer, in the presence of Doctor Bouchain, it was adjudged by the aforesaid doctor and officer truly to be the mark of the devil.

Being more tightly stretched upon the torture-rack, urged to maintain her confessions.

— Said that it was true that she is a witch and that she would maintain what she had said.

Asked how long she has been in subjugation to the devil.

— Answers that it was twenty years ago that the devil appeared to her, being in her lodgings in the form of a man dressed in a little cow-hide and black breeches. Interrogated as to what her lover was called.

— Says that she said Petit-Grignon, then, being taken down [from the rack] says upon interrogation that she is not a witch and that she can say nothing.

Asked if her lover has had carnal copulation with her, and how many times.

— To that she did not answer anything; then, making believe that she was ill, not another word could be drawn from her.

As soon as she began to confess, she asked who was alongside of her, touching her, yet none of those present could see anyone there. And it was noticed that as soon as that was said, she no longer wanted to confess anything.

Which is why she was returned to prison.

Verdict

July 9, 1652

In the light of the interrogations, answers and investigations made into the charge against Suzanne Gaudry, coupled with her confessions, from which it would appear that she has always been ill-reputed for being stained with the crime of witchcraft, and seeing that she took flight and sought refuge in this city of Valenciennes, out of fear of being apprehended by the law for this matter; seeing how her close family were also stained with the same crime, and the perpetrators executed; seeing by her own confessions that she is said to have made a pact with the devil, received the mark from him, which in the report of *sieur* Michel de Roux was judged by the medical doctor of Ronchain and the officer of *haultes oeuvres* of Cambrai, after having proved it, to be not a natural mark but a mark of the devil, to which they have sworn with an oath; and that following this, she had renounced God, Lent, and baptism and had let herself be known carnally by him, in which she received satisfaction. Also, seeing that she is said to have been a part of nocturnal carols and dances. Which are crimes of divine lèse-majesty:

For expiation of which the advice of the under-signed is that the office of Rieux can legitimately condemn the aforesaid Suzanne Gaudry to death, tying her to a gallows, and strangling her to death, then burning her body and burying it there in the environs of the woods.

At Valenciennes, the 9th of July, 1652. To each [member of the Court] 4 *livres*, 16 *sous*. . . . And for the trip of the aforementioned Roux, including an escort of one soldier, 30 *livres*.

DISCUSSION QUESTIONS

1. According to the trial record, why was Suzanne Gaudry targeted for persecution? What does this reveal about contemporary beliefs in witches and their powers?

2. How would you characterize the legal procedures used in this trial? How might the procedures help to explain the widespread consistency in the content of confessions throughout the period of witchcraft persecutions?

3. What does this document suggest about the religious anxieties of the times?

5.

Commercial Endeavors

David Pieterzen DeVries, *Voyages from Holland to America* (1655)

During the seventeenth century, the Dutch Republic entered its golden age as the center of a thriving maritime economy. Like other European states at the time, Holland expanded its commercial markets and established permanent colonies in newly explored regions of North America. The Dutch thus contributed to Europeans' growing knowledge of the topography, peoples, and cultures of the New World. In this excerpt, a French-born Dutch merchant and colonist, David DeVries (1593–1655), describes a violent conflict in 1643 between Dutch settlers and Native Americans in the area around modern New York City. The conflict was sparked by the Native Americans' refusal to relinquish their land. DeVries's account provides a vivid testimony of the clash between the two societies.

The 24th of February, sitting at the table with the governor, he began to state his intentions, that he had a mind to *wipe the mouths* of the Indians; that he had been dining at the house of Jan Claesz. Damen, where Maryn Adriaensz. and Jan Claesz.

Damen, together with Jacob Planck, had presented a petition to him to begin this work. I answered him that there was no sufficient reason to undertake it. . . . But it appeared that my speaking was of no avail. He had, with his co-murderers, determined to commit the murder, deeming it a Roman deed, and to do it without warning the inhabitants in the open lands, that each one might take care of himself against the retaliation of the Indians, for he could not kill all the Indians. When I had expressed all these things in full, sitting at the table, and the meal was over, he told me he wished me to go to the large hall, which he had been lately adding to his house. Coming to it, there stood all his soldiers ready to cross the river to Pavonia to commit the murder. Then spoke I again to Governor William Kieft: "Stop this work; you wish to break the mouths of the Indians, but you will also murder our own nation, for there are none of the farmers who are aware of it. My own dwelling, my people, cattle, corn, and tobacco will be lost." He answered me, assuring me that there would be no danger; that some soldiers should go to my house to protect it. But that was not done. So was this business begun between the 25th and 26th of February in the year 1643. I remained that night at the governor's, sitting up. I went and sat in the kitchen, when, about midnight, I heard a great shrieking, and I ran to the ramparts of the fort, and looked over to Pavonia. Saw nothing but firing, and heard the shrieks of the Indians murdered in their sleep. I returned again to the house by the fire. Having sat there awhile, there came an Indian with his squaw, whom I knew well, and who lived about an hour's walk from my house, and told me that they two had fled in a small skiff; that they had betaken themselves to Pavonia; that the Indians from Fort Orange had surprised them; and that they had come to conceal themselves in the fort. I told them that they must go away immediately; that there was no occasion for them to come to the fort to conceal themselves; that they who had killed their people at Pavonia were not Indians, but the Swannekens, as they call the Dutch, had done it. They then asked me how they should get out of the fort. I took them to the door, and there was no sentry there, and so they betook themselves to the woods. When it was day, the soldiers returned to the fort, having massacred or murdered eighty Indians, and considering they had done a deed of Roman valor, in murdering so many in their sleep; where infants were torn from their mother's breasts, and hacked to pieces in the presence of the parents, and the pieces thrown into the fire and in the water, and other sucklings were bound to small boards, and then cut, stuck, and pierced, and miserably massacred in a manner to move a heart of stone. Some were thrown into the river, and when the fathers and mothers endeavored to save them, the soldiers would not let them come on land, but made both parents and children drown, — children from five to six years of age, and also some old and decrepit persons. Many fled from this scene, and concealed themselves in the neighboring sedge, and when it was morning, came out to beg a piece of bread, and to be per-

From David Pieterzen DeVries, *Voyages from Holland to America, a.d. 1632 to 1644*, trans. Henry C. Murphy (New York: Billin and Brothers, 1853), 167–71.

mitted to warm themselves; but they were murdered in cold blood and tossed into the water. Some came by our lands in the country with their hands, some with their legs cut off, and some holding their entrails in their arms, and others had such horrible cuts and gashes, that worse than they were could never happen. . . . This is indeed a disgrace to our nation, who have so generous a governor in our Fatherland as the Prince of Orange, who has always endeavored in his wars to spill as little blood as possible. As soon as the Indians understood that the Swannekens had so treated them, all the men whom they could surprise on the farm-lands, they killed; but we have never heard that they have ever permitted women or children to be killed. They burned all the houses, farms, barns, grain, haystacks, and destroyed everything they could get hold of. So there was an open destructive war begun. They also burnt my farm, cattle, corn, barn, tobacco-house, and all the tobacco. My people saved themselves in the house where I lived, which was made with embrasures, through which they defended themselves. Whilst my people were in this state of alarm, the Indian whom I had aided to escape from the fort came there, and told the other Indians that I was a good chief, that I had helped him out of the fort, and that the killing of the Indians took place contrary to my wish. Then they all cried out together to my people that they would not shoot them; that if they had not destroyed my cattle they would not do it; that they would not burn my house; that they would let my little brewery stand, though they had melted the copper-kettle, in order to make darts for their arrows; but hearing now that it (the massacre) had been done contrary to my wish, they all went away, and left my house unbesieged. When now the Indians had destroyed so many farms and men in revenge for their people, I went to Governor William Kieft, and asked him if it was not as I had said it would be, that he would only effect the spilling of Christian blood.

DISCUSSION QUESTIONS

1. Based on this account, what are DeVries's attitudes toward the Native Americans? How do his attitudes differ from those of the governor and the soldiers who carried out his orders?

2. Why do you think DeVries described the massacre as a disgrace to his nation?

3. What does this account reveal about the Dutch settlers' way of life?

COMPARATIVE QUESTIONS

1. How do the Edict of Nantes, "Of Cannibals," and Galileo's letter support scholars who argue that amidst the conflicts of this period, many European leaders and thinkers increasingly gave precedence to secular concerns over religious ones?

2. Despite the gradual trend in Europe toward secularization during the seventeenth century, what do Galileo's letter and Suzanne Gaudry's trial records reveal about the continued importance of religion in shaping Europeans' understanding of the everyday world?

3. What do "Of Cannibals," the witchcraft trial, and DeVries's account suggest about the role of violence in European society and culture? Do you see any similarities between Montaigne's and DeVries's attitudes toward this role?

4. In what ways is Galileo's emphasis on the value of observation and personal experience reflected in the Gaudry trial? What does this suggest about the impact of the new science on traditional beliefs?

State Building and the Search for Order, 1648–1690

The wars over religion not only had left bitter memories in late-seventeenth-century Europe but also had ruined economies and weakened governments. In response, many people sought to impose order on the turbulent world in a variety of ways. As the first four documents reveal, politically, the quest for stability fueled the development of two rival systems of state building — absolutism and constitutionalism. Despite their differences, rulers within both systems centralized power and expanded bureaucracies, casting an increasingly wide net over their subjects' lives. Although not everyone submitted willingly to the expansion of state power, such resistance was typically fruitless. As the final document shows, the sinews of state power extended beyond Europe as European nations (in this case France) continued their quest for land, treasure, and prestige in the New World.

1.
Civil War and Social Contract
Thomas Hobbes, *Leviathan* (1651)

The seventeenth century was particularly turbulent in England, where Protestants and Catholics, royalists and parliamentary supporters, vied for power. Thomas Hobbes (1588–1679), an English philosopher with close aristocratic and royalist ties, viewed England's troubles as an indictment of traditional political thinking. According to Hobbes, in their natural state humans were violent and prone to war. Absolute authority was the only way to counter this threat to social order. Whether this authority rested in a king or parliament was immaterial to Hobbes; what mattered was that it gained its power from a so-

---

From Thomas Hobbes, *Leviathan*, Renascence Editions, at www.uoregon.edu/~rbear/hobbes/leviathan.html.

cial contract, or "covenant," between ruler and ruled. Individuals agreed to relinquish their right to govern themselves to an absolute ruler in exchange for collective peace and defense. Hobbes published his views in 1651 in his book Leviathan, most of which he wrote during the final stage of the English civil war while living in exile in France, where he was the tutor of the future king Charles II. The excerpt that follows speaks not only to Hobbes's understanding of human nature, absolute authority, and the social contract but also to the relationship among them.

Of the Difference of Manners

By manners, I mean not here decency of behavior; as how one man should salute another, or how a man should wash his mouth, or pick his teeth before company, and such other points of the small morals; but those qualities of mankind that concern their living together in peace and unity. . . .

. . . [I]n the first place, I put for a general inclination of all mankind a perpetual and restless desire of power after power, that ceaseth only in death. And the cause of this is not always that a man hopes for a more intensive delight than he has already attained to, or that he cannot be content with a moderate power, but because he cannot assure the power and means to live well, which he hath present, without the acquisition of more. And from hence it is that kings, whose power is greatest, turn their endeavors to the assuring it at home by laws, or abroad by wars: and when that is done, there succeedeth a new desire; in some, of fame from new conquest; in others, of ease and sensual pleasure; in others, of admiration, or being flattered for excellence in some art or other ability of the mind. . . .

Of the Natural Condition of Mankind as Concerning Their Felicity and Misery

Nature hath made men so equal in the faculties of body and mind as that, though there be found one man sometimes manifestly stronger in body or of quicker mind than another, yet when all is reckoned together the difference between man and man is not so considerable as that one man can thereupon claim to himself any benefit to which another may not pretend as well as he. For as to the strength of body, the weakest has strength enough to kill the strongest, either by secret machination or by confederacy with others that are in the same danger with himself.

And as to the faculties of the mind, setting aside the arts grounded upon words, and especially that skill of proceeding upon general and infallible rules, called science, which very few have and but in few things, as being not a native faculty born with us, nor attained, as prudence, while we look after somewhat else, I find yet a greater equality amongst men than that of strength. For prudence is but experience, which equal time equally bestows on all men in those things they equally apply themselves unto. That which may perhaps make such equality incredible is but a vain conceit of one's own wisdom, which almost all men think they have in a greater degree than the vulgar; that is, than all men but themselves, and a few others, whom by fame, or for concurring with themselves, they approve. For such is the nature of men that howsoever they may acknowledge many others to be more witty, or more eloquent or more learned, yet they will hardly believe there be many so wise as themselves; for they see their own wit at hand, and other men's at a distance. But this proveth rather that men are in that point equal, than unequal. For there is not ordinarily a greater sign of the equal distribution of anything than that every man is contented with his share.

From this equality of ability ariseth equality of hope in the attaining of our ends. And therefore if any two men desire the same thing, which nevertheless they cannot both enjoy, they become enemies; and in the way to their end (which is principally their own conservation, and sometimes their delectation only) endeavor to destroy or subdue one another. And from hence it comes to pass that where an invader hath no more to fear than another man's single power, if one plant, sow, build, or possess a convenient seat, others may probably be expected to come prepared with forces united to dispossess and deprive him, not only of the fruit of his labor, but also of his life or liberty. And the invader again is in the like danger of another. . . .

. . . [M]en have no pleasure (but on the contrary a great deal of grief) in keeping company where there is no power able to overawe them all. For every man looketh that his companion should value him at the same rate he sets upon himself, and upon all signs of contempt or undervaluing naturally endeavors, as far as he dares (which amongst them that have no common power to keep them in quiet is far enough to make them destroy each other), to extort a greater value from his contemners, by damage; and from others, by the example. So that in the nature of man, we find three principal causes of quarrel. First, competition; secondly, diffidence; thirdly, glory. The first maketh men invade for gain; the second, for safety; and the third, for reputation. The first use violence, to make themselves masters of other men's persons, wives, children, and cattle; the second, to defend them; the third, for trifles, as a word, a smile, a different opinion, and any other sign of undervalue, either direct in their persons or by reflection in their kindred, their friends, their nation, their profession, or their name. Hereby it is manifest that during the time men live without a common power to keep them all in awe, they are in that condition which is called war; and such a war as is of every man against every man. For war consisteth not in battle only, or the act of fighting, but in a tract of time, wherein the will to contend by battle is sufficiently known: and therefore the notion of time is to be considered in the nature of war, as it is in the nature of weather. For as the nature of foul weather lieth not in a shower or two of rain, but in an inclination thereto of many days together: so the nature of war consisteth not in actual fighting, but in the known disposition thereto during all the time there is no assurance to the contrary. All other time is peace.

Whatsoever therefore is consequent to a time of war, where every man is enemy to every man, the same consequent to the time wherein men live without other security than what their own strength and their own invention shall furnish them withal. In such condition there is no place for industry, because the fruit thereof is uncertain: and consequently no culture of the earth; no navigation, nor use of the commodities that may be imported by sea; no commodious building; no instruments of moving and removing such things as require much force; no knowledge of the face of the earth; no account of time; no arts; no letters; no society; and which is worst of all, continual fear, and danger of violent death; and the life of man, solitary, poor, nasty, brutish, and short. . . .

Of the Causes, Generation, and Definition of a Commonwealth

The final cause, end, or design of men (who naturally love liberty, and dominion over others) in the introduction of that restraint upon themselves, in which we see them live in Commonwealths, is the foresight of their own preservation, and of a more contented life thereby; that is to say, of getting themselves out from that miserable condition of war which is necessarily consequent, as hath been shown, to the natural passions of men when there is no visible power to keep them in awe, and tie them by fear of punishment to the performance of their covenants. . . .

The only way to erect such a common power, as may be able to defend them from the invasion of foreigners, and the injuries of one another, and thereby to secure them in such sort as that by their own industry and by the fruits of the earth they may nourish themselves and live contentedly, is to confer all their power and strength upon one man, or upon one assembly of men, that may reduce all their wills, by plurality of voices, unto one will: which is as much as to say, to appoint one man, or assembly of men, to bear their person; and every one to own and acknowledge himself to be author of whatsoever he that so beareth their person shall act, or cause to be acted, in those things which concern the common peace and safety; and therein to submit their wills, every one to his will, and their judgments to his judgment. This is more than consent, or concord; it is a real unity of them all in one and the same person, made by covenant of every man with every man, in such manner as if every man should say to every man: I authorize and give up my right of governing myself to this man, or to this assembly of men, on this condition; that thou give up, thy right to him, and authorize all his actions in like manner. This done, the multitude so united in one person is called a COMMONWEALTH; in Latin, CIVITAS. This is the generation of that great LEVIATHAN, or rather, to speak more reverently, of that mortal god to which we owe, under the immortal God, our peace and defense. For by this authority, given him by every particular man in the Commonwealth, he hath the use of so much power and strength conferred on him that, by terror thereof, he is enabled to form the wills of them all, to peace at home, and mutual aid against their enemies abroad. And in him consisteth the essence of the Commonwealth; which, to define it, is: one person, of whose acts a great multitude, by mutual covenants one with another, have made themselves every one the author, to the end he may use the strength and means of them all as he shall think expedient for their peace and common defense. . . .

Of the Rights of Sovereigns by Institution

A Commonwealth is said to be instituted when a multitude of men do agree, and covenant, every one with every one, that to whatsoever man, or assembly of men, shall be given by the major part the right to present the person of them all, that is to say, to be their representative; every one, as well he that voted for it as he that voted against it, shall authorize all the actions and judgments of that man, or assembly of men, in the same manner as if they were his own, to the end to live peaceably amongst themselves, and be protected against other men.

From this institution of a Commonwealth are derived all the rights and faculties of him, or them, on whom the sovereign power is conferred by the consent of the people assembled.

First, because they covenant, it is to be understood they are not obliged by former covenant to anything repugnant hereunto. And consequently they that have already instituted a Commonwealth, being thereby bound by covenant to own the actions and judgments of one, cannot lawfully make a new covenant amongst themselves to be obedient to any other, in anything whatsoever, without his permission. And therefore, they that are subjects to a monarch cannot without his leave cast off monarchy and return to the confusion of a disunited multitude; nor transfer their person from him that beareth it to another man, other assembly of men: for they are bound, every man to every man, to own and be reputed author of all that already is their sovereign shall do and judge fit to be done; so that any one man dissenting, all the rest should break their covenant made to that man, which is injustice: and they have also every man given the sovereignty to him that beareth their person; and therefore if they depose him, they take from him that which is his own, and so again it is injustice. Besides, if he that attempteth to depose his sovereign be killed or punished by him for such attempt, he is author of his own punishment, as being, by the institution, author of all his sovereign shall do; and because it is injustice for a man to do anything for which he may be punished by his own authority, he is also upon that title unjust. And whereas some men have pretended for their disobedience to their sovereign a new covenant, made, not with men but with God, this also is unjust: for there is no covenant with God but by mediation of somebody that representeth God's person, which none doth but God's lieutenant who hath the sovereignty under God. But this pretence of covenant with God is so evident a lie, even in the pretenders' own consciences, that it is not only an act of an unjust, but also of a vile and unmanly disposition.

Secondly, because the right of bearing the person of them all is given to him they make sovereign, by covenant only of one to another, and not of him to any of them, there can happen no breach of covenant on the part of the sovereign; and consequently none of his subjects, by any pretence of forfeiture, can be freed from his subjection. That he which is made sovereign maketh no covenant with his subjects before hand is manifest; because either he must make it with the whole multitude, as one party to the covenant, or he must make a several covenant with every man. With the whole, as one party, it is impossible, because as they are not one person: and if he make so many several covenants as there be men, those covenants after he hath the sovereignty are void; because what act soever can be pretended by any one of them for breach thereof is the act both of himself, and of all the rest, because done in the person, and by the right of every one of them in particular. Besides, if any one or more of them pretend a breach of the covenant made by the sovereign at his institution, and others or one other of his subjects, or himself alone, pretend there was no such breach, there is in this case no judge to decide the controversy: it returns therefore to the sword again; and every man recovereth the right of protecting himself by his own strength, contrary to the design they had in the institution. It is therefore in vain to grant sovereignty by way of precedent covenant. The opinion that any monarch receiveth his power by covenant, that is to say, on condition, proceedeth from want of understanding this easy truth: that covenants being but words, and breath, have no force to oblige, contain, constrain, or protect any man, but what it has from the public sword; that is, from the untied hands of that man, or assembly of men, that hath the sovereignty, and whose actions are avouched by them all, and performed by the strength of them all, in him united. But when an assembly of men is made sovereign, then no man imagineth any such covenant to have passed in the institution: for no man is so dull as to say, for example, the people of Rome made a covenant with the Romans to hold the sovereignty on such or such conditions; which not performed, the Romans might lawfully depose the Roman people. That men see not the reason to be alike in a monarchy and in a popular government proceedeth from the ambition of some that are kinder to the government of an assembly, whereof they may hope to participate, than of monarchy, which they despair to enjoy.

Thirdly, because the major part hath by consenting voices declared a sovereign, he that dissented must now consent with the rest; that is, be contented to avow all the actions he shall do, or else justly be destroyed by the rest. For if he voluntarily entered into the congregation of them that were assembled, he sufficiently declared thereby his will, and therefore tacitly covenanted, to stand to what the major part should ordain: and therefore if he refuse to stand thereto, or make protestation against any of their decrees, he does contrary to his covenant, and therefore unjustly. And whether he be of the congregation or not, and whether his consent be asked or not, he must either submit to their decrees or be left in the condition of war he was in before; wherein he might without injustice be destroyed by any man whatsoever.

Fourthly, because every subject is by this institution author of all the actions and judgments of the sovereign instituted, it follows that whatsoever he doth, can be no injury to any of his subjects; nor ought he to be by any of them accused of injustice. For he that doth anything by authority from another doth therein no injury to him by whose authority he acteth: but by this institution of a Commonwealth every particular man is author of all the sovereign doth; and consequently he that complaineth of injury from his sovereign complaineth of that whereof he himself is author, and therefore ought not to accuse any man but himself; no, nor himself of injury, because to do injury to oneself is impossible. It is true that they that have sovereign power may commit iniquity, but not injustice or injury in the proper signification.

Fifthly, and consequently to that which was said last, no man that hath sovereign power can justly be put to death, or otherwise in any manner by his subjects punished. For seeing every subject is author of the actions of his sovereign, he punisheth another for the actions committed by himself.

DISCUSSION QUESTIONS

1. How does Hobbes describe human nature? How might the events of the English civil war have shaped his views?

2. What is Hobbes's definition of the "Leviathan"? How is his definition linked to his understanding of the basis and role of absolute authority?

3. What does Hobbes mean by the "covenant" between sovereign and subject? How did this differ from the traditional understanding of absolute authority based on divine right?

4. According to Hobbes, did subjects bound by this covenant have the right to challenge sovereign power? Why or why not?

2.
The Consent of the Governed

John Locke, *The Second Treatise of Government* (1690)

Hobbes's fellow Englishman, John Locke (1632–1704), likewise viewed the tumults of his day with a critical eye. Although the English civil war ended with the restoration of Charles II to the throne, new troubles loomed. Charles openly sympathized with Catholics, as did his brother and heir, James II. Fearful of the ties between Catholicism and French absolutism, in 1678 Parliament denied the right of a Catholic to inherit the crown. Charles resisted this move, sparking a succession crisis. Locke fled to the Dutch Republic in 1683 with his patron, the Earl of Shaftesbury, who opposed a Catholic monarch. While abroad, Locke worked on his Two Treatises of Government, *which he published upon his return to England after the Glorious Revolution of 1688. A selection from the* Second Treatise *follows. As it reveals, although Locke shared Hobbes's interest in the origins of civil society, his anti-absolutist stance stood in sharp contrast to Hobbes's position. For Locke, ultimate authority rests in the will of the majority of propertied men who, in exchange for protection, endow the state with the authority to rule over them. Yet this power is not limitless. Just as the majority grants the state its power, so too can it justifiably resist it if it fails to fulfill its part of the social contract.*

Of the Beginning of Political Societies

Men being, as has been said, by nature, all free, equal, and independent, no one can be put out of this estate, and subjected to the political power of another, without his own consent. The only way whereby any one divests himself of his natural liberty, and puts on the bonds of civil society, is by agreeing with other men to join and unite into a community for their comfortable, safe, and peaceable living one amongst another, in a secure enjoyment of their properties, and a greater security

From John Locke, *Second Treatise on Government,* at www.ilt.columbia.edu/academic/digitexts/locke/second/locke2nd.txt.

against any, that are not of it. This any number of men may do, because it injures not the freedom of the rest; they are left as they were in the liberty of the state of nature. When any number of men have so consented to make one community or government, they are thereby presently incorporated, and make one body politic, wherein the majority have a right to act and conclude the rest. . . .

And thus every man, by consenting with others to make one body politic under one government, puts himself under an obligation, to every one of that society, to submit to the determination of the majority, and to be concluded by it; or else this original compact, whereby he with others incorporates into one society, would signify nothing, and be no compact, if he be left free, and under no other ties than he was in before in the state of nature. For what appearance would there be of any compact? what new engagement if he were no farther tied by any decrees of the society, than he himself thought fit, and did actually consent to? This would be still as great a liberty, as he himself had before his compact, or any one else in the state of nature hath, who may submit himself, and consent to any acts of it if he thinks fit. . . .

Whosoever therefore out of a state of nature unite into a community, must be understood to give up all the power, necessary to the ends for which they unite into society, to the majority of the community, unless they expressly agreed in any number greater than the majority. And this is done by barely agreeing to unite into one political society, which is all the compact that is, or needs be, between the individuals, that enter into, or make up a commonwealth. And thus that, which begins and actually constitutes any political society, is nothing but the consent of any number of freemen capable of a majority to unite and incorporate into such a society. And this is that, and that only, which did, or could give beginning to any lawful government in the world.

Of the Ends of Political Society and Government

If man in the state of nature be so free, as has been said; if he be absolute lord of his own person and possessions, equal to the greatest, and subject to nobody, why will he part with his freedom? why will he give up this empire, and subject himself to the dominion and control of any other power? To which it is obvious to answer, that though in the state of nature he hath such a right, yet the enjoyment of it is very uncertain, and constantly exposed to the invasion of others: for all being kings as much as he, every man his equal, and the greater part no strict observers of equity and justice, the enjoyment of the property he has in this state is very unsafe, very unsecure. This makes him willing to quit a condition, which, however free, is full of fears and continual dangers: and it is not without reason, that he seeks out, and is willing to join in society with others, who are already united, or have a mind to unite, for the mutual preservation of their lives, liberties and estates, which I call by the general name, property.

The great and chief end, therefore, of men's uniting into commonwealths, and putting themselves under government, is the preservation of their property. To which in the state of nature there are many things wanting.

First, There wants an established, settled, known law, received and allowed by common consent to be the standard of right and wrong, and the common measure to decide all controversies between them: for though the law of nature be plain and intelligible to all rational creatures; yet men being biased by their interest, as well as ignorant for want of study of it, are not apt to allow of it as a law binding to them in the application of it to their particular cases.

Secondly, In the state of nature there wants a known and indifferent judge, with authority to determine all differences according to the established law: for every one in that state being both judge and executioner of the law of nature, men being partial to themselves, passion and revenge is very apt to carry them too far, and with too much heat, in their own cases; as well as negligence, and unconcernedness, to make them too remiss in other men's.

Thirdly, In the state of nature there often wants power to back and support the sentence when right, and to give it due execution, They who by any injustice offended, will seldom fail, where they are able, by force to make good their injustice; such resistance many times makes the punishment dangerous, and frequently destructive, to those who attempt it.

Thus mankind, notwithstanding all the privileges of the state of nature, being but in an ill condition, while they remain in it, are quickly driven into society. Hence it comes to pass, that we seldom find any number of men live any time together in this state. The inconveniences that they are therein exposed to, by the irregular and uncertain exercise of the power every man has of punishing the transgressions of others, make them take sanctuary under the established laws of government, and therein seek the preservation of their property. It is this makes them so willingly give up every one his single power of punishing, to be exercised by such alone, as shall be appointed to it amongst them; and by such rules as the community, or those authorized by them to that purpose, shall agree on. And in this we have the original right and rise of both the legislative and executive power, as well as of the governments and societies themselves.

For in the state of nature, to omit the liberty he has of innocent delights, a man has two powers.

The first is to do whatsoever he thinks fit for the preservation of himself, and others within the permission of the law of nature: by which law, common to them all, he and all the rest of mankind are one community, make up one society, distinct from all other creatures. And were it not for the corruption and viciousness of degenerate men, there would be no need of any other; no necessity that men should separate from this great and natural community, and by positive agreements combine into smaller and divided associations.

The other power a man has in the state of nature, is the power to punish the crimes committed against that law. Both these he gives up, when he joins in a private, if I may so call it, or particular politic society, and incorporates into any commonwealth, separate from the rest of mankind.

The first power, viz. of doing whatsoever he thought for the preservation of himself, and the rest of mankind, he gives up to be regulated by laws made by the society, so far forth as the preservation of himself, and the rest of that society shall require; which laws of the society in many things confine the liberty he had by the law of nature.

Secondly, The power of punishing he wholly gives up, and engages his natural force, (which he might before employ in the execution of the law of nature, by his own single authority, as he thought fit) to assist the executive power of the society, as the law thereof shall require: for being now in a new state, wherein he is to enjoy many conveniences, from the labor, assistance, and society of others in the same community, as well as protection from its whole strength; he is to part also with as much of his natural liberty, in providing for himself, as the good, prosperity, and safety of the society shall require; which is not only necessary, but just, since the other members of the society do the like.

But though men, when they enter into society, give up the equality, liberty, and executive power they had in the state of nature, into the hands of the society, to be so far disposed of by the legislative, as the good of the society shall require; yet it being only with an intention in every one the better to preserve himself, his liberty, and property; (for no rational creature can be supposed to change his condition with an intention to be worse) the power of the society, or legislative constituted by them, can never be supposed to extend farther, than the common good; but is obliged to secure every one's property, by providing against those three defects above mentioned, that made the state of nature so unsafe and uneasy. And so whoever has the legislative or supreme power of any commonwealth, is bound to govern by established standing laws, promulgated and known to the people, and not by extemporary decrees; by indifferent and upright judges, who are to decide controversies by those laws; and to employ the force of the community at home, only in the execution of such laws, or abroad to prevent or redress foreign injuries, and secure the community from inroads and invasion. And all this to be directed to no other end, but the peace, safety, and public good of the people.

Discussion Questions

1. According to Locke, what is man's natural state? What are its chief characteristics?

2. Why would men relinquish the natural state to form a government? What advantages does government offer?

3. How does Locke describe the relationship between a government and its subjects? What are its terms and conditions?

4. How does Locke's proposed system guard against absolute or arbitrary power?

3.
Opposing Serfdom

Ludwig Fabritius, *The Revolt of Stenka Razin* (1670)

Despite its geographic and cultural isolation from the rest of Europe, Russia followed France's lead down the path of absolutism. In the process, Czar Alexei (r. 1645–1676) legally combined millions of slaves and free peasants into a single serf class bound to the land and their aristocratic masters. Not everyone passively accepted this fate, however. In 1667, a Cossack named Stenka Razin (c. 1630–1671) led a revolt against serfdom that gained considerable support among people whose social and economic status was threatened by the czar's policies, including soldiers from peasant stock. Razin's ultimate defeat at the hands of the czar explains the close ties between the Russian government's enhanced power and the enforcement of serfdom. A Dutch soldier, Ludwig Fabritius (1648–1729), who lived in Russia from 1660 to 1677 while employed as a military expert in the Russian army, wrote the following account of one stage of the revolt.

Then Stenka with his company started off upstream, rowing as far as Tsaritsyn, whence it took him only one day's journey to Panshin, a small town situated on the Don. Here he began straightaway quietly gathering the common people around him, giving them money, and promises of great riches if they would be loyal to him and help to exterminate the treacherous boyars.[1]

This lasted the whole winter, until by about spring he had assembled 4,000 to 5,000 men. With these he came to Tsaritsyn and demanded the immediate surrender of the fortress; the rabble soon achieved their purpose, and although the governor tried to take refuge in a tower, he soon had to give himself up as he was deserted by one and all. Stenka immediately had the wretched governor hanged; and all the goods they found belonging to the Tsar and his officers as well as to the merchants were confiscated and distributed among the rabble.

Stenka now began once more to make preparations. Since the plains are not cultivated, the people have to bring their corn from Nizhniy-Novgorod and Kazan down the Volga in big boats known as *nasady*, and everything destined for Astrakhan has first to pass Tsaritsyn. Stenka Razin duly noted this, and occupied the whole of the Volga, so that nothing could get through to Astrakhan. Here he captured a few hundred merchants with their valuable goods, taking possession of all kinds of fine linen, silks, striped silk material, sables, soft leather, ducats, talers, and many thousands of rubles in Russian money and merchandise of every description. . . .

In the meantime four regiments of *streltsy* [musketeers] were dispatched from Moscow to subdue these brigands. They arrived with their big boats and as they were not used to the water, were easily beaten. Here Stenka Razin gained possession of a large amount of ammunition and artillery-pieces and everything else he required. While the above-mentioned [musketeers] were sent from Moscow, about 5,000 men were ordered up from Astrakhan by water and by land to capture Stenka Razin. As soon as he had finished with the former, he took up a good position, and, being in possession of reliable information regarding our forces, he left Tsaritsyn and came to meet us half way at Chernyy Yar, confronting us before we had suspected his presence or received any information about him. We stopped at Chernyy Yar for a few days and sent out scouts by water and by land, but were unable to obtain any definite information. On 10 July [*sic:* June] a council of war was held at

---

From Anthony Glenn Cross, ed., *Russia under Western Eyes, 1517–1825* (London: Elek Books, 1971), 120–23.

[1]This term refers to a class of noblemen.

which it was decided to advance and seek out Stenka. The next morning, at 8 o'clock, our look-outs on the water came hurriedly and raised the alarm as the Cossacks were following at their heels. We got out of our boats and took up battle positions. General Knyaz Semen Ivanovich Lvov went through the ranks and reminded all the men to do their duty and to remember the oath they had taken to His Majesty the Tsar, to fight like honest soldiers against these irresponsible rebels, whereupon they all unanimously shouted: "Yes, we will give our lives for His Majesty the Tsar, and will fight to the last drop of our blood."

In the meantime Stenka prepared for battle and deployed on a wide front; to all those who had no rifle he gave a long pole, burnt a little at one end, and with a rag or small hook attached. They presented a strange sight on the plain from afar, and the common soldiers imagined that, since there were so many flags and standards, there must be a host of people. They [the common soldiers] held a consultation and at once decided that this was the chance for which they had been waiting so long, and with all their flags and drums they ran over to the enemy. They began kissing and embracing one another and swore with life and limb to stand together and to exterminate the treacherous boyars, to throw off the yoke of slavery, and to become free men.

The general looked at the officers and the officers at the general, and no one knew what to do; one said this, and another that, until finally it was decided that they and the general should get into the boats and withdraw to Astrakhan. But the rascally [musketeers] of Chernyy Yar stood on the walls and towers, turning their weapons on us and opened fire; some of them ran out of the fortress and cut us off from the boats, so that we had no means of escape. In the meantime those curs of ours who had gone over to the Cossacks came up from behind. We numbered about eighty men, officers, noblemen, and clerks. Murder at once began. Then, however, Stenka Razin ordered that no more officers were to be killed, saying that there must be a few good men among them who should be pardoned, whilst those others who had not lived in amity with their men should be condemned to well-deserved punishment by the Ataman and his *Krug*. A *Krug* is a meeting convened by the order of the Ataman, at which the Cossacks stand in a circle with the standard in the center; the Ataman then takes his place beside his best officers, to whom he divulges his wishes, ordering them to make these known to the common brothers and to hear their opinion on the matter. . . .

A *Krug* was accordingly called and Stenka asked through his chiefs how the general and his officers had treated the soldiers under their command. Thereupon the unscrupulous curs, [musketeers] as well as soldiers, unanimously called out that there was not one of them who deserved to remain alive, and they all asked that their father Stepan Timofeyevich Razin should order them to be cut down. This was granted with the exception of General Knyaz Semen Ivanovich Lvov, whose life was specially spared by Stenka himself. The officers were now brought in order of rank out of the tower, into which they had been thrown bound hand and foot the previous day, their ropes were cut and they were led outside the gate. When all the bloodthirsty curs had lined up, each was eager to deal his former superior the first blow, one with the sword, another with the lance, another with the scimitar, and others again with martels, so that as soon as an officer was pushed into the ring, the curs immediately killed him with their many wounds; indeed, some were cut to pieces and straightaway thrown into the Volga. My stepfather, Paul Rudolf Beem, and Lt. Col. Wundrum and many other officers, senior and junior, were cut down before my eyes.

My own time had not yet come: this I could tell by the wonderful way in which God rescued me, for as I — half-dead — now awaited the final blow, my [former] orderly, a young soldier, came and took me by my bound arms and tried to take me down the hill. As I was already half-dead, I did not move and did not know what to do, but he came back and took me by the arms and led me, bound as I was, through the throng of curs, down the hill into the boat and immediately cut my arms free, saying that I should rest in peace here and that he would be responsible for me and do his best to save my life. . . . Then my guardian angel told me not to leave the boat, and left me. He returned in the evening and brought me a piece of bread which I enjoyed since I had had nothing to eat for two days.

The following day all our possessions were looted and gathered together under the main flag, so that both our bloodthirsty curs and the Cossacks got their share.

DISCUSSION QUESTIONS

1. What do you think motivated Razin and his followers to take action?

2. Why were Razin and his forces able to defeat the czar's soldiers?

3. With whom do you think Fabritius's sympathies lay, and why?

4.
Fighting for Empire

A True and Exact Relation of the Raising of the Siege of Vienna (1683)

As the decision by Tsar Alexei (r. 1645–1676) to enserf millions of Russian peasants suggests, rulers in central and eastern Europe developed their own form of absolutism, which reflected the conditions and challenges specific to their regions. The following anonymous eyewitness account of the raising of the siege of the Austrian capital, Vienna, in 1683 provides an example of just how formidable the conditions and challenges could be. Although the Holy Roman Emperor Leopold I (r. 1658– 1705) had expanded his authority over the patchwork of ethnic groups under his rule, he still faced the growing presence of the Ottoman Turks to the east. As they pushed into the heart of Austrian Habsburg territory and surrounded Vienna in 1683, the Turks seemed poised for victory. All appeared lost for the Austrian troops

From "A True and Exact Relation of the Raising of the Siege of Vienna and the Victory Obtained Over the Ottoman Army" (London: 1683), 59–62, 65–66.

until a Polish detachment under the leadership of King Jan Sobieski (r. 1674–1696) arrived. Together they took the Turkish army by surprise and saved the beleaguered city. For the eyewitness, the impact of this "signal victory" extended far beyond the walls of Vienna, opening the door for Austrian dominance of eastern Europe. His optimism was not unfounded, for by 1699, the Turkish sultan had relinquished almost all of Hungary to the Austrians.

September 12th

After a Siege of Sixty days, accompanied with a Thousand Difficulties, Sicknesses, Want of Provisions, and great Effusion of Blood, after a Million of Cannon and Musquet Shot, Bombs, Granadoes, and all sorts of Fire Works, which has changed the Face of the fairest and most flourishing City in the World, disfigured and ruined most part of the best Palaces of the same, and chiefly those of the Emperor; and damaged in many places the Beautiful Tower and Church of St. *Stephen*, with many Sumptuous Buildings. After a Resistance so vigorous, and the Loss of so many brave Officers and Soldiers, whose Valor and Bravery deserve Immortal Glory. After so many Toils endured, so many Watchings and so many Orders so prudently distributed by Count *Staremburgh*, and so punctually executed by the other Officers.

After so many new Retrenchments, Pallizadoes, Parapets, new Ditches in the Ravelins, Bastions, Courtins, and principal Streets and Houses in the Town: Finally, after a Vigorous Defense and a Resistance without parallel, Heaven favorably heard the Prayers and Tears of a Cast-down and Mournful People, and retorted the Terror on a powerful Enemy, and drove him from the Walls of *Vienna*, who since the Fifteenth of *July* last early in the Morning, to the Twelfth of *September*, had so Vigorously attacked it with Two hundred thousand Men; and by endless Workings, Trenchings, and Minings, reduced it almost to its last gasp.

Count *Staremburgh*, who sustained this great Burden, assisted by so many Gallant Officers, having given Notice to the Christian Army, by Discharge of Musquets from the Tower of St. *Stephen*, of the Extremity whereto the City was reduced, they discovered on the Twelfth of this Month, early in the Morning, the Christian Troops marching down the Neighboring Mountains of *Kalemberg*, and heard continually the Discharges of their Artillery against the *Turks*, who being advanced thither, were fortified with Parapets of Earth and great Stones, to hinder the Descent of the Christian Army from the Mountains, who notwithstanding did advance. The Vanguard of the Horse and Foot, seconded by the Polish Horse, had a long Skirmish with the *Turks*, disputing every Foot of Ground; but seeing themselves totally vanquished by the Christian Forces, who had surmounted all the Difficulties of the Mountains, and drawn down their Cannon in spite of them, they retired Fighting, leaving to the Christians all their Camps full of Pavillions, Tents, Barracks, and Eight Pieces of Cannon (with which they had raised a Battery on that side Four days before) and retreated towards their Principal Camp, between the Villages of *Hernalls, Haderkling,* and *Jezing;* but as they passed by the Bastion of *Melck* they fired their Cannon furiously on them: The Christians being ravished with the Victory, pursued them with so much heat, that they were not only forced to leave their great Camps, but likewise all their others; flying towards *Hungary*. And it is certain, had not the Night come on, they had totally defeated and routed the *Ottoman Army.* [. . .]

In the Night the Christians made themselves Masters of all the *Turks* Camp. Afterwards Four Companies of our Foot entered into the Enemies Approaches with Torches and lighted Straw, but found nothing but Dead Bodies; they took possession of the Enemies Artillery, some whereof were brought into the City. All the night long we saw Fires at a distance, the *Turk* having fired as many of their Camps as so sudden a flight would give them leave, and retreated from the *Island* by favor of a Bridge which they had made below the River, upon one of the Arms of the *Danube*, the Christians having seized the Bridge above, on the same River.

On Monday Morning we saw all the Camps and Fields covered with Soldiers as well *Poles* as *Germans*. The *City* was relieved on *Sunday* about Five of the Clock in the Afternoon, and every bodies curiosity carried them to see the Camp, after they had been shut up above two Months.

The King of *Poland* having in the mean time with the greatest Vigor repulsed the Enemy on his side and put them to flight, leaving the Plunder of their Camp behind them, which consisted of a very Rich Tent of the Grand Visier, his Colors, Two Poles with the Horse Tails, their usual Signal of War, and his Guidon or Standard, set with Diamonds, his Treasure designed for the Payment of the Army, and in short, all his Equipage was possessed by the *Polanders*. As for the rest of the Tents, Baggage, Artillery, Ammunition, and Provisions enough to load Eight thousand Wagons, was divided among our Army.

Night coming on, we could no longer pursue, having followed the Enemy about a Mile from their Camp, and our Army having been all that time without Eating and Drinking, we were forced to found a Retreat to refresh them. We had all that Night to rest in, and the Enemy to save themselves. The next day being the Thirteenth we continued not the pursuit for the same reason, which without doubt we might have done with great advantage, since they fled in much disorder toward St. *Godart* to get over the River *Raab*. We are building a Bridge at *Alltemburgh* in *Hungary*, and our Armies will march very suddenly. On Sunday Night, after the Battle, his Imperial Majesty came to *Cloister Nuburgh*, Four hours from *Vienna*, from whence he sent the next day to compliment the King of *Poland* and the Electors upon their good success the day before.

On the Fourteenth, Count *Staremburgh* came to his Imperial Majesty (who received him with all manner of demonstrations of Affection and Esteem) and gave him a Relation of several considerable passages during the Siege: A short time after the Emperor embarked on the *Danube*, and landed above the Bridge before the Town, and entered the City at the *Stuben Gate*, at Landing he was received by the Electors of *Bavaria* and *Saxony*, who were attended by their Guards and a great many Noble Men. It being impossible to remove in so short a time such a number of Dead Bodies, both *Turks*, *Christians*, and *Horses*, whereof the stench was so great on the Road, that it was enough to have caused an Infection. [. . .]

September 19th

The Emperor is gone this day to Lintz: We are now beginning to cleanse the City of its Rubbish, and carry off the Dead Carcasses of Man and Beast. The *Turks* had a *French Ingineer* in their Camp, who hath done very much hurt to this City, and ruined us 50 Pieces of Cannon: There was also a great many *French* among the *Janizaries*, and many were found among the Dead with *French* Silver and Gold in their Pockets. There are daily brought in a great number of *Turks* Prisoners since the flight of the Grand Visier. It is intended to set the *Turks* that are already, and shall be hereafter taken, at Work on the reparation of our *Bastions* and *Courtins*. The Sieur *Kaunitz*, the Emperor's Resident at the Port, who was found in the *Grand Visier* Tent, is now in this City.

This moment comes the News that *Friday* last the *17th*, a part of the *Turks Army* fled away in such haste, within sight of *Raab*, as if ours were at their backs; the Officer who brought it, added that in his way from *Raab* he met with but two *Turks*, whom he brought Prisoners to *Bruckham* of *Ceytha*, where he sold them for four Pecks of Oats. All the Enemies or Rebels who had got into the Isle of *Schut*, are retired thence. There are gone down from hence some Boats full of Infantry towards *Hungary*. We are in hopes to hear shortly of some great Enterprise on the *Turks*. Here are daily brought in abundance of young Children whom the *Turks* had taken Captive; they ravished the young Maids and Women, and cut off the Heads of the old Men and Women.

Here is News from *Gratz*, that Count *Budiani* (who hath desired Count *Strasoldo* to intercede for him to the Emperor) had commanded 8000 *Hussars* of his Troops, under the Command of his Son and the Count *Nadasti*, to fall on 2000 *Turks* encamped near *Canisa*, and that they have put them all to the Sword. *Baron Buroni* is dead, and his Son revolted from the Rebels, and begs the Emperors Pardon. The *Turks* who are Prisoners, unanimously affirm, that the Grand Visier hath caused *Ibrahim Bassa* Visier of *Buda* to be strangled for first giving Ground at the Battle before *Vienna*. Part of the *Ottoman Army* is arrived near *Greekish Weissenberg*.

Since this Signal Victory obtained by the Christian Army (who some days had refreshed themselves) we are certainly informed they passed *Presbourgh* the 23th of *September*, in pursuit of the scattered Forces of the Ottoman Army, who fled to *Stollweissembourgh*; so that a few days will bring us an Accompt of what has passed between them. This Victory hath already given this advantage to our Affairs, that the Count of *Trausmondorse* [Trautmannsdorf] had taken and confiscated the Castles and Revenues of those who had done Homage to the *Turk*; and it was resolved to do the like in *Hungary*.

DISCUSSION QUESTIONS

1. What does this account reveal about military technology and tactics at the time?
2. How does the eyewitness portray Leopold I? What does this portrayal suggest about his method of rule?

3. How do the religious differences between the two camps shape the content and tone of this account of the raising of the siege?

5.
In Search of the Northwest Passage

Jacques Marquette, *Exploring the Mississippi* (1673)

As European colonization of the New World became more competitive, France was especially eager to gain the upper hand. Beginning with a narrow band of settlements in the St. Lawrence River valley, the French pushed westward in the second half of the seventeenth century to establish a vast inland empire. Jesuit missionaries appeared early on the scene to convert and proselytize the Indians living there. To this end, they immersed themselves in native cultures and languages, sending detailed written reports back to Europe. Below is an excerpt from one of these reports composed by Jacques Marquette (1636–1675), a Jesuit who gained fame for his exploration of the Mississippi River. Although various tribes had told French officials, missionaries, and traders about a great river running to a far-off sea, they did not know what "sea" exactly — the Pacific Ocean or the Gulf of Mexico? The latter was an appealing prospect because it would allow the French to connect their North American and Caribbean colonies. Appointed by the colonial governor, Marquette and Louis Jolliet (1645–1700), a French Canadian fur trader, set out in the summer of 1673, traveling through a web of waterways and rivers until they reached the Mississippi. They followed the river south to the border of the modern states of Arkansas and Louisiana, by which time they knew that they were near the Gulf. Along the way, Marquette and Jolliet met various Indian nations, including the Peoria nation of the Illinois confederacy described here.

IV. Of the Great River Called Mississippi; Its Most Notable Features; of Various Animals, and Especially the Pisikious, or Wild Cattle, Their Shape and Nature; Of the First Villages of the Illinois, Where the French Arrived

We are here, then, on this famous river, all of whose peculiar features I have endeavored to note carefully. The Mississippi River has its source in various lakes in the country of the northern nations. It is narrow at the place where the Meskousing empties into it. The current, which flows southward, is slow and gentle. To the right, a great range of high mountains is seen, while on the left are beautiful lands. In various places, the stream is divided by islands. On sounding, we found ten fathoms of water. Its breadth is very uneven. . . . We slowly followed its course, which runs toward the south and

---

From Allan Greer, ed., *The Jesuit Relations: Natives and Missionaries in Seventeenth-Century North America* (Boston: Bedford/St. Martin's, 2000), 194–202.

southeast, as far as the forty-second degree of latitude. Here we saw plainly that it had changed completely. There are hardly any woods or mountains, and the islands are more beautiful and are covered with finer trees. We saw only deer and cattle, bustards, and swans without wings because they drop their plumage in this country. From time to time, we came upon monstrous fish,[1] one of which struck our canoe with such violence that I thought that it was a great tree, about to break the canoe to pieces. On another occasion, we saw on the water a monster[2] with a head of a tiger, a sharp nose like that of a skunk, with whiskers and straight, erect ears; the head was gray and the neck quite black. We saw no more creatures of this sort. When we cast our nets into the water, we caught sturgeons, and a very extraordinary kind of fish. It resembles the trout, but its mouth is larger and near its nose — which is smaller, as are its eyes; it is a large thing shaped like a woman's bust, three fingers wide and a cubit long, at the end of which is a disk as wide as one's hand. This frequently causes it to fall backward when it leaps out of the water. When we reached the parallel of 41 degrees, 28 minutes, following the same direction, we found that the main game fowl was the wild turkey, while the main game animal was the *pisikious*, or wild cattle.[3] . . .

We continued to advance, but as we knew not where we were going — for we had proceeded over one hundred leagues without discovering anything except animals and birds — we remained on our guard. Thus, we would make only a small fire on land to prepare our evening meal, and after supper we would remove ourselves as far from it as possible and pass the night in our canoes that we anchored in the river at some distance from the shore. Even so, we always posted one of the party as a sentinel, for fear of a surprise. Proceeding still in a southerly and south-southwesterly direction, we found ourselves at the parallel of forty-one degrees . . . without having discovered anything.

Finally, on the 25th of June, we perceived at the water's edge some human tracks and a narrow and somewhat beaten path leading to a fine meadow. We stopped to examine it, and thinking that it was a trail that led to some village of Indians, we resolved to go and reconnoiter it. We left our two canoes under the guard of our people, strictly charging them not to allow themselves to be taken by surprise, and then Monsieur Jolliet and I set off on a rather dangerous mission for two men who exposed themselves, alone, to the mercy of a barbarous and unknown people. We silently followed the narrow path, and after walking about two leagues, we discovered a village on the bank of a river and two others on a hill distant about half a league from the first. At this point, we heartily commended ourselves to God, and after imploring his aid, we went on, but no one noticed us. We approached so near that we could even hear the Indians talking. We therefore decided that it was time to reveal ourselves. Stopping and advancing no further, we began to yell as loudly as we could. On hearing the shout, the Indians quickly issued from their cabins, and having probably recognized us as Frenchmen, especially when they saw a black

---

[1]Catfish.
[2]Wildcat.
[3]American buffalo/bison.

robe — or, at least, having no cause for distrust, as we were only two men and had given them notice of our arrival — they appointed four old men to come and speak to us. Two of these bore tobacco pipes, finely ornamented and adorned with various feathers. They walked slowly and raised their pipes toward the sun, seemingly offering them to it to be smoked by the sun, though they never spoke a word. It took them rather a long time to make their way to us from their village. Finally, when they had drawn near, they stopped to look at us attentively. I was reassured when I observed these ceremonies, which they perform only among friends. . . . I therefore spoke to them first, asking them who they were. They replied that they were Illinois, and as a token of peace, they offered us their pipes to smoke. Afterward, they invited us to enter their village, where all the people impatiently awaited us. These pipes for smoking tobacco are called calumets in this country. This word has come so much into use that, in order to be understood, I shall be obliged to use it, for I shall often have to speak of these pipes.

V. How the Illinois Received the Father in Their Village

At the door of the cabin where we would be received stood an old man who awaited us in a rather surprising posture, which constitutes a part of the ceremony that they observe when they receive strangers. This man was standing stark naked, with his hands extended and lifted toward the sun as if he wished to protect himself from its rays, which nevertheless shone upon his face through his fingers. When we came near him, he paid us this compliment: "How beautiful the sun is, O Frenchmen, when you come to visit us! All our village awaits you, and you shall enter all our cabins in peace." Having said this, he brought us into his own cabin, where there was a crowd of people who devoured us with their eyes, though they observed a profound silence. . . .

After we had taken our places, the usual civility of the country was paid to us, which consisted in offering us the calumet. This must not be refused, unless one wishes to be considered an enemy, or at least impolite, though it is enough to make even a pretense of smoking. After we had smoked, the assembly honored us by smoking in their turn. While they were passing the calumet, we received an invitation on behalf of the great captain of all the Illinois to proceed to his village, where he wished to hold a council with us. We went there with a large escort, for all these people, who had never seen any Frenchman among them, could not cease looking at us. They lay on the grass beside the trail; they went ahead of us and then retraced their steps to come and see us again. All this was done noiselessly and with marks of great respect for us.

When we reached the village, we saw the great captain at the entrance of his cabin standing between two old men, all three naked and holding their calumet turned toward the sun. He harangued us in a few words, congratulating us upon our arrival. Afterward, he offered us his calumet and invited us to smoke as we entered his cabin, where we received all their usual kind attentions.

Seeing all assembled and silent, I spoke to them by four presents that I gave them. By the first, I told them that we were journeying peacefully to visit the nations dwelling along the river as far as the sea. By the second, I announced to them that

God, who had created them, had taken pity on them, inasmuch as after they had so long been ignorant of him, he wished to make himself known to all the peoples. I was sent by Him for that purpose, and it was up to them to acknowledge and obey Him. By the third, I said that the great captain of the French wished to inform them that it was he who established peace everywhere and that it was he who had subdued the Iroquois. Finally, by the fourth, we begged them to give us all the information that they had about the sea and about the nations we must pass to reach it.

When I had finished my speech, the captain arose, and resting his hand upon the head of a little slave[4] whom he wished to give us, he spoke thus: "I thank you, Black Robe and you, O Frenchman," addressing Monsieur Jolliet, "for having taken so much trouble to come to visit us. Never has the earth been so beautiful or the sun so bright as today. Never has our river been so calm or so clear of rocks, which your canoes have removed as they traveled. Never has our tobacco tasted so good or our corn appeared so fine as we now see them. Here is my son, whom I give you so that you will know my heart. I beg you to have pity on me and on all of my nation. It is you who know the Great Spirit who has made us all. It is you who speak to Him and who hear his words. Beg Him to give me life and health and to come and dwell with us, in order to make us know him." Having said this, he placed the little slave beside us and gave us a second present, in the form of a very mysterious calumet, upon which they place more value than upon a slave. By this gift, he expressed to us the esteem that he had for Monsieur the governor, based on what we had told him of the latter. By a third, he begged us on behalf of all his nation not to go farther, on account of the great dangers to which we would expose ourselves.

I replied that I feared not death and that I believed there was no greater happiness than that of losing my life for the glory of Him who has made all. This is what these poor people cannot understand.

VI. Of the Character of the Illinois; Of Their Habits and Customs; And of the Esteem That They Have for the Calumet, or Tobacco Pipe, and of the Dance They Perform in Its Honor

When one speaks the word *Illinois*, it is as if one said in their language, "the men," as if the other Indians were merely animals. It must also be admitted that they have an air of humanity that we have not observed in the other nations that we have seen upon our route. The shortness of my stay among them did not allow me to secure all the information that I would have desired, but among all their customs, the following is what I have observed.

They are divided into many villages, some of which are quite distant from that of which we speak, which is called Peoria. This causes some difference in their language,

---

[4]In the pre- and early contact years, slaves among North American Indians were usually captives taken in war. Treatment of slaves varied, with some being treated as servants and others as members of the tribe. The children of slaves most often became full tribal members through intermarriage. [Ed.]

which, on the whole, resembles Algonquin, so that we easily understood each other. They are of a gentle and tractable disposition, as we discovered by the reception that they gave us. They have several wives, of whom they are extremely jealous. They watch them very closely and cut off their noses or ears when they misbehave. I saw several women who bore the marks of their misconduct.

Their bodies are well made; they are active and very skillful with bows and arrows. They also use guns, which they buy from our Indian allies who trade with our French. They use them especially to terrify their enemies with the noise and smoke, as these adversaries do not use guns and have never seen any, since they live too far to the west. They are warlike and make themselves dreaded by the distant tribes to the south and west where they go to procure slaves. These they barter, selling them at a high price to other nations in exchange for other wares. Those very distant Indians against whom they wage war have no knowledge of Europeans, nor do they know anything of iron or of copper, and they have only stone knives.

When the Illinois go to war, the whole village must be notified by a loud shout, which is uttered at the doors of the cabins the night and the morning before their departure. The captains are distinguished from the soldiers by wearing red sashes. These are made, with considerable skill, from the hair of bears and wild cattle. They paint their faces with red ocher, great quantities of which are found at a distance of some days' journey from the town.

They live by hunting, game being plentiful in that country, and on corn, of which they always have a good crop. Consequently, they have never suffered from famine. . . .

They are liberal in cases of illness and think that the effect of the medicines administered to them is in proportion to the presents given to the physician. Their garments consist only of skins. The women are always clad very modestly and very becomingly, while the men do not take the trouble to cover themselves.

There remains no more, except to speak of the calumet. There is nothing more mysterious or more respected among them. Less honor is paid to the crowns and scepters of kings than the Indians bestow upon this object. It seems to be the god of peace and of war, the arbiter of life and of death. It has but to be carried upon one's person and displayed to enable one to walk safely through the midst of enemies, who, in the heat of battle, will lay down their arms when it is shown. For that reason, the Illinois gave me one, to serve as a safeguard among all the nations through whom I had to pass during my voyage. There is one calumet for peace and one for war, which are distinguished solely by the color of the feathers with which they are adorned: Red is a sign of war. They also use it to put an end to their disputes, to strengthen their alliances, and to speak to strangers. It is fashioned from a red stone, polished like marble, and bored in such a manner that one end serves as a receptacle for the tobacco, while the other fits into the stem. The stem is a piece of wood two feet long, as thick as an ordinary cane, and bored through the middle. It is ornamented with the heads and necks of various birds of gorgeous plumage, and all along its length are attached long red, green, and other colors. They have a great regard for it, because they look upon it as the calumet of the sun, and, in fact, they offer it to the latter to smoke when they wish to obtain a calm, or rain, or fine weather. They refrain from bathing and from eating fresh fruit at the beginning of summer until after they have performed a dance in its honor.

DISCUSSION QUESTIONS

1. How would you characterize Marquette as an observer of the Mississippi River valley and the native peoples living there? What caught his attention and why?

2. How does he describe the Illinois people and their culture? Can we take his description at face value? Why or why not?

3. Although Marquette was a European writing for a European audience, in what ways does he take the native voice into account?

COMPARATIVE QUESTIONS

1. What similarities and/or differences do you see between Locke's and Hobbes's views of human nature and government?

2. How do these views compare to Marquette's description of the Illinois?

3. What do the first three documents suggest about the basis of authority in constitutional and absolutist states?

4. What do the accounts of Stenka Razin's revolt and the raising of the siege of Vienna suggest about the role of the military in the growth of absolutism in central and eastern Europe?

The Atlantic System and Its Consequences, 1690–1740

The growth of European domestic economies and overseas colonization during the eighteenth century infused Europe with money, new products, and a new sense of optimism about the future. Yet, as the first document illustrates, the good times came at a horrible price for millions of African slaves who formed the economic backbone of the Atlantic system by toiling on plantations in New World colonies. Meanwhile, Europeans back home enjoyed slave-produced goods. New forms of social interaction emerged hand in hand with new consumption patterns, most notably at coffeehouses. The second document gives us a flavor of early coffeehouse culture in London, where these establishments first appeared in Europe. Changes were also under way on the political front, with the stabilization of the European state system. Consequently, states such as Russia shone more brightly over the political landscape while others lost their luster. The third document brings to life Russia's new prominence through its leader's own words. The fourth and fifth documents reveal that intellectual circles were also ablaze with change as scholars and writers cast political, social, and religious issues in a new critical and secular light.

1.
Captivity and Enslavement

Olaudah Equiano, *The Interesting Narrative of the Life of Olaudah Equiano Written by Himself* (1789)

The autobiography of Olaudah Equiano (c. 1745–1797) puts a human face on the eighteenth-century Atlantic slave trade and its human consequences. As he describes, he was born in what is now Nigeria and was captured by local raiders and sold into slavery in his early teens. He gained his freedom in 1766 and soon thereafter became a vocal supporter of the English abolitionist movement. He published his autobiography in 1789, a best seller in its day, with numerous editions published in Britain and America. In the following excerpt, Equiano recounts his journey on the slave ship that took him away from his homeland, his freedom, and his very identity. Millions of others shared this same fate. Scholars have recently challenged this account, pointing to new evidence that suggests Equiano was born a slave in South Carolina, so probably early parts of his autobiography drew on the oral history of other slaves rather than on Equiano's personal experience. Regardless of where the truth lies, his book is invaluable as one of the very few texts written in English during the eighteenth century by a person of African descent.

The first object which saluted my eyes when I arrived on the coast was the sea, and a slave ship which was then riding at anchor and waiting for its cargo. These filled me with astonishment, which was soon converted into terror when I was carried on board. I was immediately handled and tossed up to see if I were sound by some of the crew, and I was now persuaded that I had gotten into a world of bad spirits and that they were going to kill me. Their complexions too differing so much from ours, their long hair and the language they spoke (which was very different from any I had ever heard) united to confirm me in this belief. Indeed such were the horrors of my views and fears at the moment that, if ten thousand worlds had been my own, I would have freely parted with them all to have exchanged my condition with that of the meanest slave in my own country. When I looked round the ship too and saw a large furnace or copper boiling and a multitude of black people of every description chained together, every one of their countenances expressing dejection and sorrow, I no longer doubted of my fate; and quite overpowered with horror and anguish, I fell motionless on the deck and fainted. When I recovered a little I found some black people about me, who I believed were some of those who had brought me on board and had been receiving their pay; they talked to me in order to cheer me, but all in vain. I asked them if we were not to be eaten by those white men with horrible looks, red faces, and loose hair. They told me I was not, and one of the crew brought me a small portion of spirituous liquor in a wine glass, but being afraid of him I would not take it out of his hand. One of the blacks therefore took it from him and gave it to me, and I took a little down my palate, which instead of reviving me, as they thought it would, threw me into the greatest consternation at the strange feeling it produced, having never tasted such any liquor before. Soon after this the blacks who brought me on board went off, and left me abandoned to despair.

I now saw myself deprived of all chance of returning to my native country or even the least glimpse of hope of gaining the shore, which I now considered as friendly; and I even wished for my former slavery in preference to my present situation, which was filled with horrors of every kind, still heightened by my ignorance of

From Paul Edwards, ed., *Equiano's Travels: His Autobiography*, abridged (London: Heinemann, 1967), 25–32.

what I was to undergo. I was not long suffered to indulge my grief; I was soon put down under the decks, and there I received such a salutation in my nostrils as I had never experienced in my life: so that with the loathsomeness of the stench and crying together, I became so sick and low that I was not able to eat, nor had I the least desire to taste anything. I now wished for the last friend, death, to relieve me; but soon, to my grief, two of the white men offered me eatables, and on my refusing to eat, one of them held me fast by the hands and laid me across I think the windlass, and tied my feet while the other flogged me severely. I had never experienced anything of this kind before, and although, not being used to the water, I naturally feared that element the first time I saw it, yet nevertheless could I have got over the nettings I would have jumped over the side, but I could not; and besides, the crew used to watch us very closely who were not chained down to the decks, lest we should leap into the water: and I have seen some of these poor African prisoners most severely cut for attempting to do so, and hourly whipped for not eating. This indeed was often the case with myself. In a little time after, amongst the poor chained men I found some of my own nation, which in a small degree gave ease to my mind. I inquired of these what was to be done with us; they gave me to understand we were to be carried to these white people's country to work for them. I then was a little revived, and thought if it were no worse than working, my situation was not so desperate: but still I feared I should be put to death, the white people looked and acted, as I thought, in so savage a manner; for I had never seen among my people such instances of brutal cruelty, and this not only shewn towards us blacks but also to some of the whites themselves. One white man in particular I saw, when we were permitted to be on deck, flogged so unmercifully with a large rope near the foremast that he died in consequence of it, and they tossed him over the side as they would have done a brute. This made me fear these people the more, and I expected nothing less than to be treated in the same manner. . . . At last, when the ship we were in had got in all her cargo, they made ready with many fearful noises, and we were all put under deck so that we could not see how they managed the vessel. But this disappointment was the last of my sorrow. The stench of the hold while we were on the coast was so intolerably loathsome that it was dangerous to remain there for any time, and some of us had been permitted to stay on the deck for the fresh air; but now that the whole ship's cargo were confined together it became absolutely pestilential. The closeness of the place and the heat of the climate, added to the number in the ship, which was so crowded that each had scarcely room to turn himself, almost suffocated us. This produced copious perspirations, so that the air soon became unfit for respiration from a variety of loathsome smells, and brought on a sickness among the slaves, of which many died, thus falling victims to the improvident avarice, as I may call it, of their purchasers. This wretched situation was again aggravated by the galling of the chains, now become insupportable, and the filth of the necessary tubs, into which the children often fell and were almost suffocated. The shrieks of the women and the groans of the dying rendered the whole a scene of horror almost inconceivable. Happily perhaps for myself I was soon reduced so low here that it was thought necessary to keep me almost always on deck, and from my extreme youth I was not put in fetters. In this situation I expected every hour to share the fate of my companions, some of whom were almost daily brought upon deck at the point of death, which I began to hope would soon put an end to my miseries. . . . At last we came in sight of the island of Barbados, at which the whites on board gave a great shout and made many signs of joy to us. We did not know what to think of this, but as the vessel drew nearer we plainly saw the harbor and other ships of different kinds and sizes, and we soon anchored amongst them off Bridgetown. Many merchants and planters now came on board, though it was in the evening. They put us in separate parcels and examined us attentively. They also made us jump, and pointed to the land, signifying we were to go there. . . . We were not many days in the merchant's custody before we were sold after their usual manner, which is this: On a signal given, (as the beat of a drum) the buyers rush at once into the yard where the slaves are confined, and make choice of that parcel they like best. The noise and clamor with which this is attended and the eagerness visible in the countenances of the buyers serve not a little to increase the apprehensions of the terrified Africans, who may well be supposed to consider them as the ministers of that destruction to which they think themselves devoted. In this manner, without scruple, are relations and friends separated, most of them never to see each other again. I remember in the vessel in which I was brought over, in the men's apartment there were several brothers who, in the sale, were sold in different lots; and it was very moving on this occasion to see and hear their cries at parting. O, ye nominal Christians! might not an African ask you, Learned you this from your God who says unto you, Do unto all men as you would men should do unto you?

DISCUSSION QUESTIONS

1. What are Equiano's impressions of the white men on the ship and their treatment of the slaves? How does this treatment reflect the slave traders' primary concerns?

2. What message do you think Equiano sought to convey to his readers? Based on this message, to whom do you think his book especially appealed?

2.
A "Sober and Wholesome Drink"

A Brief Description of the Excellent Vertues of That Sober and Wholesome Drink, Called Coffee (1674)

The expansion of the slave trade in the late seventeenth and eighteenth centuries was directly linked to Europeans' appetite for the commodities slave labor produced, including coffee. European travelers and merchants had first noticed people drinking coffee in the Middle East in the late sixteenth century, and its consumption slowly spread from there into Europe. With the drink came the rise of a new type of gathering place, the cof-

Transcription of original, as reproduced in Markman Ellis, ed., *Eighteenth-Century Coffee-House Culture*, vol. 1, *Restoration Satire* (London: Pickering & Chatto, 2006), 129.

feehouse. In 1652, a Greek merchant who had learned to make coffee while working in a Turkish trading port opened the first coffeehouse in western Europe in London. The number of coffeehouses in London, and eventually all over Europe, exploded when western European trading nations moved into the business of coffee production. Coffeehouses became places for men to meet for company and conversation, often with a political bent. The broadsheet transcribed here illuminates the origins of coffeehouse culture as merchants sought to entice customers to partake in the "sober and wholesome drink" and the sociability of the coffeehouse. Composed of two poems, the broadsheet was printed in 1674, most likely as an advertisement for coffee, coffeehouses, and the retail coffee business of Paul Greenwood situated in the heart of London's textile district. The first poem contrasts the detrimental effects of alcohol with the "sober and merry" effects of coffee. The second describes the rules of behavior coffeehouse patrons were expected to follow. Scholars have suggested that, despite its slightly satirical tone, the poem is an accurate portrayal of the regulations governing coffeehouses and may have been printed on large sheets of paper and posted on the walls of coffeehouses in London.

A Brief Description of the Excellent Vertues of that Sober and Wholesome Drink, called Coffee, and its incomparable effects in preventing or curing most diseases incident to humane bodies (London, printed for Paul Greenwood . . . who selleth the best Arabian Coffee-Powder and Chocolate, made in Cake or in Roll, after the Spanish Fashion, &c., 1674).[1]

When the sweet Poison of the Treacherous Grape,
Had Acted on the world a General Rape;
Drowning our very Reason and our Souls
In such deep Seas of large o'reflowing Bowls,
That New Philosophers Swore they could feel
The Earth to Stagger, as her Sons did Reel:
When Foggy Ale, leavying up mighty Trains
Of muddy Vapors, had besieg'd our Brains;
And Drink, Rebellion, and Religion too,
Made Men so Mad, they knew not what to do;
Then Heaven in Pity, to Effect our Cure,
And stop the Ragings of that Calenture,
First sent amongst us this All-*healing-Berry*,
At once to make us both *Sober* and *Merry*.
        Arabian coffee, a Rich Cordial

---

[1]**Chocolate, made in Cake or in Roll, after the *Spanish* Fashion:** chocolate is made from the fermented, roasted, and ground beans of the cocoa tree (*Theobroma cacao*). Imported from Spanish America, chocolate was sold as a bitter paste made up into small cylindrical cakes or rolls, which were used in the preparation of hot drinks with the addition of water, sugar, and sometimes eggs. Only in the nineteenth century was eating chocolate developed.

To Purse and Person Beneficial,
Which of so many Vertues doth partake
Its Country's called *Felix* for its sake.[2]
From the Rich Chambers of the Rising Sun,

. . .

COFFEE arrives, that Grave and wholesome Liquor,
That heals the Stomack, makes the Genius quicker,
Relieves the Memory, Revives the Sad,
And cheers the Spirits, without making Mad;

. . .

Its constant Use the sullenest Griefs will Rout,
Remove the Dropsie, gives ease to the Gout,[3]

. . .

A Friendly Entercourse[4] it doth Maintain
Between the Heart, the Liver, and the Brain,

. . .

Nor have the LADIES reason to Complain,
As fumbling Doe-littles[5] are apt to Faign;
COFFEE's no Foe to their obliging Trade,
By it Men rather are more active made;
'Tis stronger Drink, and base adulterate Wine;
Enfeebles Vigor, and makes Nature Pine;
Loaden with which, th' Impotent Sott is Led
Like a Sowe'd Hogshead to a Misses Bed;[6]
But this Rare Settle-Brain prevents those Harms,[7]
Conquers Old Sherry, and brisk Claret Charms.
Sack, I defie thee with an open Throat,
Whilst Truly COFFEE is my Antedote

---

[2]**Country's called *Felix*:** Arabia Felix (Arabia the happy), the name of one of three zones of the Arabian peninsula in classical geography, roughly corresponding to modern Yemen.

[3]**Dropsie . . . Gout:** dropsy, a morbid condition characterized by the accumulation of watery fluid in the serous cavities; gout, a disease characterized by the painful inflammation of the smaller joints (*Oxford English Dictionary*).

[4]**Entercourse:** intercourse, communication between something, here the heart, liver, and brain.

[5]**fumbling Doe-littles:** one who does little, a lazy person (*OED*).

[6]**th'Impotent . . . to a Misses Bed:** a complicated disparagement: a sot is one who dulls or stupefies himself with drink, here to the state of impotence, who must be induced to visit a young woman's bed, like a pickled or soused pig's head (an unwieldy and unrewarding dish).

[7]**Settle-Brain:** something that calms the brain (*OED*).

. . .

The RULES and ORDERS of the COFFEE-HOUSE.[8]
Enter Sirs Freely, But first if you please,
Peruse our Civil-Orders,[9] which are these.
First, Gentry, Tradesmen, all are welcome hither,
And may without Affront sit down Together:
Pre-eminence of Place, none here should Mind,[10]
But take the next fit Seat that he can find:
Nor need any, if Finer Persons come,
Rise up for to assigne to them his Room;
To limit Mens Expense, we think not fair,
But let him forfeit Twelve-pence that shall Swear:
He that shall any Quarrel begin,
Shall give each Man a Dish t'Atone the Sin;
And so shall He, whose Complements extend
So far to drink in COFFEE to his Friend;
Let Noise of loud Disputes be quite forborn,
No Maudlin Lovers[11] here in Corners Mourn,
But all be Brisk, and Talk, but not too much
On Sacred things, Let none presume to touch,
Nor Profane Scripture, or sawcily wrong
Affairs of State[12] with an Irreverent Tongue:
Let Mirth be Innocent, an each Man see,
That all his Jests without Reflection be;
To keep the House more Quiet, and from Blame,
We Banish hence Cards, Dice, and every Game:
Nor can allow of Wagers, that Exceed

---

[8]**The Rules . . . COFFEE-HOUSE:** an ironic title for a satire on coffee-house sociability. "Rules and Orders" is a commonplace phrase in legal discourse, signifying the administrative regulations of certain judicial institutions, especially courts of law, or the body of rules followed by an assembly.

[9]**Civil-Orders:** the civil laws. A term in legal debate current in the period.

[10]**Pre-eminence of Place, none here should Mind:** seats around the table in the coffee-room were not organized hierarchically, referring to the custom in coffee-houses, that each man should take the next free seat around the table.

[11]**Maudlin Lovers:** men who discuss their illicit gallantries and amors in a mawkish or sentimental manner, one of the ordeals of the coffee-house.

[12]**Affairs of State:** transactions concerning the state or nation, politics. The coffee-houses had come to be emblematic locations for debate on public affairs by those outside the court and ministry, where it was still assumed that ordinary people did not need to know about the state and its affairs.

Five shillings, which oft-times much Trouble Breed;
Let all that's lost, or forfeited be spent
In such Good Liquor as the House doth Vent,
And Customers endeavor to their Powers,
For to observe still seasonable Howers.
Lastly, let each Man what he calls for Pay,
And so you're welcome to come every Day.

DISCUSSION QUESTIONS

1. What does the imprint of the broadsheet suggest about changing consumption patterns at the time and their links to Europe's growing worldwide economic links?

2. According to the first poem, what were the medicinal effects of coffee? How might these effects have contributed to coffeehouses' growing popularity?

3. Based on the "Rules and Orders," what type of people frequented early coffeehouses? How would you describe their social interactions there?

4. Why do you think these rules legislated against swearing, disputes, and noise in coffeehouses?

3.
In Defense of Military Action

Tsar Peter I, *Letter to His Son, Alexei* (October 11, 1715)
and
Alexei's Response (October 31, 1715)

During the eighteenth century, European states turned much of their attention to the political and military scene burgeoning within Europe, vying to keep one step ahead of their rivals. Russian Tsar Peter I (r. 1689–1725) was especially successful at this game, transforming Russia into a great European power with all the trappings of a Western absolutist state, including a strong army and centralized bureaucracy, during his reign. Peter wrote the following letter to Alexei, who was then his only son and heir, during the Great Northern War against Sweden, which Peter ultimately won to Russia's great advantage. The letter explains the Tsar's relentless drive toward greatness on the European stage. Alexei's response reveals not only the striking differences in personality between the two men but also the tension that marked their tumultuous relationship.

From *A Source Book for Russian History from Early Times to 1917*, vol. II (New Haven and London: Yale University Press, 1972), 338–39.

[Peter to Alexei, October 11, 1715:]

Declaration to my son:

Everyone knows how, before the beginning of this war, our people were hemmed in by the Swedes, who not only stole the essential ports of our fatherland . . . but cut us off from communication with the whole world. And also later, in the beginning of this war (which enterprise was and is directed by God alone), oh, what great persecution we had to endure from those eternal enemies of ours because of our incompetence in the art of war, and with what sorrow and endurance we went to this school and, with the help of the above-mentioned guide, achieved a creditable degree [of effectiveness]. We were thus found worthy of looking on this enemy now trembling before us, trembling, perhaps, even more than we did before him. All this has been accomplished with the help of God through my modest labors and through those of other equally zealous and faithful sons of Russia.

However, when, considering this great blessing given by God to our fatherland, I think of my successor, a grief perhaps as strong as my joy gnaws me, when I see you, my heir, unfit for the management of state affairs (for it is not the fault of God, who has not deprived you of mind or health; for although not of a very strong constitution, you are not very weak either). But above all, you have no wish to hear anything about military affairs, which opened to us the way from darkness to light, so that we who were unknown before are now honored. I do not teach you to be inclined to wage war without a just cause, but to love this art and to endow and learn it by all means, for it is one of the two activities necessary for government: order and defense.

I have no wish to give you many examples, but I will mention only the Greeks, who are of the same religion as we. Did they not perish because they laid their arms aside, and were they not vanquished because of their peaceableness? Desirous of tranquil living, they always gave way to their enemy, who changed their tranquillity into endless servitude to tyrants. Perhaps you think that it can all be left to the generals; but this is really not so, for everyone looks up to his chief, to comply with his desires, which is an obvious fact. Thus, in the days of my brother's reign [Theodore, 1676–82], everyone liked clothes and horses above all things, and now they like arms. They may not be really interested in one or the other; but in what the chief is interested all take an interest, and to what he is indifferent, all are indifferent. And if they turn away so lightly from the frivolous pastimes, which are only a pleasure to man, how much more easily will they abandon so burdensome a game as war!

Furthermore, you do not learn anything because you have no desire to learn it, and you have no knowledge of military affairs. Lacking all knowledge, how can you direct these affairs? How can you reward the diligent and punish the negligent when you yourself do not understand their work? You will be forced to look into people's mouths like a young bird. Do you pretend to be unfit for military work because of weak health? But that is no reason. I ask of you not work, but good will, which no malady can destroy. Ask anyone who remembers my brother whom I spoke of but now, who was, beyond comparison, sicklier than you and could not ride spirited horses, but he had a great liking for them and was always looking at them and kept them before his eyes. . . . So you see, not everything is done by great labor, but also by a strong desire. You say to yourself, perhaps, that many rulers do not themselves go to war, and yet campaigns are still carried on. This is true when, although not going themselves, they have a desire for it, as had the late French king [Louis XIV], who went to war himself but little, and who yet had a great taste for it and showed such magnificent deeds in war that his wars were called the theater and school for the whole world. But he had a taste not only for war, but also for other affairs and for manufactures, through all of which he procured glory for his state more than anybody else.

Now that I have gone into all this, I return again to my original point, thinking of you. I am a man, and subject to death. To whom shall I leave all this sowing, done with God's help, and that harvest which has already grown? To one who, like the idle slave in the Gospel, buried his talent in the ground (which means that he threw away everything that God had given him)? I also keep thinking of your wicked and stubborn disposition; for how many times I used to scold you for that, and not only scold but beat you, and also how many years I have now gone without speaking to you, and all without success! . . .

I have pondered this with much grief, and, seeing that I can in no wise dispose you toward good, I have deemed it appropriate to write to you this last admonition, and to wait a short time for you to mend your ways, and that *not hypocritically* [Peter's emphasis]. If you do not, know that I shall totally disinherit you like a gangrenous member; and do not imagine that, because you are my only son, I write this only to frighten you; I will do it indeed (with God's consent), because I have never spared my own life for my fatherland and people, nor do I now; therefore how can I spare you, unworthy one? Better a good stranger than an unworthy kinsman.

Peter

October 11, 1715

Saint Petersburg

[Alexei to Peter, October 31, 1715:]

Most gracious sovereign and father:

I have read [the letter] that was given me on your behalf on October 27, 1715, after the funeral of my wife. I have nothing to say about it, except that if you wish to disinherit me of the Russian crown because of my worthlessness, let it be as you will. Most humbly I ask you for this very thing, Sire, for I consider myself unqualified and unfit for this task, being most deficient in memory (without which it is impossible to accomplish anything). All my mental and physical capacities are weakened by various illnesses, and I have become unfit to rule such a people, which task requires a man less rotten than I. Therefore, I do not make a claim, nor will I make claim in the future, to the inheritance of the Russian throne after you — God give you health for many years — even if I did not have a brother (but now, thank God, I have one [note: Prince Peter, born to Peter and Catherine on October 29, 1715], God give him health); let God be my witness [in this matter], and to show that I testify truthfully I write this with my own hand.

I entrust my children to your will and ask only for maintenance for myself to the end of my life. This is submitted to your decision and merciful will.

Your most humble slave and son Alexei
Saint Petersburg
October 31, 1715

DISCUSSION QUESTIONS

1. Why do you think Peter regarded the "art of war" as so important to government, and what did he gain by practicing it?

2. In what ways was Peter critical of his son, and why?

3. Whom does Peter single out as a political role model, and why is this significant?

4. What do these letters reveal about the Tsar's personality?

4.
Challenging Absolutism

Montesquieu, *Persian Letters: Letter 37* (1721)

As Europe's economy expanded, so did its intellectual horizons with the birth of the Enlightenment in the 1690s. Charles-Louis de Secondat, Baron of Montesquieu (1689–1755), was an especially important literary figure on this front. In 1721 he published Persian Letters, *in which he uses fictional characters to explore an array of topics with the critical, reasoning spirit characteristic of the period. Letter 37 points to one of his and other Enlightenment authors' main targets: the French king, Louis XIV (r. 1643–1715) and his absolutist state. Written by one of the book's two main characters, a Persian traveler in France named Usbek, to a friend back home, the letter explicitly criticizes the king's vanity, ostentation, and life at court. The letter implicitly passes even more serious judgment on the aging ruler in noting his esteem for "oriental policies." Montesquieu condemns these same policies elsewhere in his letters as inhumane and unjust.*

Usbek to Ibben, at Smyrna

The King of France is old. We have no examples in our histories of such a long reign as his. It is said that he possesses in a very high degree the faculty of making himself obeyed: he governs with equal ability his family, his court, and his kingdom: he has often been heard to say, that, of all existing governments, that of the Turks, or that of our august Sultan, pleased him best: such is his high opinion of Oriental statecraft.[1]

I have studied his character, and I have found certain contradictions which I cannot reconcile. For example, he has a minister who is only eighteen years old,[2] and a mistress [Madame de Maintenon] who is fourscore; he loves his religion, and yet he cannot abide those [the Jansenists] who assert that it ought to be strictly observed; although he flies from the noise of cities, and is inclined to be reticent, from morning till night he is engaged in getting himself talked about; he is fond of trophies and victories, but he has as great a dread of seeing a good general at the head of his own troops, as at the head of an army of his enemies. It has never I believe happened to anyone but himself, to be burdened with more wealth than even a prince could hope for, and yet at the same time steeped in such poverty as a private person could ill brook.

He delights to reward those who serve him; but he pays as liberally the assiduous indolence of his courtiers, as the labors in the field of his captains; often the man who undresses him, or who hands him his serviette at table, is preferred before him who has taken cities and gained battles; he does not believe that the greatness of a monarch is compatible with restriction in the distribution of favors; and, without examining into the merit of a man, he will heap benefits upon him, believing that his selection makes the recipient worthy; accordingly, he has been known to bestow a small pension upon a man who had run off two leagues from the enemy, and a good government on another who had gone four.

Above all, he is magnificent in his buildings; there are more statues in his palace gardens [at Versailles] than there are citizens in a large town. His bodyguard is as strong as that of the prince before whom all the thrones of the earth tremble;[3] his armies are as numerous, his resources as great, and his finances as inexhaustible.

Paris, the 7th of the moon of Maharram, 1713.

From Montesquieu, *Persian Letters*, vol. I, trans. John Davidson (London: Privately printed, 1892), 85–86.

[1]When Louis XIV was in his sixteenth year, some courtiers discussed in his presence the absolute power of the Sultans, who dispose as they like of the goods and the lives of their subjects. "That is something like being a king," said the young monarch. Marshal d'Estrées, alarmed at the tendency revealed in that remark, rejoined, "But, sire, several of these emperors have been strangled even in my time." [Ed.]

[2]Barbezieux, son of Louvois, Louis's youngest minister, held office at twenty-three, not eighteen; and he was dead in 1713. [Ed.]

[3]The Shah of Persia. [Ed.]

DISCUSSION QUESTIONS

1. What contradictions does Usbek see in Louis's character, and what do they reveal about his method of rule?

2. In what ways does this letter reflect Montesquieu's general interest in the foundation of good government?

3. Based on this letter, why do you think that scholars regard Montesquieu as a herald of the Enlightenment?

5.
Questioning Women's Submission
Mary Astell, *Reflections upon Marriage* (1706)

Like Montesquieu, English author Mary Astell (1666–1731) helped to usher in the Enlightenment by surveying society with a critical eye. First published anonymously in 1700, Reflections upon Marriage, *one of her best-known books, highlights Astell's keen interest in the institution of marriage, education, and relations between the sexes. Only the third edition (published in 1706) divulged her gender, but still not her name. As the following excerpt reveals, Astell held a dim view of women's inequality in general and of their submissive role in marriage in particular. She argues that one should abhor the use of arbitrary power within the state, and so, too, within the family. Among the book's principal goals was to present spinsterhood as a viable alternative to marriage. Perhaps not surprisingly, Astell herself never married.*

These Reflections being made in the Country, where the Book that occasioned them came but late to Hand, the *Reader* is desired to excuse their Unseasonableness as well as other Faults; and to believe that they have no other Design than to Correct some Abuses, which are not the less because Power and Prescription seem to Authorize them. If any are so needlessly curious as to enquire from what Hand they come, they may please to know, that it is not good Manners to ask, since the Title-Page does not tell them: We are all of us sufficiently Vain, and without doubt the Celebrated Name of *Author*, which most are so fond of, had not been avoided but for very good Reasons: To name but one; *Who will care to pull upon themselves an Hornet's nest?* 'Tis a very great Fault to regard rather who it is that Speaks, than what is Spoken; and either to submit to Authority, when we should only yield to Reason; or if Reason press too hard, to think to ward it off by Personal Objections and Reflections. Bold Truths may pass while the Speaker is Incognito, but are not

From Bridget Hill, ed., *The First English Feminist: Reflections upon Marriage and Other Writings by Mary Astell* (New York: St. Martin's Press, 1986), 69–76.

endured when he is known; few Minds being strong enough to bear what Contradicts their Principles and Practices without Recriminating when they can. And tho' to tell the Truth be the most Friendly Office, yet whosoever is so hardy as to venture at it, shall be counted an Enemy for so doing.

Thus far the old Advertisement, when the Reflections first appeared, A.D.1700.

But the *Reflector*, who hopes *Reflector* is not bad English, now Governor is happily of the feminine Gender, had as good or better have said nothing; For People by being forbid, are only excited to a more curious Enquiry. A certain Ingenuous Gentleman (as she is informed) had the Good-Nature to own these Reflections, so far as to affirm that he had the Original M.S. in his Closet, a Proof she is not able to produce, and so to make himself responsible for all their Faults, for which she returns him all due Acknowledgment. However, the Generality being of Opinion, that a Man would have had more Prudence and Manners than to have Published such unseasonable Truths, or to have betrayed the *Arcana Imperii* of his Sex, she humbly confesses, that the Contrivance and Execution of this Design, which is unfortunately accused of being so destructive to the government, of the Men I mean, is entirely her own. She neither advised with Friends, nor turned over Ancient or Modern Authors, nor prudently submitted to the Correction of such as are, or such as *think* they are good Judges, but with an *English* Spirit and Genius, set out upon the Forlorn Hope, meaning no hurt to any body, nor designing any thing but the Publick Good, and to retrieve, if possible, the Native Liberty, the Rights and Privileges of the Subject.

Far be it from her to stir up Sedition of any sort, none can abhor it more; and she heartily wishes that our Masters would pay their Civil and Ecclesiastical Governors the same Submission, which they themselves extract from their Domestic Subjects. Nor can she imagine how she any way undermines the Masculine Empire, or blows the Trumpet of Rebellion to the Moiety of Mankind. Is it by exhorting Women, not to expect to have their own Will in any thing, but to be entirely Submissive, when once they have made choice of a Lord and Master, though he happen not to be so Wise, so Kind, or even so Just a Governor as was expected? She did not indeed advise them to think his Folly Wisdom, nor his Brutality that Love and Worship he promised in his Matrimonial Oath, for this required a Flight of Wit and Sense much above her poor Ability, and proper only to Masculine Understandings. However she did not in any manner prompt them to Resist, or to Abdicate the Perjured Spouse, though the Laws of GOD and the Land make special Provision for it, in a case wherein, as is to be feared, few Men can truly plead Not Guilty.

Tis true, through Want of Learning, and of that Superior Genius which Men as Men lay claim to, she was ignorant of the *Natural Inferiority* of our Sex, which our Masters lay down as a Self-Evident and Fundamental Truth.[1] She saw nothing in the

---

[1]Possibly a reference to William Nichols, D.D., *The Duty of Inferiours Towards Their Superiours in Five Practical Discourses* (1701), in which he argued that man possesses "a higher state of natural perfection and dignity, and thereupon puts in a just claim of superiority, which everything which is of more worth has a right to, over that which has less" (pp. 87–88). [Ed.]

Reason of Things, to make this either a Principle or a Conclusion, but much to the contrary; it being Sedition at least, if not Treason to assert it in this Reign. For if by the Natural Superiority of their Sex, they mean that every Man is by Nature superior to every Woman, which is the obvious meaning, and that which must be stuck to if they would speak Sense, it would be a Sin in *any* Woman to have Dominion over *any* Man, and the greatest Queen ought not to command but to obey her Footman, because no Municipal Laws can supersede or change the Law of Nature; so that if the dominion of the Men be such, the *Salique Law*, as unjust as *English Men* have ever thought it, ought to take place over all the Earth, and the most glorious Reigns in the *English, Danish, Castilian,* and other Annals, were wicked Violations of the Law of Nature!

If they mean that *some* Men are superior to *some* Women, this is no great Discovery; had they turned the Tables they might have seen that *some* Women are Superior to *some* Men. Or had they been pleased to remember their Oaths of Allegiance and Supremacy, they might have known that *One* Woman is superior to *All* the Men in these Nations, or else they have sworn to very little purpose. And it must not be supposed, that their Reason and Religion would suffer them to take Oaths, contrary to the Law of Nature and Reason of things.

By all which it appears, that our Reflector's Ignorance is very pitiable, it may be her Misfortune but not her Crime, especially since she is willing to be better informed, and hopes she shall never be so obstinate as to shut her Eyes against the Light of Truth, which is not to be charged with Novelty, how late soever we may be blessed with the Discovery. Nor can Error, be it as Ancient as it may, ever plead Prescription against Truth. And since the only way to remove all Doubts, to answer all Objections, and to give the Mind entire Satisfaction is not by *Affirming*, but by *Proving*, so that every one may see with their *own* Eyes, and Judge according to the best of their *own* Understandings, She hopes it is no Presumption to insist on this Natural Right of Judging for her self, and the rather, because by quitting it, we give up all the Means of Rational Conviction. Allow us then as many Glasses as you please to help our Sight, and as many good Arguments as you can afford to Convince our Understandings: But don't exact of us we beseech you, to affirm that we see such things as are only the Discovery of Men who have quicker Senses; or that we understand and Know what we have by Hearsay only, for to be so excessively Complaisant, is neither to see nor to understand.

That the Custom of the World has put Women, generally speaking, into a State of Subjection, is not denied; but the Right can no more be proved from the Fact, than the Predominancy of Vice can justify it. A certain great Man has endeavored to prove by Reasons not contemptible, that in the Original State of things the Woman was the Superior, and that her Subjection to the Man is an Effect of the Fall, and the Punishment of her Sin. And that Ingenious Theorist Mr. *Whiston*[2] asserts,

---

[2] William Whiston (1667–1752), divine, mathematician, and Newtonian. Author of many works including *A New Theory of the Earth* (1696). He succeeded Newton as the Lucasian Professor and did much to popularize Newton's ideas. In 1710 he was deprived of his chair for casting doubt on the doctrine of the Trinity. [Ed.]

That before the Fall there was a greater equality between the two Sexes. However this be 'tis certainly no Arrogance in a Woman to conclude, that she was made for the Service of GOD, and that this is her End. Because GOD made all Things for Himself, and a Rational Mind is too noble a Being to be Made for the Sake and Service of any Creature. The Service she at any time becomes obliged to pay to a Man, is only a Business by the Bye. Just as it may be any Man's Business and Duty to keep Hogs; he was not Made for this, but if he hires himself out to such an Employment, he ought conscientiously to perform it. Nor can anything be concluded to the contrary from St. *Paul's* Argument, *I Cor. II.* For he argues only for Decency and Order, according to the present Custom and State of things. Taking his Words strictly and literally, they prove too much, in that *Praying and Prophecying in the Church* are allowed the Women, provided they do it with their Head Covered, as well as the Men; and no inequality can be inferred from hence, their Reverence to the Sacred Oracles who engage them in such Disputes. And therefore the blame be theirs, who have unnecessarily introduced them in the present Subject, and who by saying that the *Reflections* were not agreeable to Scripture, oblige the Reflector to shew that those who affirm it must either mistake her Meaning, or the Sense of Holy Scripture, or both, if they think what they say, and do not find fault merely because they resolve to do so. For had she ever writ any thing contrary to those sacred Truths, she would be the first in pronouncing its Condemnation.

But what says the Holy Scripture? It speaks of Women as in a State of Subjection, and so it does of the *Jews* and *Christians* when under the Dominion of the *Chaldeans* and *Romans,* requiring of the one as well as of the other a quiet submission to them under whose Power they lived. But will any one say that these had a *Natural Superiority* and Right to Dominion? that they had a superior Understanding, or any Pre-eminence, except what their greater Strength acquired? Or that the other were subjected to their Adversaries for any other Reason but the Punishment of their sins, and in order to their Reformation? Or for the Exercise of their Vertue, and because the Order of the World and the Good of Society required it?

If Mankind had never sinned, Reason would always have been obeyed, there would have been no struggle for Dominion, and Brutal Power would not have prevailed. But in the lapsed State of Mankind, and now that Men will not be guided by their Reason but by their Appetites, and do not what they *ought* but what they *can,* the Reason, or that which stands for it, the Will and Pleasure of the Governor is to be the Reason of those who will not be guided by their own, and must take place for Order's sake, although it should not be conformable to right Reason. Nor can there be any Society great or little, from Empires down to private Families, with a last Resort, to determine the Affairs of that Society by an irresistible Sentence. Now unless this Supremacy be fixed somewhere, there will be a perpetual Contention about it, such is the love of Dominion, and let the Reason of things be what it may, those who have least Force, or Cunning to supply it, will have the Disadvantage. So that since Women are acknowledged to have least Bodily strength, their being commanded to obey is in pure kindness to them and for their Quiet and Security, as well as for the Exercise of their Vertue. But does it follow that Domestic Governors have more Sense than their Subjects, any more than that other Governors have? We do not find that any Man thinks the worse of his own Understanding because another has superior Power; or concludes himself less capable of a Post of Honor and Authority, because he is not Preferred to it. How much time would lie on Men's hands, how empty would the Places of Concourse be, and how silent most Companies, did Men forbear to Censure their Governors, that is in effect to think themselves Wiser. Indeed Government would be much more desirable than it is, did it invest the Possessor with a superior Understanding as well as Power. And if mere Power gives a Right to Rule, there can be no such thing as Usurpation; but a Highway-Man so long as he has strength to force, has also a Right to require our Obedience.

Again, if Absolute Sovereignty be not necessary in a State, how comes it to be so in a family? or if in a Family why not in a State; since no Reason can be alledged for the one that will not hold more strongly for the other? If the Authority of the Husband so far as it extends, is sacred and inalienable, why not of the Prince? The Domestic Sovereign is without Dispute Elected, and the Stipulations and Contract are mutual, is it not then partial in Men to the last degree, to contend for, and practice that Arbitrary Dominion in their Families, which they abhor and exclaim against in the State? For if Arbitrary Power is evil in itself, and an improper Method of Governing Rational and Free Agents, it ought not to be Practiced any where; Nor is it less, but rather more mischievous in Families than in Kingdoms, by how much 100000 Tyrants are worse than one. What though a Husband can't deprive a Wife of Life without being responsible to the Law, he may however do what is much more grievous to a generous Mind, render Life miserable, for which she has no Redress, scarce Pity which is afforded to every other Complainant. It being thought a Wife's Duty to suffer everything without Complaint. *If all Men are born free,* how is it that all Women are born slaves? as they must be if the being subjected to the *inconstant, uncertain, unknown, arbitrary Will* of Men, be the *perfect Condition of Slavery?* and if the Essence of Freedom consists, as our Masters say it does, in having a *standing Rule to live by?* And why is Slavery so much condemned and strove against in one Case, and so highly applauded, and held so necessary and so sacred in another?

DISCUSSION QUESTIONS

1. According to Mary Astell, what is women's customary status in society, and why? What evidence does Astell present to challenge this status?

2. What does the language Astell uses reveal about her style of thinking and basic intellectual beliefs?

3. Why do you think scholars characterize *Reflections upon Marriage* as a "feminist" work?

COMPARATIVE QUESTIONS

1. Although Equiano, the coffeehouse broadsheet, and the *Persian Letters* belong to different literary genres, what do they reveal about late-seventeenth- and eighteenth-century Europeans and their customs?

2. Both Louis XIV and Peter I cast themselves as absolute rulers. Do the documents support this claim? If so, how?

3. In what ways does Astell's discussion of the evils of arbitrary power foreshadow Montesquieu's concerns?

4. In what ways do Equiano and Astell challenge conventional Christian authority and beliefs? What does this suggest about the place of Christianity in European society and culture at the time?

The Promise of Enlightenment, 1740–1789

The following documents represent some of the many voices of the Enlightenment, an intellectual and cultural movement during the eighteenth century that captured the minds of middle- and upper-class people across Europe and in British North America. Enlightenment writers were united by their belief that reason was the key to humanity's advancement as the basis of truth, liberty, and justice. They cultivated and disseminated their ideals through letters, published works, and personal exchanges, particularly at gatherings known as *salons*, which were organized by upper-class women. By midcentury, people as diverse as the king of Prussia and a French artisan began to echo the Enlightenment principle that progress depended on destroying all barriers to reason, including religious intolerance and outmoded economic and judicial practices.

1.
Spreading Enlightenment
Marie-Thérèse Geoffrin and M. d'Alembert, *The Salon of Madame Geoffrin* (1765)

Since its beginnings as an intellectual movement against absolutism, the Enlightenment had become a formidable force of change by the mid-eighteenth century. The role of salons was crucial in this regard, providing an arena for the discussion and dissemination of Enlightenment ideas by bringing innovative intellectuals, writers, and artists together in private homes on a regular basis. Madame Marie-Thérèse Geoffrin (1699–1777)

From Charles de Nouy, ed., *Correspondance inédite du roi Stanislaw-Auguste Poniatowski et de Madame Geoffrin* (Geneva: Satine, 1970; reprint of 1875 edition). Trans. Lynn Hunt as published in *Connecting with the Past*, 164–68.

presided over the most influential salon in Paris at the time, as described in the mem-
oirs of a beneficiary of her patronage, M. d'Alembert. In addition to nurturing the in-
tellectual scene in Paris, Geoffrin also cultivated it abroad by corresponding with
important European leaders, including King Stanislaw of Poland, to whom she wrote the
following letter in 1765. Together, the following two documents elucidate the life of a
woman who was actively engaged in Enlightenment thinking.

Much has been said respecting Madame Geoffrin's goodness, to what a point it was active, restless, obstinate. But it has not been added, and which reflects the greatest honor upon her, that, as she advanced in years, this habit constantly increased. For the misfortune of society, it too often happens that age and experience produce a directly contrary effect, even in very virtuous characters, if virtue be not in them a powerful sentiment indeed, and of no common stamp. The more disposed they have been at first to feel kindness towards their fellow creatures, the more, finding daily their ingratitude, do they repent of having served them, and even consider it almost as a reproach to themselves to have loved them. Madame Geoffrin had learnt, from a more reflected study of mankind, from taking a view of them more *enlightened* by reason and justice, that they are more weak and vain than wicked; that we ought to compassionate their weakness, and bear with their vanity, that they may bear with ours. . . .

The passion of *giving*, which was an absolute necessity to her, seemed born with her, and tormented her, if I may say so, even from her earliest years. While yet a child, if she saw from the window any poor creature asking alms, she would throw what- ever she could lay her hands upon to them; her bread, her linen, and even her clothes. She was often scolded for this *intemperance* of charity, sometimes even punished, but nothing could alter the disposition, she would do the same the very next day. . . .

Always occupied with those whom she loved, always anxious about them, she even anticipated every thing which might interrupt their happiness. A young man,[1] for whom she interested herself very much, who had till that moment been wholly absorbed in his studies, was suddenly seized with an unfortunate passion, which rendered study, and even life itself insupportable to him. She succeeded in curing him. Some time after she observed that the same young man mentioned to her, with great interest, an amiable woman with whom he had recently become ac- quainted. Madame Geoffrin, who knew the lady, went to her. "I am come," she said, "to intreat a favor of you. Do not evince too much friendship for **** or too much desire to see him, he will be soon in love with you, he will be unhappy, and I shall be no less so to see him suffer; nay, you yourself will be a sufferer, from conscious- ness of the sufferings you occasion him." This woman, who was truly amiable, promised what Madame Geoffrin desired, and kept her word.

As she had always among the circle of her society persons of the highest rank and birth, as she appeared even to seek an acquaintance with them, it was supposed

---

[1]This young man was M. d'Alembert himself.

that this flattered her vanity. But here a very erroneous opinion was formed of her; she was in no respect the dupe of such prejudices, but she thought that by managing the humors of these people, she could render them useful to her friends. "You think," said she, to one of the latter, for whom she had a particular regard, "that it is for my own sake I frequent ministers and great people. Undeceive yourself, — it is for the sake of you, and those like you who may have occasion for them. . . ."

Mme. Geoffrin Writes to the King of Poland

I am sending to you a banker named Claudel who is returning to Warsaw. He will have with him a printed memoir on a new kind of mill. The more I have learned about it, the more I see that this machine is very well-known. Your Majesty is best advised to invite a miller to come from France; he will know how to set it up and show how to use it, and use of it can spread from there.

Prince Sulkowski [a Polish nobleman] met Mr. Hennin at my salon. Mr. Hennin had been for a long time in Warsaw, and they talked together about Poland. I see with pain that it has a very bad government [Stanislaw was elected king only in 1764]; it seems almost impossible to make it better. . . .

I sent you the catalogue of the diamonds of Madame de Pompadour [King Louis XV's mistress had died recently and her diamonds were auctioned off]. . . .

Do not forget, my dear son, to send the memoir on commerce to Mr. Riancourt when he returns. . . .

I cannot report any news yet on your project for paintings; I am very sad about the death of poor Carle Vanloo [a leading French painter who died in July 1765]. It was a horrible loss for the arts.

DISCUSSION QUESTIONS

1. Based on these documents, how would you characterize Geoffrin's personality? In what ways was she "enlightened"?

2. What impressions do the documents offer of her salon and how it functioned?

3. What does Geoffrin's letter to Stanislaw suggest about the range of her interests? How was this typical of Enlightenment thinkers?

2.
An Enlightened Worker
Jacques-Louis Ménétra, *Journal of My Life* (1764–1802)

Although the philosophes — the writers of the Enlightenment — directed their message to the educated elite, Journal of My Life *by Jacques-Louis Ménétra (b. 1738) suggests that at least some people from the lower classes heard it too. Born in Paris, Ménétra learned to read and write in local parish schools. Following his father's example, he became a master glazier. He began his journal in 1764 and organized it principally around his recollections of his journeyman's "tour de France" from 1757 to 1764. The document here reveals not only his quick wit and sense of adventure but also his affinity for the intellectual spirit of criticism that characterized the Enlightenment. As the excerpt demonstrates, alongside the tales of his amusements, Ménétra commented on many of the fundamental issues of the day, including the question of religious tolerance. It is printed as originally written, without punctuation.*

I went to Paris to see Denongrais   Madame la Police had been interfering with business   she made up her mind to sell her property and to retire with her cuckold of a husband to her native village for she'd put by quite a bit in the course of her work   I was all for it   She said to me   I see clearly from what you've just said that you never loved me   She was right for never had a woman touched my heart except for sensual pleasure and nothing else   I promised her to come say my farewells and they've yet to be said

Since it was the good season we went to Champigny and went with some friends of mine to what are called *guinguettes* [open-air cafés with music and dancing — Trans.] Sundays and holidays we went to dance in front of the castle and other days usually with the people from the *guinguette* we played tennis or went visiting the local festivals   One holiday in a village one league from Montigny people were playing tennis on the square when Du Tillet showed up accompanied by the lord the magistrate or sheriff and the priest   I heard somebody say   That's the Parisian over there I wondered what this was all about   It's because they know you're good at tennis said my friend   they're going to propose a match   In fact six young men came and politely gave each of us a racket   My friend said no since he didn't know how to play but he said   But as for my friend he'll give you a good show   I declined   They insisted   the lord the sheriff and the priest joined in   I played   applause   hands were heard to clap   They took us to the castle (and) gave us refreshment

I was greatly applauded   I promised again that the fellows from Montigny and I would be waiting for them next Sunday   People came from all around I was all over the court and we had a good time   we won and whatever else they were well entertained   My friend went all out because M Trudaine had wanted to see me play and when I passed in front of him he and the people around him said to me Courage   So I answered that that was one thing I wasn't lacking

One day I followed the game warden   Since I had no rifle I let him run all over the fields and went to a village where I had seen the curate pay his respects to M Trudaine   who recognized me   and said I was pretty nimble at tennis and took me to his presbytery for a drink

After some idle talk we finally got onto the subject of religion   We talked about the mysteries of the sacraments. . . . I spoke passionately about the suffer-

From Jacques-Louis Ménétra, *Journal of My Life*, intro. Daniel Roche. Trans. Arthur Goldhammer (New York: Columbia University Press, 1986), 129–30.

ings that had been inflicted on men who worshiped the same God except for a few matters of opinion And (I said that) the Roman religion should be tolerant if it followed the maxims of its lawgiver   that because of its mysteries it was absurd and that all mysteries were in my opinion nothing but lies   And that so long as they sold indulgences and gave remission for sins in exchange for money   fear of hell which was like purgatory just an invention of the first impostors   that Jesus had never spoken of purgatory   And that all those sacraments were nothing but pure inventions to make money and impress the vulgar   And that he himself who was a very intelligent man was not capable of making his God   chewing him and then swallowing him   That we mistreated those peoples who did not share our belief (and who) according to the Church should have been damned because all the priests went around saying   Outside the Church there is no salvation And that we accused those who worship idols of being idolators when we prostrate ourselves before statues   We even worship a piece of dough which we eat in the firm belief that it is God And those idolators only worship all those things to keep from being hurt by them and other things in the hope of getting some good out of them while we on the other hand we were real man-eaters   After praying to him and worshipping him in order to satisfy him we've got to eat him too

He answered me with objections as many others had answered me   His one and only response was to say to me   All these mysteries must be believed because the Church believes them   he said to me   My friend you are enlightened   It is necessary that for the sake of government nations live always in ignorance and credulity   I answered him So be it

DISCUSSION QUESTIONS

1. Why do you think Ménétra was so critical of the Catholic Church?

2. How do Ménétra's criticisms echo those of great Enlightenment thinkers?

3. What does the priest mean when he describes Ménétra as enlightened?

4. How would you characterize Ménétra's style of writing?

3.
Reforming the Law

Cesare Beccaria, *On Crimes and Punishments* (1764)

Intellectuals in Paris were not alone in their faith in the power of human reason to understand and reshape the world around them. Like-minded thinkers across Europe embraced the Enlightenment spirit in their own pursuit of knowledge and progress for humanity. For Cesare Beccaria (1738–1794), this pursuit centered on a critical study

From Cesare Beccaria, *On Crimes and Punishments and Other Writings*, ed. Richard Bellamy (Cambridge: Cambridge University Press, 1995), 7–8, 39–44.

of existing criminal law. An Italian aristocrat and doctor of laws, Beccaria joined a circle of intellectuals in Milan committed to a broad program of reform, including the creation of a rational and centralized system of equal justice for all. One of the circle's founders was an official in a local prison with firsthand knowledge of the physical and legal plight of prisoners. In his book On Crimes and Punishments, *Beccaria takes up their cause by systematically examining the traditional legal and penal system. As he argues, many criminal justice practices not only are arbitrary, cruel, and ineffective, but also do not serve the greatest public good. Such practices include the use of torture to secure confessions (discussed in the excerpt that follows), the indiscriminate power of judges, and the use of capital punishment. Beccaria analyzes these and other outmoded forms of justice, calling for change. His book had a broad influence on European law, and was translated into French and English, serving as a model for legal reform.*

For the most part, men leave the care of the most important regulations either to common sense or to the discretion of individuals whose interests are opposed to those most foresighted laws which distribute benefits to all and resist the pressures to concentrate those benefits in the hands of a few, raising those few to the heights of power and happiness, and sinking everyone else in feebleness and poverty. It is, therefore, only after they have experienced thousands of miscarriages in matters essential to life and liberty, and have grown weary of suffering the most extreme ills, that men set themselves to right the evils that beset them and to grasp the most palpable truths which, by virtue of their simplicity, escape the minds of the common run of men who are not used to analyzing things, but instead passively take on a whole set of second-hand impressions of them derived more from tradition than from enquiry.

If we open our history books we shall see that the laws, for all that they are or should be contracts amongst free men, have rarely been anything but the tools of the passions of a few men or the offspring of a fleeting and haphazard necessity. They have not been dictated by a cool observer of human nature, who has brought the actions of many men under a single gaze and has evaluated them from the point of view of whether or not they conduce to *the greatest happiness shared among the greater number.* Blessed are those very few nations which have not waited for the slow succession of coincidence and contingencies to bring about some tentative movement towards the good from out of the extremities of evil, but which have sped with good laws through the intervening stages. And that philosopher who had the courage to scatter out among the multitudes from his humble, despised study the first seeds of those beneficial truths that would be so long in bearing fruit, deserves the gratitude of all humanity.

We have discovered the true relations between sovereign and subjects and between nation and nation. Commerce has been stimulated by philosophic truths disseminated by the press, and there is waged among nations a silent war by trade, which is the most humane sort of war and more worthy of reasonable men. Such is the progress we owe to the present enlightened century. But there are very few who have scrutinized and fought against the savagery and the disorderliness of the procedures of criminal justice, a part of legislation which is so prominent and so neglected in almost the whole of Europe. How few have ascended to general principles to expose and root out the errors that have built up over the centuries, so curbing, as far as it is within the power of disseminated truths to do, the all too free rein that has been given to misdirected force, which has, up to now, provided an entrenched and legitimized example of cold-blooded atrocity. And yet, the groans of the weak, sacrificed to cruel indifference and to wealthy idleness, the barbarous tortures that have been elaborated with prodigal and useless severity, to punish crimes unproven or illusory, the horrors of prison, compounded by that cruelest tormentor of the wretched, uncertainty, ought to have shaken into action that rank of magistrates who guide the opinions and minds of men.

Of Torture

The torture of a criminal while his trial is being put together is a cruelty accepted by most nations, whether to compel him to confess a crime, to exploit the contradictions he runs into, to uncover his accomplices, to carry out some mysterious and incomprehensible metaphysical purging of his infamy, [or, lastly, to expose other crimes of which he is guilty but with which he has not been charged].

No man may be called guilty before the judge has reached his verdict; nor may society withdraw its protection from him until it has been determined that he has broken the terms of the compact by which that protection was extended to him. By what right, then, except that of force, does the judge have the authority to inflict punishment on a citizen while there is doubt about whether he is guilty or innocent? This dilemma is not a novelty: either the crime is certain or it is not; if it is certain, then no other punishment is called for than what is established by law and other torments are superfluous because the criminal's confession is superfluous; if it is not certain, then an innocent man should not be made to suffer, because, in law, such a man's crimes have not been proven. Furthermore, I believe it is a willful confusion of the proper procedure to require a man to be at once accuser and accused, in such a way that physical suffering comes to be the crucible in which truth is assayed, as if such a test could be carried out in the sufferer's muscles and sinews. This is a sure route for the acquittal of robust ruffians and the conviction of weak innocents. Such are the evil consequences of adopting this spurious test of truth, but a test worthy of a cannibal, that the ancient Romans, for all their barbarity on many other counts, reserved only for their slaves, the victims of a fierce and overrated virtue.

What is the political purpose of punishment? The instilling of terror in other men. But how shall we judge the secret and secluded torture which the tyranny of custom visits on guilty and innocent alike? It is important that no established crime go unpunished; but it is superfluous to discover who committed a crime which is buried in shadows. A misdeed already committed, and for which there can be no redress, need be punished by a political society only when it influences other people by holding out the lure of impunity. If it is true that, from fear or from virtue, more men observe the laws than break them, the risk of torturing an innocent ought to be accounted all the greater, since it is more likely that any given man has observed the laws than that he has flouted them.

Another absurd ground for torture is the purging of infamy, that is, when a man who has been attainted by the law has to confirm his own testimony by the dislocation of his bones. This abuse should not be tolerated in the eighteenth century. It presupposes that pain, which is a sensation, can purge infamy, which is a mere moral relation. . . .

The third ground for torture concerns that inflicted on suspected criminals who fall into inconsistency while being investigated, as if both the innocent man who goes in fear and the criminal who wishes to cover himself would not be made to fall into contradiction by fear of punishment, the uncertainty of the verdict, the apparel and magnificence of the judge, and by their own ignorance, which is the common lot both of most knaves and of the innocent; as if the inconsistencies into which men normally fall even when they are calm would not burgeon in the agitation of a mind wholly concentrated on saving itself from a pressing danger.

. . . Every act of our will is always proportional to the force of the sensory impression which gives rise to it; and the sensibility of every man is limited. Therefore, the impression made by pain may grow to such an extent that, having filled the whole of the sensory field, it leaves the torture victim no freedom to do anything but choose the quickest route to relieving himself of the immediate pain. . . . And thus the sensitive but guiltless man will admit guilt if he believes that, in that way, he can make the pain stop. All distinctions between the guilty and the innocent disappear as a consequence of the use of the very means which was meant to discover them.

This truth is also felt, albeit indistinctly, by those very people who apparently deny it. No confession made under torture can be valid if it is not given sworn confirmation when it is over; but if the criminal does not confirm his crime, he is tortured afresh. Some learned men and some nations do not allow this vicious circle to be gone round more than three times; other nations and other learned men leave it to the choice of the judge, in such a way that, of two men equally innocent or equally guilty, the hardy and enduring will be acquitted and the feeble and timid will be convicted by virtue of the following strict line of reasoning: *I, the judge, had to find you guilty of such and such a crime; you, hardy fellow, could put up with the pain, so I acquit you; you, feeble fellow, gave in, so I convict you. I know that the confession extorted from you in the midst of your agonies would carry no weight, but I shall torture you afresh if you do not confirm what you have confessed.*

A strange consequence which necessarily follows from the use of torture is that the innocent are put in a worse position than the guilty. For, if both are tortured, the former has everything against him. Either he confesses to the crime and is convicted, or he is acquitted and has suffered an unwarranted punishment. The criminal, in contrast, finds himself in a favorable position, because if he staunchly withstands the torture he must be acquitted and so has commuted a heavier sentence into a lighter one. Therefore, the innocent man cannot but lose and the guilty man may gain.

DISCUSSION QUESTIONS

1. According to Beccaria, why is torture a customary practice?

2. Why doesn't he agree with this practice? What is the basis of his reasoning? Do you find it convincing? Why or why not?

3. What similarities and/or differences do you see between Beccaria's recommendations for reform and practices in contemporary criminal justice systems?

4. In what ways does Beccaria's choice of language echo fundamental Enlightenment ideas?

4.
Reforming Commerce

Adam Smith, *An Inquiry into the Nature and Causes of the Wealth of Nations* (1776)

Although philosophes embraced human reason as an essential tool of understanding, their views on what reason revealed varied widely. Beccaria trained his lens on crimes and punishments. The work of Scottish philosopher Adam Smith (1723–1790) is an example of another, equally enduring approach. A professor of moral philosophy with interests in law and economics, Smith, too, was concerned with how to promote the good of society, specifically through the "progress of opulence" that was so visible in the eighteenth century economic boom. He set forth his explanation in masterful fashion in An Inquiry into the Nature and Causes of the Wealth of Nations *published in 1776. The excerpt here reveals one of the pillars of Smith's argument, namely that economic markets should be left to their own devices, free from the government regulations that prevailed in his day. In this way, Smith declared, individual self-interest "led by an invisible hand" of competition could come to the fore, which was naturally compatible with society's general welfare.*

By restraining, either by high duties, or by absolute prohibitions, the importation of such goods from foreign countries as can be produced at home, the monopoly of the home market is more or less secured to the domestic industry employed in producing them. . . .

That this monopoly of the home market frequently gives great encouragement to that particular species of industry which enjoys it, and frequently turns towards that employment a greater share of both the labor and stock of the society than would otherwise have gone to it, cannot be doubted. But whether it tends either to

From Adam Smith, *An Inquiry into the Nature and Causes of the Wealth of Nations*, 2 ed., vol. II (Oxford: The Clarendon Press, 1880), 25–30.

increase the general industry of the society, or to give it the most advantageous di-rection, is not, perhaps, altogether so evident.

The general industry of the society never can exceed what the capital of the society can employ. As the number of workmen that can be kept in employment by any particular person must bear a certain proportion to his capital, so the number of those that can be continually employed by all the members of a great society, must bear a certain proportion to the whole capital of that society, and never can exceed that proportion. No regulation of commerce can increase the quantity of in-dustry in any society beyond what its capital can maintain. It can only divert a part of it into a direction into which it might not otherwise have gone; and it is by no means certain that this artificial direction is likely to be more advantageous to the society than that into which it would have gone of its own accord.

Every individual is continually exerting himself to find out the most advanta-geous employment for whatever capital he can demand. It is his own advantage, in-deed, and not that of the society, which he has in view. But the study of his own advantage naturally or rather necessarily, leads him to prefer that employment which is most advantageous to the society.

First, every individual endeavors to employ his capital as near home as he can, and consequently as much as he can in the support of domestic industry; provided always that he can thereby obtain the ordinary, or not a great deal less than the or-dinary, profits of stock. . . .

. . . Home is in this manner the center, if I may say so, round which the capi-tals of the inhabitants of every country are continually circulating, and towards which they are always tending, though by particular causes they may sometimes be driven off and repelled from it towards more distant employments. But a capi-tal employed in the home trade, it has already been shown, necessarily puts into motion a greater quantity of domestic industry, and gives revenue and employ-ment to a greater number of the inhabitants of the country, than an equal capital employed in the foreign trade of consumption; and one employed in the foreign trade of consumption has the same advantage over an equal capital employed in the carrying trade. Upon equal, or only nearly equal profits, therefore, every individ-ual naturally inclines to employ his capital in the manner in which it is likely to af-ford the greatest support to domestic industry, and to give revenue and employment to the greatest number of people of his own country.

Secondly, every individual who employs his capital in the support of domes-tic industry, necessarily endeavors so to direct that industry, that its produce may be of the greatest possible value.

The produce of industry is what it adds to the subject or materials upon which it is employed. In proportion as the value of this produce is great or small, so will likewise be the profits of the employer. But it is only for the sake of profit that any man employs a capital in the support of industry; and he will always, therefore, en-deavor to employ it in the support of that industry of which the produce is likely to be of the greatest value, or to exchange for the greatest quantity either of money or of other goods.

But the annual revenue of every society is always precisely equal to the exchangeable value of the whole annual produce of its industry, or rather is precisely the same thing with that exchangeable value. As every individual, therefore, endeavors as much as he can both to employ his capital in the support of domestic industry, and so to direct that industry that its produce may be of the greatest value, every individual necessarily labors to render the annual revenue of the society as great as he can. He generally, indeed, neither intends to promote the public interest, nor knows how much he is promoting it. By preferring the support of domestic to that of foreign industry, he intends only his own security; and by directing that industry in such a manner as its produce may be of the greatest value, he intends only his own gain, and he is in this, as in many other cases, led by an invisible hand to promote an end which was no part of his intention. Nor is it always the worse for the society that it was no part of it. By pursuing his own interest he frequently promotes that of the society more effectually than when he really intends to promote it. . . .

What is the species of domestic industry which his capital can employ, and of which the produce is likely to be of the greatest value, every individual, it is evident, can, in his local situation, judge much better than any statesman or lawgiver can do for him. The statesman, who should attempt to direct private people in what manner they ought to employ their capitals, would not only load himself with a most unnecessary attention, but assume an authority which could safely be trusted, not only to no single person, but to no council or senate whatever, and which would nowhere be so dangerous as in the hands of a man who had folly and presumption enough to fancy himself fit to exercise it.

To give the monopoly of the home market to the produce of domestic industry, in any particular art or manufacture, is in some measure to direct private people in what manner they ought to employ their capitals, and must, in almost all cases, be either a useless or a hurtful regulation. If the produce of domestic can be brought there as cheap as that of foreign industry, the regulation is evidently useless. If it cannot, it must generally be hurtful. It is the maxim of every prudent master of a family, never to attempt to make at home what it will cost him more to make than to buy. . . .

What is prudence in the conduct of every private family, can scarce be folly in that of a great kingdom. If a foreign country can supply us with a commodity cheaper than we ourselves can make it, better buy it of them with some part of the produce of our own industry, employed in a way in which we have some advantage. The general industry of the country, being always in proportion to the capital which employs it, will not thereby be diminished, no more than that of the above-mentioned artificers, but only left to find out the way in which it can be employed with the greatest advantage. It is certainly not employed to the greatest advantage, when it is thus directed towards an object which it can buy cheaper than it can make. The value of its annual produce is certainly more or less diminished, when it is thus turned away from producing commodities evidently of more value than the commodity which it is directed to produce. According to the supposition, that commodity could be purchased from foreign countries cheaper than it can be made at home. It could, therefore, have been purchased with a part only of the commodities, or, what is the same thing, with a part only of the price of the commodities, which the industry employed by an equal capital would have produced at home, had it been left to follow its natural course. The industry of the country, therefore, is thus turned away from a more to a less advantageous employment, and the exchangeable value of its annual produce, instead of being increased, according to the intention of the lawgiver, must necessarily be diminished by every such regulation.

DISCUSSION QUESTIONS

1. Why does Smith argue against the regulation of commerce? What evidence does he cite to support his argument?

2. Why does Smith think that allowing individuals to pursue economic gain freely is advantageous to society as a whole?

3. How does this excerpt support the view held by scholars that Smith helped to lay the theoretical foundations of modern capitalist society?

4. How does Smith reflect broader Enlightenment ideas?

5.
Enlightened Monarchy
Frederick II, *Political Testament* (1752)

The Enlightenment's triumph is perhaps best reflected in the politics of the second half of the eighteenth century. Rather than working to suppress the philosophes' calls for change, rulers across continental Europe embraced them as a means of enhancing their power and prestige. They did so at their own discretion, however, and often with an iron hand, as the case of King Frederick II of Prussia (r. 1740–1786) vividly reveals. A devotee of the Enlightenment as well as an exemplary soldier and statesman, Frederick transformed Prussia into a leading European state during his reign. In his Political Testament *of 1752, excerpted here, he outlines his political philosophy, which blended Enlightenment ideals with an uncompromising view of his own power.*

One must attempt, above all, to know the special genius of the people which one wants to govern in order to know if one must treat them leniently or severely, if they are inclined to revolt . . . to intrigue. . . .

[The Prussian nobility] has sacrificed its life and goods for the service of the state, its loyalty and merit have earned it the protection of all its rulers, and it is

From George L. Mosse, Rondo E. Cameron, Henry Bertram Hill, and Michael B. Petrovich, eds., *Europe in Review* (Chicago: Rand McNally and Company, 1957), 111–12.

one of the duties [of the ruler] to aid those [noble] families which have become impoverished in order to keep them in possession of their lands: for they are to be regarded as the pedestals and the pillars of the state. In such a state no factions or rebellions need be feared . . . it is one goal of the policy of this state to preserve the nobility.

A well conducted government must have an underlying concept so well integrated that it could be likened to a system of philosophy. All actions taken must be well reasoned, and all financial, political and military matters must flow towards one goal: which is the strengthening of the state and the furthering of its power. However, such a system can flow but from a single brain, and this must be that of the sovereign. Laziness, hedonism, and imbecility, these are the causes which restrain princes in working at the noble task of bringing happiness to their subjects . . . a sovereign is not elevated to his high position, supreme power has not been confined to him in order that he may live in lazy luxury, enriching himself by the labor of the people, being happy while everyone else suffers. The sovereign is the first servant of the state. He is well paid in order that he may sustain the dignity of his office, but one demands that he work efficiently for the good of the state, and that he, at the very least, pay personal attention to the most important problems. . . .

You can see, without doubt, how important it is that the King of Prussia govern personally. Just as it would have been impossible for Newton to arrive at his system of attractions if he had worked in harness with Leibnitz and Descartes, so a system of politics cannot be arrived at and continued if it has not sprung from a single brain. . . . All parts of the government are inexorably linked with each other. Finance, politics, and military affairs are inseparable; it does not suffice that one be well administered; they must all be . . . a Prince who governs personally, who has formed his [own] political system, will not be handicapped when occasions arise where he has to act swiftly: for he can guide all matters towards the end which he has set for himself. . . .

Catholics, Lutherans, Reformed, Jews, and other Christian sects live in this state, and live together in peace: if the sovereign, actuated by a mistaken zeal, declares himself for one religion or another, parties will spring up, heated disputes ensue, little by little persecutions will commence, and, in the end, the religion persecuted will leave the fatherland and millions of subjects will enrich our neighbors by their skill and industry.

It is of no concern in politics whether the ruler has a religion or whether he has none. All religions, if one examines them, are founded on superstitious systems, more or less absurd. It is impossible for a man of good sense, who dissects their contents, not to see their error; but these prejudices, these errors and mysteries were made for men, and one must know enough to respect the public and not to outrage its faith, whatever religion be involved.

DISCUSSION QUESTIONS

1. Based on this excerpt, in what ways does the term *enlightened despot* apply to Frederick II? How is he enlightened? How is he despotic?

2. What reasons does Frederick advance in favor of religious tolerance?

3. According to Frederick, what should be the one goal of government?

COMPARATIVE QUESTIONS

1. How do Ménétra's and Frederick II's attitudes toward organized religion overlap?

2. What similarities and differences do you see between Frederick II's and Beccaria's views on the basis of good government?

3. What do Geoffrin and Beccaria reveal about the means by which Enlightenment ideas spread? Why is this significant to understanding the Enlightenment's development?

4. In what ways do the documents by Adam Smith, Frederick II, and Beccaria reflect Enlightenment thinkers' intense interest in the relationship between the individual and secular society?

The Cataclysm of Revolution, 1789–1799

W hen the Estates General convened at Versailles in May 1789, no one could have foreseen what lay ahead: ten years of upheaval that established the model of modern revolution and set the course of modern politics. The following documents illuminate the French Revolution in the making, from the politically charged months preceding the convocation of the Estates General to the formation of a republic and a government of terror designed to destroy enemies of the Revolution both within and without. At each stage, the revolutionaries remained committed to the Enlightenment principle of using reason to reshape society and government. The second document, a political cartoon of the Old Regime, visually brings to life why so many people clamored for change. Even so, they were not always in control of events either in France or beyond, as peasants, working-class city folk, and even slaves from the French colony of Saint Domingue (modern-day Haiti) rose up with their own demands, taking the Revolution in even more radical directions.

1.
Defining the Nation

Abbé Sieyès, *What Is the Third Estate?* (1789)

Although in 1788 King Louis XVI (r. 1774–1792) agreed to call the Estates General, he left a thorny procedural question for the deputies to answer: Would the assembly vote by order or by head? The debate over this question galvanized the nation in the months

From Lynn Hunt, ed. and trans., *The French Revolution and Human Rights: A Brief Documentary History* (Boston: Bedford/St. Martin's, 1996), 65–70.

preceding the opening of the Estates General in May 1789, thanks in part to pamphlets like the one that follows. Written by a middle-class clergyman, Abbé Emmanuel-Joseph Sieyès (1748–1836), this pamphlet's message was clear: the privileged few should not determine the nation's future, as a traditional vote by order would ensure by allowing the clergy and nobility to join forces to block any decision contrary to their liking. Rather, government should rest in the hands of the people whose labor and skills sustain society, the Third Estate. In forging his argument, Sieyès forcefully condemned traditional political and social structures while granting the Third Estate a voice on the national stage.

The plan of this work is quite simple. We must ask ourselves three questions.

1. What is the Third Estate? Everything.
2. What has it been until now in the political order? Nothing.
3. What does it want? To become something. . . .

What does a Nation require to survive and prosper? *Private* employment and *public* offices.

Private employment includes four classes of work:

1. Since the land and water provide the raw material for the needs of mankind, the first class, in logical order, includes all those families attached to work in the countryside.

2. Between the initial sale of raw materials and their consumption or usage as finished goods, labor of various sorts adds more value to these goods. In this way human industry manages to improve on the blessings of Nature and to multiply the value of the raw materials two, ten, or a hundredfold. Such is the second class of work.

3. Between production and consumption, as also between the different stages of production, there are a host of intermediary agents, useful both to producers and consumers; these are the merchants and wholesale traders. Wholesale traders constantly weigh demand according to place and time and speculate on the profit that they can make on storage and transport; merchants actually sell the goods on the markets, whether wholesale or retail. This type of utility designates the third class of work.

4. Besides these three classes of hard-working and useful Citizens who occupy themselves with the *things* fit to be consumed or used, society also needs a multitude of private occupations and services *directly* useful or agreeable to the *person*. This fourth class embraces all those occupations from the most distinguished scientific and liberal professions down to the least esteemed domestic servants.

These are the kinds of work that sustain society. Who carries them out? The Third Estate.

In the present state of affairs public offices can also be ranked in four well-known categories: the Sword [the army], the Robe [the courts], the Church, and the Administration. Detailed analysis is not necessary to show that the Third Estate makes up everywhere $^{19}/_{20}$ths of their number, except that it is charged with all the really hard work, all the work that the privileged order refuses to perform. Only the lucrative and most honored places are taken by the members of the privileged order. Should we praise them for this? We could do so only if the Third [Estate] was unwilling or unable to fill these offices. We know the truth of the matter, but the Third Estate has nonetheless been excluded. They are told, "Whatever your services, whatever your talents, you will only go so far and no further. Honors are not for your sort." A few rare exceptions, noteworthy as they are bound to be, are only a mockery, and the language encouraged on these exceptional occasions is but an additional insult.

If this exclusion is a social crime committed against the Third Estate, can we say at least that it is useful to the public good? Ah! Are the effects of monopoly now known? If it discourages those whom it pushes aside, does it not also render those it favors less competent? Is it not obvious that every piece of work kept out of free competition will be made more expensively and less well?

When any office is deemed the prerogative of a separate order among the citizens, has no one noticed that a salary has to be paid not only to the man who does the work but also to all those of the same caste who do not and even to entire families of both those who work and those who do not? Has no one noticed that this state of affairs, so abjectly respected among us, nonetheless seems contemptible and shameful in the history of ancient Egypt and in the stories of voyages to the Indies? But let us leave aside those considerations which though broadening our purview and perhaps enlightening would only slow our pace. It suffices here to have made the point that the supposed usefulness of a privileged order to the public service is nothing but a mirage; that without that order, all that is most arduous in this service is performed by the Third Estate; that without the privileged the best places would be infinitely better filled; that such places should naturally be the prize and reward for recognized talents and services; and that if the privileged have succeeded in usurping all the lucrative and honored posts, this is at once an odious iniquity committed against the vast majority of the citizenry and an act of treason against the public good.

Who therefore dares to say that the Third Estate does not contain within itself all that is needed to form a complete Nation? The Third Estate is like a strong and robust man with one arm still in chains. If we remove the privileged order, the Nation will not be something less but something more. Thus, what is the Third Estate? All, but an all that is shackled and oppressed. What would it be without the privileged order? All, but an all that is free and flourishing. Nothing can be done without it [the Third Estate]; everything would be infinitely better without the other two orders.

It does not suffice to have demonstrated that the privileged, far from being useful to the Nation, can only weaken and harm it; it must be proved further that the noble order[1] is not even part of society itself: It may very well be a burden for the Nation but it cannot be a part of it.

First, it is not possible to assign a place to the caste of nobles among the many elements that make up a Nation. I know that there are too many individuals whose infirmities, incapacity, incurable laziness, or excessively bad morals make them essentially foreigners to the work of society. The exception and the abuse always accompany the rule, especially in a vast empire. But at least we can agree that the fewer the abuses, the better ordered the state. The worst-off state of all would be the one in which not only isolated individual cases but also an entire class of citizens would glory in inactivity amidst the general movement and would contrive to consume the best part of what is produced without having contributed anything to its making. Such a class is surely foreign to the Nation because of its *idleness.*

The noble order is no less foreign amongst us by reason of its *civil* and *public* prerogatives.

What is a Nation? A body of associates living under a *common* law and represented by the same *legislature.*

Is it not more than certain that the noble order has privileges, exemptions, and even rights that are distinct from the rights of the great body of citizens? Because of this, it does not belong to the common order, it is not covered by the law common to the rest. Thus its civil rights already make it a people apart inside the great Nation. It is truly *imperium in imperio* [a law unto itself].

As for its *political* rights, the nobility also exercises them separately. It has its own representatives who have no mandate from the people. Its deputies sit separately, and even when they assemble in the same room with the deputies of the ordinary citizens, the nobility's representation still remains essentially distinct and separate: it is foreign to the Nation by its very principle, for its mission does not emanate from the people, and by its purpose, since it consists in defending, not the general interest, but the private interests of the nobility.

The Third Estate therefore contains everything that pertains to the Nation and nobody outside of the Third Estate can claim to be part of the Nation. What is the Third Estate? EVERYTHING. . . .

---

[1][Sieyès's own note] I do not speak of the clergy here. In my way of thinking, the clergy is not an order but rather a profession charged with a public service. In the clergy, it is not the person who is privileged but the office, which is very different. . . . The word *caste* refers to a class of men who, without functions and without usefulness and by the sole fact that they exist, enjoy the privileges attached to their person. From this point of view, which is the true one in my opinion, there is only one order, that of the nobility. They are truly a people apart but a false people, which not being able to exist by itself by reason of its lack of useful organs, attaches itself to a real Nation like those plant growths which can only survive on the sap of the plants that they tire and suck dry. The Clergy, the Robe, the Sword, and the Administration are four classes of public trustees that are necessary everywhere. Why are they accused in France of *aristocraticism*? It is because the noble caste has usurped all the good positions; it has done so as if this was a patrimonial property exploited for its personal profit rather than in the spirit of social welfare.

By Third Estate is meant the collectivity of citizens who belong to the common order. Anybody who holds a legal privilege of any kind leaves that common order, stands as an exception to the common law, and in consequence does not belong to the Third Estate. . . . It is certain that the moment a citizen acquires privileges contrary to common law, he no longer belongs to the common order. His new interest is opposed to the general interest; he has no right to vote in the name of the people. . . .

What is the will of a Nation? It is the result of individual wills, just as the Nation is the aggregate of the individuals who compose it. It is impossible to conceive of a legitimate association that does not have for its goal the common security, the common liberty, in short, the public good. No doubt each individual also has his own personal aims. He says to himself, "protected by the common security, I will be able to peacefully pursue my own personal projects, I will seek my happiness where I will, assured of encountering only those legal obstacles that society will prescribe for the common interest, in which I have a part and with which my own personal interest is so usefully allied." . . .

Advantages which differentiate citizens from one another lie outside the purview of citizenship. Inequalities of wealth or ability are like the inequalities of age, sex, size, etc. In no way do they detract from the *equality* of citizenship. These individual advantages no doubt benefit from the protection of the law; but it is not the legislator's task to create them, to give privileges to some and refuse them to others. The law grants nothing; it protects what already exists until such time that what exists begins to harm the common interest. These are the only limits on individual freedom. I imagine the law as being at the center of a large globe; we the citizens, without exception, stand equidistant from it on the surface and occupy equal places; all are equally dependent on the law, all present it with their liberty and their property to be protected; and this is what I call the *common rights* of citizens, by which they are all alike. All these individuals communicate with each other, enter into contracts, negotiate, always under the common guarantee of the law. If in this general activity somebody wishes to get control over the person of his neighbor or usurp his property, the common law goes into action to repress this criminal attempt and puts everyone back in their place at the same distance from the law. . . .

It is impossible to say what place the two privileged orders ought to occupy in the social order: this is the equivalent of asking what place one wishes to assign to a malignant tumor that torments and undermines the strength of the body of a sick person. It must be *neutralized*. We must re-establish the health and working of all the organs so thoroughly that they are no longer susceptible to these fatal schemes that are capable of sapping the most essential principles of vitality.

Discussion Questions

1. What is the traditional status of the Third Estate? How does Sieyès want to change it, and why?
2. Why do you think Sieyès was so critical of nobility in particular? What do these criticisms reveal about his political principles?

3. How effective do you think this pamphlet is as a work of political propaganda, and why?

2.
The People under the Old Regime

Political Cartoon (1815)

This cartoon depicts a man carrying three figures on his back. Chained and bloodied, the man struggles beneath the weight not only of the riders' rotund physiques but also of the numerous privileges they enjoy, as recorded on the papers each holds in his hand. In the front sits an aristocrat, or perhaps Louis XVI himself, brandishing a whip and

his claim to feudal rights. A bishop clings to his shoulder, wielding his own set of pow-ers, the Inquisition and the annual church tax (dîme). Behind him sits a judge, re-splendent in his robe, who trumpets the nobility's domination of the regional courts (parlements). Their beast of burden is none other than the French people, symbolically depicted here as the naked and emaciated man whom the riders control with reins, chains, and a blindfold. Although this cartoon was first published in 1815, it captures the mood of thousands of French men and women on the eve of the Revolution just as powerfully as Sieyès and other pamphleteers had done in words.

DISCUSSION QUESTIONS

1. What is the primary message of this cartoon?

2. What images in particular do you think convey this message most effectively, and why?

3. In what ways do these images reflect the mixture of social and political conflicts that ultimately helped to fuel the French Revolution?

3.
Establishing Rights

National Assembly, *The Declaration of the Rights of Man and of the Citizen* (1789)

Promulgated by the fledgling National Assembly in August 1789, The Declaration of the Rights of Man and of the Citizen *gave the Revolution a clear sense of purpose and direction after the dizzying series of events of that summer. In it, the delegates set forth the guiding principles of the new government, echoing many of the ideals of in-fluential eighteenth-century thinkers. The document also marked the definitive end of the Old Regime by presenting the protection of individual rights, not royal prerogative, as the cornerstone of political authority. The deputies' work was not done, however, for they regarded the declaration as a preliminary step toward their primary goal: to write a constitution for the country that would transform it into an enlightened constitu-tional monarchy. This goal was met with the Constitution of 1791, to which the dec-laration was attached.*

The representatives of the French people, organized as a National Assembly, be-lieving that the ignorance, neglect, or contempt of the rights of man are the sole cause of public calamities and of the corruption of governments, have determined to set forth in a solemn declaration the natural, inalienable, and sacred rights of man, in order that this declaration, being constantly before all the members of the social body, shall remind them continually of their rights and duties; in order that

From James Harvey Robinson, *Readings in European History*, vol. II (Boston: Ginn and Com-pany, 1906), 409–11.

the acts of the legislative power, as well as those of the executive power, may be compared at any moment with the objects and purposes of all political institutions and may thus be more respected; and, lastly, in order that the grievances of the citizens, based hereafter upon simple and incontestable principles, shall tend to the maintenance of the constitution and redound to the happiness of all. Therefore the National Assembly recognizes and proclaims, in the presence and under the auspices of the Supreme Being, the following rights of man and of the citizen:

Article 1. Men are born and remain free and equal in rights. Social distinctions may be founded only upon the general good.

2. The aim of all political association is the preservation of the natural and imprescriptible rights of man. These rights are liberty, property, security, and resistance to oppression.

3. The principle of all sovereignty resides essentially in the nation. No body nor individual may exercise any authority which does not proceed directly from the nation.

4. Liberty consists in the freedom to do everything which injures no one else; hence the exercise of the natural rights of each man has no limits except those which assure to the other members of the society the enjoyment of the same rights. These limits can only be determined by law.

5. Law can only prohibit such actions as are hurtful to society. Nothing may be prevented which is not forbidden by law, and no one may be forced to do anything not provided for by law.

6. Law is the expression of the general will. Every citizen has a right to participate personally, or through his representative, in its formation. It must be the same for all, whether it protects or punishes. All citizens, being equal in the eyes of the law, are equally eligible to all dignities and to all public positions and occupations, according to their abilities, and without distinction except that of their virtues and talents.

7. No person shall be accused, arrested, or imprisoned except in the cases and according to the forms prescribed by law. Any one soliciting, transmitting, executing, or causing to be executed, any arbitrary order, shall be punished. But any citizen summoned or arrested in virtue of the law shall submit without delay, as resistance constitutes an offense.

8. The law shall provide for such punishments only as are strictly and obviously necessary, and no one shall suffer punishment except it be legally inflicted in virtue of a law passed and promulgated before the commission of the offense.

9. As all persons are held innocent until they shall have been declared guilty, if arrest shall be deemed indispensable, all harshness not essential to the securing of the prisoner's person shall be severely repressed by law.

10. No one shall be disquieted on account of his opinions, including his religious views, provided their manifestation does not disturb the public order established by law.

11. The free communication of ideas and opinions is one of the most precious of the rights of man. Every citizen may, accordingly, speak, write, and print

with freedom, but shall be responsible for such abuses of this freedom as shall be defined by law.

12. The security of the rights of man and of the citizen requires public military forces. These forces are, therefore, established for the good of all and not for the personal advantage of those to whom they shall be intrusted.

13. A common contribution is essential for the maintenance of the public forces and for the cost of administration. This should be equitably distributed among all the citizens in proportion to their means.

14. All the citizens have a right to decide, either personally or by their representatives, as to the necessity of the public contribution; to grant this freely; to know to what uses it is put; and to fix the proportion, the mode of assessment and of collection and the duration of the taxes.

15. Society has the right to require of every public agent an account of his administration.

16. A society in which the observance of the law is not assured, nor the separation of powers defined, has no constitution at all.

17. Since property is an inviolable and sacred right, no one shall be deprived thereof except where public necessity, legally determined, shall clearly demand it, and then only on condition that the owner shall have been previously and equitably indemnified.

DISCUSSION QUESTIONS

1. In delineating the rights of the individual, how did the National Assembly respond to Enlightenment writers' calls for reforms?

2. According to this document, what are the fundamental roles of government and the individual citizen?

3. How does the document define political sovereignty, and how is this definition related to the deputies' collective sense of identity and purpose?

4.
Defending Terror

Maximilien Robespierre, *Report on the Principles of Political Morality* (1794)

Despite the momentous events of the first two years of the Revolution, even more radical changes were yet to come. With pressures mounting at home and the threat of war looming abroad, in 1792 the National Convention abolished the monarchy and established the first French Republic. A year later, the government set up the Committee of Public Safety to defend the Revolution from its enemies. To this end, the committee instituted a set of

From Richard Bienvenu, ed., *The Ninth of Thermidor: The Fall of Robespierre* (New York: Oxford University Press, 1968), 33–36, 38–39.

emergency measures known as the Terror to crush all forms of dissent. Maximilien Robespierre (1758–1794), the leader of the committee, was a driving force behind the radicalization of the Revolution. In a speech delivered to the National Convention on February 5, 1794, excerpted here, he set forth his political vision. As he argued, virtue was the soul of the Republic. With the Republic fighting for its very survival, terror flowed from virtue in the form of swift and firm justice; neither could succeed without the other. At the time, Robespierre and his allies were the targets of increasingly strong criticism, for many believed that the Terror had achieved its goals and should now be dismantled. Robespierre met his critics head on, holding up terror as the sword of liberty.

What is the goal toward which we are heading? The peaceful enjoyment of liberty and equality; the reign of that eternal justice whose laws have been inscribed, not in marble and stone, but in the hearts of all men, even in that of the slave who forgets them and in that of the tyrant who denies them.

We seek an order of things in which all the base and cruel passions are enchained, all the beneficent and generous passions are awakened by the laws; where ambition becomes the desire to merit glory and to serve our country; where distinctions are born only of equality itself; where the citizen is subject to the magistrate, the magistrate to the people, and the people to justice; where our country assures the well-being of each individual, and where each individual proudly enjoys our country's prosperity and glory; where every soul grows greater through the continual flow of republican sentiments, and by the need of deserving the esteem of a great people; where the arts are the adornments of the liberty which ennobles them and commerce the source of public wealth rather than solely the monstrous opulence of a few families.

In our land we want to substitute morality for egotism, integrity for formal codes of honor, principles for customs, a sense of duty for one of mere propriety, the rule of reason for the tyranny of fashion, scorn of vice for scorn of the unlucky, self-respect for insolence, grandeur of soul for vanity, love of glory for the love of money, good people in place of good society. We wish to substitute merit for intrigue, genius for wit, truth for glamor, the charm of happiness for sensuous boredom, the greatness of man for the pettiness of the great, a people who are magnanimous, powerful, and happy, in place of a kindly, frivolous, and miserable people — which is to say all the virtues and all the miracles of the republic in place of all the vices and all the absurdities of the monarchy.

We want, in a word, to fulfill nature's desires, accomplish the destiny of humanity, keep the promises of philosophy, absolve providence from the long reign of crime and tyranny. Let France, formerly illustrious among the enslaved lands, eclipsing the glory of all the free peoples who have existed, become the model for the nations, the terror of oppressors, the consolation of the oppressed, the ornament of the world — and let us, in sealing our work with our blood, see at least the early dawn of universal bliss — that is our ambition, that is our goal.

What kind of government can realize these wonders? Only a democratic or republican government — these two words are synonyms, despite the abuses in common speech, because an aristocracy is no closer than a monarchy to being a republic. Democracy is not a state in which the people, continually meeting, regulate for themselves all public affairs, still less is it a state in which a tiny fraction of the people, acting by isolated, hasty, and contradictory measures, decide the fate of the whole society. Such a government has never existed, and it could exist only to lead the people back into despotism.

Democracy is a state in which the sovereign people, guided by laws which are of their own making, do for themselves all that they can do well, and by their delegates do all that they cannot do for themselves.

It is therefore in the principles of democratic government that you should seek the rules for your political conduct.

But, in order to lay the foundations of democracy among us and to consolidate it, in order to arrive at the peaceful reign of constitutional laws, we must finish the war of liberty against tyranny and safely cross through the storms of the revolution: that is the goal of the revolutionary system which you have put in order. You should therefore still base your conduct upon the stormy circumstances in which the republic finds itself; and the plan of your administration should be the result of the spirit of revolutionary government, combined with the general principles of democracy.

Now, what is the fundamental principle of popular or democratic government, that is to say, the essential mainspring which sustains it and makes it move? It is virtue. I speak of the public virtue which worked so many wonders in Greece and Rome and which ought to produce even more astonishing things in republican France — that virtue which is nothing other than the love of the nation and its laws.

But as the essence of the republic or of democracy is equality, it follows that love of country necessarily embraces the love of equality.

There are important consequences to be drawn immediately from the principles we have just explained.

Since the soul of the Republic is virtue, equality, and since your goal is to found, to consolidate the Republic, it follows that the first rule of your political conduct ought to be to relate all your efforts to maintaining equality and developing virtue; because the first care of the legislator ought to be to fortify the principle of the government. Thus everything that tends to excite love of country, to purify morals, to elevate souls, to direct the passions of the human heart toward the public interest, ought to be adopted or established by you. Everything which tends to concentrate them in the abjection of selfishness, to awaken enjoyment for petty things and scorn for great ones, ought to be rejected or curbed by you. Within the scheme of the French revolution, that which is immoral is impolitic, that which is corrupting is counter-revolutionary. Weakness, vice, and prejudices are the road to royalty. Dragged too often, perhaps, by the weight of our former customs, as much as by the imperceptible bent of human frailty, toward false ideas and faint-hearted sentiments, we have less cause to guard ourselves against too much energy than against too much weakness. The greatest peril, perhaps, that we have to avoid is not that of zealous fervor, but rather of weariness in doing good works and of timidity in displaying our own courage. Maintain, then, the sacred power of the republican government, instead of letting it decline. I do not need to say that I have no wish here to justify any excess.

The most sacred principles can indeed be abused. It is up to the wisdom of the government to pay heed to circumstances, to seize the right moments, to choose the proper means; because the manner of preparing great things is an essential part of the talent for performing them, just as wisdom is itself an element of virtue.

We deduce from all this a great truth — that the characteristic of popular government is to be trustful towards the people and severe towards itself.

Here the development of our theory would reach its limit, if you had only to steer the ship of the Republic through calm waters. But the tempest ranges, and the state of the revolution in which you find yourselves imposes upon you another task.

This great purity of the French revolution's fundamental elements, the very sublimity of its objective, is precisely what creates our strength and our weakness: our strength, because it gives us the victory of truth over deception and the rights of public interest over private interests; our weakness, because it rallies against us all men who are vicious, all those who in their hearts plan to despoil the people, and all those who have despoiled them and want impunity, and those who reject liberty as a personal calamity, and those who have embraced the revolution as a livelihood and the Republic as if it were an object of prey. Hence the defection of so many ambitious or greedy men who since the beginning have abandoned us along the way, because they had not begun the voyage in order to reach the same goal. One could say that the two contrary geniuses that have been depicted competing for control of the realm of nature, are fighting in this great epoch of human history to shape irrevocably the destiny of the world, and that France is the theater of this mighty struggle. Without, all the tyrants encircle you; within, all the friends of tyranny conspire — they will conspire until crime has been robbed of hope. We must smother the internal and external enemies of the Republic or perish with them. Now, in this situation, the first maxim of your policy ought to be to lead the people by reason and the people's enemies by terror.

If the mainspring of popular government in peacetime is virtue, amid revolution it is at the same time [both] virtue and *terror*: virtue, without which terror is fatal; terror, without which virtue is impotent. Terror is nothing but prompt, severe, inflexible justice; it is therefore an emanation of virtue. It is less a special principle than a consequence of the general principle of democracy applied to our country's most pressing needs.

It has been said that terror was the mainspring of despotic government. Does your government, then, resemble a despotism? Yes, as the sword which glitters in the hands of liberty's heroes resembles the one with which tyranny's lackeys are armed. Let the despot govern his brutalized subjects by terror; he is right to do this, as a despot. Subdue liberty's enemies by terror, and you will be right, as founders of the Republic. The government of the revolution is the despotism of liberty against tyranny.

DISCUSSION QUESTIONS

1. According to Robespierre, what is the central goal of the Revolution?

2. Describe Robespierre's notion of virtue. How is it related to his vision for the Revolution's future?

3. In his view, what methods can governments use to defend virtue, and why?

4. Historians have long debated whether the radical Revolution marked the beginning of true democracy or justified totalitarianism. Based on Robespierre's speech, what evidence do you find to support these two contradictory ideas?

5.
Dissent on Trial

Olympe de Gouges, *Letters on the Trial* (1793)

Once in place, the program of the Terror quickly gained momentum. All forms of dissent were deemed counterrevolutionary, and tribunals were set up to try and convict political suspects. The following excerpts from the trial record of French author and activist Olympe de Gouges (1748–1793) illuminate the instruments and ideals of the Terror in action. De Gouges, the daughter of a butcher, had already gained fame by protesting women's exclusion from full political participation in the Revolution in her 1791 tract, Declaration of the Rights of Woman. *In 1793, she aimed the power of her pen at the Terror. Having caught the attention of the police, de Gouges was imprisoned, and upon her interrogation before the Revolutionary Tribunal in November, she met the same fate as thousands of others at the time: death by guillotine.*

> Audience of . . . 12 Brumaire, Year II of the Republic,
> Case of Olympe de Gouges.

Questioned concerning her name, surname, age, occupation, place of birth, and residence. Replied that her name was Marie Olympe de Gouges, age thirty-eight, *femme de lettres*, a native of Montauban, living in Paris, rue du Harlay, Section Pont-Neuf.

The clerk read the act of accusation, the tenor of which follows.

Antoine-Quentin Fouquier-Tinville, public prosecutor before the Revolutionary Tribunal, etc.

States that, by an order of the administrators of police, dated last July 25, signed Louvet and Baudrais, it was ordered that Marie Olympe de Gouges, widow of Aubry, charged with having composed a work contrary to the expressed desire of the entire nation, and directed against whoever might propose a form of government other than that of a republic, one and indivisible, be brought to the prison called l'Abbaye, and that the documents be sent to the public prosecutor of the

From Darline Gay Levy, Harriet Branson Applewhite, Mary Durham Johnson, eds. and trans., *Women in Revolutionary Paris, 1789–1795* (Urbana: University of Illinois Press, 1979), 255–59.

Revolutionary Tribunal. Consequently, the accused was brought to the designated prison and the documents delivered to the public prosecutor on July 26. The following August 6, one of the judges of the Revolutionary Tribunal proceeded with the interrogation of the above-mentioned de Gouges woman.

From the examination of the documents deposited, together with the interrogation of the accused, it follows that against the desire manifested by the majority of Frenchmen for republican government, and in contempt of laws directed against whoever might propose another form of government, Olympe de Gouges composed and had printed works which can only be considered as an attack on the sovereignty of the people because they tend to call into question that concerning which it [the people] formally expressed its desire; that in her writing, entitled *Les Trois urnes, ou le Salut de la patrie*, there can be found the project of the liberty-killing faction which wanted to place before the people the approbation of the judgment of the tyrant condemned by the people itself; that the author of this work openly provoked civil war and sought to arm citizens against one another by proposing the meeting of primary assemblies to deliberate and express their desire concerning either monarchical government, which the national sovereignty had abolished and proscribed; concerning the one and indivisible republican [form], which it had chosen and established by the organ of its representatives; or, finally, concerning the federative [form], which would be the source of incalculable evils and which would destroy liberty infallibly.

. . . The public prosecutor stated next that it is with the most violent indignation that one hears the de Gouges woman say to men who for the past four years have not stopped making the greatest sacrifices for liberty; who on August 10, 1792, overturned both the throne and the tyrant; who knew how to bravely face the arms and frustrate the plots of the despot, his slaves, and the traitors who had abused the public confidence — to men who have submitted tyranny to the avenging blade of the law — that Louis Capet [Louis XVI] still reigns among them.

There can be no mistaking the perfidious intentions of this criminal woman, and her hidden motives, when one observes her in all the works to which, at the very least, she lends her name, calumniating and spewing out bile in large doses against the warmest friends of the people, their most intrepid defender. . . .

On the basis of the foregoing exposé the public prosecutor drew up this accusation against Marie Olympe de Gouges, widow Aubry, for having maliciously and purposefully composed writings attacking the sovereignty of the people (whose desire, when these were written, had been pronounced for republican government, one and indivisible) and tending towards the reestablishment of the monarchical government (which it [the people] had formally proscribed) as well as the federative [form] (against which it [the people] had forcefully protested); for having had printed up and distributed several copies of one of the cited works tending towards these ends, entitled, *Les Trois urnes, ou le Salut de la patrie*; for having been stopped in her distribution of a greater number of copies as well as in her posting of the cited work only by the refusal of the bill-poster and by her prompt arrest; for having sent this work to her son, employed in the army of the Vendée as *officier de l'état major*; for having, in other manuscripts and printed works — notably, in the manuscript entitled *La France sauvée, ou le Tyran détrôné* as well as in the poster entitled *Olympe de Gouges au Tribunal Révolutionnaire* — sought to degrade the constituted authorities, calumniate the friends and defenders of the people and of liberty, and spread defiance among the representatives and the represented, which is contrary to the laws. . . .

Consequently, the public prosecutor asks that he be given official notice by the assembled Tribunal of this indictment, etc., etc.

In this case only three witnesses were heard, one of whom was the citizen bill-poster, who stated that, having been asked to post a certain number of copies of printed material with the title *Les Trois urnes*, he refused when he found out about the principles contained in this writing.

When the accused was questioned sharply about when she composed this writing, she replied that it was some time last May, adding that what motivated her was that seeing the storms arising in a large number of *départments* . . . she had the idea of bringing all parties together by leaving them all free in the choice of the kind of government which would be most suitable for them; that furthermore, her intentions had proven that she had in view only the happiness of her country.

Questioned about how it was that she, the accused, who believed herself to be such a good patriot, had been able to develop, in the month of June, means which she called conciliatory concerning a fact which could not longer be in question because the people, at that period, had formally pronounced for republican government, one and indivisible, she replied that this was also the [form of government] she had voted for as the preferable one; that for a long while she had professed only republican sentiments. . . .

Asked to declare whether she acknowledged authorship of a manuscript work found among her papers entitled *La France sauvée ou le Tyran détrôné*, she replied yes.

Asked why she had placed injurious and perfidious declamations against the most ardent defenders of the rights of the people in the mouth of the person who in this work was supposed to represent the Capet woman [Marie-Antoinette], she replied that she had the Capet woman speaking the language appropriate for her; that besides, the handbill for which she was brought before the Tribunal had never been posted; that to avoid compromising herself she had decided to send twenty-four copies to the Committee of Public Safety, which, two days later, had her arrested.

The public prosecutor pointed out to the accused, concerning this matter, that if her placard entitled *Les Trois urnes* had not been made public, this was because the bill-poster had not been willing to take it upon himself. The accused was in agreement with this fact.

Questioned about whether, since her detention, she had not sent a copy to her son along with a letter, she said that the fact was exact and that her intention concerning this matter had been to apprise him of the cause of her arrest; that besides, she did not know whether her son had received it, not having heard from him in a long while and not knowing at all what could have become of him.

Asked to speak concerning various phrases in the placard entitled *Olympe de Gouges, défenseur de Louis Capet*, a work written by her at the time of the former's trial, and concerning the placard entitled *Olympe de Gouges au Tribunal Révolutionnaire* as well, she responded only with oratorical phrases and persisted in saying that she was and always had been a good *citoyenne*, that she had never intrigued.

Asked to express herself and to reply precisely concerning her sentiments with respect to the faithful representatives of the people whom she had insulted and calumniated in her writings, the accused replied that she had not changed, that she still held to her same opinion concerning them, and that she had looked upon them as ambitious persons.

In her defense the accused said that she had ruined herself in order to propagate the principles of the Revolution and that she was the founder of popular societies of her sex, etc.

During the résumé of the charge brought by the public prosecutor, the accused, with respect to the facts she was hearing articulated against her, never stopped her smirking. Sometimes she shrugged her shoulders; then she clasped her hands and raised her eyes towards the ceiling of the room; then, suddenly, she moved on to an expressive gesture, showing astonishment; then gazing next at the court, she smiled at the spectators, etc.

Here is the judgment rendered against her.

The Tribunal, based on the unanimous declaration of the jury, stating that (1) it is a fact that there exist in the case writings tending towards the reestablishment of a power attacking the sovereignty of the people [and] (2) that Marie Olympe de Gouges, calling herself widow Aubry, is proven guilty of being the author of these writings, and admitting the conclusions of the public prosecutor, condemns the aforementioned Marie Olympe de Gouges, widow Aubry, to the punishment of death in conformity with Article One of the law of last March 29, which was read, which is conceived as follows: "Whoever is convicted of having composed or printed works or writings which provoke the dissolution of the national representation, the reestablishment of royalty, or of any other power attacking the sovereignty of the people, will be brought before the Revolutionary Tribunal and punished by death," and declares the goods of the aforementioned Marie Olympe de Gouges acquired for the republic. . . .

. . . The execution took place the same day [13 Brumaire] towards 4 p.m.; while mounting the scaffold, the condemned, looking at the people, cried out: "Children of the Fatherland, you will avenge my death." Universal cries of "Vive la République" were heard among the spectators waving hats in the air.

DISCUSSION QUESTIONS

1. What was the basis of the charges against de Gouges?

2. What do these charges and the ensuing judgment reveal about the political principles of the Terror?

3. How were these ideals at odds with those of de Gouges?

4. Do you think that de Gouges's gender influenced the tribunal's attitudes toward her? If so, why?

6.
Liberty for All?

François Dominique Toussaint L'Ouverture,
Revolution in the Colonies (1794–1795)

In declaring that all men are born free and equal, the National Convention unleashed a debate with momentous consequences. Did blacks fall within the category of "all men"? This question proved explosive in the French colony of Saint Domingue. News of the Revolution's progress traveled quickly to the island, prompting slaves in the north to launch an insurrection against their white masters in August 1791. Their revolt sparked more than a decade of war. The former slave François Dominique Toussaint L'Ouverture (1743–1803) became the most prominent black leader of the revolution. Allied first with Spain in 1793, which controlled much of the island, he and his troops joined the French the following year, for reasons he explained in the letter excerpted here to the chief French commander in northern Saint Domingue. The letter is followed by extracts from a proclamation made by Toussaint to local dissenters in 1795 that further illuminate his revolutionary principles and actions.

Toussaint L'Ouverture to General Etienne Laveaux

May 1794

It is very true, general, that I was led into error by the enemies of the Republic [of France] and of mankind, but who is the man who can hope to avoid all the traps of the wicked? Indeed, I fell into their nets, but not without reason . . . the Spanish offered me their protection, and freedom for all those who fought for the kings' cause;[1] and having always fought to possess this same freedom, I clung to their offer, seeing myself abandoned by the French, my brothers.[2] But an experience a little later opened my eyes to these treacherous protectors; and being aware of their deceit and villainy, I saw clearly that their intentions were to make us cut each other's throats in order to reduce our numbers and oppress those remaining in chains and cause them to sink back into their former slavery. No, they never would reach their

---

From Gérard M. Laurent, *Toussaint L'Ouverture à Travers sa Correspondance (1794–1798)*. Trans. Katharine J. Lualdi (Madrid, 1953), 103–04, 169–72.

[1]The royalist government of Spain jumped at the opportunity to expand its holdings once the slave revolts had begun. To this end, they joined forces with the royalist government of Britain, which had been at war with France since February 1793, to destroy France's hold on the colony.
[2]In 1793, Toussaint had written to Laveaux, offering to join the French in exchange for a full amnesty for black rebels and freedom for all slaves. Laveaux rejected the offer, and Toussaint continued fighting for royalist Spain. By spring 1794, the situation had changed radically. Not only had British and Spanish forces gained control of most of the island, making Laveaux desperate for Toussaint's support, but the National Convention had also sanctioned the abolition of slavery.

base goal! And in our turn we will avenge ourselves of these wretched beings in every respect. Thus let us unite forever and, forgetting the past, henceforth concern ourselves only with crushing our enemies. . . .

Toussaint L'Ouverture to the People of Verrettes

March 1795

Brothers and sisters,

The moment has arrived when the thick veil that was blocking the light must fall. One must no longer forget the decrees of the National Convention. Its principles, its love of liberty, are unchanging, and henceforth, there can be no hope of this sacred edifice crumbling. . . .

I have learned with infinite joy about the return of some citizens of Verrettes to the bosom of the Republic; they will find the happiness that eluded them at the instigation of the soldiers of tyranny and royalty.

. . . To give them help, console them regarding past faults and prompt them to abjure the errors in which they were insidiously nourished, is an absolute duty and the sacred maxim of the French for all republicans.

This is why not only by virtue of the powers entrusted by General Laveaux, but also animated by the feelings of humanity and brotherhood with which I am filled, I must remind the citizens of Verrettes of their errors; but as much as they are detrimental to the interests of the Republic, as much I feel that their return, if sincere, can be advantageous to the growth of our success. . . .

The French are brothers; the English, the Spanish, and royalists are ferocious beasts who caress them only in order to suck their blood, that of their wives, and of their children at leisure, until satiation.

Citizens, I am not searching here to make a show of your faults. . . . You have returned to the bosom of the Republic, and well! Since then the past is forgotten; your duty is now to unite all of your physical and moral means to revive your parish and let the principles of sacred liberty germinate.

DISCUSSION QUESTIONS

1. What connections can you identify between the ideals of the French Revolution and those of Toussaint as expressed in the preceding documents?

2. What was Toussaint's ultimate goal as a leader in the revolution, whether fighting for the Spanish or the French?

3. What do these documents reveal about Toussaint's strategies for achieving his goal?

COMPARATIVE QUESTIONS

1. In what ways does the message of the political cartoon echo that of Sieyès in his pamphlet? How did the *Declaration of the Rights of Man and of the Citizen* address such concerns?

2. Based on Robespierre's speech and the trial record of Olympe de Gouges, in what ways did the Terror undermine the basic tenets of the *Declaration of the Rights of Man and of the Citizen*?

3. In what ways were de Gouges and Toussaint fighting a similar battle?

4. Taken collectively, how do these documents allow us to chart the course that the Revolution took between 1789 and 1795?

CHAPTER 20

Napoleon and the Revolutionary Legacy, 1800–1830

The end of the Terror in 1794 opened a new chapter in European history — one marked by the extraordinary rise of Napoleon Bonaparte (1769–1821). Between 1795 and 1799, Napoleon transformed himself from a humble artillery officer in the Revolutionary Army into the ruler of France. The first document describes a key stage in this transformation, Napoleon's invasion of Egypt in 1798. Although the campaign ultimately failed, it foreshadowed Napoleon's subsequent attempts to colonize large parts of Europe along similar lines. Napoleon's defeat in the Battle of the Nations in 1813 set the stage for a new era in European politics. Napoleon's enemies met at the Congress of Vienna to negotiate the terms of peace united by their singular desire to restore the old order. The second document reveals the allied powers in action as they worked to maintain traditional authority through the force of arms and conservative ideology. Yet, as the third document indicates, the revolutionary legacy was still a powerful force threatening the status quo. The fourth document shows the cultural response to the shifting European landscape — romanticism — which strove to strip away artifice and expose truth as revealed in nature and the human imagination. The final document suggests that, for all its creative potential, contemporary society was viewed by some Europeans with fear and uncertainty.

1.
Napoleon in Egypt
The Chronicle of Abd al-Rahman al-Jabartî (1798)

While the Directory government that came to power in 1795 worked to establish order in France, Napoleon (1769–1821) continued the Revolution's policy of conquest and annexation abroad, first in Italy (1796–1797) and then in Egypt (1798–1801). At the time, Egypt was France's most important trading partner outside of the Caribbean; it was also a key base for challenging British interests in Asia. Egyptian historian Abd al-Rahman al-Jabartî's (1753–c. 1826) account of the first six months of the French invasion offers a native's perspective of Napoleon. In the excerpt here, Jabartî views Napoleon's actions skeptically through the lens of his own culture. His skepticism proved well founded, for Napoleon failed to colonize Egypt. Even so, he retained his reputation as a great military leader, preparing the way for his mastery of France and much of Europe through a blend of authoritarian policies and revolutionary principles similar to those used in Egypt.

On Monday news arrived that the French had reached Damanhur and Rosetta, bringing about the flight of their inhabitants to Fuwwa and its surroundings. Contained in this news was mention of the French sending notices throughout the country demanding impost for the upkeep of the military. Furthermore they printed a large proclamation in Arabic, calling on the people to obey them and to raise their "Bandiera." In this proclamation were inducements, warnings, all manner of wiliness and stipulations. Some copies were sent from the provinces to Cairo and its text is:

In the name of God, the Merciful, the Compassionate. There is no god but God. He has no son, nor has He an associate in His Dominion.

On behalf of the French Republic which is based upon the foundation of liberty and equality, General Bonaparte, Commander-in-Chief of the French armies makes known to all the Egyptian people that for a long time the Sanjaqs[1] who lorded it over Egypt have treated the French community basely and contemptuously and have persecuted its merchants with all manner of extortion and violence. Therefore the hour of punishment has now come.

Unfortunately this group of Mamlūks,[2] imported from the mountains of Circassia and Georgia have acted corruptly for ages in the fairest land that is to be found upon the face of the globe. However, the Lord of the Universe, the Almighty, has decreed the end of their power.

O ye Egyptians, they may say to you that I have not made an expedition hither for any other object than that of abolishing your religion; but this is a pure falsehood and you must not give credit to it, but tell the slanderers that I have not come to you except for the purpose of restoring your rights from the hands of the oppressors and that I more than the Mamluks, serve God. . . .

And tell them also that all people are equal in the eyes of God and the only circumstances which distinguish one from the other are reason, virtue, and knowledge. But amongst the Mamlūks, what is there of reason, virtue, and knowledge, which would distinguish them from others and qualify them alone to possess everything which sweetens life in this world? Wherever fertile land is found it is appropriated to

---

From Shmuel Moreh, trans., *Napoleon in Egypt: Al-Jabartî's Chronicle of the French Occupation, 1798* (Princeton: Markus Wiener, 1993), 24–33.

[1]Sanjaqs: Provincial governors in the Ottoman Empire.
[2]Mamlūks: Descendants of medieval slave-soldiers who enjoyed considerable political power until the French invasion.

the Mamlūks; and the handsomest female slaves, and the best horses, and the most desirable dwelling-places, all these belong to them exclusively. If the land of Egypt is a fief of the Mamlūks, let them then produce the title-deed, which God conferred upon them. But the Lord of the Universe is compassionate and equitable toward mankind, and with the help of the Exalted, from this day forward no Egyptian shall be excluded from admission to eminent positions nor from acquiring high ranks, therefore the intelligent and virtuous and learned (*"ulamā"*) amongst them, will regulate their affairs, and thus the state of the whole population will be rightly adjusted. . . .

Blessing on blessing to the Egyptians who will act in concert with us, without any delay, for their condition shall be rightly adjusted, and their rank raised. Blessing also, upon those who will abide in their habitations, not siding with either of the two hostile parties, yet when they know us better, they will hasten to us with all their hearts. But woe upon woe to those who will unite with the Mamlūks and assist them in the war against us, for they will not find the way of escape, and no trace of them shall remain. . . .

Here is an explanation of the incoherent words and vulgar constructions which he put into this miserable letter.

His statement "In the name of God, the Merciful, the Compassionate. There is no god but God. He has no son, nor has He an associate in His Dominion." In mentioning these three sentences there is an indication that the French agree with the three religions, but at the same time they do not agree with them, not with any religion. They are consistent with the Muslims in stating the formula "In the name of God," in denying that He has a son or an associate. They disagree with the Muslims in not mentioning the two Articles of Faith, in rejecting the mission of Muhammad, and the legal words and deeds which are necessarily recognized by religion. They agree with the Christians in most of their words and deeds, but disagree with them by not mentioning the Trinity, and denying the mission and furthermore in rejecting their beliefs, killing the priests and destroying the churches. Then, their statement "On behalf of the French Republic, etc.," that is, this proclamation is sent from their Republic, that means their body politic, because they have no chief or sultan with whom they all agree, like others, whose function is to speak on their behalf. For when they rebelled against their sultan six years ago and killed him, the people agreed unanimously that there was not to be a single ruler but that their state, territories, laws, and administration of their affairs, should be in the hands of the intelligent and wise men among them. They appointed persons chosen by them and made them heads of the army, and below them generals and commanders of thousands, two hundreds, and tens, administrators and advisers, on condition that they were all to be equal and none superior to any other in view of the equality of creation and nature. They made this the foundation and basis of their system. This is the meaning of their statement "based upon the foundation of liberty and equality." . . . They follow this rule: great and small, high and low, male and female are all equal. Sometimes they break this rule according to their whims and inclinations or reasoning. Their women do not veil themselves and have no modesty; they do not care whether they uncover their private parts. Whenever a Frenchman has to perform an act of nature he does so wherever he happens to be, even in full view of people, and he goes away as he is, without washing his private parts after defecation. If he is a man of taste and refinement he wipes himself with whatever he finds, even with a paper with writing on it, otherwise he remains as he is. They have intercourse with any woman who pleases them and vice versa. Sometimes one of their women goes into a barber's shop, and invites him to shave her pubic hair. If he wishes he can take his fee in kind. It is their custom to shave both their moustaches and beard. Some of them leave the hair of their cheeks only. . . .

His saying *qad hattama* etc. (has decreed) shows that they are appointing themselves controllers of God's secrets, but there is no disgrace worse than disbelief. . . .

His statement *wa-qūlū li'l-muftariyīn* (but tell the slanderers) is the plural of *muftari* (slanderer) which means liar, and how worthy of this description they are. The proof of that is his saying "I have not come to you except for the purpose of restoring your rights from the hands of the oppressors," which is the first lie he uttered and a falsehood which he invented. Then he proceeds to something even worse than that, may God cast him into perdition, with his words: "I more than the Mamluks serve God. . . ." There is no doubt that this is a derangement of his mind, and an excess of foolishness. . . .

His saying [all people] are equal in the eyes of God the Almighty, this is a lie and stupidity. How can this be when God has made some superior to others as is testified by the dwellers in the Heavens and on the Earth? . . .

May God hurry misfortune and punishment upon them, may He strike their tongues with dumbness, may He scatter their hosts, and disperse them, confound their intelligence, and cause their breath to cease. He has the power to do that, and it is up to Him to answer.

DISCUSSION QUESTIONS

1. What strategy did Napoleon use in his proclamation to garner the support of the Egyptian people?

2. What does this strategy suggest about Napoleon's personal ambitions and method of rule?

3. Why is Jabartî critical of Napoleon's intentions as stated in his proclamation?

4. What do Jabartî's criticisms suggest about the differences between French and Egyptian culture?

2.
The Conservative Order

Prince Klemens von Metternich,
Results of the Congress at Laybach (1821)

Upon Napoleon's defeat in 1813, the allied powers met at the Congress of Vienna in 1814–1815 to establish the political landscape of post-Napoleonic Europe. Here they adopted a two-pronged strategy firmly rooted in conservative doctrine. First, they determined the boundaries of European states and restored as many nations as possible

*to their former rulers; then they agreed to convene meetings, or congresses, periodi-
cally to confront any future threats to order. Austria's chief negotiator, Prince Klemens von Metternich (1773–1859), was the mastermind of the congress system and
a chief spokesman for conservatism. In the excerpt that follows, Metternich assumes
both roles as he writes to Tsar Alexander I of Russia about the results of the Congress
at Laybach in 1821. The major powers had assembled at Laybach to discuss an uprising to secure a constitution in the kingdom of Naples. Along with Alexander, the
Austrian emperor and the king of Naples also agreed to armed intervention to suppress the revolt. Metternich praises Alexander for his decision while clearly enumer-
ating his own political principles, which favored monarchies over republics, tradition
over revolution.*

Before the separation of the monarchs and their Cabinets, may I be permitted to
place in the hands of your Imperial Majesty one word of gratitude and homage? Of
gratitude, Sire, for you deserve it, not on my part, nor on that of Austria, but from
society at large.

You must do me the justice to admit that I discerned long ago the evil which
has been lately unmasked with such awful intensity. You must also remember, Sire,
that, although I knew the evil, I did not despair of the remedy. This remedy has
begun to take effect; it is the intimate moral union between your Imperial Majesty
and your august allies, each being free in his actions. The merit, Sire, belongs to
you: for your situation was the most free, and certainly not so near to the danger
as that of the other monarchs. Your Imperial Majesty has done an immense good;
your conscience must tell you so; and that is the only recompense which a good
man earnestly seeks after; it is the only one which can reach the man placed by
providence above other men.

There is but one act of homage which I consider worthy of your Imperial
Majesty. Placed as I am between the Emperor, my master, and your Imperial
Majesty, grave duties rest upon me. The first is perhaps the most difficult — that of
seeking and finding the truth. The day when I lose confidence in my own calcula-
tions I shall regard myself as guilty in the eyes of my master and those of your Imperial Majesty. My homage, Sire, must simply be to tell you all my thoughts.

Society would have been irretrievably lost but for the measures which have
been taken during the last few months. These measures could not have arrested its
fall unless they had rested on the most correct principles. Such being the case, the
dawn of a better future begins to appear: the day will succeed if we continue to
walk on in the path in which we have placed ourselves. One single false principle,
and the night will be upon us, and chaos will succeed that night.

There are two means of enabling us to continue in this path: — Reciprocal and
unrestrained confidence, and a frank understanding of the principles on which our
conduct must be grounded.

From Klemens von Metternich, *Memoirs of Prince Metternich*, vol. 3, 1815–1829, ed. Richard
Metternich, trans. Mrs. Alexander Napier (New York: Howard Fertig, 1970; reprint of 1881
edition), 535–39.

This confidence, Sire, is what the mind has most difficulty in seizing. It has been, and would for ever have been, an insurmountable difficulty, if Providence had not created two sovereigns such as your Imperial Majesty and the Emperor Francis. You know each other perfectly, and this is ever necessary to a good understanding.

To establish for the future that perfect agreement of conduct so decisive for the fate of Europe, it is necessary to lay the foundation as simply as possible on clear, precise principles, and to secure their application by reciprocal engagements no less clear and precise. A great distance separates us, and this inconvenience we must remedy.

I will now state the principles, and point out the engagements to be made.

It is demonstrated that a vast and dangerous conspiracy has since 1814 acquired sufficient strength and means of action to enable it to seize upon a number of places in the public administration. This conspiracy was less evident to the eyes of the world as long as it did not court discovery, and contented itself with the domain of theory. In that domain nothing is surprising: discussions, pretensions, contradictions belong to it by full right. From the day that I saw sound doctrines attacked with impunity, and observed that they ran the risk of being suppressed altogether, I recognized revolution, with its inevitable consequences, disorder, anarchy, and death, where others saw only light fighting with prejudice. Up to that time the conspiracy had only reconnoitered its ground and prepared it. It has grown, and it must grow, thanks to the instruments which a too deplorable folly has allowed it to create for itself.

It has not been slow in descending from the intellectual sphere into that of material facts. One word was sufficient to gain public favor. That word was Constitution, of all words the least precise, the most open to variety of interpretation, and the easiest to make popular, for it acts on the mass of the people through their hopes. Tell men that by means of a single word you will ensure them their rights, a liberty which the mass always confound with license, a career for their ambition, and success in all their enterprises, and you will have no trouble in making them listen to you. The mass once agitated, they give up everything: they listen, but do not care to comprehend. When the people do really comprehend, they are the first to re-establish order.

This ground taken, as the last resource, authority has been attacked. The factious have had recourse to arms; triumph seemed to them quite certain.

The clear and precise aim of the factious is one and uniform. It is the overthrow of everything legally existing. The ambitious and successful are always impatient and ardent in their demands. Every day in a revolution is equivalent to the career of a man. The day past is nothing, the present day is everything, and that will be nothing tomorrow. Influence, place, fortune, all that human passions most covet, are suspended and attached to the tree of liberty like prizes on the pole at a fair. The people do not want urging to flock to it in crowds. Go to the fair they must, and to get there everything must be overturned.

The principle which the monarchs must oppose to this plan of universal destruction is the preservation of everything legally existing. The only way to arrive at this end is by allowing no innovations.

Your Imperial Majesty knows me well enough to be assured that no person is farther removed than I am from any narrow views of administration. It is simply the attainment of real good that I desire, and on every occasion consider my duty to maintain. But the more positive I am of this the more I am convinced that it is impossible at the same time to preserve and to reform with any justice or reason when the mass of the people is in agitation; it is then like an individual in a state of irritation, threatened with fever, or already yielding to its ravages.

Let the Governments govern, and authority be something more than a name, for it is nothing without power.

By ruling, it really ameliorates the situation, but let authority remove nothing from the foundations on which it rests; let it act, but not concede. It should exercise its rights, but not discuss them. It should be just (and to be so it must be strong), and should respect all rights as it would have its own respected.

In one word, Sire, let us be conservative; let us walk steadily and firmly on well-known paths; let us not deviate from those lines in word or deed: we shall thus be strong, and shall come at last to a time when improvements may be made with as much chance of success as there is now certainty of failure.

Discussion Questions

1. What does this document reveal about the inner workings of the congress system and the reasons for its success?

2. According to Metternich, what are the underlying principles that should guide the system and why? If applied in practice, what benefits do they provide for society?

3. What specific aspects of the revolutionary legacy does Metternich target for criticism? What dangers does he think they pose? How should governments respond?

3.
Challenge to Autocracy

Peter Kakhovsky, *The Decembrist Insurrection in Russia* (1825)

Guided by the Laybach agreement, the Austrians quickly suppressed the uprising in Naples but challenges to the conservative order continued to loom on the horizon. Across Europe, people longing for constitutional rights and national independence chafed under the Vienna settlement and joined secret societies to agitate for change. When Tsar Alexander I died unexpectedly in December 1825, Russia became embroiled in the turmoil. Secret societies took this opportunity to orchestrate a revolt of the army at St. Petersburg on December 14 against Alexander's brother Nicholas as the new tsar. They favored Alexander's other brother, Constantine, who they thought

From Anatole G. Mazour, *The First Russian Revolution, 1825* (Stanford: Stanford University Press, 1961, 1937), 274–77.

would promote constitutional reform but who had, in fact, refused the crown. Nicholas I (r. 1825–1855) suppressed the uprising the same day. Peter Kakhovsky (1797–1826) was among the captured rebel leaders who were interrogated by a special committee set up for the investigation and eradication of secret societies in Russia. As the committee was preparing its final report for the tsar, Kakhovsky wrote this letter in February 1826 to one of the committee's members, General V. Levashev, defending his cause. Kakhovsky's impassioned words did nothing to change either his fate or that of Russia, however. He was executed in July and, for the remainder of his reign, Nicholas kept a tight lid on all forms of dissent.

Your Excellency,
Dear Sir!

The uprising of December 14 is a result of causes related above. I see, Your Excellency, that the Committee established by His Majesty is making a great effort to discover all the members of the secret Society. But the government will not derive any notable benefit from that. We were not trained within the Society but were already ready to work when we joined it. The origin and the root of the Society one must seek in the spirit of the time and in our state of mind. I know a few belonging to the secret Society but am inclined to think the membership is not very large. Among my many acquaintances who do not adhere to the secret societies very few are opposed to my opinions. Frankly I state that among thousands of young men there are hardly a hundred who do not passionately long for freedom. These youths, burning with pure and strong love for the welfare of their Fatherland, toward true enlightenment, are growing mature.

The people have conceived a sacred truth — that they do not exist for governments, but that governments must be organized for them. This is the cause of struggle in all countries; peoples, after tasting the sweetness of enlightenment and freedom, strive toward them; and governments, surrounded by millions of bayonets, make efforts to repel these peoples back into the darkness of ignorance. But all these efforts will prove in vain; impressions once received can never be erased. Liberty, that torch of intellect and warmth of life, was always and everywhere the attribute of peoples emerged from primitive ignorance. We are unable to live like our ancestors, like barbarians or slaves.

But even our ancestors, though less educated, enjoyed civil liberty. During the time of Tsar Aleksei Mikhailovich the National Assembly, including representatives of various classes of the people, still functioned and participated in important affairs of the State. In his reign five such Assemblies were summoned. Peter I, who killed everything national in the State, also stamped out our feeble liberty. This liberty disappeared outwardly but lived within the hearts of true citizens; its advancement was slow in our country. Wise Catherine II expanded it a little; Her Majesty inquired from the Petersburg Free Economic Society concerning the value and consequences of the emancipation of peasants in Russia. This great beneficial thought lived in the heart of the Empress, whom the people loved. Who among Russians of her day and time could have read her INSTRUCTION without emotion?

The INSTRUCTION alone redeems all the shortcoming of that time, characteristic of that century.

Emperor Alexander promised as much; he, it could be said, enormously stirred the minds of the people toward the sacred rights of humanity. Later he changed his principles and intentions. The people became frightened, but the seed had sprouted and the roots grew deep. So rich with various revolutions are the latter half of the past century and the events of our own time that we have no need to refer to distant ones. We are witnesses of great events. The discovery of the New World and the United States, by virtue of its form of government, have forced Europe into rivalry with her. The United States will shine as an example even to distant generations. The name of Washington, the friend and benefactor of the people, will pass from generation to generation; the memory of his devotion to the welfare of the Fatherland will stir the hearts of citizens. In France the revolution which began so auspiciously turned, alas, at the end from a lawful into a criminal one. However, not the people but court intrigues and politics were responsible for that. The revolution in France shook all the thrones of Europe and had a greater influence upon the governments and peoples than the establishment of the United States.

The dominance of Napoleon and the war of 1813 and 1814 united all the European nations, summoned by their monarchs and fired by the call to freedom and citizenship. By what means were countless sums collected among citizens? What guided the armies? They preached freedom to us in Manifestoes, Appeals, and in Orders! We were lured and, kindly by nature, we believed, sparing neither blood nor property. Napoleon was overthrown! The Bourbons were called back to the throne of France and, submitting to circumstances, gave that brave, magnanimous nation a constitution, pledging themselves to forget that past. The Monarchs united into a Holy Alliance; congresses sprang into existence, informing the nations that they were assembled to reconcile all classes and introduce political freedom. But the aim of these congresses was soon revealed; the nations learned how greatly they had been deceived. The Monarchs thought only of how to retain their unlimited power, to support their shattered thrones, and to extinguish the last spark of freedom and enlightenment.

Offended nations began to demand what belonged to them and had been promised to them — chains and prisons became their lot! Crowns transgressed their pledges, the constitution of France was violated at its very base. Manuel, the representative of the people, was dragged from the Chamber of Deputies by gendarmes! Freedom of the press was restricted, the army of France, against its own will, was sent to destroy the lawful liberty of Spain. Forgetting the oath given by Louis XVIII, Charles X compensates émigrés and for that purpose burdens the people with new taxes. The government interferes with the election of deputies, and in the last elections, among the deputies only thirty-three persons were not in the service and payment of the King, the rest being sold to the Ministers. The firm, courageous Spanish people at the cost of blood rose for the liberty of their country, saved the King, the Monarchy, and the honor of the Fatherland; of their own volition the people themselves received Ferdinand as King. The King took the oath to safeguard the rights of the people. As early as the year 1812, Alexander I recognized the constitution of Spain.

Then the Alliance itself assisted France by sending her troops, and thus aided in dishonoring her army in the invasion of Spain. Ferdinand, arrested in Cadiz, was sentenced to death. He summoned Riego, swore to be once more loyal to the constitution and to expel the French troops from his territory, and begged Riego to spare his life. Honest men are apt to be trustful. Riego gave guaranty to the Cortes for the King, and he was freed. And what was the first step of Ferdinand? By his order Riego was seized, arrested, poisoned and, half-alive, that saint-martyr hero who renounced the throne offered to him, friend of the people, savior of the King's life, by the King's order is now taken through the streets of Madrid in the shameful wagon pulled by a donkey, and is hanged like a criminal. What an act! Whose heart would not shudder at it? Instead of the promised liberty the nations of Europe found themselves oppressed and their educational facilities curtailed. The prisons of Piedmont, Sardinia, Naples, and, in general, of the whole of Italy and Germany were filled with chained citizens. The lot of the people became so oppressive that they began to regret the past and to bless the memory of Napoleon the conqueror! These are the incidents which enlightened their minds and made them realize that it was impossible to make agreements with Sovereigns. . . .

The story told to Your Excellency that, in the uprising of December 14 the rebels were shouting "Long live the Constitution!" and that the people were asking "What is Constitution, the wife of His Highness the Grand Duke?" is not true. It is an amusing invention. We knew too well the meaning of a constitution and we had a word that would equally stir the hearts of all classes — LIBERTY!

. . .

The events of December are calamitous for us and, of course, must be distressing to the Emperor. Yet the events of this date should be fortunate for His Imperial Highness. After all, it was necessary sometime for the Society to begin its activities, but hardly could it have been so precipitate as in this instance. I swear to God, I wish the kind Sovereign prosperity! May God aid him in healing the wounds of our Fatherland and to become a friend and benefactor of the people. . . .

Most obedient and devoted servant of Your Excellency,

PETER KAKHOVSKY

DISCUSSION QUESTIONS

1. Why does Kakhovsky begin by denying broad membership in secret societies? What point is he trying to make about the source of Russians' political discontent?

2. How does Kakhovsky portray the Vienna settlement and its impact on European society and politics?

3. Kakhovsky was well versed in political history and had traveled widely in Europe before the Decembrist revolt. How did this knowledge and experience shape his views? What does this suggest about the power of the revolutionary legacy in post-Napoleonic Europe?

4.
The Romantic Imagination

John Keats, *Letter to Benjamin Bailey* (1817)

The political and social unrest of the first half of the nineteenth century found cultural expression in the artistic movement known as romanticism. As a whole, the movement shunned classical rules and models and instead embraced emotion, creative genius, and the imagination. Poetry was an especially vibrant vehicle for romantic sensibility. Despite his untimely death at the age of twenty-five, John Keats (1795–1821) became one of the major poets of the romantic period. Born to a lower-middle-class English family, Keats knew from childhood that he wanted to be a poet but he also knew that he had to support himself. Thus, he trained as a physician, writing and publishing his poems on the side. Influenced by his reading of William Wordsworth's poem Tintern Abbey *in 1817, Keats began to explore the nature of the human imagination in his own thinking; he published his first volume of poetry the same year. Rather than focusing on the imaginative process, Keats argued that a poet could lose all sense of self in the study of the external world, finding happiness and beauty as a result. In the letter excerpted here to a close friend, Keats outlines his early views on the imagination and its power to unveil truth.*

I wish you knew all that I think about Genius and the Heart — and yet I think you are thoroughly acquainted with my innermost breast in that respect or you could not have known me even thus long and still hold me worthy to be your dear friend. In passing however I must say of one thing that has pressed upon me lately and encreased my Humility and capability of submission and that is this truth — Men of Genius are great as certain ethereal Chemicals operating on the Mass of neutral intellect [but] they have not any individuality, any determined Character. I would call the top and head of those who have a proper self Men of Power.

But I am running my head into a Subject which I am certain I could not do justice to under five years' s[t]udy . . . and moreover long to be talking about the Imagination. . . . O I wish I was as certain of the end of all your troubles as that of your momentary start about the authenticity of the Imagination. I am certain of nothing but of the holiness of the Heart's affections and the truth of Imagination. What the imagination seizes as Beauty must be truth — whether it existed before or not — for I have the same Idea of all our Passions as of Love: they are all in their sublime, creative of essential Beauty. In a Word, you may know my favorite Speculation by my first Book and the little song I sent in my last — which is a representation from the fancy of the probable mode of operating in these Matters. The Imagination may be compared to Adam's dream — he awoke and found it truth.[1]

From John Keats, *The Letters of John Keats, 1814–1821*, vol. 1, ed. Hyder E. Rollins (Cambridge: Harvard University Press, 1958), 184–85.

[1]Genesis 2:21–25.

I am the more zealous in their affair, because I have never yet been able to perceive how any thing can be known for truth by consequitive reasoning — and yet it must be — Can it be that even the greatest Philosopher ever arrived at his goal without putting aside numerous objections? . . . It is 'a Vision in the form of Youth' a Shadow of reality to come — and this consideration has further conv[i]nced me for it has come as auxiliary to another favorite Speculation of mine, that we shall enjoy our-selves here after by having what we called happiness on Earth repeated in a finer tone and so repeated. And yet such a fate can only befall those who delight in sen-sation rather than hunger as you do after Truth — Adam's dream will do here and seems to be a conviction that Imagination and its empyreal reflection is the same as human Life and its spiritual repetition. But as I was saying — the simple imagi-native Mind may have its rewards in the repeti[ti]on of its own silent Working com-ing continually on the spirit with a fine suddenness — to compare great things with small — have you never by being surprised with an old Melody — in a delicious place — by a delicious voice, fe[l]t over again your very speculations and surmises at the time it first operated on your soul? Do you not remember forming to you-self the singer's face more beautiful that it was possible and yet with the elevation of the Moment you did not think so? Even then you were mounted on the Wings of Imagination so high — that the Prototype must be here after — that delicious face you will see — What a time! . . .

DISCUSSION QUESTIONS

1. How does Keats describe the imagination? How is it linked to human emotion?
2. Why does Keats contrast the imagination to logic and reason? In what ways was he reacting against Enlightenment ideals?
3. Based on Keats' use of language, why do you think modern scholars characterize him as a "romantic" writer? Do you think he saw himself in this way?

5.
Technology's Wrath

Mary Shelley, *Frankenstein* (1818)

While Keats embraced the wonders and creative potential of the human imagination, others feared the destructive force such creativity could unleash. English writer Mary Shelley (1797–1851) explored this fear in her novel Frankenstein. *She was well ac-quainted with the artistic and political currents of her day; she was married to Percy Bysshe Shelley, a romantic poet, and her mother, writer Mary Wollstonecraft, had de-fended the egalitarian ideals of the French Revolution. Inspired by a ghost-story com-petition to write the novel, Mary Shelley tells the tale of a Swiss scientific progeny,*

From Mary Shelley, *Frankenstein*, Second Edition, ed. Johanna Smith (New York: Bedford/ St. Martin's, 2000), 56–60.

Victor Frankenstein, who is at once a Romantic artist and modern inventor. While studying at university, Frankenstein embarks on a daring project to create life from death in his laboratory, described in the excerpt below. Only after he succeeds does he realize the horror of what he has done. Although he infused life into lifeless matter through the power of his imagination and technological prowess, he is no longer master of his creation. As the novel continues, the "miserable monster" born at Frankenstein's hand is rejected by all who see him, prompting him to vent his despair and anger onto his creator.

One of the phenomena which had peculiarly attracted my attention was the structure of the human frame, and, indeed, any animal endued with life. Whence, I often asked myself, did the principle of life proceed? It was a bold question, and one which has ever been considered as a mystery; yet with how many things are we upon the brink of becoming acquainted, if cowardice or carelessness did not restrain our enquiries. I revolved these circumstances in my mind, and determined thenceforth to apply myself more particularly to those branches of natural philosophy which relate to physiology. Unless I had been animated by an almost supernatural enthusiasm, my application to this study would have been irksome, and almost intolerable. To examine the causes of life, we must first have recourse to death. I became acquainted with the science of anatomy: but this was not sufficient; I must also observe the natural decay and corruption of the human body. In my education my father had taken the greatest precautions that my mind should be impressed with no supernatural horrors. I do not ever remember to have trembled at a tale of superstition, or to have feared the apparition of a spirit. Darkness had no effect upon my fancy; and a churchyard was to me merely the receptacle of bodies deprived of life, which, from being the seat of beauty and strength, had become food for the worm. Now I was led to examine the cause and progress of this decay, and forced to spend days and nights in vaults and charnel-houses. My attention was fixed upon every object the most insupportable to the delicacy of the human feelings. I saw how the fine form of man was degraded and wasted; I beheld the corruption of death succeed to the blooming cheek of life; I saw how the worm inherited the wonders of the eye and brain. I paused, examining and analyzing all the minutiæ of causation, as exemplified in the change from life to death, and death to life, until from the midst of this darkness a sudden light broke in upon me — a light so brilliant and wondrous, yet so simple, that while I became dizzy with the immensity of the prospect which it illustrated, I was surprised, that among so many men of genius who had directed their enquiries towards the same science, I alone should be reserved to discover so astonishing a secret.

Remember, I am not recording the vision of a madman. The sun does not more certainly shine in the heavens, than that which I now affirm is true. Some miracle might have produced it, yet the stages of the discovery were distinct and probable. After days and nights of incredible labor and fatigue, I succeeded in discovering the cause of generation and life; nay, more, I became myself capable of bestowing animation upon lifeless matter.

The astonishment which I had at first experienced on this discovery soon gave place to delight and rapture. After so much time spent in painful labor, to arrive at once at the summit of my desires, was the most gratifying consummation of my toils. But this discovery was so great and overwhelming, that all the steps by which I had been progressively led to it were obliterated, and I beheld only the result. What had been the study and desire of the wisest men since the creation of the world was now within my grasp. Not that, like a magic scene, it all opened upon me at once: the information I had obtained was of a nature rather to direct my endeavors so soon as I should point them towards the object of my search, than to exhibit that object already accomplished. . . .

I see by your eagerness, and the wonder and hope which your eyes express, my friend, that you expect to be informed of the secret with which I am acquainted; that cannot be: listen patiently until the end of my story, and you will easily perceive why I am reserved upon that subject. I will not lead you on, unguarded and ardent as I then was, to your destruction and infallible misery. Learn from me, if not by my precepts, at least by my example, how dangerous is the acquirement of knowledge, and how much happier that man is who believes his native town to be the world, than he who aspires to become greater than his nature will allow.

When I found so astonishing a power placed within my hands, I hesitated a long time concerning the manner in which I should employ it. Although I possessed the capacity of bestowing animation, yet to prepare a frame for the reception of it, with all its intricacies of fibers, muscles, and veins, still remained a work of inconceivable difficulty and labor. I doubted at first whether I should attempt the creation of a being like myself, or one of simpler organization; but my imagination was too much exalted by my first success to permit me to doubt of my ability to give life to an animal as complex and wonderful as man. The materials at present within my command hardly appeared adequate to so arduous an undertaking; but I doubted not that I should ultimately succeed. I prepared myself for a multitude of reverses; my operations might be incessantly baffled, and at last my work be imperfect: yet, when I considered the improvement which every day takes place in science and mechanics, I was encouraged to hope my present attempts would at least lay the foundations of future success. Nor could I consider the magnitude and complexity of my plan as any argument of its impracticability. It was with these feelings that I began the creation of a human being. As the minuteness of the parts formed a great hindrance to my speed, I resolved, contrary to my first intention, to make the being of a gigantic stature; that is to say, about eight feet in height, and proportionably large. After having formed this determination, and having spent some months in successfully collecting and arranging my materials, I began.

No one can conceive the variety of feelings which bore me onwards, like a hurricane, in the first enthusiasm of success. Life and death appeared to me ideal bounds, which I should first break through, and pour a torrent of light into our dark world. A new species would bless me as its creator and source; many happy and excellent natures would owe their being to me. No father could claim the gratitude of his child so completely as I should deserve theirs. Pursuing these reflections, I thought, that if I could bestow animation upon lifeless matter, I might in process of time (although I now found it impossible) renew life where death had apparently devoted the body to corruption.

These thoughts supported my spirits, while I pursued my undertaking with unremitting ardor. My cheek had grown pale with study, and my person had become emaciated with confinement. Sometimes, on the very brink of certainty, I failed; yet still I clung to the hope which the next day or the next hour might realize. One secret which I alone possessed was the hope to which I had dedicated myself; and the moon gazed on my midnight labors, while, with unrelaxed and breathless eagerness, I pursued nature to her hiding-places. Who shall conceive the horrors of my secret toil, as I dabbled among the unhallowed damps of the grave, or tortured the living animal to animate the lifeless clay? My limbs now tremble, and my eyes swim with the remembrance; but then a resistless, and almost frantic, impulse, urged me forward; I seemed to have lost all soul or sensation but for this one pursuit. It was indeed but a passing trance, that only made me feel with renewed acuteness so soon as, the unnatural stimulus ceasing to operate, I had returned to my old habits. I collected bones from charnel-houses; and disturbed, with profane fingers, the tremendous secrets of the human frame. In a solitary chamber, or rather cell, at the top of the house, and separated from all the other apartments by a gallery and staircase, I kept my workshop of filthy creation: my eye-balls were staring from their sockets in attending to the details of my employment. The dissecting room and the slaughter-house furnished many of my materials; and often did my human nature turn with loathing from my occupation, whilst, still urged on by an eagerness which perpetually increased, I brought my work near to a conclusion. . . .

It was on a dreary night in November, that I beheld the accomplishment of my toils. With an anxiety that almost amounted to agony, I collected the instruments of life around me, that I might infuse a spark of being into the lifeless thing that lay at my feet. It was already one in the morning; the rain pattered dismally against the panes, and my candle was nearly burnt out, when, by the glimmer of the half-extinguished light, I saw the dull yellow eye of the creature open; it breathed hard, and a convulsive motion agitated its limbs.

How can I describe my emotions at this catastrophe, or how delineate the wretch whom with such infinite pains and care I had endeavored to form? His limbs were in proportion, and I had selected his features as beautiful. Beautiful! — Great God! His yellow skin scarcely covered the work of muscles and arteries beneath; his hair was of a lustrous black, and flowing; his teeth of a pearly whiteness; but these luxuriances only formed a more horrid contrast with his watery eyes, that seemed almost of the same color as the dun white sockets in which they were set, his shriveled complexion and straight black lips.

The different accidents of life are not so changeable as the feelings of human nature. I had worked hard for nearly two years, for the sole purpose of infusing life into an inanimate body. For this I had deprived myself of rest and health. I had desired it with an ardor that far exceeded moderation; but now that I had finished, the beauty of the dream vanished, and breathless horror and disgust filled my heart. Unable to endure the aspect of the being I had created, I rushed out of the room, and continued a long time traversing my bedchamber, unable to compose my mind to sleep. At length lassitude succeeded to the tumult I had before endured; and I threw myself on the bed in my clothes, endeavoring to seek a few moments of forgetfulness. But it was in vain; I slept, indeed, but I was disturbed by the wildest dreams. I thought I saw Elizabeth, in the bloom of health, walking in the streets of Ingolstadt. Delighted and surprised, I embraced her; but as I imprinted the first kiss on her lips, they became livid with the hue of death; her features appeared to change, and I thought that I held the corpse of my dead mother in my arms; a shroud enveloped her form, and I saw the graveworms crawling in the folds of the flannel. I started from my sleep with horror; a cold dew covered my forehead, my teeth chattered, and every limb became convulsed; when, by the dim and yellow light of the moon, as it forced its way through the window shutters, I beheld the wretch—the miserable monster whom I had created. He held up the curtain of the bed; and his eyes, if eyes they may be called, were fixed on me. His jaws opened, and he muttered some inarticulate sounds, while a grin wrinkled his cheeks. He might have spoken, but I did not hear; one hand was stretched out, seemingly to detain me, but I escaped, and rushed down stairs. I took refuge in the courtyard belonging to the house which I inhabited; where I remained during the rest of the night, walking up and down in the greatest agitation, listening attentively, catching and fearing each sound as if it were to announce the approach of the demoniacal corpse to which I had so miserably given life.

Oh! no mortal could support the horror of that countenance. A mummy again endued with animation could not be so hideous as that wretch. I had gazed on him while unfinished; he was ugly then; but when those muscles and joints were rendered capable of motion, it became a thing such as even Dante could not have conceived.

I passed the night wretchedly. Sometimes my pulse beat so quickly and hardly, that I felt the palpitation of every artery; at others, I nearly sank to the ground through languor and extreme weakness. Mingled with this horror, I felt the bitterness of disappointment; dreams that had been my food and pleasant rest for so long a space were now become a hell to me; and the change was so rapid, the overthrow so complete!

DISCUSSION QUESTIONS

1. Describe Frankenstein's process of creation. What drew him to embark on his project to create life? How did he go about realizing his dream?

2. How does Frankenstein describe the humanlike monster he creates?

3. What prompts Frankenstein to doubt the goodness of his creation? What hints does he provide as to the causes of his own downfall?

4. What messages do you think Mary Shelley may have been trying to convey in this novel about contemporary society and politics?

COMPARATIVE QUESTIONS

1. Al-Jabartî was highly critical of the French in Egypt because, from his perspective, they embraced the ideals of equality and liberty yet often placed restrictions on their meanings in practice. In what ways does Peter Kakhovsky share this

view? What does this suggest about contradictions in Napoleon's method of rule and their long-term consequences?

2. Compare the political principles of Metternich and Peter Kakhovsky. How did they differ? How were their differences rooted in the legacy of the French Revolution and Napoleonic conquests?

3. Peter Kakhovsky targets Tsar Alexander's political views as a cause of the Decembrist rebellion. How did Metternich seek to shape these views and their translation into practice?

4. In his letter, Keats enumerates the creative possibilities of the human imagination. Describe his tone. Is he optimistic or pessimistic about this potential? How does his attitude compare to Mary Shelley's view of human creativity as embodied in her character Frankenstein?

CHAPTER 21

Industrialization and Social Ferment, 1830–1850

The nineteenth century was a time of momentous economic and social change as factories sprang up across much of Europe and railroad tracks crisscrossed the landscape. Although Britain initially led the way in industrial growth, the Continent soon began to catch up. For the middle classes, industrialization opened the door to new riches and prestige. By contrast, for the men, women, and children who labored in factories and mines, it meant little more than a life of drudgery, poverty, and often extreme physical hardship. The first two documents that follow expose industrialization's effects on the everyday world, from the grueling regime of factory work to the demands of running the ideal middle-class household. The third and fourth documents demonstrate that, as industrialization picked up pace, people became increasingly aware of its human costs and the need to address them. Some social critics promoted reform within existing governmental structures; others sought to abolish them completely, giving rise to one of the most significant ideological consequences of the new age, the birth of communism. Yet the immediate impact of communism was far less visible than the intensity of nationalist fervor unleashed by the revolutions of 1848, as the fifth document suggests. Against this backdrop, Europe's place in the world also underwent a shift. As the final document reveals, Europeans adopted new political and economic strategies overseas that laid the foundations for imperialism.

1.
Establishing New Work Habits

Factory Rules in Berlin (1844)

Industrialization did not simply create new social classes, new jobs, and new problems; it also created new work habits regimented by the pace of machines and the time clock. It fell on factory owners and managers to instill these habits in the workforce to ensure efficient and consistent levels of production. This was no easy task, because most people, whether former peasants or skilled workers, were traditionally accustomed to controlling their own time. The list of rules distributed to the employees of the Foundry and Engineering Works of the Royal Overseas Trading Company in Berlin provides a telling example of one approach to this challenge. This document also illustrates the spread of industrialization eastward across continental Europe.

In every large works, and in the co-ordination of any large number of workmen, good order and harmony must be looked upon as the fundamentals of success, and therefore the following rules shall be strictly observed.

Every man employed in the concern named below shall receive a copy of these rules, so that no one can plead ignorance. Its acceptance shall be deemed to mean consent to submit to its regulations.

(1) The normal working day begins at all seasons at 6 a.m. precisely and ends, after the usual break of half an hour for breakfast, an hour for dinner and half an hour for tea, at 7 p.m., and it shall be strictly observed.

Five minutes before the beginning of the stated hours of work until their actual commencement, a bell shall ring and indicate that every worker employed in the concern has to proceed to his place of work, in order to start as soon as the bell stops.

The doorkeeper shall lock the door punctually at 6 a.m., 8.30 a.m., 1 p.m. and 4.30 p.m.

Workers arriving 2 minutes late shall lose half an hour's wages; whoever is more than 2 minutes late may not start work until after the next break, or at least shall lose his wages until then. Any disputes about the correct time shall be settled by the clock mounted above the gatekeeper's lodge.

These rules are valid both for time- and for piece-workers, and in cases of breaches of these rules, workmen shall be fined in proportion to their earnings. The deductions from the wage shall be entered in the wage-book of the gatekeeper whose duty they are; they shall be unconditionally accepted as it will not be possible to enter into any discussions about them.

(2) When the bell is rung to denote the end of the working day, every workman, both on piece- and on day-wage, shall leave his workshop and the yard, but is not allowed to make preparations for his departure before the bell rings. Every breach of this rule shall lead to a fine of five silver groschen to the sick fund. Only those who have obtained special permission by the overseer may stay on in the workshop in order to work. — If a workman has worked beyond the closing bell, he must give his name to the gatekeeper on leaving, on pain of losing his payment for the overtime.

(3) No workman, whether employed by time or piece, may leave before the end of the working day, without having first received permission from the overseer

From Sidney Pollard and C. Holmes, *Documents of European Economic History*, vol. I: *The Process of Industrialization, 1750–1870* (New York: St. Martin's Press, 1968), 534–36.

and having given his name to the gatekeeper. Omission of these two actions shall lead to a fine of ten silver groschen payable to the sick fund.

(4) Repeated irregular arrival at work shall lead to dismissal. This shall also apply to those who are found idling by an official or overseer, and refuse to obey their order to resume work.

(5) Entry to the firm's property by any but the designated gateway, and exit by any prohibited route, e.g., by climbing fences or walls, or by crossing the Spree, shall be punished by a fine of fifteen silver groschen to the sick fund for the first offences, and dismissal for the second.

(6) No worker may leave his place of work otherwise than for reasons connected with his work.

(7) All conversation with fellow-workers is prohibited; if any worker requires information about his work, he must turn to the overseer, or to the particular fellow-worker designated for the purpose.

(8) Smoking in the workshops or in the yard is prohibited during working hours; anyone caught smoking shall be fined five silver groschen for the sick fund for every such offence.

(9) Every worker is responsible for cleaning up his space in the workshop, and if in doubt, he is to turn to his overseer. — All tools must always be kept in good condition, and must be cleaned after use. This applies particularly to the turner, regarding his lathe.

(10) Natural functions must be performed at the appropriate places, and whoever is found soiling walls, fences, squares, etc., and similarly, whoever is found washing his face and hands in the workshop and not in the places assigned for the purpose, shall be fined five silver groschen for the sick fund.

(11) On completion of his piece of work, every workman must hand it over at once to his foreman or superior, in order to receive a fresh piece of work. Pattern makers must on no account hand over their patterns to the foundry without express order of their supervisors. No workman may take over work from his fellow-workman without instruction to that effect by the foreman.

(12) It goes without saying that all overseers and officials of the firm shall be obeyed without question, and shall be treated with due deference. Disobedience will be punished by dismissal.

(13) Immediate dismissal shall also be the fate of anyone found drunk in any of the workshops.

(14) Untrue allegations against superiors or officials of the concern shall lead to stern reprimand, and may lead to dismissal. The same punishment shall be meted out to those who knowingly allow errors to slip through when supervising or stock-taking.

(15) Every workman is obliged to report to his superiors any acts of dishonesty or embezzlement on the part of his fellow workmen. If he omits to do so, and it is shown after subsequent discovery of a misdemeanor that he knew about it at the time, he shall be liable to be taken to court as an accessory after the fact and the wage due to him shall be retained as punishment. Conversely, anyone denouncing a theft in such a way as to allow conviction of the thief shall receive a reward of two

Thaler, and, if necessary, his name shall be kept confidential. — Further, the gate-keeper and the watchman, as well as every official, are entitled to search the baskets, parcels, aprons, etc. of the women and children who are taking dinners into the works, on their departure, as well as search any worker suspected of stealing any article whatever. . . .

(18) Advances shall be granted only to the older workers, and even to them only in exceptional circumstances. As long as he is working by the piece, the workman is entitled merely to his fixed weekly wage as subsistence pay; the extra earnings shall be paid out only on completion of the whole piece contract. If a workman leaves before his piece contract is completed, either of his own free will, or on being dismissed as punishment, or because of illness, the partly completed work shall be valued by the general manager with the help of two overseers, and he will be paid accordingly. There is no appeal against the decision of these experts.

(19) A free copy of these rules is handed to every workman, but whoever loses it and requires a new one, or cannot produce it on leaving, shall be fined 2½ silver groschen, payable to the sick fund.

DISCUSSION QUESTIONS

1. As delineated in the rules, what new modes of discipline did factory work require, and why?

2. What was the principal method used to encourage compliance with these rules?

3. Based on this document, how would you describe a typical day in this factory for the workers employed there?

2.
New Rules for the Middle Class

Sarah Stickney Ellis,
Characteristics of the Women of England (1839)

As working-class women toiled in factories, the growing ranks of middle-class women faced their own challenges. Many social commentators expected middle-class women to focus on their homes and families, thereby transforming them into bastions of order, tranquility, and proper behavior. Writers such as Sarah Stickney Ellis (1812–1872) offered ample advice on fulfilling such expectations. Published in 1839, The Women of England *was the first in Ellis's series of hugely successful conduct guides for women. In the following excerpt, she discusses a range of topics to help her female readers cultivate their "highest attributes" as pillars of family life, which, Ellis argues, required unwavering self-sacrifice and service. Her words portray the domestic ideal that, in reality, eluded many women, either by choice or circumstance. Even so, the book reveals much about changing attitudes toward women during the industrial age.*

From Sarah Stickney Ellis, *The Women of England: Their Social Duties and Domestic Habits* (New York: Henry G. Langley, 1844), 8–10.

Perhaps it may be necessary to be more specific in describing the class of women to which this work relates. It is, then, strictly speaking, to those who belong to that great mass of the population of England which is connected with trade and manufactures; — or, in order to make the application more direct, to that portion of it who are restricted to the services of from one to four domestics, — who, on the one hand, enjoy the advantages of a liberal education, and, on the other, have no pretension to family rank. . . .

It is from the class of females above described, that we naturally look for the highest tone of moral feeling, because they are at the same time removed from the pressing necessities of absolute poverty, and admitted to the intellectual privileges of the great; and thus, while they enjoy every facility in the way of acquiring knowledge, it is their still higher privilege not to be exempt from the domestic duties which call forth the best energies of the female character.

Where domestics abound, and there is a *hired* hand for every kindly office, it would be a work of supererogation for the mistress of the house to step forward, and assist with her own; but where domestics are few, and the individuals who compose the household are thrown upon the consideration of the mothers, wives, and daughters for their daily comfort, innumerable channels are opened for the overflow of those floods of human kindness, which it is one of the happiest and most ennobling duties of woman to administer to the weary frame, and to pour into the wounded mind.

It is perhaps the nearest approach we can make towards any thing like a definition of what is most striking in the characteristics of the women of England, to say, that the nature of their domestic circumstances is such as to invest their characters with the threefold recommendation of *promptitude in action, energy of thought, and benevolence of feeling.* With all the responsibilities of family comfort and social enjoyment resting upon them, and unaided by those troops of menials who throng the halls of the affluent and the great, they are kept alive to the necessity of making their own personal exertions conducive to the great end of promoting the happiness of those around them. They cannot sink into supineness, or suffer any of their daily duties to be neglected, but some beloved member of the household is made to feel the consequences, by enduring inconveniences which it is alike their pride and their pleasure to remove. The frequently recurring avocations of domestic life admit of no delay. When the performance of any kindly office has to be asked for, solicited, and re-solicited, it loses more than half its charm. It is therefore strictly in keeping with the fine tone of an elevated character to be beforehand with expectation, and thus to show, by the most delicate yet most effectual of all human means, that the object of attention, even when unheard and unseen, has been the subject of kind and affectionate solicitude.

By experience in these apparently minute affairs, a woman of kindly feeling and properly disciplined mind, soon learns to regulate her actions also according to the principles of true wisdom, and hence arises that energy of thought for which the women of England are so peculiarly distinguished. Every passing event, however insignificant to the eye of the world, has its crisis, every occurrence its emergency, every cause its effect; and upon these she has to calculate with precision, or the machinery of household comfort is arrested in its movements, and thrown into disorder.

Woman, however, would but ill supply the place appointed her by Providence, were she endowed with no other faculties than those of promptitude in action and energy of thought. Valuable as these may be, they would render her but a cold and cheerless companion, without the kindly affections and tender offices that sweeten human life. It is a high privilege, then, which the women of England enjoy, to be necessarily, and by the force of circumstances, thrown upon their affections, for the rule of their conduct in daily life. "What shall I do to gratify myself—to be admired—or to vary the tenor of my existence?" are not the questions which a woman of right feelings asks on first awaking to the avocations of the day. Much more congenial to the highest attributes of woman's character, are inquiries such as these: "How shall I endeavor through this day to turn the time, the health, and the means permitted me to enjoy, to the best account?—Is any one sick? I must visit their chamber without delay, and try to give their apartment an air of comfort, by arranging such things as the wearied nurse may not have thought of. Is any one about to set off on a journey? I must see that the early meal is spread, or prepare it with my own hands, in order that the servant, who was working last night, may profit by unbroken rest. Did I fail in what was kind or considerate to any of the family yesterday? I will meet her this morning with a cordial welcome, and show, in the most delicate way I can, that I am anxious to atone for the past. Was any one exhausted by the last day's exertion? I will be an hour before them this morning, and let them see that their labor is so much in advance. Or, if nothing extraordinary occurs to claim my attention, I will meet the family with a consciousness that, being the least engaged of any member of it, I am consequently the most at liberty to devote myself to the general good of the whole, by cultivating cheerful conversation, adapting myself to the prevailing tone of feeling, and leading those who are least happy, to think and speak of what will make them more so."

Who can believe that days, months, and years spent in a continual course of thought and action similar to this, will not produce a powerful effect upon the character, and not only upon the individual who thinks and acts alone, but upon all to whom her influence extends? In short, the customs of English society have so constituted women the guardians of the comfort of their homes, that, like the Vestals of old, they cannot allow the lamp they cherish to be extinguished, or to fail for want of oil, without an equal share of degradation attaching to their names.

In other countries, where the domestic lamp is voluntarily put out, in order to allow the women to resort to the opera, or the public festival, they are not only careless about their home comforts, but necessarily ignorant of the high degree of excellence to which they might be raised. In England there is a kind of science of good household management, which, if it consisted merely in keeping the house respectable in its physical character, might be left to the effectual working out of hired hands; but, happily for the women of England, there is a philosophy in this science, by which all their highest and best feelings are called into exercise. Not only must the house be neat and clean, but it must be so ordered as to suit the tastes of all, as far as may be, without annoyance or offence to any. Not only must a constant system of activity be established, but peace must be preserved, or happiness will be destroyed. Not only must elegance be called in, to adorn and beautify the whole, but strict integrity must be maintained by the minutest calculation as to lawful means, and self, and self-gratification, must be made the yielding point in every disputed case. Not only must an appearance of outward order and comfort be kept up, but around every domestic scene there must be a strong wall of confidence, which no internal suspicion can undermine, no external enemy break through.

DISCUSSION QUESTIONS

1. How does Ellis define middle-class English women, and why does she address her book specifically to them?

2. According to Ellis, what are a middle-class woman's principal domestic duties, and why?

3. What do a woman's domestic duties suggest about the status of middle-class women in English society at the time?

3.
The Division of Labor Illustrated

Punch *Magazine, "Capital and Labour"* (1843)

Coal-fired steam engines were at the heart of the Industrial Revolution. They fueled the rapid spread of railroads and new textile machinery, which in turn fueled an increased demand for coal. Miners, young and old, worked under very difficult conditions to

CAPITAL AND LABOUR.

From Michael Freeman, *Railways and the Victorian Imagination* (New Haven: Yale University Press, 1999), plate 108. © *Punch* Magazine, 1843.

keep pace. This was especially true in Britain, the hub of the Industrial Revolution, where the output of coal and iron doubled between 1830 and 1850. The miners' plight sparked calls for reform, particularly regarding the widespread use of child labor. As the cartoon on page 149 suggests, people recognized that industrialization had profoundly altered traditional socioeconomic relations, with capitalistic "money men" exploiting human labor for monetary gain. The cartoon appeared in the British magazine Punch *in 1843 to coincide with a parliamentary report on the employment of children.*

DISCUSSION QUESTIONS

1. How does the top portion of the cartoon portray the lifestyle of British capitalists? What images stand out in particular?

2. How does this portrait contrast to that of the people in the mine shown in the bottom portion? Why do you think the illustrator chose to depict so many different kinds of people rather than focus exclusively on miners?

3. What is the relationship between the top and bottom parts of the cartoon? How are their meanings interdependent?

4.
What Is the Proletariat?

Friedrich Engels, *Draft of a Communist Confession of Faith*
(1847)

When Friedrich Engels (1820–1895) composed the following draft of a communist "confession of faith" in 1847, the Industrial Revolution was in full swing in Great Britain and rapidly gaining ground on the continent. Engels observed the impact of this process on the working class with a critical eye. Two years earlier, he had joined forces with another critic of industrialization, Karl Marx (1818–1883). Together they launched an ideological revolution with the publication of the Communist Manifesto *in 1848, which set forth a new understanding of industrial society and its problems and proposed a new set of solutions centered on the abolition of capitalist, "private" property. Engels's "confession of faith" illuminates key landmarks on his and Marx's intellectual journey, for it was among the materials Marx used to compose the Manifesto. The confession was debated and approved in 1847 at the first congress of the Communist League. Although the first six questions reveal Engels's debt to the utopian principle of the community of property, those remaining reflect his and Marx's distinct historical vision.*

From John E. Toews, ed., *The Communist Manifesto with Related Documents* (Boston: Bedford/St. Martin's, 1999), 99–104.

Draft of a Communist Confession of Faith

June 9, 1847

QUESTION 1: *Are you a Communist?*

ANSWER: Yes.

QUESTION 2: *What is the aim of the Communists?*

ANSWER: To organize society in such a way that every member of it can develop and use all his capabilities and powers in complete freedom and without thereby infringing the basic conditions of this society.

QUESTION 3: *How do you wish to achieve this aim?*

ANSWER: By the elimination of private property and its replacement by community of property.

QUESTION 4: *On what do you base your community of property?*

ANSWER: Firstly, on the mass of productive forces and means of subsistence resulting from the development of industry, agriculture, trade and colonization, and on the possibility inherent in machinery, chemical, and other resources of their infinite extension.

Secondly, on the fact that in the consciousness or feeling of every individual there exist certain irrefutable basic principles which, being the result of the whole of historical development, require no proof.

QUESTION 5: *What are such principles?*

ANSWER: For example, every individual strives to be happy. The happiness of the individual is inseparable from the happiness of all, etc.

QUESTION 6: *How do you wish to prepare the way for your community of property?*

ANSWER: By enlightening and uniting the proletariat.

QUESTION 7: *What is the proletariat?*

ANSWER: The proletariat is that class of society which lives exclusively by its labor and not on the profit from any kind of capital; that class whose weal and woe, whose life and death, therefore, depend on the alternation of times of good and bad business; in a word, on the fluctuations of competition.

QUESTION 8: *Then there have not always been proletarians?*

ANSWER: No. There have always been poor and working classes; and those who worked were almost always the poor. But there have not always been proletarians, just as competition has not always been free.

QUESTION 9: *How did the proletariat arise?*

ANSWER: The proletariat came into being as a result of the introduction of the machines which have been invented since the middle of the last century and the most important of which are: the steam-engine, the spinning machine, and the power loom. These machines, which were very expensive and could therefore only be purchased by rich people, supplanted the workers of the time, because by the use of machinery it was possible to produce commodities more quickly and cheaply than could the workers with their imperfect spinning wheels and hand-looms. The machines thus delivered industry entirely into the hands of the big capitalists and rendered the workers' scanty property which consisted mainly of their tools, looms, etc., quite worthless, so that the capitalist was left with everything, the worker with nothing. In this way the factory system was introduced. Once the capitalists saw how advantageous this was for them, they sought to extend it to more and more branches of labor. They divided work more and more between the workers so that workers who formerly had made a whole article now produced only a part of it. Labor simplified in this way produced goods more quickly and therefore more cheaply and only now was it found in almost every branch of labor that here also machines could be used. As soon as any branch of labor went over to factory production it ended up, just as in the case of spinning and weaving, in the hands of the big capitalists, and the workers were deprived of the last remnants of their independence. We have gradually arrived at the position where almost *all* branches of labor are run on a factory basis. This has increasingly brought about the ruin of the previously existing middle class, especially of the small master craftsmen, completely transformed the previous position of the workers, and two new classes which are gradually swallowing up all other classes have come into being, namely:

I. The class of the big capitalists, who in all advanced countries are in almost exclusive possession of the means of subsistence and those means (machines, factories, workshops, etc.) by which these means of subsistence are produced. This is the *bourgeois* class, or the *bourgeoisie*.
II. The class of the completely propertyless, who are compelled to sell their labor to the first class, the bourgeois, simply to obtain from them in return their means of subsistence. Since the parties to this trading in labor are not *equal*, but the bourgeois have the advantage, the propertyless must submit to the bad conditions laid down by the bourgeois. This class, dependent on the bourgeois, is called the class of the *proletarians* or the *proletariat*.

QUESTION 10: *In what way does the proletarian differ from the slave?*

ANSWER: The slave is sold once and for all, the proletarian has to sell himself by the day and by the hour. The slave is the property of one master and for that very reason has a guaranteed subsistence, however wretched it may be. The proletarian is, so to speak, the slave of the entire bourgeois *class*, not of one master, and therefore has no guaranteed subsistence, since nobody buys his labor if he does not need it. The slave is accounted a *thing* and not a member of civil society. The proletarian is recognized as a *person*, as a member of civil society. The slave *may*, therefore, have a better subsistence than the proletarian but the latter stands at a higher stage of development. The slave frees himself by *becoming a proletarian*, abolishing from the totality of property relationships *only* the relationship of *slavery*. The proletarian can free himself only by abolishing *property in general*.

QUESTION 11: *In what way does the proletarian differ from the serf?*

ANSWER: The serf has the piece of land, that is, of an instrument of production, in return for handing over a greater or lesser portion of the yield. The proletarian works with instruments of production which belong to someone else who, in return for his labor, hands over to him a portion, determined by competition, of the products. In the case of the serf, the share of the laborer is determined by his own labor, that is, by himself. In the case of the proletarian it is determined by competition, therefore in the first place by the bourgeois. The serf has guaranteed subsistence, the proletarian has not. The serf frees himself by driving out his feudal lord and becoming a property owner himself, thus entering into competition and joining for the time being the possessing class, the privileged class. The proletarian frees himself by doing away with property, competition, and all class differences.

QUESTION 12: *In what way does the proletarian differ from the handicraftsman?*

ANSWER: As opposed to the proletarian, the so-called handicraftsman, who still existed nearly everywhere during the last century and still exists here and there, is at most a *temporary* proletarian. His aim is to acquire capital himself and so to exploit other workers. He can often achieve this aim where the craft guilds still exist or where freedom to follow a trade has not yet led to the organization of handwork on a factory basis and to intense competition. But as soon as the factory system is introduced into handwork and competition is in full swing, this prospect is eliminated and the handicraftsman becomes more and more a proletarian. The handicraftsman therefore frees himself *either* by becoming a bourgeois or in general passing over into the middle class, *or,* by becoming a proletarian as a result of competition (as now happens in most cases) and joining the movement of the proletariat — i.e., the more or less conscious communist movement.

QUESTION 13: *Then you do not believe that community of property has been possible at any time?*

ANSWER: No. Communism has only arisen since machinery and other inventions made it possible to hold out the prospect of an all-sided development, a happy existence, for all members of society. Communism is the theory of a liberation which was not possible for the slaves, the serfs, or the handicraftsmen, but only for the proletarians and hence it belongs of necessity to the 19th century and was not possible in any earlier period.

QUESTION 14: *Let us go back to the sixth question. As you wish to prepare for community of property by the enlightening and uniting of the proletariat, then you reject revolution?*

ANSWER: We are convinced not only of the uselessness but even of the harmfulness of all conspiracies. We are also aware that revolutions are not made deliberately and arbitrarily but that everywhere and at all times they are the necessary consequence of circumstances which are not in any way whatever dependent either on the will or on the leadership of individual parties or of whole classes. But we also see that the development of the proletariat in almost all countries of the world is forcibly repressed by the possessing classes and that thus a revolution is being forcibly worked for by the opponents of communism. If, in the end, the oppressed proletariat is thus driven into a revolution, then we will defend the cause of the proletariat just as well by our deeds as now by our words.

QUESTION 15: *Do you intend to replace the existing social order by community of property at one stroke?*

ANSWER: We have no such intention. The development of the masses cannot be ordered by decree. It is determined by the development of the conditions in which these masses live, and therefore proceeds gradually.

QUESTION 16: *How do you think the transition from the present situation to community of property is to be effected?*

ANSWER: The first, fundamental condition for the introduction of community of property is the political liberation of the proletariat through a democratic constitution.

QUESTION 17: *What will be your first measure once you have established democracy?*

ANSWER: Guaranteeing the subsistence of the proletariat.

QUESTION 18: *How will you do this?*

ANSWER: I. By limiting private property in such a way that it gradually prepares the way for its transformation into social property, e.g., by progressive taxation, limitation of the right of inheritance in favor of the state, etc., etc.

    II. By employing workers in national workshops and factories and on national estates.

    III. By educating all children at the expense of the state.

QUESTION 19: *How will you arrange this kind of education during the period of transition?*

ANSWER: All children will be educated in state establishments from the time when they can do without the first maternal care.

QUESTION 20: *Will not the introduction of community of property be accompanied by the proclamation of the community of women?*

ANSWER: By no means. We will only interfere in the personal relationship between men and women or with the family in general to the extent that the maintenance of the existing institution would disturb the new social order. Besides, we are well aware that the family relationship has been modified in the course of history by the property relationships and by periods of development, and that consequently the ending of private property will also have a most important influence on it.

QUESTION 21: *Will nationalities continue to exist under communism?*

ANSWER: The nationalities of the peoples who join together according to the principle of community will be just as much compelled by this union to merge with one another and thereby supersede themselves as the various differences between estates and classes disappear through the superseding of their basis — private property.

QUESTION 22: *Do Communists reject the existing religions?*

ANSWER: All religions which have existed hitherto were expressions of historical stages of development of individual peoples or groups of peoples. But communism is that stage of historical development which makes all existing religions superfluous and supersedes them.

DISCUSSION QUESTIONS

1. According to Engels's confession, what were the central goals of the communists, and how did they aim to achieve them?

2. How does Engels define the proletariat, and what sets it apart from other types of workers?

3. How does Engels's confession explicitly link communist ideology to industrialization? What place did revolution have in this ideology?

5.
The Poetry of Freedom

Sándor Petofi, *"National Song"* of Hungary (1848)

As news of the February Revolution in Paris spread, it inspired people seeking change to take to the streets across Europe, including in Hungary. Long under Habsburg control, in the 1830s a growing segment of the Hungarian population advocated for national self-determination. They faced stiff opposition, however, from the absolutist, autocratic court in Vienna, which ultimately erupted into violence there and in another Hungarian city, Pest — part of modern-day Budapest. On March 15, 1848, a group of intellectuals gathered in front of the new Hungarian National Museum in Pest to outline their demands for their nation. Among those leaders was the popular radical poet Sándor Petofi (1823–1849), who recited his poem, "National Song," urging bystanders to free Hungary from Habsburg tyranny. Tens of thousands of supporters thronged the city within hours. Although the ensuing revolution was ultimately crushed, in 1991 the National Assembly of Hungary designated March 15 as one of three national days commemorating Hungary's statehood.

RISE, Magyar! is the country's call!
The time has come, say one and all:
Shall we be slaves, shall we be free?
This is the question, now agree!
For by the Magyar's God above
 We truly swear,
We truly swear the tyrant's yoke
 No more to bear!

Alas! till now we were but slaves;
Our fathers resting in their graves
Sleep not in freedom's soil. In vain
They fought and died free homes to gain.
But by the Magyar's God above
 We truly swear,
We truly swear the tyrant's yoke
 No more to bear!

From Eva March Tappan, ed., *Russia, Austria-Hungary, The Balkan States and Turkey: The World's Story. A History of the World in Story, Song, and Art*, vol. VI (Boston: Houghton Mifflin, 1914), 408–10.

A miserable wretch is he
Who fears to die, my land, for thee!
His worthless life who thinks to be
Worth more than thou, sweet liberty!
Now by the Magyar's God above
        We truly swear,
We truly swear the tyrant's yoke
        No more to bear!

The sword is brighter than the chain,
Men cannot nobler gems attain;
And yet the chain we wore, oh, shame!
Unsheath the sword of ancient fame!
For by the Magyar's God above
        We truly swear,
We truly swear the tyrant's yoke
        No more to bear!

The Magyar's name will soon once more
Be honored as it was before!
The shame and dust of ages past
Our valor shall wipe out at last.
For by the Magyar's God above
        We truly swear,
We truly swear the tyrant's yoke
        No more to bear!

And where our graves in verdure rise,
Our children's children to the skies
Shall speak the grateful joy they feel,
And bless our names the while they kneel.
For by the Magyar's God above
        We truly swear,
We truly swear the tyrant's yoke
        No more to bear!

DISCUSSION QUESTIONS

1. Based on this poem, what drove Petofi and his fellow revolutionaries to action, and what did they hope to achieve?

2. Why do you think this poem was so successful in helping to rally people behind the revolution?

3. Despite the revolutionaries' initial successes, ethnic divisions in Hungary ultimately helped to seal the revolution's downfall. In what ways might this poem have contributed to such divisions?

6.
Imperialism and Opium
Commissioner Lin, *Letter to Queen Victoria* (1839)

The Industrial Revolution was not the only factor reshaping the European economy in the first half of the nineteenth century. With the abolition of slavery by Great Britain and many other nations, European governments shifted their focus away from their Caribbean plantation colonies toward new colonies in Asia and Africa. British merchants took the lead in opening up China to trade with the West, armed with an extremely addictive commodity — opium. For them, the importation of the drug into China was a legitimate commercial enterprise. The Chinese government held a different view, however, as the letter below reveals. The Chinese emperor had appointed Lin Tse-hsü (1785–1850) to address the opium problem, which he proposed to do with a two-pronged strategy: cutting off the supply of opium and punishing all users and sellers, including foreign traders. Lin wrote to British Queen Victoria (r. 1837–1901) seeking support for this policy. There is no evidence that she ever received his letter, excerpted here, but it was published later in the London Times. *Ultimately, Britain waged the first of two Opium Wars (1839–1842) to secure the continuation of the opium trade and gain a territorial foothold in the region.*

We find that your country is distant from us, . . . that your foreign ships come hither striving the one with the other for our trade, and for the simple reason of their strong desire to reap a profit. Now, out of the wealth of our Inner Land, if we take a part to bestow upon foreigners from afar, it follows, that the immense wealth which the said foreigners amass, ought properly speaking to be portion of our own native Chinese people. By what principle of reason then, should these foreigners send in return a poisonous drug, which involves in destruction those very natives of China? Without meaning to say that the foreigners harbor such destructive intentions in their hearts, we yet positively assert that from their inordinate thirst after gain, they are perfectly careless about the injuries they inflict upon us! And such being the case, we should like to ask what has become of that conscience which heaven has implanted in the breasts of all men?

We have heard that in your own country opium is prohibited with the utmost strictness and severity: — this is a strong proof that you know full well how hurtful it is to mankind. Since then you do not permit it to injure your own country, you ought not to have the injurious drug transferred to another country, and above all others, how much less to the Inner Land! Of the products which China exports to your foreign countries, there is not one which is not beneficial to mankind in some shape or other. There are those which serve for food, those which are useful, and those which are calculated for re-sale; — but all are beneficial. . . .

From William H. McNeill and Mitsuko Iriye, eds., *Modern Asia and Africa* (New York: Oxford University Press, 1971), 113–18.

On the other hand, the things that come from your foreign countries are only calculated to make presents of, or serve for mere amusement. It is quite the same to us if we have them, or if we have them not. If then these are of no material consequence to us of the Inner Land, what difficulty would there be in prohibiting and shutting our market against them? It is only that our heavenly dynasty most freely permits you to take off her tea, silk, and other commodities, and convey them for consumption everywhere, without the slightest stint or grudge, for no other reason, but that where a profit exists, we wish that it be diffused abroad for the benefit of all the earth!

Your honorable nation takes away the products of our central land, and not only do you thereby obtain food and support for yourselves, but moreover, by reselling these products to other countries you reap a threefold profit. Now if you would only not sell opium, this threefold profit would be secured to you: how can you possibly consent to forego it for a drug that is hurtful to men, and an unbridled craving after gain that seems to know no bounds! Let us suppose that foreigners came from another country, and brought opium into England, and seduced the people of your country to smoke it, would not you, the sovereign of the said country, look upon such a procedure with anger, and in your just indignation endeavor to get rid of it? Now we have always heard that your highness possesses a most kind and benevolent heart, surely then you are incapable of doing or causing to be done unto another, that which you should not wish another to do unto you! . . .

Suppose the subject of another country were to come to England to trade, he would certainly be required to comply with the laws of England, then how much more does this apply to us of the celestial empire! Now it is a fixed statute of this empire, that any native Chinese who sells opium is punishable with death, and even he who merely smokes it, must not less die. Pause and reflect for a moment: if you foreigners did not bring the opium hither, where should our Chinese people get it to re-sell? It is your foreigners who involve our simple natives in the pit of death, and are they alone to be permitted to escape alive? If so much as one of those deprive one of our people of his life, he must forfeit his life in requital for that which he has taken: — how much more does this apply to him who by means of opium destroys his fellow-men? Does the havoc which he commits stop with a single life? Therefore it is that those foreigners who now import opium into the Central Land are condemned to be beheaded and strangled by the new statute. . . .

Our celestial empire rules over ten thousand kingdoms! Most surely do we possess a measure of godlike majesty which you cannot fathom! Still we cannot bear to slay or exterminate without previous warning, and it is for this reason that we now clearly make known to you the fixed laws of our land. If the foreign merchants of your said honorable nation desire to continue their commercial intercourse, they then must tremblingly obey our recorded statutes, they must cut off for ever the source from which the opium flows, and on no account make an experiment of our laws in their own persons! Let then your highness punish those of your subjects who may be criminal, do not endeavor to screen or conceal them, and thus you will secure peace and quietness to your possessions, thus will you more than ever display a proper sense of respect and obedience, and thus may we unitedly enjoy the common blessing of peace and happiness.

DISCUSSION QUESTIONS

1. How does Lin describe economic relations between Britain and China? Which country benefits the most according to his view? Why is this important to his argument against the import of opium?

2. Why does Lin set opium apart from the other goods imported by Britain into China? How does he describe the drug's effects on the Chinese people?

3. Why does Lin accuse the British government of hypocrisy in its attitudes toward opium?

4. How would you describe Lin's tone in this letter? What does it suggest about how he viewed Western culture in general?

COMPARATIVE QUESTIONS

1. How do Ellis's conduct guide and the Berlin factory rules reflect the regimentation of daily life that characterized industrial society?

2. In what ways was Engels reacting against the portrayal of working- and middle-class life found in Ellis's guide, the Berlin factory rules, and the *Punch* cartoon?

3. How is the idea of liberty central to Engels's discussion and to the "National Song" of Hungary?

4. Based on the first four documents, how did the Industrial Revolution create a new social and economic order in Europe? What does Commissioner Lin's letter suggest about the impact of these changes on China?

CHAPTER 22

Politics and Culture of the Nation-State, 1850–1870

The second half of the nineteenth century marked the dawning of a new age in European politics and culture. After the failed revolutions of 1848 to 1849, politicians, artists, intellectuals, and the general public cast aside the promises of idealists and claimed to see society as it really was: combative, competitive, and inherently disordered. To master this unruly scene and strengthen state power from above, European leaders embraced tough-minded politics (realpolitik). With the rise of realpolitik came the decline of the Concert of Europe, which had favored a balance of power over national aspirations. The first document reflects Russia's response to this changing landscape as the country struggled to modernize. The second and third documents allow us to see two masters of realpolitik at work — the Italian count Camillo di Cavour (1810–1861) and the Prussian Otto von Bismarck (1815–1898). The biological research of Charles Darwin (1809–1882) reflects the scientific dimensions of the new age, as the fourth document reveals. His work gave scientific authority to the idea that human beings had evolved from more primitive life forms. As the final document shows, some people applied evolution to the development of human societies, arguing that only the toughest and most advanced would prosper.

1.
Ending Serfdom in Russia
Peter Kropótkin, *Memoirs of a Revolutionist* (1861)

Largely engineered by French emperor Napoleon III to advance his territorial ambitions, the Crimean War (1853–1856) opened the door to a major shift in the distribution of European power. With the death toll mounting at the hands of France and

From Peter Kropótkin, *Memoirs of a Revolutionist* (New York: Horizon Press, 1968), 133–36.

*its allies, Russia asked for peace. Russia's defeat marked the end of its role as a main-
stay of the Concert of Europe, and also revealed the country's inability to compete in
the rapidly changing industrial world. Among Russia's greatest liabilities was the institution of serfdom — binding the peasant population to the land — which inhibited
the growth of a modern labor force and fostered widespread discontent. After years of
discussion and debate, Russian tsar Alexander II (r. 1855–1881) chose a momentous
solution to combat these problems: on March 3, 1861, he issued the Emancipation
Manifesto officially abolishing serfdom. In the following excerpt from his memoirs published in 1899, Prince Peter Kropótkin (1842–1921) provides a firsthand glimpse of
how people in St. Petersburg reacted to the emancipation decree and of its impact on
one of his family estates. At the time, Kropótkin was a student at a select military school
in St. Petersburg, the Corps of Pages, and he later gained fame as a revolutionary and
anarchist.*

I was at the corps, having to take part in the military parade at the riding-school. I
was still in bed, when my soldier servant, Ivánoff, dashed in with the tea tray, ex-
claiming, "Prince, freedom! The manifesto is posted on the Gostínoi Dvor" (the
shops opposite the corps).

"Did you see it yourself?"

"Yes. People stand round; one reads, the others listen. It *is* freedom!"

In a couple of minutes I was dressed, and out. A comrade was coming in.

"Kropótkin, freedom!" he shouted. "Here is the manifesto. My uncle learned
last night that it would be read at the early mass at the Isaac Cathedral; so we went.
There were not many people there; peasants only. The manifesto was read and distributed after the mass. They well understood what it meant. When I came out of
the church, two peasants, who stood in the gateway, said to me in such a droll way,
'Well, sir? now — all gone?'" And he mimicked how they had shown him the way
out. Years of expectation were in that gesture of sending away the master.

I read and re-read the manifesto. It was written in an elevated style by the old
Metropolitan of Moscow, Philarète, but with a useless mixture of Russian and Old
Slavonian which obscured the sense. . . . Notwithstanding all this, one thing was
evident: serfdom was abolished, and the liberated serfs would get the land and their
homesteads. They would have to pay for it, but the old stain of slavery was removed.
They would be slaves no more; the reaction had *not* got the upper hand.

We went to the parade; and when all the military performances were over,
Alexander II, remaining on horseback, loudly called out, "The officers to me!" They
gathered round him, and he began, in a loud voice, a speech about the great event
of the day.

"The officers . . . the representatives of the nobility in the army" — these scraps of
sentences reached our ears — "an end has been put to centuries of injustice . . . I expect sacrifices from the nobility . . . the loyal nobility will gather round the throne" . . .
and so on. Enthusiastic hurrahs resounded amongst the officers as he ended.

We ran rather than marched back on our way to the corps, — hurrying to be
in time for the Italian opera, of which the last performance in the season was to be

given that afternoon; some manifestation was sure to take place then. Our military attire was flung off with great haste, and several of us dashed, lightfooted, to the sixth-story gallery. The house was crowded.

During the first entr'acte the smoking-room of the opera filled with excited young men, who all talked to one another, whether acquainted or not. We planned at once to return to the hall, and to sing, with the whole public in a mass choir, the hymn "God Save the Tsar."

However, sounds of music reached our ears, and we all hurried back to the hall. The band of the opera was already playing the hymn, which was drowned immediately in enthusiastic hurrahs coming from all parts of the hall. I saw Bavéri, the conductor of the band, waving his stick, but not a sound could be heard from the powerful band. Then Bavéri stopped, but the hurrahs continued. I saw the stick waved again in the air; I saw the fiddle-bows moving, and musicians blowing the brass instruments, but again the sound of voices overwhelmed the band. Bavéri began conducting the hymn once more, and it was only by the end of that third repetition that isolated sounds of the brass instruments pierced through the clamor of human voices.

The same enthusiasm was in the streets. Crowds of peasants and educated men stood in front of the palace, shouting hurrahs, and the Tsar could not appear without being followed by demonstrative crowds running after his carriage. . . .

Where were the uprisings which had been predicted by the champions of slavery? Conditions more indefinite than those which had been created by the Polozhénie (the emancipation law) could not have been invented. If anything could have provoked revolts, it was precisely the perplexing vagueness of the conditions created by the new law. And yet, except in two places where there were insurrections, and a very few other spots where small disturbances entirely due to misunderstandings and immediately appeased took place, Russia remained quiet, — more quiet than ever. With their usual good sense, the peasants had understood that serfdom was done away with, that "freedom had come," and they accepted the conditions imposed upon them, although these conditions were very heavy.

I was in Nikólskoye in August, 1861, and again in the summer of 1862, and I was struck with the quiet, intelligent way in which the peasants had accepted the new conditions. They knew perfectly well how difficult it would be to pay the redemption tax for the land, which was in reality an indemnity to the nobles in lieu of the obligations of serfdom. But they so much valued the abolition of their personal enslavement that they accepted the ruinous charges — not without murmuring, but as a hard necessity — the moment that personal freedom was obtained. For the first months they kept two holidays a week, saying that it was a sin to work on Friday; but when the summer came they resumed work with even more energy than before.

When I saw our Nikólskoye peasants, fifteen months after the liberation, I could not but admire them. Their inborn good nature and softness remained with them, but all traces of servility had disappeared. They talked to their masters as equals talk to equals, as if they never had stood in different relations.

DISCUSSION QUESTIONS

1. As described by Kropótkin, how did people react to the emancipation decree?
2. According to Kropótkin, how did the decree challenge traditional social boundaries?
3. How does Kropótkin describe Alexander II, and what do you think his description suggests about the tsar's power at the time?

2.

Fighting for Italian Nationalism

Camillo di Cavour, *Letter to King Victor Emmanuel*

(July 24, 1858)

As prime minister of the northern Italian kingdom of Piedmont-Sardinia, Camillo di Cavour was among the most skilled practitioners of realpolitik in mid-nineteenth-century Europe. Politically fragmented, Italy had long been a battleground for European rulers, sowing the seeds of the movement for Italian unification (Risorgimento). *Cavour capitalized on this movement to guide Italy down the path of nationhood. His target was Austria, who dominated most of the peninsula. His strategy was to draw them into war with the help of French emperor, Napoleon III. To this end, Cavour met secretly with Napoleon in July 1858. In the letter excerpted here, Cavour summarizes the terms of their agreement for the Piedmontese king Victor Emmanuel II (r. Italy 1861–1878). It reflects Cavour's pragmatic, calculated approach to the unification process, which culminated in 1861 with the formal establishment of the united kingdom of Italy.*

As soon as I entered the Emperor's study, he raised the question which was the purpose of my journey. He began by saying that he had decided to support Piedmont with all his power in a war against Austria, provided that the war was undertaken for a nonrevolutionary end which could be justified in the eyes of diplomatic circles — and still more in the eyes of French and European public opinion.

Since the search for a plausible excuse presented our main problem before we could agree, I felt obliged to treat that question before any others. . . . The Emperor came to my aid, and together we set ourselves to discussing each state in Italy, seeking grounds for war. It was very hard to find any. After we had gone over the whole peninsula without success, we arrived at Massa and Carrara, and there we discovered what we had been so ardently seeking. After I had given the Emperor a description of that unhappy country, of which he already had a clear enough idea anyway, we agreed on instigating the inhabitants to petition Your Majesty, asking protection and even demanding the annexation of the Duchies to Piedmont. This

From Denis Mack Smith, ed., *The Making of Italy, 1796–1870* (New York: Harper & Row, 1968), 238–42.

Your Majesty would decline, but you would take note of the Duke of Modena's oppressive policy and would address him a haughty and menacing note. The Duke, confident of Austrian support, would reply impertinently. Thereupon Your Majesty would occupy Massa, and the war could begin.

As it would be the Duke of Modena who would look responsible, the Emperor believes the war would be popular not only in France, but in England and the rest of Europe, because the Duke is considered, rightly or wrongly, the scapegoat of despotism. . . .

The Emperor readily agreed that it was necessary to drive the Austrians out of Italy once and for all, and to leave them without an inch of territory south of the Alps or west of the Isonzo. But how was Italy to be organized after that? After a long discussion, which I spare Your Majesty, we agreed more or less to the following principles, recognizing that they were subject to modification as the course of the war might determine. The valley of the Po, the Romagna, and the Legations would form a kingdom of Upper Italy under the House of Savoy. Rome and its immediate surroundings would be left to the Pope. The rest of the Papal States, together with Tuscany, would form a kingdom of central Italy. The Neapolitan frontier would be left unchanged. These four Italian states would form a confederation on the pattern of the German Bund, the presidency of which would be given to the Pope to console him for losing the best part of his estates.

This arrangement seemed to me fully acceptable. Your Majesty would be legal sovereign of the richest and most powerful half of Italy, and hence would in practice dominate the whole peninsula.

After we had settled the fate of Italy, the Emperor asked me what France would get, and whether Your Majesty would cede Savoy and the County of Nice. I answered that Your Majesty believed in the principle of nationalities and realized accordingly that Savoy ought to be reunited with France; and that consequently you were ready to make this sacrifice. . . .

Then we proceeded to examine how the war could be won, and the Emperor observed that we would have to isolate Austria so that she would be our sole opponent. That was why he deemed it so important that the grounds for war be such as would not alarm the other continental powers. Better still if they were also popular in England. He seemed convinced that what we had decided would fulfill this double purpose. The Emperor counts positively on England's neutrality; he advised me to make every effort to influence opinion in that country to compel the government (which is a slave to public opinion) not to side with Austria. He counts, too, on the antipathy of the Prince of Prussia toward the Austrians to keep Prussia from deciding against us. As for Russia, Alexander has repeatedly promised not to oppose Napoleon's Italian projects. Unless the Emperor is deluding himself, which I am not inclined to believe after all he told me, it would simply be a matter of a war between France and ourselves on one side and Austria on the other.

The Emperor nevertheless believes that, even reduced to these proportions, there remain formidable difficulties. There is no denying that Austria is very strong. . . .

Once agreed on military matters, we equally agreed on the financial question, and I must inform Your Majesty that this is what chiefly preoccupies the Emperor.

Nevertheless he is ready to provide us with whatever munitions we need, and to help us negotiate a loan in Paris. As for contributions from other Italian provinces in money and material, the Emperor believes we should insist on something, but use great caution. All these questions which I here relate to you as briefly as possible were discussed with the Emperor from eleven o'clock in the morning to three o'clock in the afternoon.

DISCUSSION QUESTIONS

1. Why did Napoleon III agree to help Cavour in planning Piedmont's war against Austria? What did each seek to gain through the agreement?

2. Why did Cavour and Napoleon think it important to consider public opinion in devising the grounds for war?

3. How did the two men think Italy should be organized after the war? What does this reveal about the methods of state building in the mid-nineteenth century?

3.
Realpolitik and Otto von Bismarck
Rudolf von Ihering, *Two Letters* (1866)

Like Cavour, Prussian prime minister Otto von Bismarck (1815–1898) embraced the principles of realpolitik. Through his military and diplomatic strategies, Bismarck took advantage of the collapse of the Concert of Europe and made the dream of a united Germany a reality. Bismarck had many detractors, however, including liberals like jurist Rudolf von Ihering (1818–1892). In the excerpts here from two letters he wrote in 1866, von Ihering provides a contemporary assessment of realpolitik in action during the war with Austria, a pivotal period in Bismarck's quest for German unification. The war erupted in June 1866, and by early July, Prussia was triumphant. At first, Bismarck's tactics shocked von Ihering. Yet the allure of German unity proved irresistible to him and other liberals, and they soon embraced the sense of military superiority that came to define German nationalism.

(*To J. Glaser, Giessen, 1 May.*) . . . Never, probably, has a war been incited so shamelessly and with such horrifying frivolity as the one that Bismarck is currently trying to start against Austria. My innermost feelings are revolted by this violation of every legal and moral principle. God knows I am no friend of Austria; on the contrary, I have always been regarded as one of her enemies — that is to say of her political system, not of the Austrian people whom I have learned to love . . . —; I am devoted to the idea of Prussian influence in north Germany, even though I have

From Walter Michael Simon, *Germany in the Age of Bismarck* (London: Allen and Unwin, 1968), 110–13.

little sympathy for the present political system in Prussia. But I would rather cut off my hand than to use it in such a disgusting operation as Prussian policy is now launching against Austria — the common sense of any honest man cannot even comprehend the depths of this perfidy. We ask ourselves in amazement: is it really true that what the whole world knows to be lies can be proclaimed from on high as the truth? Austria is supposed to be mobilizing against Prussia! Any child knows that the opposite is the case. . . . The saddest thing about it all is that once the struggle is under way principles of right and wrong must come in absolutely tragic conflict with interests. Whom should we wish victorious, Austria or Prussia? We have no choice, we must come down on the side of the *unjust* cause, because we cannot tolerate the possibility of Austria gaining the upper hand in Germany. Everyone here detests this war, nobody can be comfortable with the idea that it will have the result that we *must* desire — the hegemony of Prussia. That is our situation. Germans taking up arms against Germans, civil war, a plot of three or four Powers against one, with not even an appearance of legality, without popular participation, created by a few diplomats alone, a conspiracy against your poor country, which causes even the enemies of Austria to sympathize with her and in which they would have to desire her victory — if this victory did not mean our own ruin! . . . The war would be unthinkable if Austria had not for decades been doing everything to make it impossible even for her friends in Germany to take sides with her and putting the most menacing weapons in the hands of her enemies. . . . Everyone agrees on the crying injustice that is being done to Austria, and yet, as I say, thousands here would not lift a finger for her cause, people feel that that would mean turning against one's own cause; for with very few exceptions the general opinion here is that the free development of Germany would be incompatible with Austrian supremacy. This may be wrong, but I am merely stating the fact. There is just as little affection for the German princes: here also one finds the same collision between undoubted historical justice and a total inability to work up any enthusiasm for it. It is sad to be in conflict with one's own feelings — we ought to desire victory for the just cause in this instance too, but we cannot!

(*To B. Windscheid, Giessen, 19 August.*) . . . I think I must be dreaming when I think of how much has happened in the short space of a few weeks; it seems that it must be years. I am only now gradually coming to my senses again; at one time I was quite dizzy from the pace of events. What a surging of emotions — of deep fear, anxious hesitation, joyous exultation, apprehensive suspense, furious indignation, profound pity, and in the end once more a rejoicing of the soul, an ecstasy of happiness such as my heart has never before known! Oh, my dear friend, what enviable luck to be living at this time, to have seen this turning-point in German history with which there has been nothing to compare for a thousand years. For years I have envied the Italians that they succeeded in what seemed for us to lie only in the distant future, I have wished for a German Cavour and Garibaldi as Germany's political messiah. And overnight he has appeared in the person of the much-abused Bismarck. Should we not think we are dreaming if the impossible becomes possible? Like you I was afraid at the prospect of war, I was convinced of the notion that the Austrians, experienced in the practical school of war, would be superior to the Prussians. Has intelligence and moral energy ever in history celebrated such a triumph over crude force? There is something wonderful about this spirit that animates little Prussia, this spirit that lifts us all out of a state of impotence and ignominy and gives to the name of Germany in Europe a lustre and a tone that it has not had for a thousand years. I bow before the genius of Bismarck, who has achieved a masterpiece of political planning and action such as are only rarely to be found in history. How marvelously the man spun all the threads of the great web, how firmly and safely so that none of them broke, how precisely he knew and used all the ways and means — his king, Napoleon, his army, the administration, Austria and her forces — in short, a masterpiece of calculation. I have forgiven the man everything he has done up to now, more, I have convinced myself that it was necessary; what seemed to us, the uninitiated, as criminal arrogance has turned out in the end to have been an indispensable means to the goal. He is one of the greatest men of the century; it is a real revelation to have lived at the same time as such a man; a man of action like that, not heedless action but action inspired and prepared both politically and morally, is worth a hundred men of liberal principles and of powerless honesty!

Nine weeks ago I should not have believed that I would write a paean of praise to Bismarck, but I cannot help myself! I leave it to my stubborn colleagues from Swabia and Bavaria to abuse him, to concentrate everything disgusting they can think of on the name of Bismarck. Incorrigible doctrinaires! For years, they have yelled and drunk themselves hoarse for German unity, and when someone comes on the scene and achieves the impossible by transferring German unity from a book of student songs into reality they cry "crucify him."

DISCUSSION QUESTIONS

1. What does von Ihering reveal about Bismarck's political methods in these two letters?
2. Why do you think von Ihering was conflicted in his attitudes about these methods?
3. How do von Ihering's opinions change between the time he wrote the first and second letters, and what do you think accounts for this change?

4.
Evolutionary Principles

Charles Darwin, *The Descent of Man* (1871)

As Otto von Bismarck (1815–1898) and other realpolitikers were transforming European political views during the late nineteenth century, the English naturalist Charles Darwin (1809–1882) was transforming scientific views. In 1859, Darwin published On the Origin of Species, *in which he argued that animal species evolved over time through a process of natural selection by which the strongest and most well adapted to*

From Charles Darwin, *The Descent of Man and Selection in Relation to Sex* (New York: D. Appleton and Company, 1896), 606–9, 612–13, 618–19.

any given environment survived. The biblical story of creation had no place in Darwin's conclusions, and this incited considerable debate. The debate intensified twelve years later when Darwin applied his theory of evolution directly to humans in The Descent of Man and Selection in Relation to Sex, *excerpted here.*

The main conclusion here arrived at, and now held by many naturalists who are well competent to form a sound judgment, is that man is descended from some less highly organized form. The grounds upon which this conclusion rests will never be shaken, for the close similarity between man and the lower animals in embryonic development, as well as in innumerable points of structure and constitution, both of high and of the most trifling importance, — the rudiments which he retains, and the abnormal reversions to which he is occasionally liable, — are facts which cannot be disputed. They have long been known, but until recently they told us nothing with respect to the origin of man. Now when viewed by the light of our knowledge of the whole organic world, their meaning is unmistakable. The great principle of evolution stands up clear and firm, when these groups of facts are considered in connection with others such as the mutual affinities of the members of the same group, their geographical distribution in past and present times, and their geological succession. It is incredible that all these facts should speak falsely. He who is not content to look, like a savage, at the phenomena of nature as disconnected, cannot any longer believe that man is the work of a separate act of creation. . . .

We have seen that man incessantly presents individual differences in all parts of his body and in his mental faculties. These differences or variations seem to be induced by the same general causes, and to obey the same laws as with the lower animals. In both cases similar laws of inheritance prevail. Man tends to increase at a greater rate than his means of subsistence; consequently he is occasionally subjected to a severe struggle for existence, and natural selection will have effected whatever lies within its scope. . . .

Through the means just specified, aided perhaps by others as yet undiscovered, man has been raised to his present state. But since he attained to the rank of manhood, he has diverged into distinct races, or as they may be more fitly called, subspecies. Some of these, such as the Negro and European, are so distinct that, if specimens had been brought to a naturalist without any further information, they would undoubtedly have been considered by him as good and true species. Nevertheless all the races agree in so many unimportant details of structure and in so many mental peculiarities, that these can be accounted for only by inheritance from a common progenitor; and a progenitor thus characterized would probably deserve to rank as man. . . .

By considering the embryological structure of man, — the homologies which he presents with the lower animals, — the rudiments which he retains, — and the reversions to which he is liable, we can partly recall in imagination the former condition of our early progenitors; and can approximately place them in their proper place in the zoological series. We thus learn that man is descended from a hairy, tailed quadruped, probably arboreal in its habits, and an inhabitant of the Old World. . . .

The belief in God has often been advanced as not only the greatest, but the most complete of all the distinctions between man and the lower animals. It is however impossible, . . . to maintain that this belief is innate or instinctive in man. On the other hand a belief in all-pervading spiritual agencies seems to be universal; and apparently follows from a considerable advance in man's reason, and from a still greater advance in his faculties of imagination, curiosity and wonder. I am aware that the assumed instinctive belief in God has been used by many persons as an argument for His existence. But this is a rash argument, as we should thus be compelled to believe in the existence of many cruel and malignant spirits, only a little more powerful than man; for the belief in them is far more general than in a beneficent Deity. The idea of a universal and beneficent Creator does not seem to arise in the mind of man, until he has been elevated by long-continued culture. . . .

I am aware that the conclusions arrived at in this work will be denounced by some as highly irreligious; but he who denounces them is bound to show why it is more irreligious to explain the origin of man as a distinct species by descent from some lower form, through the laws of variation and natural selection, than to explain the birth of the individual through the laws of ordinary reproduction. The birth both of the species and of the individual are equally parts of that grand sequence of events, which our minds refuse to accept as the result of blind chance. The understanding revolts at such a conclusion. . . .

The main conclusion arrived at in this work, namely that man is descended from some lowly organized form, will, I regret to think, be highly distasteful to many. But there can hardly be a doubt that we are descended from barbarians. The astonishment which I felt on first seeing a party of Fuegians on a wild and broken shore will never be forgotten by me, for the reflection at once rushed into my mind — such were our ancestors. These men were absolutely naked and bedaubed with paint, their long hair was tangled, their mouths frothed with excitement, and their expression was wild, startled, and distrustful. They possessed hardly any arts, and like wild animals lived on what they could catch; they had no government, and were merciless to every one not of their own small tribe. He who has seen a savage in his native land will not feel much shame, if forced to acknowledge that the blood of some more humble creature flows in his veins. For my own part I would as soon be descended from that heroic little monkey, who braved his dreaded enemy in order to save the life of his keeper, or from that old baboon, who descending from the mountains, carried away in triumph his young comrade from a crowd of astonished dogs — as from a savage who delights to torture his enemies, offers up bloody sacrifices, practices infanticide without remorse, treats his wives like slaves, knows no decency, and is haunted by the grossest superstitions.

Man may be excused for feeling some pride at having risen, though not through his own exertions, to the very summit of the organic scale; and the fact of his having thus risen, instead of having been aboriginally placed there, may give him hope for a still higher destiny in the distant future. But we are not here concerned with hopes or fears, only with the truth as far as our reason permits us to discover it; and I have given the evidence to the best of my ability. We must, however, acknowledge, as it seems to me, that man with all his noble qualities, with sympathy which feels for the most debased, with benevolence which extends not only to other men but to the humblest living creature, with his god-like intellect which has penetrated into the movements and constitution of the solar system — with all these exalted powers — Man still bears in his bodily frame the indelible stamp of his lowly origin.

DISCUSSION QUESTIONS

1. What evidence does Darwin supply to support his theory of human evolution?
2. How does this evidence call into question the relationship between religion and science?
3. How does Darwin voice the concern for realism and concrete facts that marked the general mood of his day?

5.
Social Evolution
Walter Bagehot, *Physics and Politics* (1872)

The ramifications of Darwin's work extended beyond the field of biology when people began to use evolutionary principles to explain, justify, and perpetuate the social and political inequalities of the day. For English writer Walter Bagehot (1826–1877), Darwin's theories provided a perfect lens for understanding the development of human society, and why, in his view, some nations were more "advanced" than others. Progress is not inevitable, Bagehot asserted, but rather stems most conspicuously from a nation's ability to master the art of war. A great admirer of Napoleon III, Bagehot believed that militarism was essential to nation building and cultural advancement. This theme is at the heart of his 1872 book, Physics and Politics, *excerpted here. By "physics," Bagehot meant science, more specifically Darwinism.*

The Use of Conflict

"The difference between progression and stationary inaction," says one of our greatest living writers, "is one of the great secrets which science has yet to penetrate." I am sure I do not pretend that I can completely penetrate it; but it undoubtedly seems to me that the problem is on the verge of solution, and that scientific successes in kindred fields by analogy suggest some principles which wholly remove many of its difficulties, and indicate the sort of way in which those which remain may hereafter be removed too.

But what is the problem? Common English, I might perhaps say common civilized thought, ignores it. Our habitual instructors, our ordinary conversation, our

---

From Walter Bagehot, *Physics and Politics* (New York: D. Appleton and Co., 1873), 41–44, 49.

inevitable and ineradicable prejudices tend to make us think that "Progress" is the normal fact in human society, the fact which we should expect to see, the fact which we should be surprised if we did not see. But history refutes this. The ancients had no conception of progress; they did not so much as reject the idea; they did not even entertain the idea. Oriental nations are just the same now. Since history began they have always been what they are. Savages, again, do not improve; they hardly seem to have the basis on which to build, much less the material to put up anything worth having. Only a few nations, and those of European origin, advance; and yet these think — seem irresistibly compelled to think — such advance to be inevitable, natural, and eternal. Why then is this great contrast?

In solving, or trying to solve, the question, we must take notice of this remarkable difference, and explain it, too, or else we may be sure our principles are utterly incomplete, and perhaps altogether unsound. But what then is that solution, or what are the principles which tend towards it? Three laws, or approximate laws, may, I think, be laid down, with only one of which I can deal in this paper, but all three of which it will be best to state, that it may be seen what I am aiming at.

First. In every particular state of the world, those nations which are strongest tend to prevail over the others; and in certain marked peculiarities the strongest tend to be the best.

Secondly. Within every particular nation the type or types of character then and there most attractive tend to prevail; and the most attractive, though with exceptions, is what we call the best character.

Thirdly. Neither of these competitions is in most historic conditions intensified by extrinsic forces, but in some conditions, such as those now prevailing in the most influential part of the world, both are so intensified.

These are the sort of doctrines with which, under the name of "natural selection" in physical science, we have become familiar; and as every great scientific conception tends to advance its boundaries and to be of use in solving problems not thought of when it was started, so here, what was put forward for mere animal history may, with a change of form, but an identical essence, be applied to human history.

The discussion of these three principles cannot be kept quite apart except by pedantry; but it is almost exclusively with the first — that of the competition between nation and nation, or tribe and tribe (for I must use these words in their largest sense, and so as to include every cohering aggregate of human beings) — that I can deal now; and even as to that I can but set down a few principal considerations.

The progress of the military art is the most conspicuous, I was about to say the most *showy*, fact in human history.

The cause of this military growth is very plain. The strongest nation has always been conquering the weaker; sometimes even subduing it, but always prevailing over it. Every intellectual gain, so to speak, that a nation possessed was in the earliest times made use of — was *invested* and taken out — in war; all else perished. Each nation tried constantly to be the stronger, and so made or copied the best weapons; by conscious and unconscious imitation each nation formed a type of character suitable to war and conquest. Conquest improved mankind by the intermixture of strengths; the armed truce, which was then called peace, improved them by the competition of training and the consequent creation of new power. Since the long-headed men first drove the short-headed men out of the best land in Europe, all European history has been the history of the superposition of the more military races over the less military — of the efforts, sometimes successful, sometimes unsuccessful, of each race to get more military; and so the art of war has constantly improved.

DISCUSSION QUESTIONS

1. According to Bagehot, why do some societies progress and others do not?
2. How does the idea of natural selection factor into Bagehot's understanding of progress?
3. Why does Bagehot think that military skill is particularly important to human advancement?

COMPARATIVE QUESTIONS

1. How would you compare the political methods and goals of Alexander II, Cavour, and Bismarck?
2. Why did these methods and goals help to end the Concert of Europe?
3. How do Darwin and Bagehot's ideas support the principles of realpolitik?
4. What do these documents reveal about how Europeans built a sense of national identity in the late nineteenth century?

Industry, Empire, and Everyday Life, 1870–1890

The dual phenomena of industry and empire transformed Europe and the world during the late nineteenth century. With domestic industries booming, European leaders looked abroad for new markets and raw materials. The widespread belief that a nation's imperial holdings were an indication of its strength and racial superiority also fueled the quest for empire. As the first two documents show, this quest was a source of unity and discord on both sides of the Atlantic Ocean. The third document illuminates Germany's especially striking success in melding industrial growth and imperial expansion, which raised concerns throughout Europe, particularly in Great Britain. The fourth document points to the political repercussions of economic development as workers joined together to demand a say in the workplace. Industry and empire found artistic expression as well. Heavily influenced by Asian art and architecture, some visual artists abandoned tradition to depict scenes from nature and society as they appeared at any given moment. In the process, they also set their work apart from the photographic realism of the camera, a popular industrial invention. The final document allows us to see this creative process through the eyes of French painter, Edgar Degas (1834–1917).

1.
Defending Conquest

Jules Ferry, *Speech before the French National Assembly* (1883)

French politician Jules Ferry (1832–1893) fueled his country's quest to compete in the Continent's race to conquer foreign territory in the closing decades of the nineteenth century. While serving two terms as premier during the Third Republic, Ferry took the lead in France's colonial expansion in Africa and Asia. Yet not everyone embraced his imperialist policies, including his conservative and socialist colleagues within the government. In the following speech, delivered before the National Assembly in July 1883, Ferry faced his opponents head on, defending not only the political and economic necessity of French expansionism but also its moral justness. At the same time, his critics voice their views, revealing the basis of their anticolonial sentiment.

M. JULES FERRY: Gentlemen, it embarrasses me to make such a prolonged demand upon the gracious attention of the Chamber, but I believe that the duty I am fulfilling upon this platform is not a useless one. It is as strenuous for me as for you, but I believe that there is some benefit in summarizing and condensing, in the form of arguments, the principles, the motives, and the various interests by which a policy of colonial expansion may be justified; it goes without saying that I will try to remain reasonable, moderate, and never lose sight of the major continental interests which are the primary concern of this country. What I wish to say, to support this proposition, is that in fact, just as in word, the policy of colonial expansion is a political and economic system; I wish to say that one can relate this system to three orders of ideas: economic ideas, ideas of civilization in its highest sense, and ideas of politics and patriotism.

In the area of economics, I will allow myself to place before you, with the support of some figures, the considerations which justify a policy of colonial expansion from the point of view of that need, felt more and more strongly by the industrial populations of Europe and particularly those of our own rich and hard working country: the need for export markets. Is this some kind of chimera? Is this a view of the future or is it not rather a pressing need, and, we could say, the cry of our industrial population? I will formulate only in a general way what each of you, in the different parts of France, is in a position to confirm. Yes, what is lacking for our great industry, drawn irrevocably on to the path of exportation by the [free trade] treaties of 1860, what it lacks more and more is export markets. Why? Because next door to us Germany is surrounded by barriers, because beyond the ocean, the United States of America has become protectionist, protectionist in the most extreme sense, because not only have these great markets, I will not say closed but shrunk, and thus become more difficult of access for our industrial products, but also these great states are beginning to pour products not seen heretofore onto our own markets. . . . It is not necessary to pursue this demonstration any farther. Yes, gentlemen, I am speaking to the economists, whose convictions and past services no one appreciates more than I do; I am speaking to the honorable M. Passy, whom I see here and who is one of the most authoritative representatives among us of the old school of economics [*smiles*]; I know very well what they will reply to me, what is at the bottom of their thoughts . . . the old school, the great school, gentlemen; one, M. Passy, which your name has embellished, which was led in France by Jean-Baptiste Say and by Adam Smith in England. I do not mean to treat you with any irony, M. Passy, believe me.

From Ralph A. Austin, ed., *Modern Imperialism: Western Overseas Expansion and Its Aftermath, 1776–1965* (Lexington: D. C. Heath, 1969), 69–74.

I say that I know very well the thoughts of the economists, whom I can call doctrinaires without offending M. Passy. They say to us, "The true export markets are the commercial treaties which furnish and assure them." Gentlemen, I do not look down upon commercial treaties: if we could return to the situation which existed after 1860, if the world had not been subjected to that economic revolution which is the product of the development of science and the speeding up of communications, if this great revolution had not intervened, I would gladly take up the situation which existed after 1860. It is quite true that in that epoch the competition of grain from Odessa did not ruin French agriculture, that the grain of America and of India did not yet offer us any competition; at that moment we were living under the regime of commercial treaties, not only with England, but with the other great powers, with Germany, which had not yet become an industrial power. I do not look down upon them, these treaties; I had the honor of negotiating some of less importance than those of 1860; but gentlemen, in order to make treaties, it is necessary to have two parties: one does not make treaties with the United States; this is the conviction which has grown among those who have attempted to open some sort of negotiations in this quarter, whether officially or officiously.

Gentlemen, there is a second point, a second order of ideas to which I have to give equal attention, but as quickly as possible, believe me; it is the humanitarian and civilizing side of the question. On this point the honorable M. Camille Pellatan has jeered in his own refined and clever manner; he jeers, he condemns, and he says, "What is this civilization which you impose with cannonballs? What is it but another form of barbarism? Don't these populations, these inferior races, have the same rights as you? Aren't they masters of their own houses? Have they called upon you? You come to them against their will, you offer them violence, but not civilization." There, gentlemen, is the thesis; I do not hesitate to say that this is not politics, nor is it history: it is political metaphysics. ["Ah, Ah," *on far left*].

. . . Gentlemen, I must speak from a higher and more truthful plane. It must be stated openly that, in effect, superior races have rights over inferior races. [*Movement on many benches on the far left.*]

M. JULES MAIGNE: Oh! You dare to say this in the country which has proclaimed the rights of man!

M. DE GUILLOUTET: This is a justification of slavery and the slave trade!

M. JULES FERRY: If M. Maigne is right, if the declaration of the rights of man was written for the blacks of equatorial Africa, then by what right do you impose regular commerce upon them? They have not called upon you.

M. RAOUL DUVAL: We do not want to impose anything upon them. It is you who wish to do so!

M. JULES MAIGNE: To propose and to impose are two different things!

M. GEORGES PERIN: In any case, you cannot bring about commerce by force.

M. JULES FERRY: I repeat that superior races have a right, because they have a duty. They have the duty to civilize inferior races. . . . [*Approbation from the left. New interruptions from the extreme left and from the right.*]

That is what I have to answer M. Pelletan in regard to the second point upon which he touched.

He then touched upon a third, more delicate, more serious, and upon which I ask your permission to express myself quite frankly. It is the political side of the question. The honorable M. Pelletan, who is a distinguished writer, always comes up with remarkably precise formulations. I will borrow from him the one which he applied the other day to this aspect of colonial policy.

"It is a system," he says, "which consists of seeking out compensations in the Orient with a circumspect and peaceful seclusion which is actually imposed upon us in Europe."

I would like to explain myself in regard to this. I do not like this word, "compensation," and, in effect, not here but elsewhere it has often been used in a treacherous way. If what is being said or insinuated is that any government in this country, any Republican minister could possibly believe that there are in any part of the world compensations for the disasters which we have experienced, an injury is being inflicted . . . and an injury undeserved by that government. [*Applause at the center and left.*] I will ward off this injury with all the force of my patriotism! [*New applause and bravos from the same benches.*]

Gentlemen, there are certain considerations which merit the attention of all patriots. The conditions of naval warfare have been profoundly altered. ["Very true! Very true!"]

At this time, as you know, a warship cannot carry more than fourteen days' worth of coal, no matter how perfectly it is organized, and a ship which is out of coal is a derelict on the surface of the sea, abandoned to the first person who comes along. Thence the necessity of having on the oceans provision stations, shelters, ports for defense and revictualling. [*Applause at the center and left. Various interruptions.*] And it is for this that we needed Tunisia, for this that we needed Saigon and the Mekong Delta, for this that we need Madagascar, that we are at Diégo-Suarez and Vohemar [two Madagascar ports] and will never leave them! [*Applause from a great number of benches.*] Gentlemen, in Europe as it is today, in this competition of so many rivals which we see growing around us, some by perfecting their military or maritime forces, others by the prodigious development of an ever growing population; in a Europe, or rather in a universe of this sort, a policy of peaceful seclusion or abstention is simply the highway to decadence! Nations are great in our times only by means of the activities which they develop; it is not simply "by the peaceful shining forth of institutions" [*Interruptions on the extreme left and right*] that they are great at this hour.

As for me, I am astounded to find the monarchist parties becoming indignant over the fact that the Republic of France is following a policy which does not confine itself to that ideal of modesty, of reserve, and, if you will allow me the expression, of bread and butter [*Interruptions and laughter on the left*] which the representatives of fallen monarchies wish to impose upon France. [*Applause at the center.*]

. . . [The Republican Party] has shown that it is quite aware that one cannot impose upon France a political ideal conforming to that of nations like independent Belgium and the Swiss Republic; that something else is needed for France: that she cannot be merely a free country, that she must also be a great country, exercizing all of her rightful influence over the destiny of Europe, that she ought to propagate this influence throughout the world and carry everywhere that she can her language, her customs, her flag, her arms, and her genius. [*Applause at center and left.*]

DISCUSSION QUESTIONS

1. Why does Ferry consider colonial expansion to be an economic necessity?

2. Aside from its economic benefits, why, according to Ferry, is colonial expansion justified?

3. How does Ferry appeal to nationalist sentiment to defend his imperialist stance, and why?

4. What is the basis of his critics' arguments against imperialism?

2.
Imperialism and Anti-Imperialism

Rudyard Kipling, *The White Man's Burden*
and
Editorial from the San Francisco Call (1899)

The debate over imperialism was not confined to European shores; it also exploded onto the American scene when the United States gained control of Puerto Rico, Guam, and the Philippines in February 1899 after its victory in the Spanish-American War. Rudyard Kipling (1865–1936) published the poem "The White Man's Burden" in London and U.S. newspapers in direct response to the United States' fledging status as an imperial power. He urged Americans to share the "burden" — of implanting Western civilization among the "new-caught, sullen peoples" of East Asia — already shouldered by Europe. Born in British India and the son of a civil servant, Kipling was well versed in the ways of empire building and had already made a name for himself as the author of The Jungle Book, *among other works. The poem elicited a swift response across the United States, including the anti-imperialist editorial, which appeared in the* San Francisco Call, *that follows the poem.*

The White Man's Burden

Take up the White Man's burden —
   Send forth the best ye breed —
Go bind your sons to exile
   To serve your captives' need;

From *Rudyard Kipling's Verse: Inclusive Edition (1885–1918)* (New York: Doubleday, 1927), 371–72; "The White Man's Burden," *San Francisco Call* (Feb. 7, 1899). Reprinted on www.boondocksnet.com/ai/, Jim Zwick, ed., *Anti-Imperialism in the United States.*

To wait in heavy harness,
　On fluttered folk and wild —
Your new-caught, sullen peoples,
　Half-devil and half-child.

Take up the White Man's Burden —
　In patience to abide,
To veil the threat of terror
　And check the show of pride;
By open speech and simple,
　An hundred times made plain,
To seek another's profit,
　And work another's gain.

Take up the White Man's burden —
　The savage wars of peace —
Fill full the mouth of Famine
　And bid the sickness cease;
And when your goal is nearest
　The end for others sought,
Watch Sloth and heathen Folly
　Bring all your hope to nought.

Take up the White Man's burden —
　No tawdry rule of kings,
But toil of serf and sweeper —
　The tale of common things.
The ports ye shall not enter,
　The roads ye shall not tread,
Go make them with your living,
　And mark them with your dead.

Take up the White Man's burden —
　And reap his old reward:
The blame of those ye better,
　The hate of those ye guard —
The cry of hosts ye humor
　(Ah, slowly!) toward the light: —
"Why brought ye us from bondage,
　Our loved Egyptian night?"

Take up the White Man's burden —
　Ye dare not stoop to less —
Nor call too loud on Freedom
　To cloak your weariness;

By all ye cry or whisper,
　By all ye leave or do,
The silent, sullen peoples
　Shall weigh your Gods and you.

Take up the White Man's burden —
　Have done with childish days —
The lightly proffered laurel,
　The easy, ungrudged praise.
Comes now, to search your manhood
　Through all the thankless years,
Cold, edged with dear-bought wisdom,
　The judgment of your peers!

Editorial from the *San Francisco Call*

Rudyard Kipling has joined the ranks of those eminent British jingoes who are trying to induce the United States to help Great Britain in her imperial schemes by taking part in the Oriental imbroglio. Chamberlain and Balfour have enticed us with lofty oratory. Kipling wooes us with a song published in The Call of Sunday.

　The title of the ballad is "The White Man's Burden." Mr. Kipling sings:

Take up the White Man's burden
　Have done with childish days —
The lightly proffered laurel,
　The easy, ungrudged praise;
Comes now, to search your manhood
　Through all the thankless years,
Cold, edged with dear-bought wisdom,
　The judgment of your peers!

　By way of further information as to what we shall have to do when we have done with childish days and set about winning the approving judgment of our peers with their cold, edged, dear-bought wisdom, the poet, drawing an easy lesson from the experience of Great Britain, adds:

Take up the White Man's Burden —
　Send forth the best ye breed —
Go, bind your sons to exile
　To serve your captives' need;
To wait, in heavy harness,
　On fluttered folk and wild —
Your new-caught sullen peoples,
　Half-devil and half-child.

It seems we are to infer from this that if we do not consent to send forth the best we breed to serve in exile amid the jungles of tropic islands for the noble purpose of imposing American law and civilization upon the mongrel races, half devil and half child, we shall lose the esteem of European powers now engaged in that task, and possibly the esteem of Mr. Kipling also. It is a dilemma from which we cannot escape. Fate has ordained it and face it we must.

We might be more willing to enter upon the imperial task if our British cousins were not so outspoken in their eagerness to get us to do so. Their willingness to have us share the glory of civilizing the Orient awakens a suspicion that the glory is not altogether a profitable one. Great Britain evidently has more than she can carry and would like to divide the glory with us.

The invitation to take part is flattering to our pride, but not attractive to our common sense. We have a pretty heavy white man's burden at home and it will take something more than a song even from so strong a singer as Kipling to coax us to go to the Orient in search of an increase.

In all seriousness the eagerness of Chamberlain, Balfour, and other British leaders to get the United States involved in the affairs of the Orient and indirectly made a party to all European squabbles, is a significant sign of the times, and ought to be a sufficient warning to all intelligent Americans to avoid imperialism as they would a plague.

The pursuit of imperialism has raised up antagonists to Great Britain in every part of the world; it has imposed upon her people a heavy burden of debt and taxation; it has disturbed her politics by the continual menace of war and thus prevented the accomplishment of many needed reforms at home; and finally it has brought her into a position where without an ally she is confronted by a hostile world and is in danger of having her commerce, and perhaps even her empire, swept away at the first outbreak of war.

Rightly considered the white man's burden is to set and keep his own house in order. It is not required of him to upset the brown man's house under pretense of reform and then whip him into subjugation whenever he revolts at the treatment.

DISCUSSION QUESTIONS

1. How does Kipling define "The White Man's Burden"? What duties does he think this "burden" entails?

2. What kind of portrait does Kipling paint of non-Western peoples?

3. According to the author of the editorial from the *San Francisco Call*, why should Americans reject Kipling's appeal and avoid imperialism "as they would a plague"?

4. In what ways do these two sources expose the paradoxes of the new imperialism?

3.

Global Competition

Ernest Edwin Williams, *Made in Germany* (1896)

In the closing decades of the nineteenth century, Germany emerged as a new, seemingly unstoppable economic force. It enjoyed astounding industrial growth throughout this period and gained a substantial share of European export markets. Many people in Great Britain observed these events with dismay, seeing Germany as a threat not only to their country's long-standing industrial dominance but also to its national identity as a world power. Journalist Ernest Edwin Williams (1866–1935) fanned the flames of such fears in Made in Germany, *published in 1896. Drawing on a dizzying array of statistics, Williams painted a menacing picture of the omnipresence of German products in his readers' everyday lives. He hoped that his bleak portrait would prompt Parliament to adopt measures to protect and enhance British trade. Although his message went unheeded, it evidently struck a chord, for the book went through six editions in its first year.*

The Departing Glory

Preliminary

The Industrial Supremacy of Great Britain has been long an axiomatic commonplace; and it is fast turning into a myth, as inappropriate to fact as the Chinese Emperor's computation of his own status. This is a strong statement. But it is neither wide nor short of the truth. The industrial glory of England is departing, and England does not know it. There are spasmodic outcries against foreign competition, but the impression they leave is fleeting and vague. The phrase, "Made in Germany," is raw material for a jape at the pantomime, or is made the text for a homily by the official guardians of some particular trade, in so far as the matter concerns themselves. British Consuls, too, send words of warning home, and the number of these is increasing with significant frequency. But the nation at large is yet as little alive to the impending danger as to the evil already wrought. The man in the shop or the factory has plenty to say about the Armenian Question and the House of Lords, but about commercial and industrial matters which concern him vitally he is generally much less eloquent. The amount of interest evinced by the amateur politician seems invariably to advance with the remoteness of the matter from his daily bread. It is time to disturb the fatal torpor: even though the moment be, in one sense, unhappily chosen. The pendulum between depression and prosperity has swung to the latter, and manufacturers and merchants are flushed with the joyful contemplation of their order-books. Slackness has given way to briskness; the lean years have been succeeded by a term of fat ones. The prophet of evil commands his most attentive audiences when the times are with him. When they are good — though the good be fleeting — his words are apt to fall unheeded. . . .

From Ernest Edwin Williams, *Made in Germany*, 4th ed. (London: William Heinemann, 1896), 1–2, 7–12, 18.

As It Was

There was a time when our industrial empire was unchallenged. It was England which first emerged from the Small-Industry stage. She produced the Industrial Revolution about the middle of the last century, and well-nigh until the middle of this she developed her multitude of mills, and factories, and mines, and warehouses, undisturbed by war at home, and profiting by wars abroad. The great struggles which drained the energies of the Continental nations, sealed her industrial supremacy, and made her absolute mistress of the world-market. Thanks to them, she became the Universal Provider. English machinery, English pottery, English hardware, guns, and cutlery, English rails and bridge-work, English manufactures of well-nigh every kind formed the material of civilization all over the globe. She covered the dry land with a network of railways, and the seas were alive with her own ships freighted with her own merchandise. Between 1793 and 1815 the value of her exports had risen from £17,000,000 to £58,000,000. Her industrial dominion was immense, unquestioned, unprecedented in the history of the human race; and not unnaturally we have come to regard her rule as eternal. But careless self-confidence makes not for Empire. While she was throwing wide her gates to the world at large, her sisters were building barriers of protection against her; and, behind those barriers, and aided often by State subventions, during the middle and later years of the century, they have developed industries of their own. Of course, this was to a certain extent inevitable. England could not hope for an eternal monopoly of the world's manufactures; and industrial growths abroad do not of necessity sound the knell of her greatness. But she must discriminate in her equanimity. And most certainly she must discriminate against Germany. For Germany has entered into a deliberate and deadly rivalry with her, and is battling with might and main for the extinction of her supremacy. . . .

The German Revolution

Up to a couple of decades ago, Germany was an agricultural State. Her manufactures were few and unimportant; her industrial capital was small; her export trade was too insignificant to merit the attention of the official statistician; she imported largely for her own consumption. Now she has changed all that. Her youth has crowded into English houses, has wormed its way into English manufacturing secrets, and has enriched her establishments with the knowledge thus purloined. She has educated her people in a fashion which has made it in some branches of industry the superior, and in most the equal of the English. Her capitalists have been content with a simple style, which has enabled them to dispense with big immediate profits, and to feed their capital. They have toiled at their desks, and made their sons do likewise; they have kept a strict controlling hand on all the strings of their businesses; they have obtained State aid in several ways — as special rates to shipping ports; they have insinuated themselves into every part of the world — civilized, barbarian, savage — learning the languages, and patiently studying the wants and tastes of the several peoples. Not content with reaping the advantages of British colonization — this was accomplished with alarming facility — Germany has "protected" the simple savage on her own account, and the Imperial Eagle now floats on the breezes of the South Sea Islands, and droops in the thick air of the African littoral. Her diplomatists have negotiated innumerable commercial treaties. The population of her cities has been increasing in a manner not unworthy of England in the Thirties and Forties. Like England, too, she is draining her rural districts for the massing of her children in huge factory towns. Her yards (as well as those of England) too, are ringing with the sound of hammers upon ships being builded for the transport of German merchandise. Her agents and travelers swarm through Russia, and wherever else there is a chance of trade on any terms — are even supplying the foreigner with German goods *at a loss*, that they may achieve their purpose in the end. In a word, an industrial development, unparalleled, save in England a century ago, is now her portion. A gigantic commercial State is arising to menace our prosperity, and contend with us for the trade of the world. . . .

Made in Germany

The phrase is fluent in the mouth: how universally appropriate it is, probably no one who has not made a special study of the matter is aware. Take observations, Gentle Reader, in your own surroundings: the mental exercise is recommended as an antidote to that form of self-sufficiency which our candid friends regard as indigenous to the British climate. Your investigations will work out somewhat in this fashion. You will find that the material of some of your own clothes was probably woven in Germany. Still more probably is it that some of your wife's garments are German importations; while it is practically beyond a doubt that the magnificent mantles and jackets wherein her maids array themselves on their Sundays out are German-made and German-sold, for only so could they be done at the figure. Your governess's *fiancé* is a clerk in the City; but he also was made in Germany. The toys, and the dolls, and the fairy books which your children maltreat in the nursery are made in Germany: nay, the material of your favorite (patriotic) newspaper had the same birthplace as like as not. Roam the house over, and the fateful mark will greet you at every turn, from the piano in your drawing-room to the mug on your kitchen dresser, blazoned though it be with the legend, *A Present from Margate*. Descend to your domestic depths, and you shall find your very drain-pipes German made. You pick out of the grate the paper wrappings from a book consignment, and they also are "Made in Germany." You stuff them into the fire, and reflect that the poker in your hand was forged in Germany. As you rise from your hearthrug you knock over an ornament on your mantlepiece; picking up the pieces you read, on the bit that formed the base, "Manufactured in Germany." And you jot your dismal reflections down with a pencil that was made in Germany. At midnight your wife comes home from an opera which was made in Germany, has been here enacted by singers and conductor and players made in Germany, with the aid of instruments and sheets of music made in Germany. You go to bed, and glare wrathfully at a text on the wall; it is illuminated with an English village church, and it was "Printed in Germany." If you are imaginative and dyspeptic, you drop off to sleep only to dream that St. Peter (with a duly stamped halo round his head and a bunch of keys from the Rhineland) has refused you admission into Paradise, because you bear not the Mark of the Beast upon your forehead, and are not of German make. But you console yourself with the thought that it was only a Bierhaus Paradise any way; and you are awakened in the morning by the sonorous brass of a German band.

Is the picture exaggerated? Bear with me, while I tabulate a few figures from the Official Returns of Her Majesty's Custom House, where, at any rate, fancy and exaggeration have no play. In '95 Germany sent us linen manufactures to the value of £91,257; cotton manufactures to the value of £536,471; embroidery and needlework to the value of £11,309; leather gloves to the value of £27,934 (six times the amount imported six years earlier); and woolen manufactures to the value of £1,016,694. Despite the exceeding cheapness of toys, the value of German-made playthings for English nurseries amounted, in '95, to £459,944. In the same year she sent us books to the value of £37,218, and paper to the value of £586,835. For musical instruments we paid her as much as £563,018; for china and earthenware £216,876; for prints, engravings, and photographs, £111,825. This recital of the moneys which *in one year* have come out of John Bull's pocket for the purchase of his German-made household goods is, I submit disproof enough of any charge of alarmism. For these articles, it must be remembered, are not like oranges and guano. They are not products which we must either import or lack: — *they all belong to the category of English manufactures*, the most important of them, indeed, being articles in the preparation of which Great Britain is held pre-eminent. The total value of manufactured goods imported into the United Kingdom by Germany rose from £16,629,987 in '83 to £21,632,614 in '93: an increase of 30.08 per cent. . . .

The Significance of These Facts

These are the sober — to believers in our eternal rule, the sobering — facts. They are picked almost at random from a mass of others of like import, and I think they are sufficient to prove that my general statements are neither untrue nor unduly emphatic. And yet the data needed for the purpose of showing the parlous condition into which our trade is drifting are still largely to seek. Germany is yet in her industrial infancy; and the healthiest infant can do but poor battle against a grown man. England, with her enormous capital, and the sway she has wielded for a century over the world-market, is as that strong man. Now, to tell a strong man, conscious of his strength to an over-weening degree, that he is in peril from a half-grown youngster, is to invite his derision; and yet if a strong man, as the years advance on him, neglect himself and abuse his strength, he may fall before an energetic stripling. Germany has already put our trade in a bad way; but the worst lies in the future, and it is hard to convince the average Englishman of this. He will admit that Germany's trade has increased, and that at many points it hits our own; but here his robust insularity asserts itself. Germany has not the capital, he will tell you; her workmen are no workmen at all; her capitalists and her managers are poor bureaucratic plodders; the world will soon find out that her products are not of

English make, and so forth. And he goes on vocalizing *Rule Britannia* in his best commercial prose.

DISCUSSION QUESTIONS

1. According to Williams, what are the secrets of Germany's economic "revolution"?

2. Why does he regard Germany's industrial success as a cause for alarm, particularly in Great Britain?

3. What does this excerpt suggest about industrial growth during this period and its impact on international relations?

4.
The Advance of Unionism
Margaret Bondfield, *A Life's Work* (1948)

Despite the explosive industrial growth of the last third of the nineteenth century, life for European workers was still a struggle. They remained vulnerable to economic exploitation and fluctuations in the faster-paced, more competitive, and more complex marketplace. Workers began to take matters into their own hands by organizing formal unions to fight for better working conditions. Although men dominated the trade union movement, women found a place too, as the following excerpt from the autobiography of Margaret Bondfield (1873–1954) reveals. The daughter of a lace factory worker, Bondfield went to work at age fourteen as a draper's assistant. With the rise of consumer capitalism, shop assisting was among the fastest growing employment opportunities for women. The long days and low wages prompted Bondfield to join the newly established National Union for Shop Assistants in 1894, launching her lifelong commitment to political activism.

London: By dint of rigid economy, at the end of five years of shop life in Brighton I had saved £5, which seemed to me great wealth; but the material side of life did not bother me much. I had reached a stage in my spiritual pilgrimage which I must needs travel alone. Religion had become something personal, to be accepted or rejected; at home it was like the air — it permeated our lives, but was not discussed. I could no longer passively accept contemporary opinion on business morality, to which I applied the harsh judgments of the very young. The outward and visible sign of my protest was a sudden move to London. It was undoubtedly *the* turning-point in my life. But for that I might have become a successful business woman!

For the next three months I was nearer to starvation than at any time since. I learned the bitterness of a hopeless search for work. The kindness of a landlady who trusted me kept me going when I was penniless, and until I got a job.

From Margaret Bondfield, *A Life's Work* (London: Hutchinson & Co., 1948), 27–29, 36.

In those days the seekers after work had no Labor Exchange to help them. The best plan was to visit the wholesale firms in the City and get information about vacancies from the commercial travelers, and then journey as fast as the old horse buses allowed — perhaps right across London — only to find a queue of 150 to 200 applicants already there. Before we had stood in the queue for long a notice would be put up: "No good waiting any longer — place filled."

I have taken the whole of Oxford Street, going into every shop walking West on the one side, and every shop on the other side coming back on the chance that there might be a vacancy. I was not tall enough. I remember one man saying to me, "We never engage anyone under five feet eight inches."

Even today those first months in the great city searching for work carry the shadow of a nightmare; but finally I got a job — only to find that conditions, which I had thought peculiar to the Brighton shop, were almost universal. . . .

A small thing led me to another adventure of faith. I was hungry and I went across to Fitzroy Street to buy a penn'orth of fish and a ha'p'orth of chips, served to me in a newspaper; munching my feast, I strolled around Fitzroy Square reading the paper, in which was a letter from James Macpherson, Secretary of the National Union of Shop Assistants, Warehousemen and Clerks, urging shop assistants to join together to fight against the wretched conditions of employment. I was working about sixty-five hours a week for between £15 and £25 per annum, living in. Here I felt was the right thing to do, and at once I joined up.

My brother Frank was in London, working at Clement's House Printing Works, where he was "Father of the Chapel" and a member of the Union committee to negotiate terms for the introduction of the Linotype. He encouraged my Trade Union activities. This was a happy time for me.

My Union officers gave me all the work I could do in my scant leisure, and every kind of encouragement. They elected me on to the district council, and once I attended a national conference. For the next two years the Union utilized me for platform work in an ever-increasing degree.

Encouraged by T. Spencer Jones, the editor of our little Union paper, I ventured first to undertake reports of meetings, and later to write a few short stories under the pen-name of Grace Dare. It was quite impossible for me to write in the presence of any who might know what I was doing, and as I had not one inch of space I could call my own, I would wait till one or two of my room-mates were asleep, and then stealthily, with the feeling of a conspirator, and knowing that I was committing an offense for which I could be heavily fined, I would light my half-penny dip, hiding its glare by means of a towel thrown over the back of a chair, and set to work on my monthly article.

If my room-mates woke they were kind enough not to remember it the next morning, and although this surreptitious writing was kept up for about two years, I do not think any breach of rules was ever reported to the firm.

In those early days — 1894 to 1896 — executive committee meetings of my Union were called for Sundays, the only possible day. The committee members had often to travel long distances on night trains, arriving early on Sunday morning, sitting for the transaction of business in a stuffy room, clouded with tobacco smoke, starting back again on Sunday night to be in time for business at 7.30 or 8 a.m. on Monday; they were the pioneers, and to me they were heroes, for they had only bare expenses from the Union. . . . "Death to the Living-in System," "Abolish Fines and Deductions," "Reduce the Hours Worked in Shops," were the slogans. We had no delusions about the size of the job. We frankly told our audiences that we invited them to share in hard work for the next ten years in building up the membership. We were about 2,000 strong in a trade employing 750,000 people. "Come, pioneers! O pioneers!" we sang, and they were coming! . . .

From this time on I just lived for the Trade Union Movement. I concentrated on my job.

This concentration was undisturbed by love affairs. I had seen too much — too early — to have the least desire to join in the pitiful scramble of my work-mates. The very surroundings of shop life accentuated the desire of most shop girls to get married. Long hours of work and the living-in system deprived them of the normal companionship of men in their leisure hours, and the wonder is that so many of the women continued to be good and kind, and self-respecting, without the incentive of a great cause, or of any interest outside their job.

Many of them would toil after business hours to make their clothes, so that, from their small salaries, they could help some member of their family. Some women, much older than myself, would look forward to marriage with hope and dread — hope of economic security, and dread of the unknown ordeal of childbirth. Through what sex knowledge I was able to pass on, Mrs. Martindale resolved their fears, but it was not at all easy to transmit to them the reverence for motherhood, which I had seen at its best and highest, but which to them was too often linked with the obscene.

I had no vocation for wifehood or motherhood, but an urge to serve the Union — an urge which developed into "a sense of oneness with our kind."

DISCUSSION QUESTIONS

1. According to Bondfield, what was life like for her and her coworkers?

2. What traditional female roles did Bondfield reject to devote herself fully to union activities?

3. What does Bondfield reveal about the role of literacy and the press in working-class collective action?

5.
Artistic Expression

Edgar Degas, *Notebooks* (1863–1884)

Visual artists were not immune to the changes unfolding around them in late-nineteenth-century Europe. Beginning in the 1850s, many artists turned away from classical and romantic conventions and portrayed the world in realistic and graphic ways. Some artists pushed the boundaries of tradition further still with a new style

called impressionism. Impressionists were equally fascinated with their immediate sur-
roundings but also focused on the light, color, and movement of a single moment. Edgar
Degas (1834–1917) embodied this shift in the visual arts. A classically trained drafts-
man, Degas began his professional career in Paris in 1859, painting portraits and his-
torical subjects. For Degas, the pull of convention was ultimately no match for the novel
artistic influences energizing the Parisian art scene at the time, notably Japanese prints,
photography, and the fledgling impressionist movement. The impact on Degas was
profound. By the late 1860s, he had turned his eye to depicting modern life in motion.
The excerpts below from his private notebooks capture his artistic creativity and driv-
ing desire to portray local scenes and individuals one moment and one action at a time.

From Degas' Notebook: 1863–1867

What is certain is that putting a bit of nature in place and drawing it are two entirely different things.[1]

I don't like to hear people saying like children in front of rosy and glowing
flesh: "Oh, what life, what blood!" — the human skin is as varied in appearance, especially among us, as the rest of nature: fields, trees, mountains, water, forests. It is
possible to meet with as many resemblances between a face and a pebble as between two pebbles because everyone still wants to see a likeness between two faces.
(I am speaking in terms of the question of form, not bringing up that of coloring,
since we often find so much connection between a pebble and a fish, a mountain
and a dog's head, clouds and horses, etc.)

Therefore, it is not merely instinct which makes us say that we must search for
a method of coloring everywhere, for the affinities among what is alive, what is
dead and what vegetates. I can, for example, easily recall the color of some hair, because I got the idea that it was hair made out of polished walnutwood, or else flax,
or horse-chestnut shells. The rendering of the form will make real hair, with its
softness and lightness or its roughness or its weight out of this tone which is almost precisely that of walnutwood, flax, or horse-chestnut shell. And then one
paints in such different ways on such different supports that the same tone might
be one thing in one place, another in another. . . .

From Degas' Notebook: 1878–1884

After having done portraits seen from above, I will do them seen from below —
sitting very close to a woman and looking at her from a low viewpoint, I will see her
head in the chandelier, surrounded by crystals, etc.; do simple things like draw a

---

From Linda Nochlin, ed., *Impressionism and Post-Impressionism, 1874–1904* (Englewood
Cliffs: Prentice-Hall, 1966), 61–63.

[1]According to French poet and Degas admirer Paul Valéry (1871–1945), in this statement
Degas "meant to distinguish what he called the *mise en place*, or the conventional representation of objects, from what he called the 'drawing' or the alteration which this exact representation . . . undergoes from a particular artist's way of seeing and working." [Ed.]

profile which would not move, [the painter] himself moving, going up or down, the same for a full face — a piece of furniture, a whole living room; do a series of arm-movements of the dance, or of legs that would not move, himself turning either around or — etc. Finally study a figure or an object, no matter what, from every viewpoint. One could use a looking glass for that, one would not [have to] stir from one's place. Only the looking glass would be lowered or tilted. One would turn about. Studio projects: Set up tiers [a series of benches] all around the room so as to get used to drawing things from above and below. Only let myself paint things seen in a looking glass to get used to hatred of trompe-l'oeil.[2]

For a portrait, make someone pose on the ground floor and work on the first floor to get used to keeping hold of the forms and expressions and never draw or paint *immediately*.

For the Newspaper cut a lot. Of a dancer do either the arms or the legs or the back. Do the shoes — the hands — of the hairdresser — the badly cut coiffure . . . , bare feet in dance, action, etc., etc.

Do every kind of worn object placed, accompanied in such a way that they have the life of the man or the woman; corsets which have just been taken off, for example — and which keep the form of the body, etc., etc.

Series on instruments and instrumentalists, their shapes, twisting of the hands and arms and neck of the violinist, for example, puffing out and hollowing of the cheeks of bassoons, oboes, etc.

Do a series in aquatint on *mourning* (different blacks), black veils of deep mourning (floating on the face), black gloves, carriages in mourning, carriage of the Funeral Company, carriages like Venetian gondolas.

On smoke, smoke of smokers, pipes, cigarettes, cigars, smoke of locomotives, of high chimneys, factories, steamboats, etc. Destruction of smoke under the bridges. Steam.

On the evening. Infinite subjects. In the cafés, different values of the glass-shades reflected in the mirrors.

On the bakery, the bread: series on journeymen bakers, seen in the cellar itself or through the air vents from the street. Colors of pink flour — lovely curves of pie, still lifes on the different breads, large, oval, fluted, round, etc. Experiment, in color, on the yellows, pinks, grey-whites of breads. Perspective views of rows of breads. Charming layout of bakeries. Cakes, the wheat, the mills, the flour, the sacks, the market-porters.

No one has ever done monuments or houses from below, from beneath, up close as one sees them going by in the streets. . . .

DISCUSSION QUESTIONS

1. What subjects intrigued Degas as an artist? Why was he interested in portraying them from so many different viewpoints and positions?

---

[2]**trompe-l'oeil:** French for "deceive the eye." A style of painting intended to look photo-graphically realistic. [Ed.]

2. In what ways was this interest typical of impressionism in general?

3. How did the changing economic and social scene in Paris at the time influence Degas's interests and approach?

Comparative Questions

1. According to Ferry and Williams, what factors are key to a nation's strength, and why?

2. What do the views of Ferry and Williams suggest about changes in Europe's place within the world at large?

3. How do you think Kipling would have reacted to Ferry's defense of colonial expansion?

4. What do Williams, Bondfield, and Degas reveal about the impact of industrialization on everyday life and culture in Europe?

CHAPTER

24

Modernity and the Road to War, 1890–1914

As the twentieth century dawned, Europeans had cause for both elation and fear. On the one hand, many enjoyed unprecedented prosperity: Europe's industrial and technological forces continued to grow, and European nations controlled most of the world's surface. On the other, domestic and international tensions abounded: at home, people struggled to navigate the hazards of modern life, while abroad nation-states faced mounting competition and dissent in their quest for imperial glory. The following documents illustrate that disorder and chaos seemed to lurk around every corner — in the marketplace, a suffrage organization, an anti-imperialist placard, a defiant newspaper article, or even in one's own dreams and sexuality. Collectively, these documents reveal that the road of modernity was rocky and uncertain, casting a permanent shadow over the Enlightenment's faith in the inevitability of progress.

1.
"God Is Dead"

Friedrich Nietzsche, *The Gay Science* (1882)

Friedrich Nietzsche (1844–1900), the son of a town minister, was born at a time of rapid political, social, and economic change in Europe. In his youth, Nietzsche attended a boarding school, where he was exposed to the work of German philosopher Arthur Schopenhauer (1788–1860) and German composer Richard Wagner (1813–1883), which influenced his thinking for the rest of his life. Nietzsche also had a great passion

From Friedrich Nietzsche, *The Gay Science — With a Prelude in Rhymes and an Appendix of Songs* (New York: Vintage Books/Random House, 1974), 73–76, 163–64, 180–82, 228–29, 273–74.

for the classics, and became a philology professor at the University of Basel at the age of twenty-four. A productive and influential author, he gained fame for confronting one of his age's most significant intellectual problems — namely, many educated Europeans had abandoned traditional Christianity, but no comparable institution had stepped in to fill the moral, intellectual, and cultural void. Science was rapidly improving Europeans' knowledge of the world; however, with great discovery, came great terror when long-held beliefs were shown to be false. These and other important components of Nietzsche's philosophy — the role of art in society, the ideal of eternal recurrence, and the improvements for humanity — can be found in the following excerpts from The Gay Science.

The teachers of the purpose of existence. — Whether I contemplate men with benevolence or with an evil eye, I always find them concerned with a single task, all of them and every one of them in particular: to do what is good for the preservation of the human race. Not from any feeling of love for the race, but merely because nothing in them is older, stronger, more inexorable and unconquerable than this instinct — because this instinct constitutes *the essence* of our species, our herd. It is easy enough to divide our neighbors quickly, with the usual myopia, from a mere five paces away, into useful and harmful, good and evil men; but in any large-scale accounting, when we reflect on the whole a little longer, we become suspicious of this neat division and finally abandon it. Even the most harmful man may really be the most useful when it comes to the preservation of the species; for he nurtures either in himself or in others, through his effects, instincts without which humanity would long have become feeble or rotten. Hatred, the mischievous delight in the misfortunes of others, the lust to rob and dominate, and whatever else is called evil belongs to the most amazing economy of the preservation of the species. To be sure, this economy is not afraid of high prices, of squandering, and it is on the whole extremely foolish. Still it is *proven* that it has preserved our race so far.

I no longer know whether you, my dear fellow man and neighbor, are at all *capable* of living in a way that would damage the species; in other words, "unreasonably" and "badly." What *might* have harmed the species may have become extinct many thousands of years ago and may by now be one of those things that are not possible even for God. Pursue your best or your worst desires, and above all perish! In both cases you are probably still in some way a promoter and benefactor of humanity and therefore entitled to your eulogists — but also to your detractors. But you will never find anyone who could wholly mock you as an individual, also in your best qualities, bringing home to you to the limits of truth your boundless, fly-like, froglike wretchedness! To laugh at oneself as one would have to laugh in order to laugh *out of the whole truth* — to do that even the best so far lacked sufficient sense for the truth, and the most gifted had too little genius for that. Even laughter may yet have a future. I mean, when the proposition "the species is everything, *one* is always none" has become part of humanity, and this ultimate liberation and irresponsibility has become accessible to all at all times. Perhaps laughter will then have formed an alliance with wisdom, perhaps only "gay science" will then be left.

For the present, things are still quite different. For the present, the comedy of existence has not yet "become conscious" of itself. For the present, we still live in the age of tragedy, the age of moralities and religions. What is the meaning of the ever new appearance of these founders of moralities and religions, these instigators of fights over moral valuations, these teachers of remorse and religious wars? What is the meaning of these heroes on this stage? Thus far these have been the heroes, and everything else, even if at times it was all that could be seen and was much too near to us, has always merely served to set the stage for these heroes, whether it was machinery or coulisse or took the form of confidants and valets. (The poets, for example, were always the valets of some morality.)

It is obvious that these tragedians, too, promote the interests of the *species*, even if they should believe that they promote the interest of God or work as God's emissaries. They, too, promote the life of the species, *by promoting the faith in life.* "Life is worth living," every one of them shouts; "there is something to life, there is something behind life, beneath it; beware!"

From time to time this instinct, which is at work equally in the highest and the basest men — the instinct for the preservation of the species — erupts as reason and as passion of the spirit. Then it is surrounded by a resplendent retinue of reasons and tries with all the force at its command to make us forget that at bottom it is instinct, drive, folly, lack of reasons. Life *shall* be loved, *because*— ! Man *shall* advance himself and his neighbor, *because*— ! What names all these Shalls and Becauses receive and may yet receive in the future! . . . His inventions and valuations may be utterly foolish and overenthusiastic; he may badly misjudge the course of nature and deny its conditions — . . . and yet, whenever "the hero" appeared on the stage, something new was attained: the gruesome counterpart of laughter, that profound emotional shock felt by many individuals at the thought: "Yes, I am worthy of living!" Life and I and you and all of us became *interesting* to ourselves once again for a little while. . . .

Gradually, man has become a fantastic animal that has to fulfill one more condition of existence than any other animal: man *has to* believe, to know, from time to time *why* he exists; his race cannot flourish without a periodic trust in life — without faith in *reason in life.* And again and again the human race will decree from time to time: "There is something at which it is absolutely forbidden henceforth to laugh." The most cautious friend of man will add: "Not only laughter and gay wisdom but the tragic, too, with all its sublime unreason, belongs among the means and necessities of the preservation of the species." . . .

Our ultimate gratitude to art. — If we had not welcomed the arts and invented this kind of cult of the untrue, then the realization of general untruth that now comes to us through science — the realization that delusion and error are conditions of human knowledge and sensation — would be utterly unbearable. *Honesty* would lead to nausea and suicide. But now there is a counterforce against our honesty that helps us to avoid such consequences: art as the *good* will to appearance. . . . As an aesthetic phenomenon existence is still *bearable* for us, and art furnishes us with eyes and hands and above all the good conscience to be *able* to turn ourselves by looking upon, by looking *down* upon, ourselves and, from an artistic distance, laughing *over* ourselves or weeping *over* ourselves. We must discover the *hero* no less than the *fool* in our passion for knowledge; we must occasionally find pleasure in our folly, or we cannot continue to find pleasure in our wisdom. Precisely because we are at bottom grave and serious human beings — really, more weights than human beings — nothing does us as much good as a *fool's cap*: we need it in relation to ourselves — we need all exuberant, floating, dancing, mocking, childish, and blissful art lest we lose the *freedom above* things that our demands of us. . . . We should be *able* also to stand *above* morality — and not only to *stand* with the anxious stiffness of a man who is afraid of slipping and falling any moment, but also to *float* above it and *play*. How then could we possibly dispense with art — and with the fool? . . .

In the horizon of the infinite. — We have left the land and have embarked. We have burned our bridges behind us — indeed, we have gone farther and destroyed the land behind us. Now, little ship, look out! Beside you is the ocean: to be sure, it does not always roar, and at times it lies spread out like silk and gold and reveries of graciousness. But hours will come when you will realize that it is infinite and that there is nothing more awesome than infinity. Oh, the poor bird that felt free and now strikes the walls of this cage! Woe, when you feel homesick for the land as if it had offered more *freedom* — and there is no longer any "land."

The madman. — Have you not heard of that madman who lit a lantern in the bright morning hours, ran to the market place, and cried incessantly: "I seek God! I seek God!" — As many of those who did not believe in God were standing around just then, he provoked much laughter. Has he got lost? asked one. Did he lose his way like a child? asked another. Or is he hiding? Is he afraid of us? Has he gone on a voyage? emigrated? — Thus they yelled and laughed.

The madman jumped into their midst and pierced them with his eyes. "Whither is God?" he cried; "I will tell you. *We have killed him* — you and I. All of us are his murderers. But how did we do this? How could we drink up the sea? Who gave us the sponge to wipe away the entire horizon? What were we doing when we unchained this earth from its sun? Whither is it moving now? Whither are we moving? Away from all suns? Are we not plunging continually? Backward, sideward, forward, in all directions? Is there still any up or down? Are we not straying as through an infinite nothing? Do we not feel the breath of empty space? Has it not become colder? Is not night continually closing in on us? Do we hear nothing as yet of the noise of the gravediggers who are burying God? Do we smell nothing as yet of the divine decomposition? Gods, too, decompose. God is dead. God remains dead. And we have killed him.

"How shall we comfort ourselves, the murderers of all murderers? What was holiest and mightiest of all that the world has yet owned has bled to death under our knives: who will wipe this blood off us? What water is there for us to clean ourselves? What festivals of atonement, what sacred games shall we have to invent? Is not the greatness of this deed too great for us? Must we ourselves not become gods simply to appear worthy of it? There has never been a greater deed; and whoever is born after us — for the sake of this deed he will belong to a higher history than all history hitherto."

Here the madman fell silent and looked again at his listeners; and they, too, were silent and stared at him in astonishment. At last he threw his lantern on the ground, and it broke into pieces and went out. "I have come too early," he said then; "my time is not yet. This tremendous event is still on its way, still wandering; it has not yet reached the ears of men. Lightning and thunder require time; the light of the stars requires time; deeds, though done, still require time to be seen and heard. This deed is still more distant from them than the most distant stars — *and yet they have done it themselves.*"

It has been related further that on the same day the madman forced his way into several churches and there struck up his *requiem aeternam deo.* Led out and called to account, he is said always to have replied nothing but: "What after all are these churches now if they are not the tombs and sepulchers of God?" . . .

Preparatory human beings. — I welcome all signs that a more virile, warlike age is about to begin, which will restore honor to courage above all. For this age shall prepare the way for one yet higher, and it shall gather the strength that this higher age will require some day — the age that will carry heroism into the search for knowledge and that will *wage wars* for the sake of ideas and their consequences. To this end we now need many preparatory courageous human beings who cannot very well leap out of nothing, any more than out of the sand and slime of present-day civilization and metropolitanism — human beings who know how to be silent, lonely, resolute, and content and constant in invisible activities; human beings who are bent on seeking in all things for what in them must be *overcome*; human beings distinguished as much by cheerfulness, patience, unpretentiousness, and contempt for all great vanities as by magnanimity in victory and forbearance regarding the small vanities of the vanquished; human beings whose judgment concerning all victors and the share of chance in every victory and fame is sharp and free; human beings with their own festivals, their own working days, and their own periods of mourning, accustomed to command with assurance but instantly ready to obey when that is called for — equally proud, equally serving their own cause in both cases; more endangered human beings, more fruitful human beings, happier beings! For believe me: the secret for harvesting from existence the greatest fruitfulness and the greatest enjoyment is — to *live dangerously!* Build your cities on the slopes of Vesuvius! Send your ships into uncharted seas! Live at war with your peers and yourselves! Be robbers and conquerors as long as you cannot be rulers and possessors, you seekers of knowledge! Soon the age will be past when you could be content to live hidden in forests like shy deer. At long last the search for knowledge will reach out for its due; it will want to *rule* and *possess*, and you with it!

The greatest weight. — What, if some day or night a demon were to steal after you into your loneliest loneliness and say to you: "This life as you now live it and have lived it, you will have to live once more and innumerable times more; and there will be nothing new in it, but every pain and every joy and every thought and sigh and everything unutterably small or great in your life will have to return to you, all in the same succession and sequence — even this spider and this moonlight between the trees, and even this moment and I myself. The eternal hourglass of existence is turned upside down again and again, and you with it, speck of dust!"

Would you not throw yourself down and gnash your teeth and curse the demon who spoke thus? Or have you once experienced a tremendous moment when you would have answered him: "You are a god and never have I heard anything more divine." If this thought gained possession of you, it would change you as you are or perhaps crush you. The question in each and every thing, "Do you desire this once more and innumerable times more?" would lie upon your actions as the greatest weight. Or how well disposed would you have to become to yourself and to life *to crave nothing more fervently* than this ultimate eternal confirmation and seal?

DISCUSSION QUESTIONS

1. Much of *The Gay Science* is written in the form of a parable. Why do you think Nietzsche chose this style to express his ideas?

2. According to Nietzsche, what is the role of art in the life of humanity, and why is it so important?

3. What does the death of God signify to Nietzsche? Why did he place the words "God is dead" in the mouth of a madman?

4. How would you describe Nietzsche's beliefs about human beings in general? What did he see as their strengths and weaknesses?

2.
The Dreyfus Affair
Émile Zola, *"J'accuse!"* (January 13, 1898)

At the close of the nineteenth century, more and more Europeans embraced militant nationalism and anti-Semitism as weapons against the struggles of modern society. The combination of these forces fueled what became a defining event of the period, the Dreyfus Affair. In 1894, a Jewish captain in the French army, Alfred Dreyfus (1859–1935), was accused of spying for Germany. A military memorandum (bordereau) discovered by a secret agent in the German embassy in Paris formed the centerpiece of the military's case. Despite Dreyfus's protestations of innocence, he was convicted and imprisoned on Devil's Island. The case receded from public view for nearly two years until new evidence pointed to the real traitor, Ferdinand Walsin-Esterhazy. Forced to open an investigation, the army desperately sought a way to protect its prestige and

---

From Alain Pagès, ed., *The Dreyfus Affair, "J'Accuse" and Other Writings*, trans. Eleanor Levieux (New Haven: Yale University Press, 1996), 43–47, 50–53.

reputation. Its efforts culminated on January 12, 1898, when a panel of military judges found Esterhazy not guilty after a two-day trial conducted behind closed doors. Among Dreyfus's most ardent champions was French writer Émile Zola (1840–1902), who drafted the letter excerpted here in response to the trial. The day after the verdict, Zola's letter appeared in 300,000 copies of a special edition of the Parisian newspaper, L'Aurore. Because of Zola's popularity and his willingness to name names, his letter transformed the Dreyfus case into an international affair.

Monsieur le Président,

Will you allow me, out of my gratitude for the gracious manner in which you once granted me an audience, to express my concern for your well-deserved glory? Will you allow me to tell you that although your star has been in the ascendant hitherto, it is now in danger of being dimmed by the most shameful and indelible of stains?

You have emerged unscathed from libelous slurs, you have won the people's hearts. You are the radiant center of our apotheosis, for the Russian alliance has been indeed, for France, a patriotic celebration. And now you are about to preside over our World Fair. What a solemn triumph it will be, the crowning touch on our grand century of diligent labor, truth and liberty. But what a blot on your name (I was about to say, on your reign) this abominable Dreyfus Affair is! A court martial, acting on orders, has just dared to acquit such a man as Esterhazy. Truth itself and justice itself have been slapped in the face. And now it is too late, France's cheek has been sullied by that supreme insult, and History will record that it was during your Presidency that such a crime against society was committed.

They have dared to do this. Very well, then, I shall dare too. I shall tell the truth, for I pledged that I would tell it, if our judicial system, once the matter was brought before it through the normal channels, did not tell the truth, the whole truth. It is my duty to speak up; I will not be an accessory to the fact. If I were, my nights would be haunted by the specter of that innocent man so far away, suffering the worst kind of torture as he pays for a crime he did not commit.

And it is to you, M. le Président, that I will shout out the truth with all the revulsion of a decent man. To your credit, I am convinced that you are unaware of the truth. And to whom should I denounce the evil machinations of those who are truly guilty if not to you, the First Magistrate in the land? . . .

Ah, for anyone who knows the true details of the first affair, what a nightmare it is! Major du Paty de Clam arrests Dreyfus and has him placed in solitary confinement. He rushes to the home of Madame Dreyfus and terrifies her, saying that if she speaks up, her husband is lost. Meanwhile the unfortunate man is tearing out his hair, clamoring his innocence. And that is how the investigation proceeded, as in some fifteenth-century chronicle, shrouded in mystery and a wealth of the wildest expedients, and all on the basis of a single, childish accusation, that idiotic bordereau, which was not only a very ordinary kind of treason but also the most impudent kind of swindle, since almost all of the so-called secrets that had supposedly been turned over to the enemy were of no value. I dwell on this point because this is the egg from which the real crime — the dreadful denial of justice which has laid France low — was later to hatch. I would like to make it perfectly clear how the miscarriage of justice came about, how it is the product of Major du Paty de Clam's machinations, how General Mercier and Generals de Boisdeffre and Gonse came to be taken in by it and gradually became responsible for this error and how it is that later they felt they had a duty to impose it as the sacred truth, a truth that will not admit of even the slightest discussion. At the beginning, all they contributed was negligence and lack of intelligence. The worst we can say is that they gave in to the religious passions of the circles they move in and the prejudices wrought by esprit de corps. They let stupidity have its way.

But now, here is Dreyfus summoned before the court martial. The most utter secrecy is demanded. They could not have imposed stricter silence and been more rigorous and mysterious if a traitor had actually opened our borders to the enemy and led the German Emperor straight to Notre Dame. The entire nation is flabbergasted. Terrible deeds are whispered about, monstrous betrayals that scandalize History itself, and of course the nation bows to these rumors. No punishment can be too severe; the nation will applaud the traitor's public humiliation; the nation is adamant: the guilty man shall remain on the remote rock where infamy has placed him and he shall be devoured by remorse. But then, those unspeakable accusations, those dangerous accusations that might inflame all of Europe and had to be so carefully concealed behind the closed doors of a secret session — are they true? No, they are not! There is nothing behind all that but the extravagant, demented flights of fancy of Major du Paty de Clam. It's all a smokescreen with just one purpose: to conceal a cheap novel of the most outlandish sort. And to be convinced of this, one need only examine the formal indictment that was read before the court martial.

How hollow that indictment is! Is it possible a man has been found guilty on the strength of it? Such iniquity is staggering. I challenge decent people to read it: their hearts will leap with indignation and rebellion when they think of the disproportionate price Dreyfus is paying so far away on Devil's Island. So Dreyfus speaks several languages, does he? This is a crime. Not one compromising paper was found in his home? A crime. He occasionally pays a visit to the region he hails from? A crime. He is a hard-working man, eager to know everything? A crime. He does not get flustered? A crime. He does get flustered? A crime. And how naively it is worded! How baseless its claims are! They told us he was indicted on fourteen different counts but in the end there is actually only one: that famous bordereau; and we even find out that the experts did not all agree, that one of them, M. Gobert, was subjected to some military pressure because he dared to come to a different conclusion from the one they wanted him to reach. We were also told that twenty-three officers had come and testified against Dreyfus. We still do not know how they were questioned, but what is certain is that not all of their testimony was negative. Besides, all of them, you will notice, came from the offices of the War Department. This trial is a family conclave; they all *belong*. We must not forget that. It is the General Staff who wanted this trial; it is they who judged Dreyfus; and they have just judged him for the second time. . . .

. . . And what makes the whole business all the more odious and cynical is that they are lying with impunity and there is no way to convict them. They turn France inside out, they shelter behind the legitimate uproar they have caused, they seal mouths by making hearts quake and perverting minds. I know of no greater crime against society.

These, M. le Président, are the facts that explain how a miscarriage of justice has come to be committed. And the evidence as to Dreyfus's character, his financial situation, his lack of motives, the fact that he has never ceased to clamor his innocence — all these demonstrate that he has been a victim of Major du Paty de Clam's overheated imagination, and of the clericalism that prevails in the military circles in which he moves, and of the hysterical hunt for "dirty Jews" that disgraces our times. . . .

. . .

As I have already shown, the Dreyfus Affair was the affair of the War Office: an officer from the General Staff denounced by his fellow officers on the General Staff, sentenced under pressure from the Chiefs of the General Staff. And I repeat, he cannot emerge from his trial innocent without all of the General Staff being guilty. Which is why the War Office employed every means imaginable — campaigns in the press, statements and innuendoes, every type of influence — to cover Esterhazy, in order to convict Dreyfus a second time. . . . Where, oh where is a strong and wisely patriotic ministry that will be bold enough to overhaul the whole system and make a fresh start? I know many people who tremble with alarm at the thought of a possible war, knowing what hands our national defense is in! and what a den of sneaking intrigue, rumor-mongering and back-biting that sacred chapel has become — yet that is where the fate of our country is decided! People take fright at the appalling light that has just been shed on it all by the Dreyfus Affair, that tale of human sacrifice! Yes, an unfortunate, a "dirty Jew" has been sacrificed. Yes, what an accumulation of madness, stupidity, unbridled imagination, low police tactics, inquisitorial and tyrannical methods this handful of officers have got away with! They have crushed the nation under their boots, stuffing its calls for truth and justice down its throat on the fallacious and sacrilegious pretext that they are acting for the good of the country!

And they have committed other crimes. They have based their action on the foul press and let themselves be defended by all the rogues in Paris — and now the rogues are triumphant and insolent while law and integrity go down in defeat. It is a crime to have accused individuals of rending France apart when all those individuals ask for is a generous nation at the head of the procession of free, just nations — and all the while the people who committed that crime were hatching an insolent plot to make the entire world swallow a fabrication. It is a crime to lead public opinion astray, to manipulate it for a death-dealing purpose and pervert it to the point of delirium. It is a crime to poison the minds of the humble, ordinary people, to whip reactionary and intolerant passions into a frenzy while sheltering behind the odious bastion of anti-Semitism. France, the great and liberal cradle of the rights of man, will die of anti-Semitism if it is not cured of it. It is a crime to play on patriotism to further the aims of hatred. And it is a crime to worship the saber as a modern god when all of human science is laboring to hasten the triumph of truth and justice. . . .

That, M. le Président, is the plain truth. It is appalling. It will remain an indelible blot on your term as President. Oh, I know that you are powerless to deal with it, that you are the prisoner of the Constitution and of the people nearest to you. But as a man, your duty is clear, and you will not overlook it, and you will do your duty. Not for one minute do I despair that truth will triumph. I am confident and I repeat, more vehemently even than before, the truth is on the march and nothing shall stop it. The Affair is only just beginning, because only now have the positions become crystal clear: on the one hand, the guilty parties, who do not want the truth to be revealed; on the other, the defenders of justice, who will give their lives to see that justice is done. I have said it elsewhere and I repeat it here: if the truth is buried underground, it swells and grows and becomes so explosive that the day it bursts, it blows everything wide open along with it. Time will tell; we shall see whether we have not prepared, for some later date, the most resounding disaster.

. . .

But this letter has been a long one, M. le Président, and it is time to bring it to a close.

I accuse Lt-Col du Paty de Clam of having been the diabolical agent of a miscarriage of justice (though unwittingly, I am willing to believe) and then of having defended his evil deed for the past three years through the most preposterous and most blameworthy machinations.

I accuse General Mercier of having been an accomplice, at least by weak-mindedness, to one of the most iniquitous acts of this century.

I accuse General Billot of having had in his hands undeniable proof that Dreyfus was innocent and of having suppressed it, of having committed this crime against justice and against humanity for political purposes, so that the General Staff, which had been compromised, would not lose face.

I accuse Generals de Boisdeffre and Gonse of having been accomplices to this same crime, one out of intense clerical conviction, no doubt, and the other perhaps because of the esprit de corps which makes the War Office the Holy of Holies and hence unattackable.

I accuse General de Pellieux and Major Ravary of having led a villainous inquiry, by which I mean a most monstrously one-sided inquiry, the report on which, by Ravary, constitutes an imperishable monument of naive audacity.

I accuse the three handwriting experts, Messrs Belhomme, Varinard, and Couard, of having submitted fraudulent and deceitful reports — unless a medical examination concludes that their eyesight and their judgment were impaired.

I accuse the War Office of having conducted an abominable campaign in the press (especially in *L'Eclair* and *L'Echo de Paris*) in order to cover up its misdeeds and lead public opinion astray.

Finally, I accuse the first court martial of having violated the law by sentencing a defendant on the basis of a document which remained secret, and I accuse the second court martial of having covered up that illegal action, on orders, by having, in its own turn, committed the judicial crime of knowingly acquitting a guilty man.

In making these accusations, I am fully aware that my action comes under Articles 30 and 31 of the law of 29 July 1881 on the press, which makes libel a punishable offense. I deliberately expose myself to that law.

As for the persons I have accused, I do not know them; I have never seen them; I feel no rancor or hatred towards them. To me, they are mere entities, mere embodiments of social malfeasance. And the action I am taking here is merely a revolutionary means to hasten the revelation of truth and justice.

I have but one goal: that light be shed, in the name of mankind which has suffered so much and has the right to happiness. My ardent protest is merely a cry from my very soul. Let them dare to summon me before a court of law! Let the inquiry be held in broad daylight!

I am waiting.

M. le Président, I beg you to accept the assurance of my most profound respect.

DISCUSSION QUESTIONS

1. According to Zola, what motivated the army officers' actions against Dreyfus?

2. What does Zola mean when he describes Dreyfus's conviction and Esterhazy's acquittal as "crimes against society"?

3. Why do you think Zola felt compelled to publicize his views?

4. Many scholars argue that with the rise of mass politics during the late nineteenth century, the press played an increasingly important role in everyday life. In what ways do the form and content of Zola's letter support this argument?

3.
Rising Up against Western Imperialism

The I-ho-ch'uan (Boxers), *The Boxers Demand Death for All "Foreign Devils"* (1900)

Despite Europeans' dominant presence around the globe, at the turn of the twentieth century, their imperial hold in many places was increasingly tenuous as local resistance to foreign rule and interference mounted. The following placard, written and circulated by the Boxers at the height of their mass revolt in 1900, exposes the beliefs driving one such uprising in China, where European nations had recently made significant inroads. Lashing out against "foreign devils," the Boxers burned churches, destroyed telegraph lines and railways, and murdered Chinese

From Louis L. Snyder, ed., *The Imperialism Reader: Documents and Readings on Modern Expansionism* (Princeton: Van Nostrand, 1962), 322–23.

Christians and missionaries. As the document reveals, an amalgam of distinctive spiritual values and overt hostility to the trappings of modern "progress" fueled the Boxers' actions. Although brutally repressed, the Boxer Rebellion strengthened Chinese nationalist sentiment, which ultimately undermined Western imperialism in China.

The Gods assist the Boxers,
The Patriotic Harmonious corps,
It is because the "Foreign Devils" disturb the "Middle Kingdom."
Urging the people to join their religion,
To turn their backs on Heaven,
Venerate not the Gods and forget the ancestors.

Men violate the human obligations,
Women commit adultery,
"Foreign Devils" are not produced by mankind,
If you do not believe,
Look at them carefully.

The eyes of all the "Foreign Devils" are bluish,
No rain falls,
The earth is getting dry,
This is because the churches stop Heaven,
The Gods are angry;
The Genii are vexed;
Both come down from the mountain to deliver the doctrine.

This is no hearsay,
The practices of boxing will not be in vain;
Reciting incantations and pronouncing magic words,
Burn up yellow written prayers,
Light incense sticks
To invite the Gods and Genii of all the grottoes.

The Gods come out from grottoes,
The Genii come down from mountains,
Support the human bodies to practice the boxing.
When all the military accomplishments or tactics
Are fully learned,
It will not be difficult to exterminate the "Foreign Devils" then.

Push aside the railway tracks,
Pull out the telegraph poles,
Immediately after this destroy the steamers.

The great France
Will grow cold and downhearted.
The English and Russians will certainly disperse.
Let the various "Foreign Devils" all be killed.
May the whole Elegant Empire of the Great Ching Dynasty be ever prosperous!

DISCUSSION QUESTIONS

1. Why do the Boxers describe foreigners as "devils"?

2. What forces do the Boxers believe are on their side?

3. In addition to killing foreigners, why do you think the Boxers called for an attack on railways, telegraph lines, and steamers?

4. What type of society do the Boxers desire for China?

4.
Militant Suffrage

Emmeline Pankhurst, *Speech from the Dock* (1908)

By granting working-class men the vote in 1884, the British government hoped to make politics more unified and orderly. Yet the realization of such hopes proved elusive, in part because a new political foe had appeared on the scene: the women's suffrage movement. The founder of the Women's Social and Political Union (WSPU), Emmeline Pankhurst (1858–1928), was among the most influential voices of the movement. Although women in Britain had long been fighting for rights, the expansion of the male electorate further accentuated their political exclusion. In the following speech before a police court judge, Pankhurst defends the WSPU's tactics, which had become increasingly militant since its inception in 1903. She and two colleagues had been arrested for distributing a leaflet encouraging her supporters "to rush the House of Commons," and they faced a prison sentence for refusing to "bind themselves over" — in other words, to promise to behave properly. Pankhurst's speech reflects her belief that the WSPU's struggle was more than a quest for the vote; it was a war against a patriarchical society.

Ever since my girlhood, a period of about 30 years, I have belonged to organizations to secure for women that political power which I have felt was essential to bringing about those reforms which women need. I have tried constitutional methods. I have been womanly. When you spoke to some of my colleagues the day before yesterday about their being unwomanly, I felt that bitterness which I know every one of them felt in their hearts. We have tried to be womanly, we have tried to use

---

From Emmeline Pankhurst, "Speech from the Dock [Police Court]," in *Votes for Women* (October 29, 1908), 1.

feminine influence, and we have seen that it is of no use. Men who have been impatient have invariably got reforms for their impatience. And they have not our excuse for being impatient. . . .

Now, while I share in the feeling of indignation which has been expressed to you by my daughter, I have lived longer in the world than she has. Perhaps I can look round the whole question better than she can, but I want to say here, deliberately, to you, that we are here today because we are driven here. We have taken this action, because as women — and I want you to understand it is as women we have taken this action — it is because we realize that the condition of our sex is so deplorable that it is our duty even to break the law in order to call attention to the reasons why we do so.

I do not want to say anything which may seem disrespectful to you, or in any way give you offense, but I do want to say that I wish, sir, that you could put yourself into the place of women for a moment before you decide upon this case. My daughter referred to the way in which women are huddled into and out of these police-courts without a fair trial. I want you to realize what a poor hunted creature, without the advantages we have had, must feel.

I have been in prison. I was in Holloway Gaol for five weeks. I was in various parts of the prison. I was in the hospital, and in the ordinary part of the prison, and I tell you, sir, with as much sense of responsibility as if I had taken the oath, that there were women there who have broken no law, who are there because they have been able to make no adequate statement.

You know that women have tried to do something to come to the aid of their own sex. Women are brought up for certain crimes, crimes which men do not understand — I am thinking especially of infanticide — they are brought before a man judge, before a jury of men, who are called upon to decide whether some poor, hunted woman is guilty of murder or not. I put it to you, sir, when we see in the papers, as we often do, a case similar to that of Daisy Lord, for whom a great petition was got up in this country, I want you to realize how we women feel, because we are women, because we are not men, we need some legitimate influence to bear upon our law-makers.

Now, we have tried every way. We have presented larger petitions than were ever presented for any other reform; we have succeeded in holding greater public meetings than men have ever had for any reform, in spite of the difficulty which women have in throwing off their natural diffidence, that desire to escape publicity which we have inherited from generations of our foremothers; we have broken through that. We have faced hostile mobs at street corners, because we were told that we could not have that representation for our taxes which men have won unless we converted the whole of the country to our side. Because we have done this, we have been misrepresented, we have been ridiculed, we have had contempt poured upon us. The ignorant mob at the street corner has been incited to offer us violence, which we have faced unarmed and unprotected by the safeguards which Cabinet Ministers have. We know that we need the protection of the vote even more than men have needed it.

I am here to take upon myself now, sir, as I wish the prosecution had put upon me, the full responsibility for this agitation in its present phase. I want to address you as a woman who has performed the duties of a woman, and, in addition, has performed the duties which ordinary men have had to perform, by earning a living for her children, and educating them. In addition to that, I have been a public officer. I enjoyed for 10 years an official post under the Registrar, and I performed those duties to the satisfaction of the head of the department. After my duty of taking the census was over, I was one of the few Registrars who qualified for a special bonus, and was specially praised for the way in which the work was conducted. Well, sir, I stand before you, having resigned that office when I was told that I must either do that or give up working for this movement.

I want to make you realize that it is a point of honor that if you decide — as I hope you will not decide — to bind us over, that we shall not sign any undertaking, as the Member of Parliament did who was before you yesterday. Perhaps his reason for signing that undertaking may have been that the Prime Minister had given some assurance to the people he claimed to represent that something should be done for them. We have no such assurance. Mr. Birrell told the women who questioned him the other day that he could not say that anything would be done to give an assurance to the women that their claims should be conceded. So, sir, if you decide against us today, to prison we must go, because we feel that we should be going back to the hopeless condition this movement was in three years ago if we consented to be bound over to keep the peace which we have never broken, and so, sir, if you decide to bind us over, whether it is for three or six months, we shall submit to the treatment, the degrading treatment, that we have submitted to before.

Although the Government admitted that we are political offenders, and, therefore, ought to be treated as political offenders are invariably treated, we shall be treated as pickpockets and drunkards; we shall be searched. I want you, if you can, as a man, to realize what it means to women like us. We are driven to do this, we are determined to go on with agitation, because we feel in honor bound. Just as it was the duty of your forefathers, it is our duty to make this world a better place for women than it is today. . . .

This is the only way we can get that power which every citizen should have of deciding how the taxes she contributes to should be spent, and how the laws she has to obey should be made, and until we get that power we shall be here — we are here today, and we shall come here over and over again. You must realize how futile it is to settle this question by binding us over to keep the peace. You have tried it; it has failed. Others have tried to do it, and have failed. If you had power to send us to prison, not for six months, but for six years, for 16 years, or for the whole of our lives, the Government must not think that they can stop this agitation. It will go on.

I want to draw your attention to the self-restraint which was shown by our followers on the night of the 13th, after we had been arrested. It only shows that our influence over them is very great, because I think that if they had yielded to their natural impulses, there might have been a breach of the peace on the evening of the 13th. They were very indignant, but our words have always been, "be patient, exercise self-restraint, show our so-called superiors that the criticism of women being hysterical is not true; use no violence, offer yourselves to the violence of others." We are going to win. Our women have taken that advice; if we are in prison they will continue to take that advice.

Well, sir, that is all I have to say to you. We are here not because we are law-breakers; we are here in our efforts to become law-makers.

DISCUSSION QUESTIONS

1. How did the WSPU's tactics challenge conventional notions of proper behavior for women at the time?

2. According to Pankhurst, why was the WSPU forced to adopt such tactics?

3. Why did she think that women had both a right to and a need for political enfranchisement?

5.
Tapping the Human Psyche
Sigmund Freud, *The Interpretation of Dreams* (1900)

The fast-paced and conflict-ridden nature of life in industrial Europe undermined many people's optimism about their own and society's future. Austrian doctor Sigmund Freud (1856–1939) developed the method of psychoanalysis to tap into and cure such anxieties. After studying medicine in Vienna, in 1886 Freud opened his own practice to treat patients with nervous disorders. His clinical experience was the basis for his lifelong commitment to the scientific study of the human unconscious. In 1900, he published his most well-known work, The Interpretation of Dreams, *excerpted here. In it, he described dreams as windows into an individual's irrational desires and inner conflicts. Only by drawing out dreams' hidden meanings could a person expose the roots of his or her psychological problems. Psychoanalysis was designed to do just that, thereby laying the foundation of modern psychology.*

In the following pages, I shall demonstrate that there is a psychological technique which makes it possible to interpret dreams, and that on the application of this technique, every dream will reveal itself as a psychological structure, full of significance, and one which may be assigned to a specific place in the psychic activities of the waking state. Further, I shall endeavor to elucidate the processes which underlie the strangeness and obscurity of dreams, and to deduce from these processes the nature of the psychic forces whose conflict or co-operation is responsible for our dreams. . . .

I am proposing to show that dreams are capable of interpretation; and any contributions to the solution of the problem which have already been discussed will emerge only as possible by-products in the accomplishment of my special task. On the hypothesis that dreams are susceptible of interpretation, I at once find my-

A. A. Brill, trans. and ed., *The Basic Writings of Sigmund Freud* (New York: The Modern Library, 1938), 183, 188, 191–94, 208–9.

self in disagreement with the prevailing doctrine of dreams . . . for "to interpret a dream" is to specify its "meaning," to replace it by something which takes its position in the concatenation of our psychic activities as a link of definite importance and value. But, as we have seen, the scientific theories of the dream leave no room for a problem of dream-interpretation; since, in the first place, according to these theories, dreaming is not a psychic activity at all, but a somatic process which makes itself known to the psychic apparatus by means of symbols. . . .

I have, however, come to think differently. . . . I must insist that the dream actually does possess a meaning, and that a scientific method of dream-interpretation is possible. I arrived at my knowledge of this method in the following manner:

For years I have been occupied with the solution of certain psychopathological structures — hysterical phobias, obsessional ideas, and the like — with therapeutic intentions. . . . In the course of these psychoanalytic studies, I happened upon the question of dream-interpretation. My patients, after I had pledged them to inform me of all the ideas and thoughts which occurred to them in connection with a given theme, related their dreams, and thus taught me that a dream may be interpolated in the psychic concatenation, which may be followed backwards from a pathological idea into the patient's memory. The next step was to treat the dream itself as a symptom, and to apply to it the method of interpretation which had been worked out for such symptoms.

For this a certain psychic preparation on the part of the patient is necessary. A twofold effort is made, to stimulate his attentiveness in respect of his psychic perceptions, and to eliminate the critical spirit in which he is ordinarily in the habit of viewing such thoughts as come to the surface. For the purpose of self-observation with concentrated attention it is advantageous that the patient should take up a restful position and close his eyes; he must be explicitly instructed to renounce all criticism of the thought-formations which he may perceive. He must also be told that the success of the psychoanalysis depends upon his noting and communicating everything that passes through his mind, and that he must not allow himself to suppress one idea because it seems to him unimportant or irrelevant to the subject, or another because it seems nonsensical. He must preserve an absolute impartiality in respect to his ideas; for if he is unsuccessful in finding the desired solution of the dream, the obsessional idea, or the like, it will be because he permits himself to be critical of them. . . .

As will be seen, the point is to induce a psychic state which is in some degree analogous, as regards the distribution of psychic energy (mobile attention), to the state of the mind before falling asleep — and also, of course, to the hypnotic state. On falling asleep the "undesired ideas" emerge, owing to the slackening of a certain arbitrary (and, of course, also critical) action, which is allowed to influence the trends of our ideas; we are accustomed to speak of fatigue as the reason of this slackening; the emerging undesired ideas are changed into visual and auditory images. In the condition which it utilized for the analysis of dreams and pathological ideas, this activity is purposely and deliberately renounced, and the psychic energy thus saved (or some part of it) is employed in attentively tracking the undesired thoughts which now come to the surface. . . .

The first step in the application of this procedure teaches us that one cannot make the dream as a whole the object of one's attention, but only the individual components of its content. If I ask a patient who is as yet unpracticed: "What occurs to you in connection with this dream?" he is unable, as a rule, to fix upon anything in his psychic field of vision. I must first dissect the dream for him; then, in connection with each fragment, he gives me a number of ideas which may be described as the "thoughts behind" this part of the dream. In this first and important condition, then, the method of dream-interpretation which I employ diverges from the popular, historical and legendary method of interpretation by symbolism and approaches more nearly to the second or "cipher method." Like this, it is an interpretation in detail, not *en masse*; like this, it conceives the dream, from the outset, as something built up, as a conglomerate of psychic formations. . . .

When, after passing through a narrow defile, one suddenly reaches a height beyond which the ways part and a rich prospect lies outspread in different directions, it is well to stop for a moment and consider whither one shall turn next. We are in somewhat the same position after we have mastered this first interpretation of a dream. We find ourselves standing in the light of a sudden discovery. The dream is not comparable to the irregular sounds of a musical instrument, which, instead of being played by the hand of a musician, is struck by some external force; the dream is not meaningless, not absurd, does not presuppose that one part of our store of ideas is dormant while another part begins to awake. It is a perfectly valid psychic phenomenon, actually a wish-fulfilment; it may be enrolled in the continuity of the intelligible psychic activities of the waking state; it is built up by a highly complicated intellectual activity. . . .

It is easy to show that the wish-fulfilment in dreams is often undisguised and easy to recognize, so that one may wonder why the language of dreams has not long since been understood. There is, for example, a dream which I can evoke as often as I please, experimentally, as it were. If, in the evening, I eat anchovies, olives, or other strongly salted foods, I am thirsty at night, and therefore I wake. The waking, however, is preceded by a dream, which has always the same content, namely, that I am drinking. I am drinking long draughts of water; it tastes as delicious as only a cool drink can taste when one's throat is parched; and then I wake, and find that I have an actual desire to drink. The cause of this dream is thirst, which I perceive when I wake. From this sensation arises the wish to drink and the dream shows me this wish as fulfilled. It thereby serves a function, the nature of which I soon surmise. I sleep well, and am not accustomed to being waked by a bodily need. If I succeed in appeasing my thirst by means of the dream that I am drinking, I need not wake up in order to satisfy my thirst. It is thus a *dream of convenience*. The dream takes the place of action, as elsewhere in life.

DISCUSSION QUESTIONS

1. How did Freud's theory of dream interpretation reject contemporary scientific views about dreams?

2. What does Freud mean when he describes dreams as "wish-fulfilments"?

3. According to Freud, what is the relationship between a person's dreams and his or her waking state?

6.
The Idealized Family

Eugenics Education Society of London,
Eugenics for Citizens: Aim of Eugenics (c. 1907)

In arguing that scientists could — and should — study people's innermost desires, Freud helped to blur the boundaries between public and private life. Marriage and sexuality also came under the spotlight as Europe's falling birthrate sparked concerns that Anglo-Saxons were committing "race suicide" by not having enough children. Social Darwinists were especially vocal in their warnings of racial decay. Among the most

From www.uvm.edu/~eugenics/images/citizens.html. © Galton Institute Archive/ Wellcome Library.

famous of these was Charles Darwin's cousin Sir Francis Galton (1822–1911), who reasoned that society's efforts to protect the weakest, most vulnerable members of humanity were in fact at odds with natural selection — meaning that far from evolving to become a stronger and more talented people, society risked reverting toward mediocrity, or experiencing a "regression toward the mean." Galton created the term eugenics, defining it as "the study of the Agencies under social control, that improve or impair the racial qualities of future generations either physically or mentally." In 1907, friends of Galton's from Cambridge joined with middle-class professional men interested in eugenics to form the Eugenics Education Society, electing Galton as their first president. Their aim was practical rather than scholarly: to spread the wisdom of eugenics as widely as possible in society, with the aim of improving the population as a whole. With this goal in mind, the society published pamphlets, such as the one from which the image on page 209 was taken, to explain eugenic concepts simply enough for all people to understand.

Discussion Questions

1. How does the family in the pamphlet illustration demonstrate the Eugenics Education Society's vision of the ideal man? The ideal woman? The ideal family?

2. Why do you think the illustrator chose to show a family in classical attire rather than in turn-of-the-century clothing?

3. What parallels can be drawn between the turn-of-the-century interest in eugenics and present-day curiosity about the possibilities of genetic engineering?

4. Sir Francis Galton once wrote that eugenics "must be introduced into the national consciousness as a new religion." How might this image inspire religious sentiments?

Comparative Questions

1. In what ways do the documents in this chapter challenge liberal beliefs and values?

2. What might contemporary readers have found unsettling about the idea that women should have the right to vote or that dreams could reveal one's innermost desires? How do these ideas relate to Nietzsche's assertion that "God is dead," or that "there is no land any longer"?

3. What similarities and differences do you see in the documents' depictions of masculinity and femininity?

4. What do these authors' texts suggest about how turn-of-the-century science was used to support arguments about social issues, such as equality of the sexes, racial distinctions, anti-Semitism, and sexuality?

World War I and Its Aftermath, 1914–1929

Contemporaries dubbed World War I the "Great War" with good reason. Over the course of four years, millions died in battle — victims of advanced military technologies, outdated tactics, wretched leadership, and a desire for total victory. The first document allows us to see these horrors through two soldiers' eyes. The second document reveals that civilians contributed to the staggering death toll, for it was they who manufactured the grenades, rifles, and other weapons used on the front with such devastating effects. Yet the war's legacy did not stop there, as the last three documents attest. Civilian protests against the war unleashed the Russian Revolution, which transformed the world's political landscape. To the west, governments faced their own challenges as they struggled under the weight of postwar reconstruction and popular discontent. Among the people who capitalized on these troubled times were Benito Mussolini (1883–1945) and Adolf Hitler (1889–1945), who ushered in a new age of violent dictatorship in Europe.

1.
The Horrors of War

Fritz Franke and Siegfried Sassoon, *Two Soldiers' Views* (1914–1918)

When the war broke out in August 1914, no one foresaw the years of massive destruction and bloodshed that would follow. By late autumn, the two sides were entrenched along a line that extended from France into Belgium, and so the Western Front was born. Here millions of soldiers like Fritz Franke (1892–1915) and Siegfried Sassoon (1886–1967) faced unspeakable horrors. In the following letter written in the war's first months, Franke, a medical student from Berlin, describes trench warfare as a liv-

ing hell of shells and corpses. His description also reveals what already had become and would remain the war's defining feature in the West: immobility and stalemate. Franke paid the ultimate price for both — he was killed in May 1915. By contrast, Sassoon, a British officer, survived and became famous for poems like "Counter-Attack," which describes the war's misery and futility.

Fritz Franke

Louve, November 5th, 1914

Yesterday we didn't feel sure that a single one of us would come through alive. You can't possibly picture to yourselves what such a battle-field looks like. It is impossible to describe it, and even now, when it is a day behind us, I myself can hardly believe that such bestial barbarity and unspeakable suffering are possible. Every foot of ground contested; every hundred yards another trench; and everywhere bodies — rows of them! All the trees shot to pieces; the whole ground churned up a yard deep by the heaviest shells; dead animals; houses and churches so utterly destroyed by shell-fire that they can never be of the least use again. And every troop that advances in support must pass through a mile of this chaos, through this gigantic burial-ground and the reek of corpses.

In this way we advanced on Tuesday, marching for three hours, a silent column, in the moonlight, towards the Front and into a trench as Reserve, two to three hundred yards from the English, close behind our own infantry.

There we lay the whole day, a yard and a half to two yards below the level of the ground, crouching in the narrow trench on a thin layer of straw, in an overpowering din which never ceased all day or the greater part of the night — the whole ground trembling and shaking! There is every variety of sound — whistling, whining, ringing, crashing, rolling . . . the beastly things pitch right above one and burst and the fragments buzz in all directions, and the only question one asks is: "Why doesn't one get me?" Often the things land within a hand's breadth and one just looks on. One gets so hardened to it that at the most one ducks one's head a little if a great, big naval-gun shell comes a bit too near and its grey-green stink is a bit too thick. Otherwise one soon just lies there and thinks of other things. And then one pulls out the Field Regulations or an old letter from home, and all at once one has fallen asleep in spite of the row.

Then suddenly comes the order: "Back to the horses. You are relieved!" And one runs for a mile or so, mounts, and is a gay trooper once more; hola, away, through night and mist, in gallop and in trot!

One just lives from one hour to the next. For instance, if one starts to prepare some food, one never knows if one mayn't have to leave it behind within an hour. If you lie down to sleep, you must always be "in Alarm Order." On the road, you have just to ride behind the man in front of you without knowing where you are going, or at the most only the direction for half a day.

From A. F. Wedd, trans., *German Students' War Letters* (New York: E. P. Dutton, 1929), 123–25.

All the same, there is a lot that is pleasant in it all. We often go careering through lovely country in beautiful weather. And above all one acquires a knowledge of human nature! We all live so naturally and unconventionally here, every one according to his own instincts. That brings much that is good and much that is ugly to the surface, but in every one there is a large amount of truth, and above all strength — strength developed almost to a mania!

Siegfried Sassoon

Counter-Attack

We'd gained our first objective hours before
While dawn broke like a face with blinking eyes,
Pallid, unshaved and thirsty, blind with smoke.
Things seemed all right at first. We held their line,
With bombers posted, Lewis guns well placed,
And clink of shovels deepening the shallow trench.
    The place was rotten with dead; green clumsy legs
    High-booted, sprawled and grovelled along the saps
    And trunks, face downward, in the sucking mud,
    Wallowed like trodden sand-bags loosely filled;
    And naked sodden buttocks, mats of hair,
    Bulged, clotted heads slept in the plastering slime.
    And then the rain began — the jolly old rain!

A yawning soldier knelt against the bank,
Staring across the morning blear with fog;
He wondered when the Allemands would get busy;
And then, of course, they started with five-nines
Traversing, sure as fate, and never a dud.
Mute in the clamor of shells he watched them burst
Spouting dark earth and wire with gusts from hell,
While posturing giants dissolved in drifts of smoke.
He crouched and flinched, dizzy with galloping fear,
Sick for escape — loathing the strangled horror
And butchered, frantic gestures of the dead.

An officer came blundering down the trench:
"Stand-to and man the fire-step!" On he went . . .
Gasping and bawling, "Fire-step . . . counter-attack!"
    Then the haze lifted. Bombing on the right
    Down the old sap: machine-guns on the left;
    And stumbling figures looming out in front.
    "O Christ, they're coming at us!" Bullets spat,

From Siegfried Sassoon, *Collected Poems* (New York: Viking Press, 1949), 68–69.

And he remembered his rifle . . . rapid fire . . .
And started blazing wildly . . . then a bang
Crumpled and spun him sideways, knocked him out
To grunt and wriggle: none heeded him; he choked
And fought the flapping veils of smothering gloom,
Lost in a blurred confusion of yells and groans . . .
Down, and down, and down, he sank and drowned,
Bleeding to death. The counter-attack had failed.

DISCUSSION QUESTIONS

1. Although they fought on opposite sides, what attributes did Franke and Sassoon share?

2. Based on Franke's and Sassoon's descriptions of the battlefront, what physical and psychological effects did trench warfare have on soldiers?

3. How does Franke's letter challenge the Allies' propaganda in which German soldiers were depicted as being devoid of humanity?

2.
Mobilizing for Total War

L. Doriat, *Women on the Home Front* (1917)

The massive mobilization of the homefront made World War I like no other war fought before. Across Europe, thousands of civilians poured into factories to manufacture supplies for the troops. With casualties mounting and more and more men leaving to replenish the armed forces, women became particularly vital to sustaining the wartime labor force. Consequently, new employment opportunities arose for them, especially in traditionally masculine domains such as munitions. The following interview of a French factory worker in the city of Saint-Nazaire in Brittany by journalist L. Doriat puts a human face on this aspect of the war's impact beyond the battlefield. In it, the worker, whom Doriat never identifies, reveals her sense of patriotic duty mingled with her determination not to lose her femininity amid the din and dirt of her job.

The dwelling I enter is tidy, sun lights up the main room and makes the household objects shine; everything speaks of an orderly woman who likes her home. A few flowers in a vase on the table near which she is working prove to me that I was right about the woman I've come to see. The factory has not destroyed her feminine sense of delicacy. Without a hat she seems to me younger; she is sur-

---

From Margaret R. Higonnet, ed., *Lines of Fire: Women Writers of World War I* (New York: Plume, 1999), 129–31.

prised to see me, she confesses, because she doubted I would come. Convalescent, she hasn't worked for a whole month, which is why I am lucky enough to find her.

"The very day after my arrival, I found work, thanks to the foreman of a factory of shells who knew my husband," she hastens to tell me. "There is no comparison between this extremely hard and much more precise work and the little toy-like petards that I was making. Here it's not sheets of white metal but big 120 shells. You must also pay much more attention, a defect is serious. The factory never stops, day and night shifts of eight alternate. It's intensive production; no mawkishness here, we are not women by the arms of the machine. Scarcely any apprenticeship, one or two days and you're set.

"I am in a workshop for tempering the steel, or rather I was — will they give me back my place and my machine when I return to the workshop? At the moment of my accident, which I'll tell you about, I was doing the shop-trial of the steel for the shell, testing or inspecting the casing, of course. Right after the tempering bath, when the steel is still hot and black, the other workers and I had to tap it with a buffing wheel in order to polish the steel on a small surface of the bottom and the ogive of the shell. Doing this we handle at least a thousand shells a day, and as I told you, they are big, very heavy to manipulate. Other workers take these same pieces and make a light mark on the polished area, which must not etch the steel further than a certain depth, in a kind of test; they are equipped with a graduated sheet of metal that lets them evaluate the etched lines. If the mark is too deep, the steel is too soft; if it's too shallow, it is too hard; in either case it can't be used and goes back to be recast. The inspection requires great attentiveness. A final verification is made by a controller and as we are always required to put our number on the pieces that pass through our hands, the imperfections, the errors can be traced to their authors.

"There too you don't talk, you don't even think of it. The deafening noise of the machines, the enormous heat of the ovens near which you work, the swiftness of the movements make this precision work into painful labor. When we do it at night, the glare together with the temperature of the furnace exhausts your strength and burns your eyes. In the morning when you get home, you throw yourself on your bed without even the strength to eat a bite. There are also the lathe workshops, I've never been there; many workers learn quickly to turn a shell without needing to calibrate it; some turners do piece work; they are always the ones who hurt themselves. At the job you become very imprudent, as I told you.

"However, you see, I hurt myself too. Forgetting that my buffing machine does an incalculable number of turns a second, I brushed against it with my arm. Clothing and flesh were all taken off before I even noticed. They had to scrape the bone, bandage me every day, I was afraid of an amputation, which luckily was avoided. Only in the last few days have I been able to go without a sling and use my arm; next week I go back to the workshop. I don't want them to change my job, I'm used to my machine and a fresh apprenticeship would not please me at all. I assure you, the first day I was in this noise, near these enormous blast furnaces, opposite the huge machine at which I had to work for hours, I was afraid. We are all like that, all the more so that we are not given time to reflect. You have to understand and act quickly. Those who lose their heads don't accomplish anything, but they are rare. In general, one week suffices to turn a novice into a skilled worker.

"The foremen scold now and then, but they mustn't count it against us; doesn't everyone know that a man is an apprentice before he becomes a mechanic? But at present, however simplified, however divided up the tasks may be, you become a qualified mechanic right away.

"Yet among us there are women like myself who had never done anything; others who did not know how to sew or embroider; nothing discouraged us. As for me I don't complain, this strained activity pleases me. I can thus forget my loneliness — and not having any children, what else should I do with all my time?

"When the war is over, I will look for a job that corresponds better to my taste. I have enough education to become a cashier in a store. I will then be able to be neater than now, for you can't imagine what care it takes to stay more or less clean if you work in a metallurgy.

"A woman is always a woman; I suffered a lot from remaining for hours with my hands and face dirty with dust and smoke. Everything is a matter of habit; among us there are women who seem fragile and delicate — well! if you saw them at work, you would be stunned: it's a total transformation. As for me, I would never have thought I had so much stamina; when I remember that the least little errand wore me out before, I don't recognize myself. Certainly when the day or the night is over, you go home, the fatigue is great, but we are not more tired than the men are. True, we are more sober because we maintain better hygiene and as a result, our sources of energy are more rational and regular, we don't turn to alcohol for strength.

"Our sense of the present need, of the national peril, of hatred for the enemy, of the courage of our husbands and sons — all this pricks us on, we work with all our heart, with all our strength, with all our soul. It is not necessary to stimulate us, each one is conscious of the task assigned to her and in all simplicity she does it, convinced that she defends her country by forging the arms that will free it. We are very proud of being workers for the national defense."

On that proud phrase, I left this valiant woman, with a warm handshake to thank her and to express my admiration.

DISCUSSION QUESTIONS

1. What does this account suggest about women's role in the war effort?

2. How do both the interviewer and interviewee cast light on people's fears about the war's effects on traditional gender roles?

3. In what ways does this interview reflect the national consensus supporting the war, as fostered by government-directed propaganda campaigns?

3.
Revolutionary Marxism Defended
Vladimir Ilyich Lenin,
Letter to Nikolai Aleksandrovich Rozhkov (January 29, 1919)

As World War I dragged on, European governments faced a new foe in civilian protests. The Russian tsar was especially ill equipped for this challenge, which opened the door to revolution. By the fall of 1917, Vladimir Ilyich Lenin (1870–1924) had emerged as the leading voice of the Russian Revolution and within a matter of months, he and his Bolshevik Party seized complete control of the government. Their takeover plunged Russia into four years of civil war, further exacerbating the country's desperate economic plight. The following document is Lenin's response to a letter from a colleague that encouraged him to assume "personal dictatorship" as a means of setting Russia on the right course. Lenin dismisses the suggestion and reveals his faith in revolutionary Marxism to effect positive change, not only in Russia but also in western Europe. Ironically, several years after Lenin's death, his self-proclaimed successor, Joseph Stalin (1879–1953), instituted just such a dictatorship.

29 January 1919
Nikolai Aleksandrovich!

I was very glad to get your letter — not because of its contents but because I am hoping for a rapprochement on the general factual basis of soviet work.

The situation is not desperate, only difficult. But now there exists very serious hope of improving the food situation thanks to the victories over the counterrevolution in the south and east.

You should not be thinking of free trade — to an economist, of all people, it should be clear that free trade, given the absolute shortage of essential produce, is equivalent to frenzied, brutal speculation and the triumph of the haves over the have-nots. We should not go backward through free trade but forward through the improvement of the state monopoly, toward socialism. It is a difficult transition, but despair is impermissible and unwise. If, instead of serenading free trade, the nonparty intelligentsia or the intelligentsia close to the party would form emergency groups, small groups, and unions for all-around assistance to the food supply, it would seriously help the cause and lessen hunger.

As for "personal dictatorship," excuse the expression, but it is utter nonsense. The apparatus has already become gigantic — in some places excessively so — and under such conditions a "personal dictatorship" is entirely unrealizable and attempts to realize it would only be harmful.

From Richard Pipes, ed., *The Unknown Lenin: From the Secret Archive* (New Haven: Yale University Press, 1999), 62–63.

A turning point has occurred in the intelligentsia. The civil war in Germany and the struggle precisely along the lines of soviet power against "the universal, direct, equal, and secret ballot, that is, against the counter-revolutionary Constituent Assembly" — this struggle in Germany is breaking through even to the most stubborn intelligentsia minds and will succeed in breaking through. This is more visible from the outside. *Nul n'est prophète en son pays.*[1] At home, in Russia, they regarded this as "merely" the "savagery" of Bolshevism. But now history has shown that it is the worldwide collapse of bourgeois democracy and bourgeois parliamentarism, that you cannot get by anywhere without a civil war (*volentem ducunt fata, nolentem trahunt*[2]). The intelligentsia will have to arrive at the position of helping the workers precisely on a Soviet platform.

Then, I think, circles, organizations, committees, free unions, groups, small groups, and gatherings of the intelligentsia will grow like mushrooms and offer their selfless labor in the most difficult posts in food and transportation work. Then we will shorten and ease the birth pangs by months. Because something amazingly good and viable will be born, no matter how difficult those pangs are.

Greetings, N. Lenin

DISCUSSION QUESTIONS

1. On what grounds does Lenin reject the idea of personal dictatorship?

2. Why do you think Lenin is optimistic about the future despite Russia's bleak economic situation?

3. In what ways does this letter reflect Lenin's commitment to Marxist principles?

4.
Establishing Fascism in Italy

Benito Mussolini, *The Doctrine of Fascism* (1932)

Like millions of his fellow Italians, Benito Mussolini (1883–1945) bitterly resented the outcome of World War I. The Allies had reneged on many of their territorial promises, and Italy's economy was in shambles. Mussolini tapped into these waves of discontent when, in 1919, he founded the Fascist movement, comprising former socialists, war veterans, and others who embraced the radical right as the new symbol of authority and strength. Blaming the parliamentary government for the country's ills, the Fascists marched on Rome in 1922 to take matters into their own hands.

From Michael Oakeshott, ed. and trans., *The Social and Political Doctrines of Contemporary Europe* (Cambridge: Cambridge University Press, 1947), 164–79.

[1]"No one is a prophet in his own country."
[2]"Fate leads the willing and drags the unwilling."

Upon the king's request, Mussolini became prime minister. This marked the beginning of Mussolini's rise to political power. The following excerpt from an article by Mussolini, first published in the Enciclopedia Italiana *in 1932, illuminates the basic ideological contours of Fascism as they had developed during the first decade of his authoritarian rule.*

Fundamental Ideas

7. Against individualism, the Fascist conception is for the State; and it is for the individual in so far as he coincides with the State, which is the conscience and universal will of man in his historical existence. It is opposed to classical Liberalism, which arose from the necessity of reacting against absolutism, and which brought its historical purpose to an end when the State was transformed into the conscience and will of the people. Liberalism denied the State in the interests of the particular individual; Fascism reaffirms the State as the true reality of the individual. And if liberty is to be the attribute of the real man, and not of that abstract puppet envisaged by individualistic Liberalism, Fascism is for liberty. And for the only liberty which can be a real thing, the liberty of the State and of the individual within the State. Therefore, for the Fascist, everything is in the State, and nothing human or spiritual exists, much less has value, outside the State. In this sense Fascism is totalitarian, and the Fascist State, the synthesis and unity of all values, interprets, develops, and gives strength to the whole life of the people.

8. Outside the State there can be neither individuals nor groups (political parties, associations, syndicates, classes). Therefore Fascism is opposed to Socialism, which confines the movement of history within the class struggle and ignores the unity of classes established in one economic and moral reality in the State; and analogously it is opposed to class syndicalism. Fascism recognizes the real exigencies for which the socialist and syndicalist movement arose, but while recognizing them wishes to bring them under the control of the State and give them a purpose within the corporative system of interests reconciled within the unity of the State.

9. Individuals form classes according to the similarity of their interests, they form syndicates according to differentiated economic activities within these interests; but they form first, and above all, the State, which is not to be thought of numerically as the sum-total of individuals forming the majority of a nation. And consequently Fascism is opposed to Democracy, which equates the nation to the majority, lowering it to the level of that majority; nevertheless it is the purest form of democracy if the nation is conceived, as it should be, qualitatively and not quantitatively, as the most powerful idea (most powerful because most moral, most coherent, most true) which acts within the nation as the conscience and the will of a few, even of One, which ideal tends to become active within the conscience and the will of all — that is to say, of all those who rightly constitute a nation by reason of nature, history or race, and have set out upon the same line of development and spiritual formation as one conscience and one sole will. . . .

Political and Social Doctrine

Fascism is today clearly defined not only as a regime but as a doctrine. And I mean by this that Fascism today, self-critical as well as critical of other movements, has an unequivocal point of view of its own, a criterion, and hence an aim, in face of all the material and intellectual problems which oppress the people of the world. . . .

3. Above all, Fascism, in so far as it considers and observes the future and the development of humanity quite apart from the political considerations of the moment, believes neither in the possibility nor in the utility of perpetual peace. It thus repudiates the doctrine of Pacifism — born of a renunciation of the struggle and an act of cowardice in the face of sacrifice. War alone brings up to their highest tension all human energies and puts the stamp of nobility upon the peoples who have the courage to meet it. All other trials are substitutes, which never really put a man in front of himself in the alternative of life and death. A doctrine, therefore, which begins with a prejudice in favor of peace is foreign to Fascism; as are foreign to the spirit of Fascism. . . .

5. Such a conception of life makes Fascism the precise negation of that doctrine which formed the basis of the so-called Scientific or Marxian Socialism: the doctrine of historical Materialism, according to which the history of human civilizations can be explained only as the struggle of interest between the different social groups and as arising out of change in the means and instruments of production. That economic improvements — discoveries of raw materials, new methods of work, scientific inventions — should have an importance of their own, no one denies, but that they should suffice to explain human history to the exclusion of all other factors is absurd: Fascism believes, now and always, in holiness and in heroism, that is in acts in which no economic motive — remote or immediate — plays a part. With this negation of historical materialism, according to which men would be only by-products of history, who appear and disappear on the surface of the waves while in the depths the real directive forces are at work, there is also denied the immutable and irreparable "class struggle" which is the natural product of this economic conception of history, and above all it is denied that the class struggle can be the primary agent of social changes. . . .

6. After Socialism, Fascism attacks the whole complex of democratic ideologies and rejects them both in their theoretical premises and in their applications or practical manifestations. Fascism denies that the majority, through the mere fact of being a majority, can rule human societies; it denies that this majority can govern by means of a periodical consultation; it affirms the irremediable, fruitful and beneficent inequality of men, who cannot be leveled by such a mechanical and extrinsic fact as universal suffrage. By democratic regimes we mean those in which from time to time the people is given the illusion of being sovereign, while true effective sovereignty lies in other, perhaps irresponsible and secret, forces. Democracy is a regime without a king, but with very many kings, perhaps more exclusive, tyrannical and violent than one king even though a tyrant. . . .

8. In face of Liberal doctrines, Fascism takes up an attitude of absolute op-position both in the field of politics and in that of economics. It is not necessary to exaggerate — merely for the purpose of present controversies — the impor-tance of Liberalism in the past century, and to make of that which was one of the numerous doctrines sketched in that century a religion of humanity for all times, present and future. . . . The "Liberal" century, after having accumulated an infin-ity of Gordian knots, tried to untie them by the hecatomb of the World War. Never before has any religion imposed such a cruel sacrifice. Were the gods of Liberal-ism thirsty for blood? Now Liberalism is about to close the doors of its deserted temples because the peoples feel that its agnosticism in economics, its indifferent-ism in politics and in morals, would lead, as they have led, the States to certain ruin. In this way one can understand why all the political experiences of the con-temporary world are anti-Liberal, and it is supremely ridiculous to wish on that account to class them outside of history; as if history were a hunting ground re-served to Liberalism and its professors, as if Liberalism were the definitive and no longer surpassable message of civilization. . . .

If it is admitted that the nineteenth century has been the century of Socialism, Liberalism, and Democracy, it does not follow that the twentieth must also be the century of Liberalism, Socialism, and Democracy. Political doctrines pass; peoples remain. It is to be expected that this century may be that of authority, a century of the "Right," a Fascist century. If the nineteenth was the century of the individual (Liberalism means individualism) it may be expected that this one may be the cen-tury of "collectivism" and therefore the century of the State. . . .

10. The keystone of Fascist doctrine is the conception of the State, of its essence, of its tasks, of its ends. For Fascism the State is an absolute before which individu-als and groups are relative. Individuals and groups are "thinkable" in so far as they are within the State. The Liberal State does not direct the interplay and the mate-rial and spiritual development of the groups, but limits itself to registering the re-sults; the Fascist State has a consciousness of its own, a will of its own, on this account it is called an "ethical" State. In 1929, at the first quinquennial assembly of the regime, I said: "For Fascism, the State is not the night-watchman who is con-cerned only with the personal security of the citizens; nor is it an organization for purely material ends, such as that of guaranteeing a certain degree of prosperity and a relatively peaceful social order, to achieve which a council of administration would be sufficient, nor is it a creation of mere politics with no contact with the ma-terial and complex reality of the lives of individuals and the life of peoples. The State, as conceived by Fascism and as it acts, is a spiritual and moral fact because it makes concrete the political, juridical, economic organization of the nation and such an organization is, in its origin and in its development, a manifestation of the spirit. The State is the guarantor of internal and external security, but it is also the guardian and the transmitter of the spirit of the people as it has been elaborated through the centuries in language, custom, faith. The State is not only present, it is also past, and above all future. It is the State which, transcending the brief limit of individual lives, represents the immanent conscience of the nation. The forms in

which States express themselves change, but the necessity of the State remains. It is the State which educates citizens for civic virtue, makes them conscious of their mission, calls them to unity; harmonizes their interests in justice; hands on the achievements of thought in the sciences, the arts, in law, in human solidarity; it carries men from the elementary life of the tribe to the highest human expression of power which is Empire; it entrusts to the ages the names of those who died for its integrity or in obedience to its laws; it puts forward as an example and recommends to the generations that are to come the leaders who increased its territory and the men of genius who gave it glory. When the sense of the State declines and the disintegrating and centrifugal tendencies of individuals and groups prevail, national societies move to their decline."

11. From 1929 up to the present day these doctrinal positions have been strengthened by the whole economico-political evolution of the world. It is the State alone that grows in size, in power. It is the State alone that can solve the dramatic contradictions of capitalism. What is called the crisis cannot be overcome except by the State, within the State. . . . Fascism desires the State to be strong, organic, and at the same time founded on a wide popular basis. The Fascist State has also claimed for itself the field of economics and, through the corporative, social and educational institutions which it has created, the meaning of the State reaches out to and includes the farthest off-shoots; and within the State, framed in their respective organizations, there revolve all the political, economic and spiritual forces of the nation. A State founded on millions of individuals who recognize it, feel it, are ready to serve it, is not the tyrannical State of the medieval lord. It has nothing in common with the absolutist States that existed either before or after 1789. In the Fascist State the individual is not suppressed, but rather multiplied, just as in a regiment a soldier is not weakened but multiplied by the number of his comrades. The Fascist State organizes the nation, but it leaves sufficient scope to individuals; it has limited useless or harmful liberties and has preserved those that are essential. It cannot be the individual who decides in this matter, but only the State. . . .

13. The Fascist State is a will to power and to government. In it the tradition of Rome is an idea that has force. In the doctrine of Fascism Empire is not only a territorial, military or mercantile expression, but spiritual or moral. One can think of an empire, that is to say a nation that directly or indirectly leads other nations, without needing to conquer a single square kilometer of territory. For Fascism the tendency to Empire, that is to say, to the expansion of nations, is a manifestation of vitality; its opposite, staying at home, is a sign of decadence: peoples who rise or re-rise are imperialist, peoples who die are denunciatory. Fascism is the doctrine that is most fitted to represent the aims, the states of mind, of a people, like the Italian people, rising again after many centuries of abandonment or slavery to foreigners. But Empire calls for discipline, coordination of forces, duty, and sacrifice; this explains many aspects of the practical working of the regime and the direction of many of the forces of the State and the necessary severity shown to those who would wish to oppose this spontaneous and destined impulse of the Italy of the twentieth century, to oppose it in the name of the superseded ideologies of the nineteenth, repudiated wherever great experiments of political and social transformation have

been courageously attempted: especially where, as now, peoples thirst for authority, for leadership, for order. If every age has its own doctrine, it is apparent from a thousand signs that the doctrine of the present age is Fascism. That it is a doctrine of life is shown by the fact that it has resuscitated a faith. That this faith has conquered minds is proved by the fact that Fascism has had its dead and its martyrs.

Fascism henceforward has in the world the universality of all those doctrines which, by fulfilling themselves, have significance in the history of the human spirit.

DISCUSSION QUESTIONS

1. According to Mussolini, how is Fascism opposed to liberalism, democracy, and socialism? How is this opposition rooted in Mussolini's concept of the individual's role in the Fascist state?

2. What does Mussolini mean when he describes Fascism as "totalitarian"?

3. As elaborated here, in what ways were Mussolini's principles rooted in the legacy of World War I?

5.
A New Form of Anti-Semitism

Adolf Hitler, *Mein Kampf* (1925)

In 1923, Adolf Hitler (1889–1945) was sentenced to five years in prison at Landsberg Castle for his participation in the "Beer Hall Putsch," an attempt by his National Socialist Party to overthrow the German Democratic national government. He was treated well in prison and received many guests as he strolled the castle grounds. When a friend suggested that he write his autobiography to pass the time, Hitler was skeptical; although a gifted orator, he had written very little. After Hitler's fellow inmate, Rudolf Hess (1894–1987), agreed to transcribe it for him, however, Hitler dictated the book. Originally titled Four Years of Struggle Against Lies, Stupidity, and Cowardice, *it was published in 1925 as* My Struggle (Mein Kampf). *In it, Hitler attributed most human achievements to the German race — he called it the "Aryan" race — and argued that it had a duty to dominate the planet. The Jews, conversely, were held responsible for what Hitler viewed as the world's worst problems, including communism, modern art, pornography, prostitution, and Germany's defeat in World War I.*

Nation and Race

It is idle to argue which race or races were the original representative of human culture and hence the real founders of all that we sum up under the word "humanity." It is simpler to raise this question with regard to the present, and here

From Adolf Hitler, *Mein Kampf,* trans. Ralph Manheim (Boston: Houghton Mifflin, 1999), 290, 300, 303, 326, 643, 646, 649, 651–53.

an easy, clear answer results. All the human culture, all the results of art, science, and technology that we see before us today, are almost exclusively the creative product of the Aryan. This very fact admits of the not unfounded inference that he alone was the founder of all higher humanity, therefore representing the prototype of all that we understand by the word "man." He is the Prometheus of mankind from whose bright forehead the divine spark of genius has sprung at all times, forever kindling anew that fire of knowledge which illumined the night of silent mysteries and thus caused man to climb the path of mastery over the other beings of this earth. . . .

The mightiest counterpart to the Aryan is represented by the Jew. . . . Not through him does any progress of mankind occur, but in spite of him. . . .

He works systematically for revolutionization in a twofold sense: economic and political.

Around peoples who offer too violent a resistance to attack from within he weaves a net of enemies, thanks to his international influence, incites them to war, and finally, if necessary, plants the flag of revolution on the very battlefields.

In economics he undermines the states until the social enterprises which have become unprofitable are taken from the state and subjected to his financial control.

In the political field he refuses the state the means for its self-preservation, destroys the foundations of all national self-maintenance and defense, destroys faith in the leadership, scoffs at its history and past, and drags everything that is truly great into the gutter.

Culturally he contaminates art, literature, the theater, makes a mockery of natural feeling, overthrows all concepts of beauty and sublimity, of the noble and the good, and instead drags men down into the sphere of his own base nature.

Religion is ridiculed, ethics and morality represented as outmoded, until the last props of a nation in its struggle for existence in this world have fallen. . . .

Eastern Orientation or Eastern Policy

Only an adequately large space on this earth assures a nation of freedom of existence. . . .

The National Socialist movement must strive to eliminate the disproportion between our population and our area — viewing this latter as a source of food as well as a basis for power politics — between our historical past and the hopelessness of our present impotence. And in this it must remain aware that we, as guardians of the highest humanity on this earth, are bound by the highest obligation, and the more it strives to bring the German people to racial awareness so that, in addition to breeding dogs, horses, and cats, they will have mercy on their *own* blood, the more it will be able to meet this obligation.

. . . The demand for restoration of the frontiers of 1914 is a political absurdity of such proportions and consequences as to make it seem a crime. Quite aside from the fact that

the Reich's frontiers in 1914 were anything but logical. For in reality they were neither complete in the sense of embracing the people of German nationality, nor sensible with regard to geo-military expediency. They were not the result of a considered political action, but momentary frontiers in a political struggle that was by no means concluded; partly, in fact, they were the results of chance. . . .

. . . Moreover, the times have changed since the Congress of Vienna: *Today it is not princes and princes' mistresses who haggle and bargain over state borders; it is the inexorable Jew who struggles for his domination over the nations.* No nation can remove this hand from its throat except by the sword. Only the assembled and concentrated might of a national passion rearing up in its strength can defy the international enslavement of peoples. Such a process is and remains a bloody one.

If, however, we harbor the conviction that the German future, regardless what happens, demands the supreme sacrifice, quite aside from all considerations of political expediency as such, we must set up an aim worthy of this sacrifice and fight for it. . . .

And I must sharply attack those folkish pen-pushers who claim to regard such an acquisition of soil as a "breach of sacred human rights" and attack it as such in their scribblings. One never knows who stands behind these fellows. But one thing is certain, that the confusion they can create is desirable and convenient to our national enemies. By such an attitude they help to weaken and destroy from within our people's will for the only correct way of defending their vital needs. For no people on this earth possesses so much as a square yard of territory on the strength of a higher will or superior right. Just as Germany's frontiers are fortuitous frontiers, momentary frontiers in the current political struggle of any period, so are the boundaries of other nations' living space. And just as the shape of our earth's surface can seem immutable as granite only to the thoughtless soft-head, but in reality only represents at each period an apparent pause in a continuous development, created by the mighty forces of Nature in a process of continuous growth, only to be transformed or destroyed tomorrow by greater forces, likewise the boundaries of living spaces in the life of nations.

DISCUSSION QUESTIONS

1. How do the ideas of race and land acquisition intersect in Hitler's strategy for German domination of the world?

2. In this excerpt, how does Hitler both anticipate and respond to criticism of the genocidal action he prescribes?

3. What does Hitler's response to the so-called "folkish pen-pushers" betray about his attitude toward parliamentary democracy?

COMPARATIVE QUESTIONS

1. In what ways did communist and Fascist ideology offer radically different solutions to similar problems?

2. What do Franke, Sassoon, and the French factory worker reveal about the role of technology in World War I?

3. What specific facets of liberal ideology did Lenin, Mussolini, and Hitler reject, and why?

4. Compare and contrast Mussolini's conception of "vitality" with Hitler's ideas of "race." What does this suggest about the similarities and differences between German and Italian Fascism?

An Age of Catastrophes, 1929–1945

The Great Depression of the 1930s ushered in an age of unprecedented violence and suffering around the globe. Millions were out of work, hungry, and disillusioned. Authoritarian leaders capitalized on the downhearted, gaining widespread support with their promises to revive the economy and to restore national glory. As the first document vividly shows, the Nazi party, led by Adolf Hitler (1889–1945), was one of the most menacing of these new political forces. Western democracies responded cautiously to the Nazis, hoping to contain Hitler's ambition through a policy of appeasement rather than military might. The second document illustrates this policy in action at a critical juncture in Hitler's march toward war. Not everyone passively accepted the Fascists' rise to power, however. For example, European and North American citizens formed international brigades in Spain to fight the threat of Fascism there, as the third document illustrates. Although the ensuing civil war was dreadful in its destruction, no one was truly prepared for the horrors of World War II. The last two documents reveal that the combination of ideology and advanced technology that fueled the war was especially cruel to the civilian population, setting a dangerous precedent for the future.

1.
Socialist Nationalism
Joseph Goebbels, *Nazi Propaganda Pamphlet* (1930)

Perhaps no one better personifies the power of authoritarian rulers to manipulate the minds of millions in the 1930s than Adolf Hitler (1889–1945). Among the secrets of Hitler's success was his propaganda chief, Joseph Goebbels (1895–1945). A member of the National Socialist Party since 1922, Goebbels shared Hitler's belief that the masses were easily managed if the message directed to them was simple and repetitive. To this

From Louis L. Snyder, ed., *Documents of German History* (New Brunswick: Rutgers University Press, 1958), 414–16.

end, Goebbels wrote pamphlets, such as the one that follows, in support of the Nazi cause. In it, he reveals the virulent anti-Semitism that shaped the Nazis' political program and set them apart from other totalitarian regimes. Goebbels's tactics helped propel Hitler to national leadership in 1933.

WHY ARE WE NATIONALISTS?

We are NATIONALISTS because we see in the NATION the only possibility for the protection and the furtherance of our existence.

The NATION is the organic bond of a people for the protection and defense of their lives. He is nationally minded who understands this IN WORD AND IN DEED.

Today, in GERMANY, NATIONALISM has degenerated into BOURGEOIS PATRIOTISM, and its power exhausts itself in tilting at windmills. It says GERMANY and means MONARCHY. It proclaims FREEDOM and means BLACK-WHITE-RED.

Young nationalism has its unconditional demands. BELIEF IN THE NATION is a matter of all the people, not for individuals of rank, a class, or an industrial clique. The eternal must be separated from the contemporary. The maintenance of a rotten industrial system has nothing to do with nationalism. I can love Germany and hate capitalism; not only CAN I do it, I also MUST do it. The germ of the rebirth of our people LIES ONLY IN THE DESTRUCTION OF THE SYSTEM OF PLUNDERING THE HEALTHY POWER OF THE PEOPLE.

WE ARE NATIONALISTS BECAUSE WE, AS GERMANS, LOVE GERMANY. And because we love Germany, we demand the protection of its national spirit and we battle against its destroyers.

WHY ARE WE SOCIALISTS?

We are SOCIALISTS because we see in SOCIALISM the only possibility for maintaining our racial existence and through it the reconquest of our political freedom and the rebirth of the German state. SOCIALISM has its peculiar form first of all through its comradeship in arms with the forward-driving energy of a newly awakened nationalism. Without nationalism it is nothing, a phantom, a theory, a vision of air, a book. With it, it is everything, THE FUTURE, FREEDOM, FATHERLAND!

It was a sin of the liberal bourgeoisie to overlook THE STATE-BUILDING POWER OF SOCIALISM. It was the sin of MARXISM to degrade SOCIALISM to a system of MONEY AND STOMACH.

We are SOCIALISTS because for us THE SOCIAL QUESTION IS A MATTER OF NECESSITY AND JUSTICE, and even beyond that A MATTER FOR THE VERY EXISTENCE OF OUR PEOPLE.

SOCIALISM IS POSSIBLE ONLY IN A STATE WHICH IS FREE INSIDE AND OUTSIDE.

DOWN WITH POLITICAL BOURGEOIS SENTIMENT: FOR REAL NATIONALISM!

DOWN WITH MARXISM: FOR TRUE SOCIALISM!

UP WITH THE STAMP OF THE FIRST GERMAN NATIONAL SOCIALIST STATE!

AT THE FRONT THE NATIONAL SOCIALIST GERMAN WORKERS PARTY! . . .

WHY DO WE OPPOSE THE JEWS?

We are ENEMIES OF THE JEWS, because we are fighters for the freedom of the German people. THE JEW IS THE CAUSE AND THE BENEFICIARY OF OUR MISERY. He has used the social difficulties of the broad masses of our people to deepen the unholy split between Right and Left among our people. He has made two halves of Germany. He is the real cause for our loss of the Great War.

The Jew has no interest in the solution of Germany's fateful problems. He CANNOT have any. FOR HE LIVES ON THE FACT THAT THERE HAS BEEN NO SOLUTION. If we would make the German people a unified community and give them freedom before the world, then the Jew can have no place among us. He has the best trumps in his hands when a people lives in inner and outer slavery. THE JEW IS RESPONSIBLE FOR OUR MISERY AND HE LIVES ON IT.

That is the reason why we, AS NATIONALISTS and AS SOCIALISTS, oppose the Jew. HE HAS CORRUPTED OUR RACE, FOULED OUR MORALS, UNDERMINED OUR CUSTOMS, AND BROKEN OUR POWER.

THE JEW IS THE PLASTIC DEMON OF THE DECLINE OF MANKIND.

THE JEW IS UNCREATIVE. He produces nothing. HE ONLY HANDLES PRODUCTS. As long as he struggles against the state, HE IS A REVOLUTIONARY; as soon as he has power, he preaches QUIET AND ORDER, so that he can consume his plunder at his convenience.

ANTI-SEMITISM IS UN-CHRISTIAN. That means, then, that he is a Christian who looks on while the Jew sews straps around our necks. TO BE A CHRISTIAN MEANS: LOVE THY NEIGHBOR AS THYSELF! MY NEIGHBOR IS ONE WHO IS TIED TO ME BY HIS BLOOD. IF I LOVE HIM, THEN I MUST HATE HIS ENEMIES. HE WHO THINKS GERMAN MUST DESPISE THE JEWS. The one thing makes the other necessary.

WE ARE ENEMIES OF THE JEWS BECAUSE WE BELONG TO THE GERMAN PEOPLE. THE JEW IS OUR GREATEST MISFORTUNE.

It is not true that we eat a Jew every morning at breakfast.

It is true, however, that he SLOWLY BUT SURELY ROBS US OF EVERYTHING WE OWN.

THAT WILL STOP, AS SURELY AS WE ARE GERMANS.

DISCUSSION QUESTIONS

1. According to this pamphlet, what do the terms *nationalist* and *socialist* mean within the context of the Nazi Party?

2. Why do you think the pamphlet targets Jews as enemies of the German people?

3. What does the pamphlet suggest about the link between the Nazis' racial views and their goals for Germany's future?

2.
Seeking a Diplomatic Solution

Neville Chamberlain, *Speech on the Munich Crisis* (1938)

During the troubled 1930s, many Europeans' deep longing for peace clouded their ability to see the true nature of the Nazi threat. The British politician Neville Chamberlain (1869–1940) was no exception. He became prime minister in 1937 when Hitler's preparations for war were well under way. After annexing Austria in March 1938, Hitler turned to his next target, Czechoslovakia. Chamberlain, Benito Mussolini (1883–1945), and French premier Edouard Daladier (1884–1970) met with Hitler in Munich in September 1938 to defuse the situation; their meeting resulted in an agreement that accepted Germany's territorial claims. In his closing speech, delivered during a debate on the agreement in the House of Commons and excerpted here, Chamberlain defended his policy of appeasement toward Hitler as the key to peace. Tragically, it was instead a prelude to war.

War today — this has been said before, and I say it again — is a different thing not only in degree, but in kind from what it used to be. We no longer think of war as it was in the days of Marlborough or the days of Napoleon or even in the days of 1914. When war starts today, in the very first hour, before any professional soldier, sailor, or airman has been touched, it will strike the workman, the clerk, the man-in-the-street or in the 'bus, and his wife and children in their homes. As I listened I could not help being moved, as I am sure everybody was who heard the hon. Member for Bridgeton (Mr. Maxton) when he began to paint the picture which he himself had seen and realized what it would mean in war — people burrowing underground, trying to escape from poison gas, knowing that at any hour of the day or night death or mutilation was ready to come upon them. Remembering that the dread of what might happen to them or to those dear to them might remain with fathers and mothers for year after year — when you think of these things you cannot ask people to accept a prospect of that kind; you cannot force them into a position that they have got to accept it; unless you feel yourself, and can make them feel, that the cause for which they are going to fight is a vital cause — a cause that transcends all the human values, a cause to which you can point, if some day you win the victory, and say, "That cause is safe."

Since I first went to Berchtesgaden more than 20,000 letters and telegrams have come to No. 10, Downing Street. Of course, I have only been able to look at a tiny fraction of them, but I have seen enough to know that the people who wrote did not feel that they had such a cause for which to fight, if they were asked to go to war in order that the Sudeten Germans might not join the Reich. That is how they are feeling. That is my answer to those who say that we should have told Germany weeks

From *Parliamentary Debates. Fifth Series. Volume 339. House of Commons Official Report* (London, 1938), 544–52.

ago that, if her army crossed the border of Czechoslovakia, we should be at war with her. We had no treaty obligations and no legal obligations to Czechoslovakia and if we had said that, we feel that we should have received no support from the people of this country. . . .

As regards future policy, it seems to me that there are really only two possible alternatives. One of them is to base yourself upon the view that any sort of friendly relations, or possible relations, shall I say, with totalitarian States are impossible, that the assurances which have been given to me personally are worthless, that they have sinister designs and that they are bent upon the domination of Europe and the gradual destruction of democracies. Of course, on that hypothesis, war has got to come, and that is the view — a perfectly intelligible view — of a certain number of hon. and right hon. Gentlemen in this House. I am not sure that it is not the view of some Members of the party opposite. [An HON. MEMBER: "Yes."] Not all of them. They certainly have never put it in so many words, but it is illustrated by the observations of the hon. Member for Derby (Mr. Noel-Baker), who spoke this afternoon, and who had examined the Agreement signed by the German Chancellor and myself, which he described as a pact designed by Herr Hitler to induce us to relinquish our present obligations. That shows how far prejudice can carry a man. The Agreement, as anyone can see, is not a pact at all. So far as the question of "never going to war again" is concerned, it is not even an expression of the opinion of the two who signed the paper, except that it is their opinion of the desire of their respective peoples. I do not know whether the hon. Member will believe me or attribute to me also sinister designs when I tell him that it was a document not drawn up by Herr Hitler but by the humble individual who now addresses this House.

If the view which I have been describing is the one to be taken, I think we must inevitably proceed to the next stage — that war is coming, broadly speaking, the democracies against the totalitarian States — that certainly we must arm ourselves to the teeth, that clearly we must make military alliances with any other Powers whom we can get to work with us, and that we must hope that we shall be allowed to start the war at the moment that suits us and not at the moment that suits the other side. That is what some right hon. and hon. Gentlemen call collective security. Some hon. Members opposite will walk into any trap if it is only baited with a familiar catchword and they do it when this system is called collective security. But that is not the collective security we are thinking of or did think of when talking about the system of the League of Nations. That was a sort of universal collective security in which all nations were to take their part. This plan may give you security; it certainly is not collective in any sense. It appears to me to contain all the things which the party opposite used to denounce before the War — entangling alliances, balance of power and power politics. If I reject it, as I do, it is not because I give it a label; it is because, to my mind, it is a policy of utter despair.

If that is hon. Members' conviction, there is no future hope for civilization or for any of the things that make life worth living. Does the experience of the Great War and of the years that followed it give us reasonable hope that if some new war started that would end war any more than the last one did? No. I do not believe that war is inevitable. . . . It seems to me that the strongest argument against the inevitability of war is to be found in something that everyone has recognized or that has been recognized in every part of the House. That is the universal aversion from war of the people, their hatred of the notion of starting to kill one another again. . . .

What is the alternative to this bleak and barren policy of the inevitability of war? In my view it is that we should seek by all means in our power to avoid war, by analyzing possible causes, by trying to remove them, by discussion in a spirit of collaboration and good will. I cannot believe that such a program would be rejected by the people of this country, even if it does mean the establishment of personal contact with dictators, and of talks man to man on the basis that each, while maintaining his own ideas of the internal government of his country, is willing to allow that other systems may suit better other peoples. . . .

I am told that the policy which I have tried to describe is inconsistent with the continuance, and much more inconsistent with the acceleration of our present program of arms. I am asked how I can reconcile an appeal to the country to support the continuance of this program with the words which I used when I came back from Munich the other day and spoke of my belief that we might have peace for our time. I hope hon. Members will not be disposed to read into words used in a moment of some emotion, after a long and exhausting day, after I had driven through miles of excited, enthusiastic, cheering people — I hope they will not read into those words more than they were intended to convey. I do indeed believe that we may yet secure peace for our time, but I never meant to suggest that we should do that by disarmament, until we can induce others to disarm too. Our past experience has shown us only too clearly that weakness in armed strength means weakness in diplomacy, and if we want to secure a lasting peace, I realize that diplomacy cannot be effective unless the consciousness exists, not here alone, but elsewhere, that behind the diplomacy is the strength to give effect to it.

One good thing, at any rate, has come out of this emergency through which we have passed. It has thrown a vivid light upon our preparations for defense, on their strength and on their weakness. I should not think we were doing our duty if we had not already ordered that a prompt and thorough inquiry should be made to cover the whole of our preparations, military and civil, in order to see, in the light of what has happened during these hectic days, what further steps may be necessary to make good our deficiencies in the shortest possible time. . . .

I cannot help feeling that if, after all, war had come upon us, the people of this country would have lost their spiritual faith altogether. As it turned out the other way, I think we have all seen something like a new spiritual revival, and I know that everywhere there is a strong desire among the people to record their readiness to serve their country, wherever or however their services could be most useful. I would like to take advantage of that strong feeling if it is possible, and although I must frankly say that at this moment I do not myself clearly see my way to any particular scheme, yet I want also to say that I am ready to consider any suggestions that may be made to me, in a very sympathetic spirit.

Finally, I would like to repeat what my right hon. Friend the Chancellor of the Exchequer said yesterday in his great speech. Our policy of appeasement does not mean that we are going to seek new friends at the expense of old ones, or, indeed, at the expense of any other nations at all. I do not think that at any time there has been a more complete identity of views between the French Government and ourselves than there is at the present time. Their objective is the same as ours — to obtain the collaboration of all nations, not excluding the totalitarian States, in building up a lasting peace for Europe.

DISCUSSION QUESTIONS

1. How did Chamberlain justify his policy of appeasement?

2. According to Chamberlain, why did some people oppose a policy of appeasement?

3. What does Chamberlain's defense indicate about popular attitudes toward war and peace?

3.
The Spanish Civil War
Isidora Dolores Ibárruri Gómez,
La Pasionaria's Farewell Address (November 1, 1938)

Isidora Dolores Ibárruri Gómez (1895–1989) was born into a poor family of miners, the eighth of eleven children. At twenty-one, she married a miner who was also a trade union activist. His imprisonment in 1916 led her to become active in politics, and by 1920 she was an elected member of the Basque Communist Party, which was based in northeast Spain. Under the pseudonym "La Pasionaria" ("the Passion Flower"), she published articles in the miners' newspaper, rallying them to the communist cause. She soon rose to the top of the communist leadership and attended meetings of the Comintern as part of the Spanish delegation. A vocal opponent of fascism, she was a passionate orator for the Republicans during the Spanish Civil War, and is probably best remembered for her rallying cry — "It is better to die on your feet than to live on your knees." In the speech that follows, given on November 1, 1938, before a crowd of 15,000 in Barcelona, she praised the efforts of the anti-Fascist International Brigades — 60,000 volunteers who had come from across Europe and North America to fight alongside the Spanish Republicans. The International Brigades were dissolved for diplomatic reasons in late 1938, and many volunteers were arrested on their return home, particularly those from Great Britain because the British government had formally forbidden its citizens to participate in the Spanish Civil War.

It is very difficult to say a few words in farewell to the heroes of the International Brigades, because of what they are and what they represent. A feeling of sorrow, an infinite grief catches our throat — sorrow for those who are going away, for the

---

From Online Journal and Multimedia Companion to Cary Nelson, ed., *Anthology of Modern American Poetry* (www.english.uiuc.edu/maps/scw/farewell.htm).

soldiers of the highest ideal of human redemption, exiles from their countries, persecuted by the tyrants of all peoples — grief for those who will stay here forever mingled with the Spanish soil, in the very depth of our heart, hallowed by our feeling of eternal gratitude.

From all peoples, from all races, you came to us like brothers, like sons of immortal Spain; and in the hardest days of the war, when the capital of the Spanish Republic was threatened, it was you, gallant comrades of the International Brigades, who helped save the city with your fighting enthusiasm, your heroism and your spirit of sacrifice. — And Jarama and Guadalajara, Brunete and Belchite, Levante and the Ebro, in immortal verses sing of the courage, the sacrifice, the daring, the discipline of the men of the International Brigades.

For the first time in the history of the peoples' struggles, there was the spectacle, breathtaking in its grandeur, of the formation of International Brigades to help save a threatened country's freedom and independence — the freedom and independence of our Spanish land.

Communists, Socialists, Anarchists, Republicans — men of different colors, differing ideology, antagonistic religions — yet all profoundly loving liberty and justice, they came and offered themselves to us unconditionally.

They gave us everything — their youth or their maturity; their science or their experience; their blood and their lives; their hopes and aspirations — and they asked us for nothing. But yes, it must be said, they did want a post in battle, they aspired to the honor of dying for us.

Banners of Spain! Salute these many heroes! Be lowered to honor so many martyrs!

Mothers! Women! When the years pass by and the wounds of war are stanched; when the memory of the sad and bloody days dissipates in a present of liberty, of peace and of well-being; when the rancors have died out and pride in a free country is felt equally by all Spaniards, speak to your children. Tell them of these men of the International Brigades.

Recount for them how, coming over seas and mountains, crossing frontiers bristling with bayonets, sought by raving dogs thirsting to tear their flesh, these men reached our country as crusaders for freedom, to fight and die for Spain's liberty and independence threatened by German and Italian fascism. They gave up everything — their loves, their countries, home and fortune, fathers, mothers, wives, brothers, sisters and children — and they came and said to us: "We are here. Your cause, Spain's cause, is ours. It is the cause of all advanced and progressive mankind."

Today many are departing. Thousands remain, shrouded in Spanish earth, profoundly remembered by all Spaniards. Comrades of the International Brigades: Political reasons, reasons of state, the welfare of that very cause for which you offered your blood with boundless generosity, are sending you back, some to your own countries and others to forced exile. You can go proudly. You are history. You are legend. You are the heroic example of democracy's solidarity and universality in the face of the vile and accommodating spirit of those who interpret democratic principles with their eyes on hoards of wealth or corporate shares which they want to safeguard from all risk.

We shall not forget you; and, when the olive tree of peace is in flower, entwined with the victory laurels of the Republic of Spain — return!

Return to our side for here you will find a homeland — those who have no country or friends, who must live deprived of friendship — all, all will have the affection and gratitude of the Spanish people who today and tomorrow will shout with enthusiasm —

Long live the heroes of the International Brigades!

DISCUSSION QUESTIONS

1. How does Ibárruri Gómez's speech reflect the international character of her communist ideology?

2. According to Ibárruri Gómez, why did the volunteers of the International Brigades come to fight in Spain?

3. What role does Ibárruri Gómez think women should play in keeping the memory of the International Brigades' heroism alive, and why is national memory of the International Brigades important?

4. In this speech, Ibárruri Gómez uses the rhetoric of both nationalism and international unity. Is she successful in her effort, or are these ideologies mutually exclusive?

4.
The Final Solution

Sam Bankhalter and Hinda Kibort,
Memories of the Holocaust (1938–1945)

When Neville Chamberlain (1869–1940) detailed the horrors that modern warfare would inflict on civilians, not even he knew how true his words would prove to be. Once the war erupted, one segment of the civilian population in particular was the target of Hitler's fury: Jews. The result was the Final Solution, a technologically and bureaucratically sophisticated system of camps for incarcerating or exterminating European Jews that the Germans put into place between 1941 and 1942. Either inmates were killed on their arrival or spared to endure a different kind of death: starvation, abuse, and overwork. The two interviews that follow allow us to see the Holocaust through the eyes of its victims. The first is that of Sam Bankhalter, who was captured by the Nazis in his native Poland and sent to Auschwitz at age fourteen. The second voice is that of Hinda Kibort, a Lithuanian who was nineteen when the Nazis began their assault on the local Jewish population. In 1944, she was deported to Stutthof, a labor camp in northern Poland.

From Rhoda G. Lewin, *Witnesses to the Holocaust: An Oral History* (Boston: Twayne Publishers, 1990), 5–8, 50–55.

Sam Bankhalter

Lodz, Poland

There was always anti-Semitism in Poland. The slogan even before Hitler was "Jew, get out of here and go to Palestine." As Hitler came to power, there was not a day at school I was not spit on or beaten up.

I was at camp when the Germans invaded Poland. The camp directors told us to find our own way home. We walked many miles with airplanes over our heads, dead people on the streets. At home there were blackouts. I was just a kid, tickled to death when I was issued a flashlight and gas mask. The Polish army was equipped with buggies and horses, the Germans were all on trucks and tanks. The war was over in ten days.

The Ghetto   The German occupation was humiliation from day 1. If Jewish people were wearing the beard and sidecurls, the Germans were cutting the beard, cutting the sidecurls, laughing at you, beating you up a little bit. Then the Germans took part of Lodz and put on barbed wire, and all the Jews had to assemble in this ghetto area. You had to leave in five or ten minutes or half an hour, so you couldn't take much stuff with you. . . .

Auschwitz   We were the first ones in Auschwitz. We built it. What you got for clothing was striped pants and the striped jacket, no underwear, no socks. In wintertime you put paper in your shoes, and we used to take empty cement sacks and put a string in the top, put two together, one in back and one in front, to keep warm.

If they told you to do something, you went to do it. There was no yes or no, no choices. I worked in the crematorium for about eleven months. I saw Dr. Mengele's experiments on children, I knew the kids that became vegetables. Later in Buchenwald I saw Ilse Koch with a hose and regulator, trying to get pressure to make a hole in a woman's stomach. I saw them cutting Greek people in pieces. I was in Flossenburg for two weeks, and they shot 25,000 Russian soldiers, and we put them down on wooden logs and burned them. Every day the killing, the hanging, the shooting, the crematorium smell, the ovens, and the smoke going out.

I knew everybody, knew every trick to survive. I was one of the youngest in Auschwitz, and I was like "adopted" by a lot of the older people, especially the fathers. Whole families came into Auschwitz together, and you got to Dr. Mengele, who was saying "right, left, left, right," and you knew, right there, who is going to the gas chamber and who is not. Most of the men broke down when they knew their wives and their kids — three-, five-, nine-year-olds — went into the gas chambers. In fact, one of my brothers committed suicide in Auschwitz because he couldn't live with knowing his wife and children are dead.

I was able to see my family when they came into Auschwitz in 1944. I had a sister, she had a little boy a year old. Everybody that carried a child went automatically to the gas chamber, so my mother took the child. My sister survived, but she still suffers, feels she was a part of killing my mother. . . .

Looking Back   Once you start fighting for your life, all the ethics are gone. You live by circumstances. There is no pity. You physically draw down to the point where you cannot think any more, where the only thing is survival, and maybe a little hope that if I survive, I'm gonna be with my grandchildren and tell them the story.

In the camps, death actually became a luxury. We used to say, "Look at how lucky he is. He doesn't have to suffer any more."

I was a lucky guy. I survived, and I felt pretty good about it. But then you feel guilty living! My children — our friends are their "aunts" and "uncles." They don't know what is a grandfather, a grandmother, a cousin, a holiday sitting as a family.

As you grow older, you think about it, certain faces come back to you. You remember your home, your brothers, children that went to the crematorium. You wonder, how did your mother and father feel when they were in the gas chamber? Many nights I hear voices screaming in those first few minutes in the gas chamber, and I don't sleep.

I talk to a lot of people, born Americans, and they don't relate. They can't understand, and I don't blame them. Sometimes it's hard even for me to understand the truth of this whole thing. Did it really happen? But I saw it.

The majority of the people here live fairly good. I don't think there's a country in the world that can offer as much freedom as this country can offer. But the Nazi party exists here, now. This country is supplying anti-Semitic material to the whole world, printing it here and shipping it all over, and our leaders are silent, just as the world was silent when the Jews were being taken to the camps. How quick we forget.

When I sit in a plane, I see 65 percent of the people will pick up the sports page of the newspaper. They don't care what is on the front page! And this is where the danger lies. All you need is the economy to turn a little sour and have one person give out the propaganda. With 65 percent of the population the propaganda works, and then the other 35 percent is powerless to do anything about it.

Hinda Kibort

Kovno, Lithuania

When the Germans marched in in July 1941, school had let out for the summer, so our whole family was together, including my brother who was in the university and my little sister who was in tenth grade. We tried to leave the city, but it was just like you see in the documentaries — people with their little suitcases walking along highways and jumping into ditches because German planes were strafing, coming down very low, and people killed, and all this terror. German tanks overtook us, and we returned home.

The Occupation   We did not have time like the German Jews did, from '33 until the war broke out in '39, for step-by-step adjustments. For us, one day we were human, the next day we're subhuman. We had to wear yellow stars. Everybody could command us to do whatever they wanted. They would make you hop around in the middle of the street, or they made you lie down and stepped on you,

or spit on you, or they tore at beards of devout Jews. And there was always an audience around to laugh. . . .

The Ghetto   In September all the Jews were enclosed in a ghetto. We lived together in little huts, sometimes two families to a room. There were no schools, no
newspapers, no concerts, no theater. Officially, we didn't have any radios or books,
but people brought in many books and they circulated. We also had a couple of radios and we could hear the BBC, so we were very much aware of what was going
on with the war.

As long as we were strong and useful, we would survive. Everybody had to go
to work except children under twelve and the elderly. There were workshops in the
ghetto where they made earmuffs for the army, for instance, but mostly people went
out to work in groups, with guards. A few tried to escape, but were caught.

We did not know yet about concentration camps.

In 1943 the war turned, and we could feel a terrible tension from the guards
and from Germans we worked with on the outside. We could exchange clothing or
jewelry for food, but this was extremely dangerous because every time a column
came back from work, we were all searched. A baker, they found some bread and a
few cigarettes in his pocket. He was hanged publicly, on a Sunday. There was a
little orchard in the ghetto, a public place, and we Jews had to build a gallows there
and a Jew had to hang him. We were all driven out by the guards and had to stand
and watch this man being hanged.

November 5, 1943, was the day all the children were taken away. They brought
in Romanian and Ukrainian S.S. to do it. All five of us in our family were employed in a factory adjacent to the ghetto, so we could see through the window
what was happening. They took everybody out who stayed in the ghetto — all the
children, all the elderly. When we came back after work we were a totally childless
society! You can imagine parents coming home to — nothing. Everybody was absolutely shattered.

People were looking for answers, for omens. They turned to seances or to heaven
to look for signs. And this was the day when we heard for the first time the word
Auschwitz. There was a rumor that the children were taken there, but we didn't know
the name so we translated it as *Der Schweiz* — Switzerland. We hoped that the trains
were going to Switzerland, that the children would be hostages there.

The Transport   On July 16, 1944, the rest of the ghetto were put on cattle trains,
with only what we could carry. We had no bathrooms. There was a pail on one side
that very soon was full. We were very crowded. The stench and the lack of water and
the fear, the whole experience, is just beyond explanation.

At one time, when we were in open country, a guard opened the door and we
sat on the side and let our feet down and got some fresh air. We even tried to sing.
But then they closed it up, and we were all inside again.

Labor Camp   When we arrived at Stutthof our family was separated — the men
to one side of the camp, women to the other. My mother and sister and I had to

undress. There were S.S. guards around, men and women. In the middle of the room was a table and an S.S. man in a white coat. We came in in batches, totally naked.

I cannot describe how you feel in a situation like this. We were searched, totally, for jewelry, gold, even family pictures. We had to stand spread-eagle and spread out our fingers. They looked through the hair, they looked into the mouth, they looked in the ears, and then we had to lie down. They looked into every orifice of the body, right in front of everybody. We were in total shock.

From this room we were rushed through a room that said above the door "shower room." There were little openings in the ceiling and water was trickling through. In the next room were piles of clothing, rags, on the floor. You had to grab a skirt, a blouse, a dress, and exchange among yourselves to find what fit. The same thing with shoes. Some women got big men's shoes. I ended up with brown suede pumps with high heels and used a rock to break off the heels, so I could march and stand in line on roll calls.

After this we went into registration and they took down your profession, scholastic background, everything. We got black numbers on a white piece of cloth that had to be sewn on the sleeve. My mother and sister and I had numbers in the 54,000s. People from all over Europe — Hungarian women and Germans, Czechoslovakia, Belgium, you name it — they were there. Children, of course, were not there. When families came with children, the children were taken right away.

As prisoners of Stutthof we were taken to outside work camps. A thousand of us women were taken to dig antitank ditches, a very deep V-shaped ditch that went for miles and miles. The Germans had the idea that Russian tanks would fall into those ditches and not be able to come up again!

When we were done, 400 of us were taken by train deeper into Germany. We ended up in tents, fifty women to a tent. We had no water for washing and not even a latrine. If at night you wanted to go, you had to call a guard who would escort you to this little field, stand there watching while you were crouching down, and then escort you back.

We were covered with lice, and we became very sick and weak. But Frau Schmidt taught us to survive. She was a chemist, and she taught us what roots or grasses we could eat that weren't poisonous. She also said that to survive we have to keep our minds occupied and not think about the hunger and cold. She made us study every day! . . .

By the middle of December we had to stop working because the snow was very deep and everything was frozen. January 20, 1945, they made a selection. The strong women that could still work would be marched out, and the sick, those who couldn't walk or who had bent backs, or who were just skeletons and too weak to work, would be left behind. My mother was selected and my sister and I decided to stay behind with her.

We were left without food, with two armed guards. We thought the guards will burn the tents, with us in them. Then we heard there was a factory where they boiled people's bodies to manufacture soap. But the next day the guards put us in formation and marched us down the highway until we came to a small town.

We were put in the jail there. There we were, ninety-six women standing in a small jail cell, with no bathroom, pressed so close together we couldn't sit down, couldn't bend down. Pretty soon everybody was hysterical, screaming. Then slowly we quieted down.

In the morning when they opened the doors, we really spilled outside! They had recruited a bunch of Polish guards and they surrounded us totally, as if in a box. So there we were, ninety-six weak, emaciated women, marching down the highway with all these guards with rifles.

Then the German guards told us to run into the woods. The snow was so deep, up to our knees, and most of us were barefoot, frozen, our feet were blistered. We couldn't really run, but we spread out in a long line, with my mother and sister and I at the very end. I was near one guard, and all of a sudden I heard the sound of his rifle going "click." I still remember the feeling in the back of my spine, very strange and very scary. Then the guards began to shoot.

There was a terrible panic, screams. People went really crazy. The three of us always hand-held with my mother in the middle, but now she let go of us and ran toward the guards, screaming not to shoot her children. They shot her, and my sister and I grabbed each other by the hand and ran into the woods.

We could hear screaming and shooting, and then it got very quiet. We were afraid to move. The guards wore those awesome-looking black uniforms with the skull and crossbones insignia, and every tree looked like another guard! A few women came out from behind the trees, and eventually, ten of us made it out to the highway.

With our last strength, we made it to a small Polish village about a mile away. We knocked on doors, but they didn't let us in, and they started to throw things at us. We went to the church, and the priest said he couldn't help us because the Germans were in charge.

We were so weak we just sat there on the church steps, and late in the evening the priest came with a man who told us to go hide in a barn that was empty. We did not get any other help, whatsoever, from that whole Polish village — not medical help, not a rag to cover ourselves, not even water. Nothing.

Liberation   The next morning there was a terrible battle right in front of the barn. We were so afraid. Then it got very quiet. We opened the door, and we saw Russian tanks. We were free!

The Russians put us into an empty farmhouse. They gave us Vaseline and some rags, all they had, to cover our wounds. Then they put us on trucks and took us to a town where we found a freight train and just jumped on it.

At the border Russian police took us off the train. They grilled us. "How did you survive? You must have cooperated with the Germans." It was terrible. But finally we got identity cards — in Russia, you are nobody without some kind of I.D. — and my sister and I decided to go to the small town where we had lived. We thought somebody might have survived. . . .

Looking Back   I was a prisoner from age nineteen to twenty-three. I lost my mother and twenty-eight aunts, uncles, and cousins — all killed. To be a survivor has meant to me to be a witness because being quiet would not be fair to the ones that did not survive.

There are people writing and saying the Holocaust never happened, it's a hoax, it's Jewish propaganda. We should keep talking about it, so the next generation won't grow up not knowing how a human being can turn into a beast, not knowing the danger in keeping quiet when you see something brewing. The onlooker, the bystander, is as much at fault as the perpetrator because he lets it happen. That is why I have this fear of what is called the "silent majority."

So when a non-Jewish friend or a student asks, "What can I do?" I say, when you see something anti-Semitic happen, get up and say, "This is wrong" or "I protest." Send a letter to the newspaper saying, "This should not happen in my community," and sign your name. Then maybe somebody else will be brave enough to come forward and say that he protests, too.

DISCUSSION QUESTIONS

1. According to these accounts, what role did the ghettos play in the Final Solution?

2. Based on these interviews, what was the principal difference between camps like Auschwitz and those like Stutthof?

3. What do these accounts reveal about conditions in the camps and the inmates' strategies for survival?

4. What lessons does the Holocaust hold for the future?

5.
Atomic Catastrophe

Michihiko Hachiya, *Hiroshima Diary* (August 7, 1945)

Although World War II began in Europe, in 1941 the conflict engulfed the world as Japan and the United States entered the war on opposite sides. Despite initial successes, within a year the Japanese began to lose ground to the Allies' formidable forces. Even so, they fought on, unwilling to surrender no matter what the material and human costs. This strategy prompted Allied leaders to make a fateful decision. On August 6, 1945, an American plane dropped an atomic bomb on the Japanese city of Hiroshima, adding tens of thousands to the war's civilian death toll. Thousands more were wounded, including Dr. Michihiko Hachiya, the director of the Hiroshima Communications Hospital. Made of reinforced concrete and located approximately 1,500 meters from the hypocenter of the bomb, the hospital escaped destruction and was soon packed with patients. Dr. Hachiya was among them. Bedridden for several weeks, he began a journal documenting his experiences. The excerpt that follows is drawn from his entry for the

From Michihiko Hachiya, *Hiroshima Diary*, trans. and ed. Warner Wells, M.D. (Chapel Hill: University of North Carolina Press, 1955), 13–17, 24–25.

day after the bomb had been dropped, when he and other survivors struggled to make sense of the unprecedented scale of destruction and human suffering around them.

Dr. Tabuchi, an old friend from Ushita, came in. His face and hands had been burned, though not badly, and after an exchange of greetings, I asked if he knew what had happened.

"I was in the back yard pruning some trees when it exploded," he answered. "The first thing I knew, there was a blinding white flash of light, and a wave of intense heat struck my cheek. This was odd, I thought, when in the next instant there was a tremendous blast.

"The force of it knocked me clean over," he continued, "but fortunately, it didn't hurt me; and my wife wasn't hurt either. But you should have seen our house! It didn't topple over, it just inclined. I have never seen such a mess. Inside and out everything was simply ruined. Even so, we are happy to be alive, and what's more Ryoji, our son, survived. I didn't tell you that he had gone into the city on business that morning. About midnight, after we had given up all hope that he could possibly survive in the dreadful fire that followed the blast, he came home. "Listen!" he continued, "why don't you come on home with me? My house is certainly nothing to look at now, but it is better than here."

It was impossible for me to accept his kind offer, and I tried to decline in a way that would not hurt his feelings.

"Dr. Tabuchi," I replied, "we are all grateful for your kind offer, but Dr. Katsube just warned me that I must lie perfectly still until my wounds are healed."

Dr. Tabuchi accepted my explanation with some reluctance, and after a pause he made ready to go.

"Don't go," I said. "Please tell us more of what occurred yesterday."

"It was a horrible sight," said Dr. Tabuchi. "Hundreds of injured people who are trying to escape to the hills passed our house. The sight of them was almost unbearable. Their faces and hands were burnt and swollen; and great sheets of skin had peeled away from their tissues to hang down like rags on a scarecrow. They moved like a line of ants. All through the night, they went past our house, but this morning they had stopped. I found them lying on both sides of the road so thick that it was impossible to pass without stepping on them."

I lay with my eyes shut while Dr. Tabuchi was talking, picturing in my mind the horror he was describing. I neither saw nor heard Mr. Katsutani when he came in. It was not until I heard someone sobbing that my attention was attracted, and I recognized my old friend. I had known Mr. Katsutani for many years and knew him to be an emotional person, but even so, to see him break down made tears come to my eyes. He had come all the way from Jigozen[1] to look for me, and now that he had found me, emotion overcame him.

---

[1] A village on the Inland Sea about 10 miles southwest of Hiroshima.

He turned to Dr. Sasada and said brokenly: "Yesterday, it was impossible to enter Hiroshima, else I would have come. Even today fires are still burning in some places. You should see how the city has changed. When I reached the Misasa Bridge[2] this morning, everything before me was gone, even the castle. These buildings here are the only ones left anywhere around. The Communications Bureau seemed to loom right in front of me long before I got anywhere near here."

Mr. Katsutani paused for a moment to catch his breath and went on: "I *really* walked along the railroad tracks to get here, but even they were littered with electric wires and broken railway cars, and the dead and wounded lay everywhere. When I reached the bridge, I saw a dreadful thing. It was unbelievable. There was a man, stone dead, sitting on his bicycle as it leaned against the bridge railing. It is hard to believe that such a thing could happen!"

He repeated himself two or three times as if to convince himself that what he said was true and then continued: "It seems that most of the dead people were either on the bridge or beneath it. You could tell that many had gone down to the river to get a drink of water and had died where they lay. I saw a few live people still in the water, knocking against the dead as they floated down the river. There must have been hundreds and thousands who fled to the river to escape the fire and then drowned.

"The sight of the soldiers, though, was more dreadful than the dead people floating down the river. I came onto I don't know how many, burned from the hips up; and where the skin had peeled, their flesh was wet and mushy. They must have been wearing their military caps because the black hair on top of their heads was not burned. It made them look like they were wearing black lacquer bowls.

"And they had no faces! Their eyes, noses, and mouths had been burned away, and it looked like their ears had melted off. It was hard to tell front from back. One soldier, whose features had been destroyed and was left with his white teeth sticking out, asked me for some water, but I didn't have any. I clasped my hands and prayed for him. He didn't say anything more. His plea for water must have been his last words. The way they were burned, I wonder if they didn't have their coats off when the bomb exploded."

It seemed to give Mr. Katsutani some relief to pour out his terrifying experiences on us; and there was no one who would have stopped him, so fascinating was his tale of horror. While he was talking, several people came in and stayed to listen. Somebody asked him what he was doing when the explosion occurred.

"I had just finished breakfast," he replied, "and was getting ready to light a cigarette, when all of a sudden I saw a white flash. In a moment there was a tremendous blast. Not stopping to think, I let out a yell and jumped into an air-raid dugout. In a moment there was such a blast as I have never heard before. It was terrific! I

---

[2]A large bridge which crosses the Ōta River not far from the old Hiroshima Castle in the northern part of the city and only a few blocks from the Communications Hospital.

jumped out of the dugout and pushed my wife into it. Realizing something terrible must have happened in Hiroshima, I climbed up onto the roof of my storehouse to have a look."

Mr. Katsutani became more intense and, gesticulating wildly, went on: "Towards Hiroshima, I saw a big black cloud go billowing up, like a puffy summer cloud. Knowing for sure then that something terrible had happened in the city, I jumped down from my storehouse and ran as fast as I could to the military post at Hatsukaichi.[3] I ran up to the officer in charge and told him what I had seen and begged him to send somebody to help in Hiroshima. But he didn't even take me seriously. He looked at me for a moment with a threatening expression, and then do you know what he said? He said, 'There isn't much to worry about. One or two bombs won't hurt Hiroshima.' There was no use talking to that fool!

"I was the ranking officer in the local branch of the Ex-officer's Association, but even I didn't know what to do because that day the villagers under my command had been sent off to Miyajima[4] for labor service. I looked all around to find someone to help me make a rescue squad, but I couldn't find anybody. While I was still looking for help, wounded people began to stream into the village. I asked them what had happened, but all they could tell me was that Hiroshima had been destroyed and everybody was leaving the city. With that I got on my bicycle and rode as fast as I could towards Itsukaichi. By the time I got there, the road was jammed with people, and so was every path and byway.

"Again I tried to find out what had happened, but nobody could give me a clear answer. When I asked these people where they had come from, they would point towards Hiroshima and say, 'This way.' And when I asked where they were going, they would point toward Miyajima and say, 'That way.' Everybody said the same thing.

"I saw no badly wounded or burned people around Itsukaichi, but when I reached Kusatsu, nearly everybody was badly hurt. The nearer I got to Hiroshima the more I saw until by the time I had reached Koi,[5] they were all so badly injured, I could not bear to look into their faces. They smelled like burning hair."

Mr. Katsutani paused for a moment to take a deep breath and then continued: "The area around Koi station was not burned, but the station and the houses nearby were badly damaged. Every square inch of the station platform was packed with wounded people. Some were standing; others lying down. They were all pleading for water. Now and then you could hear a child calling for its mother. It was a living hell, I tell you. It was a living hell!"

---

[3]The next village toward Hiroshima from Jigozen.
[4]Miyajima, or "Sacred Island," one of the seven places of superlative scenic beauty in Japan, where the magnificent camphor-wood *torii* of the Itsukushima Shrine rises majestically from the sea as a gateway to the island, is plainly visible to the south of Jigozen.
[5]A railroad station on the very western limits of the city where the slopes of Chausa-yama merge with the Hiroshima delta.

All day I had listened to visitors telling me about the destruction of Hiroshima and the scenes of horror they had witnessed. I had seen my friends wounded, their families separated, their homes destroyed. I was aware of the problems our staff had to face, and I knew how bravely they struggled against superhuman odds. I knew what the patients had to endure and the trust they put in the doctors and nurses, who, could they know the truth, were as helpless as themselves.

By degrees my capacity to comprehend the magnitude of their sorrow, to share with them the pain, frustration, and horror became so dulled that I found myself accepting whatever was told me with equanimity and a detachment I would have never believed possible.

In two days I had become at home in this environment of chaos and despair.

I felt lonely, but it was an animal loneliness. I became part of the darkness of the night. There were no radios, no electric lights, not even a candle. The only light that came to me was reflected in flickering shadows made by the burning city. The only sounds were the groans and sobs of the patients. Now and then a patient in delirium would call for his mother, or the voice of one in pain would breathe out the word *eraiyo* — "the pain is unbearable; I cannot endure it!"

What kind of a bomb was it that had destroyed Hiroshima? What had my visitors told me earlier? Whatever it was, it did not make sense.

There could not have been more than a few planes. Even *my* memory would agree to that. Before the air-raid alarm there was the metallic sound of one plane and no more. Otherwise why did the alarm stop? Why was there no further alarm during the five or six minutes before the explosion occurred?

Reason as I would, I could not make the ends meet when I considered the destruction that followed. Perhaps it *was* a new weapon! More than one of my visitors spoke vaguely of a "new bomb," a "secret weapon," a "special bomb," and someone even said that the bomb was suspended from two parachutes when it burst! Whatever it was, it was beyond my comprehension. Damage of this order could have no explanation! All we had were stories no more substantial than the clouds from which we had reached to snatch them.

DISCUSSION QUESTIONS

1. How do Dr. Hachiya's friends describe the bomb's physical impact on the cityscape of Hiroshima and its residents? What images in particular stand out in their accounts?

2. Why did Dr. Hachiya find it difficult to understand what his friends described?

3. What does his confusion suggest about the nature of warfare in the new atomic era?

COMPARATIVE QUESTIONS

1. In what ways was the central message of Goebbels's pamphlet a reality for Bankhalter and Kibort?

2. How would you compare the views of Chamberlain and Ibárruri Gómez on the use of military power as an instrument of peace?

3. How might the Spanish Civil War have represented a rehearsal for World War II? How was it different from this later conflict?

4. How did the use of the atomic bomb and the implementation of the Final Solution set World War II apart from World War I?

The Cold War
and the Remaking
of Europe,
1945–1965

Despite widespread feelings of relief and joy when World War II at last came to an end, an uncertain path lay ahead for the world. With Europe in shambles, two new superpowers emerged from the rubble: the United States and the Soviet Union. Their rivalry, known as the *cold war*, would shape international affairs for decades to come. The first two documents expose the ideological and political roots of U.S. and Soviet cold war policies. The bipolarization of world politics was not the only sign of Europe's diminished international identity, as the third document shows. War-weary and bitter, colonial peoples from Asia to Africa successfully battled for independence from European rule. Campaigns for freedom also appeared on the horizon closer to home. As societal and governmental pressures reasserted traditional boundaries between men and women, the fourth document reveals that some women called for change, setting the stage for the women's liberation movement during the 1960s. The fifth document highlights an additional struggle for change, as eastern Europeans risked imprisonment and even death to challenge Soviet rule.

1.
Stalin and the Western Threat

The Formation of the Communist Information
Bureau (Cominform) (1947)

Despite his instrumental role in defeating Fascism, the head of the Soviet Union, Joseph Stalin (1879–1953), deeply mistrusted his Western allies. Convinced that their ultimate goal was to destroy communism, Stalin moved rapidly to establish a buffer zone of satellite states in eastern Europe. At a meeting in September 1947, communist leaders consolidated the Soviets' hold in the East by establishing a centralized associ-ation of communist parties — the Communist Information Bureau (Cominform). As the following document justifying their actions reveals, the Cominform embodied Stalin's belief that only by coordinating their efforts could the Soviet Union and its clients defeat the "imperialist" threat. Stalin's Western rivals worked to put their own counterstrategies in place, thus hardening the battle lines of the cold war.

The representatives of the Communist Party of Yugoslavia, the Bulgarian Workers' Party (Communists), the Communist Party of Rumania, the Hungarian Commu-nist Party, the Polish Workers' Party, the Communist Party of the Soviet Union (Bolsheviks), the Communist Party of France, the Communist Party of Czecho-slovakia and the Communist Party of Italy, having exchanged views on the inter-national situation, have agreed upon the following declaration.

Fundamental changes have taken place in the international situation as a result of the Second World War and in the post-war period.

These changes are characterized by a new disposition of the basic political forces operating in the world arena, by a change in the relations among the victor states in the Second World War, and their realignment.

While the war was on, the Allied States in the War against Germany and Japan went together and comprised one camp. However, already during the war there were differences in the Allied camp as regards the definition of both war aims and the tasks of the post-war peace settlement. The Soviet Union and the other dem-ocratic countries regarded as their basic war aims the restoration and consolida-tion of democratic order in Europe, the eradication of fascism and the prevention of the possibility of new aggression on the part of Germany, and the establish-ment of a lasting all-round cooperation among the nations of Europe. The United States of America, and Britain in agreement with them, set themselves another aim in the war: to rid themselves of competitors on the markets (Germany and Japan) and to establish their dominant position. This difference in the definition of war aims and the tasks of the post-war settlement grew more profound after the war. Two diametrically opposed political lines took shape: on the one side the pol-icy of the USSR and the other democratic countries directed at undermining im-perialism and consolidating democracy, and on the other side, the policy of the United States and Britain directed at strengthening imperialism and stifling democracy. Inasmuch as the USSR and the countries of the new democracy be-came obstacles to the realization of the imperialist plans of struggle for world domination and smashing of democratic movements, a crusade was proclaimed against the USSR and the countries of the new democracy, bolstered also by threats of a new war on the part of the most zealous imperialist politicians in the United States of America and Britain.

From United States Senate, 81st Congress, 1st Session, Document No. 48, *North Atlantic Treaty: Documents Relating to the North Atlantic Treaty* (Washington, D.C.: U.S. Government Printing Office, 1949), 117–20.

Thus two camps were formed — the imperialist and anti-democratic camp having as its basic aim the establishment of world domination of American imperialism and the smashing of democracy, and the anti-imperialist and democratic camp having as its basic aim the undermining of imperialism, the consolidation of democracy, and the eradication of the remnants of fascism.

The struggle between the two diametrically opposed camps — the imperialist camp and the anti-imperialist camp — is taking place in a situation marked by a further aggravation of the general crisis of capitalism, the weakening of the forces of capitalism and the strengthening of the forces of Socialism and democracy.

Hence the imperialist camp and its leading force, the United States, are displaying particularly aggressive activity. This activity is being developed simultaneously along all lines — the lines of strategic military measures, economic expansion and ideological struggle. The Truman-Marshall Plan is only a constituent part, the European sub-section, of the general plan for the policy of global expansion pursued by the United States in all parts of the World. The plan for the economic and political enslavement of Europe by American imperialism is being supplemented by plans for the economic and political enslavement of China, Indonesia, the South American countries. Yesterday's aggressors — the capitalist magnates of Germany and Japan — are being groomed by the United States of America for a new role, that of instruments of the imperialist policy of the United States in Europe and Asia.

The arsenal of tactical weapons used by the imperialist camp is highly diversified. It combines direct threats of violence, blackmail and extortion, every means of political and economic pressure, bribery and utilization of internal contradictions and strife in order to strengthen its own positions, and all this is concealed behind a liberal-pacifist mask designed to deceive and trap the politically inexperienced. . . .

Under these circumstances it is necessary that the anti-imperialist, democratic camp should close its ranks, draw up an agreed program of actions and work out its own tactics against the main forces of the imperialist camp, against American imperialism and its British and French allies, against the right-wing Socialists, primarily in Britain and France.

To frustrate the plan of imperialist aggression the efforts of all the democratic anti-imperialist forces of Europe are necessary. The right-wing Socialists are traitors to this cause. With the exception of those countries of the new democracy where the bloc of the Communists and the Socialists with other democratic, progressive parties forms the basis of the resistance of these countries to the imperialist plans, the Socialists in the majority of other countries, and primarily the French Socialists and the British Labourites . . . by their servility and sycophancy are helping American capital to achieve its aims, provoking it to resort to extortion and impelling their own countries on to the path of vassal-like dependence on the United States of America.

This imposes a special task on the Communist Parties. They must take into their hands the banner of defense of the national independence and sovereignty of their countries. If the Communist Parties stick firmly to their positions, if they do not let themselves be intimidated and blackmailed, if they courageously safeguard democracy and the national sovereignty, liberty and independence of their countries, if in their struggle against attempts to enslave their countries economically and politically they be able to take the lead of all the forces that are ready to fight for honor and national independence, no plans for the enslavement of the countries of Europe and Asia can be carried into effect.

This is now one of the principal tasks of the Communist Parties.

It is essential to bear in mind that there is a vast difference between the desire of the imperialists to unleash a new war and the possibility of organizing such a war. The nations of the world do not want war. The forces standing for peace are so large and so strong that if these forces be staunch and firm in defending the peace, if they display stamina and resolution, the plans of the aggressors will meet with utter failure. It should not be forgotten that the war danger hullabaloo raised by the imperialist agents is intended to frighten the nervous and unstable elements and by blackmail to win concessions for the aggressor.

The principal danger for the working class today lies in underestimating their own strength and overestimating the strength of the imperialist camp. Just as the Munich policy untied the hands of Hitlerite aggression in the past, so yielding to the new line in the policy of the United States and that of the imperialist camp is bound to make its inspirers still more arrogant and aggressive. Therefore, the Communist Parties must take the lead in resisting the plans of imperialist expansion and aggression in all spheres — state, political, economic, and ideological; they must close their ranks, unite their efforts on the basis of a common anti-imperialist and democratic platform and rally around themselves all the democratic and patriotic forces of the nation.

Resolution on Interchange of Experience and Coordination of Activities of the Parties Represented at the Conference

The Conference states that the absence of contacts among the Communist Parties participating at this Conference is a serious shortcoming in the present situation. Experience has shown that such lack of contacts among the Communist Parties is wrong and harmful. The need for interchange of experience and voluntary coordination of action of the various Parties is particularly keenly felt at the present time in view of the growing complication of the post-war international situation, a situation in which the lack of connections among the Communist Parties may prove detrimental to the working class.

In view of this, the participants in the Conference have agreed on the following:

1. To set up an Information Bureau consisting of representatives of the Communist Party of Yugoslavia, the Bulgarian Workers' Party (Communists), the Communist Party of Rumania, the Hungarian Communist Party, the Polish Workers' Party, the Communist Party of the Soviet Union (Bolsheviks), the Communist Party of France, the Communist Party of Czechoslovakia and the Communist Party of Italy.

2. To charge the Information Bureau with the organization of interchange of experience, and if need be, coordination of the activities of the Communist Parties on the basis of mutual agreement.

3. The Information Bureau is to consist of two representatives from each Central Committee, the delegations of the Central Committees to be appointed and replaced by the Central Committees.

4. The Information Bureau is to have a printed organ — a fortnightly and subsequently, a weekly. The organ is to be published in French and Russian, and when possible, in other languages as well.

5. The Information Bureau is to be located in the city of Belgrad [sic].

DISCUSSION QUESTIONS

1. According to the document, how did the relationship between the Soviet Union and its Western allies change during the postwar period, and why?

2. What does the document mean when it describes the United States as an "imperialist" power?

3. What course of action does the document set forth to undermine this power, and to what end?

4. How does this document distort the reality of Soviet actions in eastern Europe?

2.
Truman and the Soviet Threat

National Security Council, *Paper Number 68* (1950)

Although he had helped to end World War II, U.S. president Harry S. Truman (1945–1953) had little time to celebrate. Daunting challenges still lay ahead as the fragile wartime alliance between the United States and the Soviet Union collapsed. By 1949, the Soviet bloc in eastern Europe was firmly in place, and the threat of international communism loomed large with the triumph of Mao Zedong (1893–1976) in China. In response, Truman set out to devise a coherent strategy for combating the expansion of Soviet power. To this end, he commissioned the U.S. Departments of State and Defense to compile a report on the subject, which was completed in 1950 on the eve of the outbreak of the Korean War. The classified report, excerpted here, elucidates not only the basis of U.S. cold war tactics but also the fears and perceptions underlying them.

Within the past thirty-five years the world has experienced two global wars of tremendous violence. . . . During the span of one generation, the international distribution of power has been fundamentally altered. For several centuries it had proved impossible for any one nation to gain such preponderant strength that a coalition of other nations could not in time face it with greater strength. The international scene was marked by recurring periods of violence and war, but a

From National Security Council, Paper Number 68, *Foreign Relations of the United States* (Washington, D.C.: U.S. Government Printing Office, 1977), 235–92.

system of sovereign and independent states was maintained, over which no state was able to achieve hegemony.

Two complex sets of factors have now basically altered this historical distribution of power. First, the defeat of Germany and Japan and the decline of the British and French Empires have interacted with the development of the United States and the Soviet Union in such a way that power has increasingly gravitated to these two centers. Second, the Soviet Union, unlike previous aspirants to hegemony, is animated by a new fanatic faith, antithetical to our own, and seeks to impose its absolute authority over the rest of the world. Conflict has, therefore, become endemic and is waged, on the part of the Soviet Union, by violent or non-violent methods in accordance with the dictates of expediency. . . .

On the one hand, the people of the world yearn for relief from the anxiety arising from the risk of atomic war. On the other hand, any substantial further extension of the area under the domination of the Kremlin would raise the possibility that no coalition adequate to confront the Kremlin with greater strength could be assembled. It is in this context that this Republic and its citizens in the ascendancy of their strength stand in their deepest peril.

The issues that face us are momentous, involving the fulfillment or destruction not only of this Republic but of civilization itself. They are issues which will not await our deliberations. With conscience and resolution this Government and the people it represents must now take new and fateful decisions. . . .

Our overall policy at the present time may be described as one designed to foster a world environment in which the American system can survive and flourish. It therefore rejects the concept of isolation and affirms the necessity of our positive participation in the world community.

This broad intention embraces two subsidiary policies. One is a policy which we would probably pursue even if there were no Soviet threat. It is a policy of attempting to develop a healthy international community. The other is the policy of "containing" the Soviet system. . . .

As for the policy of "containment," it is one which seeks by all means short of war to (1) block further expansion of Soviet power, (2) expose the falsities of Soviet pretensions, (3) induce a retraction of the Kremlin's control and influence and (4) in general, so foster the seeds of destruction within the Soviet system that the Kremlin is brought at least to the point of modifying its behavior to conform to generally accepted international standards.

It was and continues to be cardinal in this policy that we possess superior overall power in ourselves or in dependable combination with other like-minded nations. One of the most important ingredients of power is military strength. In the concept of "containment," the maintenance of a strong military posture is deemed to be essential for two reasons: (1) as an ultimate guarantee of our national security and (2) as an indispensable backdrop to the conduct of the policy of "containment." . . .

At the same time, it is essential to the successful conduct of a policy of "containment" that we always leave open the possibility of negotiation with the U.S.S.R.

A diplomatic freeze — and we are in one now — tends to defeat the very purposes of "containment" because it raises tensions at the same time that it makes Soviet retractions and adjustments in the direction of moderated behavior more difficult. It also tends to inhibit our initiative and deprives us of opportunities for maintaining a moral ascendancy in our struggle with the Soviet system. . . .

It is quite clear from Soviet theory and practice that the Kremlin seeks to bring the free world under its dominion by the methods of the cold war. The preferred technique is to subvert by infiltration and intimidation. Every institution of our society is an instrument which it has sought to stultify and turn against our purposes. Those that touch most closely our material and moral strength are obviously the prime targets, labor unions, civil enterprises, schools, churches, and all media for influencing opinion. The effort is not so much to make them serve obvious Soviet ends as to prevent them from serving our ends, and thus to make them sources of confusion in our economy, our culture, and our body politic. The doubts and diversities that in terms of our values are part of the merit of a free system, the weaknesses and the problems that are peculiar to it, the rights and privileges that free men enjoy, and the disorganization and destruction left in the wake of the last attack in our freedoms, all are but opportunities for the Kremlin to do its evil work. Every advantage is taken of the fact that our means of prevention and retaliation are limited by those principles and scruples which are precisely the ones that give our freedom and democracy its meaning for us. None of our scruples deter those whose only code is, "morality is that which serves the revolution."

At the same time the Soviet Union is seeking to create overwhelming military force, in order to back up infiltration with intimidation. In the only terms in which it understands strength, it is seeking to demonstrate to the free world that force and the will to use it are on the side of the Kremlin, that those who lack it are decadent and doomed. In local incidents it threatens and encroaches both for the sake of local gains and to increase anxiety and defeatism in all the free world. . . .

Our position as the center of power in the free world places a heavy responsibility upon the United States for leadership. We must organize and enlist the energies and resources of the free world in a positive program for peace which will frustrate the Kremlin design for world domination by creating a situation in the free world to which the Kremlin will be compelled to adjust. Without such a cooperative effort, led by the United States, we will have to make gradual withdrawals under pressure until we discover one day that we have sacrificed positions of vital interest. . . .

In summary, we must, by means of a rapid and sustained build-up of the political, economic, and military strength of the free world, and by means of an affirmative program intended to wrest the initiative from the Soviet Union, confront it with convincing evidence of the determination and ability of the free world to frustrate the Kremlin to the new situation. Failing that, the unwillingness of the determination and ability of the free world to the Kremlin design of a world dominated by its will [*sic*]. Such evidence is the only means short of war which eventually may force the Kremlin to abandon its present course of action and to negotiate acceptable agreements on issues of major importance.

The whole success of the proposed program hangs ultimately on recognition by this Government, the American people, and all free peoples, that the cold war is in fact a real war in which the survival of the free world is at stake. Essential prerequisites to success are consultations with Congressional leaders designed to make the program the object of nonpartisan legislative support, and a presentation to the public of a full explanation of the facts and implications of the present international situation. The prosecution of the program will require of us all the ingenuity, sacrifice, and unity demanded by the vital importance of the issue and the tenacity to persevere until our national objectives have been attained.

DISCUSSION QUESTIONS

1. As described in the report, how did World War II transform the international distribution of power?
2. According to the report, in what ways did the Soviet Union pose a danger to Americans and all "free peoples"?
3. What solutions does the document set forth to counter this danger?
4. Why does the report describe the cold war as a "real" war?

3.
Throwing Off Colonialism
Ho Chi Minh, *Declaration of Independence of the Republic of Vietnam* (1945)

The devastation wrought by World War II encompassed more than the countless bombed buildings and millions of dead. The war had also fatally weakened the European powers' grip on their empires, as colonial peoples around the globe rose up against imperialist rule. A small nationalist organization — the Viet Minh — had formed in French Indochina in 1939 and achieved new prominence in the wake of World War II when the French sought to reassert their control in the region. Less than a month after Japan's surrender, the Viet Minh declared Vietnam's independence from France, as noted in the following document. It was signed by "President Ho Chi Minh" (1890– 1969) — one of the organization's original leaders — who had lived in Paris, Moscow, and China. The document explicitly draws on the language of the French Enlightenment to further the Viet Minh's cause and condemn that of France.

"All men are created equal. They are endowed by their Creator with certain unalienable rights, among these are Life, Liberty and the pursuit of happiness."

From Allan B. Cole, ed., *Conflict in Indo-China and International Repercussions: A Documentary History, 1945–1955* (Ithaca: Cornell University Press, 1956), 20–21.

This immortal statement was made in the Declaration of Independence of the United States of America in 1776. Now if we enlarge the sphere of our thoughts, this statement conveys another meaning: All the peoples on the earth are equal from birth, all the peoples have a right to live, be happy and free.

The Declaration of the Rights of Man and of the Citizen of the French Revolution in 1791 also states: "All men are born free and with equal rights, and must always be free and have equal rights."

Before the Outbreak of War

Those are undeniable truths.

Nevertheless, for more than eighty years, the French imperialists deceitfully raising the standard of Liberty, Equality, and Fraternity, have violated our Fatherland and oppressed our fellow-citizens. They have acted contrarily to the ideals of humanity and justice.

In the province of politics, they have deprived our people of every liberty.

They have enforced inhuman laws; to ruin our unity and national consciousness, they have carried out three different policies in the North, the Center, and the South of Vietnam.

They have founded more prisons than schools. They have mercilessly slain our patriots; they have deluged our revolutionary areas with innocent blood. They have fettered public opinion; they have promoted illiteracy.

To weaken our race they have forced us to use their manufactured opium and alcohol.

In the province of economics, they have stripped our fellow-citizens of everything they possessed, impoverishing the individual and devastating the land.

They have robbed us of our rice fields, our mines, our forests, our raw materials. They have monopolized the printing of bank-notes, the import and export trade; they have invented numbers of unlawful taxes, reducing our people, especially our countryfolk, to a state of extreme poverty.

They have stood in the way of our businessmen and stifled all their undertakings; they have extorted our working classes in a most savage way.

In the Autumn of the year 1940, when the Japanese fascists violated Indochina's territory to get one more foothold in their fight against the Allies, the French imperialists fell on their knees and surrendered, handing over our country to the Japanese, adding Japanese fetters to the French ones. From that day on the Vietnamese people suffered hardships yet unknown in the history of mankind. The result of this double oppression was terrific: from Quangtri to the Northern border two million people were starved to death in the early months of 1945.

On the 9th of March 1945 the French troops were disarmed by the Japanese. Once more the French either fled, or surrendered unconditionally, showing thus that not only they were incapable of "protecting" us, but that they twice sold us to the Japanese.

Yet, many times before the month of March, the Vietminh had urged the French to ally with them against the Japanese. The French colonists never answered.

On the contrary they intensified their terrorizing policy. Before taking their flight they even killed a great number of our patriots who had been imprisoned at Yenbay and Caobang.

Democratic Republic of Vietnam

Nevertheless, towards the French people our fellow-citizens have always manifested an attitude pervaded with toleration and humanity. Even after the Japanese putsch of March 1945 the Vietminh have helped many Frenchmen to reach the frontier, have delivered some of them from the Japanese jails, and never failed to protect their lives and properties.

The truth is that since the Autumn of 1940 our country had ceased to be a French colony and had become a Japanese outpost. After the Japanese had surrendered to the Allies our whole people rose to conquer political power and institute the Republic of Vietnam.

The truth is that we have wrested our independence from the Japanese and not from the French. The French have fled, the Japanese have capitulated, Emperor Bao Dai has abdicated, our people has broken the fetters which for over a century have tied us down; our people has at the same time overthrown the monarchic constitution that had reigned supreme for so many centuries and instead has established the present Republican Government.

For these reasons, we, members of the provisional Government, representing the whole population of Vietnam, have declared and renew here our declaration that we break off all relations with the French people and abolish all the special rights the French have unlawfully acquired on our Fatherland.

The whole population of Vietnam is united in a common allegiance to the Republican Government and is linked by a common will which is to annihilate the dark aims of the French imperialists.

We are convinced that the Allied nations which have acknowledged at Teheran and San Francisco the principles of self-determination and equality of status will not refuse to acknowledge the independence of Vietnam.

A people that has courageously opposed French domination for more than eighty years, a people that has fought by the Allies' side these last years against the fascists, such a people must be free, such a people must be independent.

For these reasons we, members of the Provisional Government of Vietnam, declare to the world that Vietnam has the right to be free and independent, and has in fact become a free and independent country. We also declare that the Vietnamese people is determined to make the heaviest sacrifices to maintain its independence and its Liberty.

DISCUSSION QUESTIONS

1. How does the document characterize the actions of the French in Vietnam, and why?
2. In what ways did World War II further the cause of the Viet Minh?

3. Why did the Viet Minh believe that the Vietnamese people had an undeniable right to independence?

4.
The Condition of Modern Women
Simone de Beauvoir, *The Second Sex* (1949)

Like Ho Chi Minh, Simone de Beauvoir (1908–1986) challenged traditional power structures in the postwar era. However, although she watched the growing independence movement in French Indochina with interest, her battle did not center on the plight of the colonized people. Rather, she dedicated herself to examining the condition of modern women, which, she argued, was similarly marked by injustice and discrimination. She presented her views to the world in her book The Second Sex, *published in 1949. In the following excerpt, Beauvoir outlines the fundamental premise of her work that, throughout history, women's identities have been defined by men and thus subjugated to them. Beauvoir believed that women could break free from their subservience only by taking charge of their own lives. Her views would help galvanize the women's liberation movement in the United States and Europe during the 1960s.*

A man would never get the notion of writing a book on the peculiar situation of the human male. But if I wish to define myself, I must first of all say: "I am a woman"; on this truth must be based all further discussion. A man never begins by presenting himself as an individual of a certain sex; it goes without saying that he is a man. The terms *masculine* and *feminine* are used symmetrically only as a matter of form, as on legal papers. In actuality the relation of the two sexes is not quite like that of two electrical poles, for man represents both the positive and the neutral, as is indicated by the common use of *man* to designate human beings in general; whereas woman represents only the negative, defined by limiting criteria, without reciprocity. In the midst of an abstract discussion it is vexing to hear a man say: "You think thus and so because you are a woman"; but I know that my only defense is to reply: "I think thus and so because it is true," thereby removing my subjective self from the argument. It would be out of the question to reply: "And you think the contrary because you are a man," for it is understood that the fact of being a man is no peculiarity. A man is in the right in being a man; it is the woman who is in the wrong. It amounts to this: just as for the ancients there was an absolute vertical with reference to which the oblique was defined, so there is an absolute human type, the masculine. Woman has ovaries, a uterus; these peculiarities imprison her in her subjectivity, circumscribe her within the limits of her own nature. It is often said that she thinks with her glands. Man superbly ignores the fact that his anatomy

From Simone de Beauvoir, *The Second Sex*, trans. and ed. H. M. Parshley (New York: Knopf, 1953), xvi–xx.

also includes glands, such as the testicles, and that they secrete hormones. He thinks of his body as a direct and normal connection with the world, which he believes he apprehends objectively, whereas he regards the body of woman as a hindrance, a prison, weighed down by everything peculiar to it. . . . And she is simply what man decrees; thus she is called "the sex," by which is meant that she appears essentially to the male as a sexual being. For him she is sex — absolute sex, no less. She is defined and differentiated with reference to man and not he with reference to her; she is the incidental, the inessential as opposed to the essential. He is the Subject, he is the Absolute — she is the Other. . . .

Thus it is that no group ever sets itself up as the One without at once setting up the Other over against itself. If three travelers chance to occupy the same compartment, that is enough to make vaguely hostile "others" out of all the rest of the passengers on the train. In small-town eyes all persons not belonging to the village are "strangers" and suspect; to the native of a country all who inhabit other countries are "foreigners"; Jews are "different" for the anti-Semite, Negroes are "inferior" for American racists, aborigines are "natives" for colonists, proletarians are the "lower class" for the privileged. . . .

No subject will readily volunteer to become the object, the inessential; it is not the Other who, in defining himself as the Other, establishes the One. The Other is posed as such by the One in defining himself as the One. But if the Other is not to regain the status of being the One, he must be submissive enough to accept this alien point of view. Whence comes this submission in the case of woman? . . .

. . . Throughout history they [women] have always been subordinated to men, and hence their dependency is not the result of a historical event or a social change — it was not something that *occurred*. The reason why otherness in this case seems to be an absolute is in part that it lacks the contingent or incidental nature of historical facts. A condition brought about at a certain time can be abolished at some other time, as the Negroes of Haiti and others have proved; but it might seem that a natural condition is beyond the possibility of change. In truth, however, the nature of things is no more immutably given, once for all, than is historical reality. If woman seems to be the inessential which never becomes the essential, it is because she herself fails to bring about this change. Proletarians say "We"; Negroes also. Regarding themselves as subjects, they transform the bourgeois, the whites, into "others." But women do not say "We," except at some congress of feminists or similar formal demonstration; men say "women," and women use the same word in referring to themselves. They do not authentically assume a subjective attitude. The proletarians have accomplished the revolution in Russia, the Negroes in Haiti, the Indo-Chinese are battling for it in Indo-China; but the women's effort has never been anything more than a symbolic agitation. They have gained only what men have been willing to grant; they have taken nothing, they have only received.

The reason for this is that women lack concrete means for organizing themselves into a unit which can stand face-to-face with the correlative unit. They have no past, no history, no religion of their own; and they have no such solidarity of work and interest as that of the proletariat. They are not even promiscuously herded together in the way that creates community feeling among the American Negroes, the ghetto Jews, the workers of Saint-Denis, or the factory hands of Rennault. They live dispersed among the males, attached through residence, housework, economic condition, and social standing to certain men — fathers or husbands — more firmly than they are to other women. If they belong to the bourgeoisie, they feel solidarity with men of that class, not with proletarian women; if they are white, their allegiance is to white men, not to Negro women. The proletariat can propose to massacre the ruling class, and a sufficiently fanatical Jew or Negro might dream of getting sole possession of the atomic bomb and making humanity wholly Jewish or black; but woman cannot even dream of exterminating the males. The bond that unites her to her oppressors is not comparable to any other. The division of the sexes is a biological fact, not an event in human history. . . . The couple is a fundamental unity with its two halves riveted together, and the cleavage of society along the line of sex is impossible. Here is to be found the basic trait of woman: she is the Other in a totality of which the two components are necessary to one another.

DISCUSSION QUESTIONS

1. What does Beauvoir mean when she describes women as the "Other"?

2. According to Beauvoir, how does women's status both resemble and differ from that of other oppressed groups, such as colonized peoples?

3. Why, unlike some of these groups, have women been unable to change their status?

5.
The Hungarian Uprising

Béla Lipták, *Birth of MEFESZ* (1956)

After Stalin's death in 1953, a climate of uncertainty enveloped communist parties around the world. The new leader of the Soviet Union, Nikita Khrushchev (1894–1971), attacked Stalinism and opened the door for the possibility of reform. In 1956, tens of thousands of people in eastern Europe sought to take advantage of the change in mood by protesting against Soviet rule. The Hungarian uprising in October was among the most daring and heroic of these rebellions; university students and factory workers joined together to advocate for free speech and personal liberty. This excerpt from A Testament of Revolution was written by Béla Lipták, a student in Budapest at the time of the uprising and ultimately one of the rebellion's leaders. Lipták describes the first spontaneous act of protest that led to the formation of an anticommunist student group at Budapest's Technical University. Although the protesters were brutally suppressed, they came to symbolize anticommunist courage against draconian

From Béla Lipták, *A Testament of Revolution* (College Station: Texas A&M University Press, 2001), 25–29.

oppression. In 1956, instead of choosing an individual person, Time *magazine named "the Hungarian Freedom Fighter" as Man of the Year.*

Attila and I settled down in the gallery of the aula, the large assembly hall of the Technical University. . . .

That day there must have been a couple of thousand students in the aula, but none of us was really paying much attention to what was going on. One could hear this constant murmur in the hall. It was like any other meeting in the Communist world. They talked *at* us, and our only defense against that was to not listen.

Below our gallery, on the main floor of the aula, the two rectors of the dual university, László Gillemot and Tibor Cholnoky, were at the microphone. With them were some professors, the Communist Party secretary, lesser Party officials, and the leaders of the Communist Youth Organization, the DISZ. It was the DISZ that had convened the meeting. In their uniform of blue jackets, white shirts, and red neckties, the leaders of the DISZ looked like a special breed of penguins or booby birds. Their purpose for calling the meeting was to preempt the spread of MEFESZ, the new non-Communist student association. Since the recent formation of MEFESZ in the city of Szeged, suddenly the DISZ seemed to care a lot about us. They talked about special train passes for students, cheaper textbooks, and better food and housing. We did not speak up. We never did. It was their show, and we let them do all the talking.

And talk they did. I was scraping the corrosion off my "gold" ring, which had cost me thirty-six forints and must have had some copper in its heritage, because it was turning green. I was spitting on it, rubbing it, and was just beginning to make some progress when I felt Attila's elbow in my side. He was pointing down to the speakers' platform, where there was some commotion. The murmur in the aula stopped. Now there was total silence. In startled curiosity the dozing students were beginning to wake up. We were sitting up and starting to pay attention. Now you could hear a pin drop. Then, from the middle of the tumult at the microphone, a voice rose: "I represent the MEFESZ of Szeged! I want to speak!"

It was unprecedented! Extraordinary! The air was thick with tension. We did not know who had spoken, did not understand what was happening. All we could see was that the DISZ penguins were shoving a small fellow away from the microphone. He was a student like us, and he was talking, gesticulating, but we heard nothing — the blue-jacketed DISZ had pushed him all the way to the wall.

Then the Party secretary, Mrs. Orbán, came to the microphone and admonished us, "You have only one duty! Your duty is to study!" She was almost screaming. "You don't want the MEFESZ of Szeged! You don't want any ideas from Szeged!" I could not imagine why Szeged was suddenly such a bad place. I did not particularly care what she was saying but I was hypnotized by this minihero, this crazy little guy from Szeged.

My mind raced on: I do not understand him. I do not understand what he wants. Is he out of his mind? Does he not know that he will be kicked out of the university? Not only that, he will also be thrown in jail — that is, right after they beat the shit out of him. Does he not understand that we are nobodies, that our collective name is "Shut Up"? Does he not understand that he is nothing, that I am nothing, that we have no say in anything? Does he not understand that the microphone is only for the Party collaborators and nobody, but nobody, else talks into it? Does he not know that even the penguins dare only read their prepared statements? And that even then they wait until they are told that it is their turn to read?

Attila muttered my own racing thoughts when he said, "I just don't get it!"

Then we saw the members of the military department, the only people who possessed arms at the university, marching onto the speaker's platform, and we got very quiet. My throat was dry, my breath bated. All eyes were on the officers. Then suddenly, from a distance, we heard a voice. It was that of a fifth-year architecture student, a blond, very tall young man by the name of Jancsi Danner. He yelled, "Let him speak!"

My heart stopped. Nothing like this had ever happened since the Red Army had occupied Hungary. I stared at Jancsi. His ears were red, his mouth was trembling, but he did not blink; he faced the bewildered and frightened stares of two thousand students.

"God, he has lost his marbles!" I said.

In the meantime a new and angry sort of murmur was building up, replacing the previously astonished silence, and now, a few rows in front of us, Laci Zsindely, a classmate of mine, hesitantly started to clap. It was then that the miracle occurred.

First one, then two, then four or five students joined in, and suddenly this sparse clapping turned into a hurricane, a burst of thunderous applause the likes of which I had never heard. I saw Attila clapping like a madman as he shouted to me, "Applaud or I will never speak to you again!"

I had never seen anything like it. As some of the students stood up, the ovation continued, and the Party officials around the microphone became nervous, surprised, angry—and just a bit uncertain. I had never seen them uncertain. That was something new. My flesh was creeping, and I was clapping as though my life depended on it, as if I were out of my mind. And during all this my mind was racing. Is this possible? Can we actually have a say? Can we contradict them like this, directly to their faces? Is it possible that I matter, that what I think matters? Is it possible that I do not have to hold my tongue all the time? Is it possible that I am not alone?

Now, it was total chaos. The Party secretary ran to the telephone. The rest of her penguins were white as sheets. The hands of the officers of the military department had moved to the guns on their belts while the chief of DISZ kept screaming into the microphone. And then, through all the pandemonium and over the thunderous applause, we heard his voice once more: "I represent the MEFESZ of Szeged! Allow me to speak!"

Now I really felt hypnotized. I stood up and began walking toward that voice and saw Attila doing the same thing. From other directions, another twenty, then thirty, students were also starting to move toward the voice. This was all completely spontaneous. We walked without knowing who was walking with us. We were drawn toward the speaker's stand, toward the angry but scared penguins, who had encircled the boy from MEFESZ. The circle thinned as we got closer and we just started pushing the whole group toward the microphone. I saw my hand rise, reaching for one of the fat penguins. . . . But then I saw the microphone. Five more meters and we would have it! I pushed with all my might. The DISZ resistance faltered. Now, Jancsi Danner grabbed the microphone and proclaimed, "I ask the representative of the students of Szeged to speak!"

There was a deafening ovation that took quite a while to taper off until there was total silence. I saw the six-foot-four Jancsi Danner reaching down to his waist as he gave the microphone to the diminutive delegate from Szeged. I just stood in the protective ring around him, and my eyes filled with tears as he started to speak in a strong voice: "Fellow students! Hungarians!"

I saw the flash of cameras. I saw strangers rushing to the telephones. Floodlights started to glare and film cameras begun to buzz. And the little fellow from Szeged was oblivious to it all as he started to speak: "Once again, the wind of freedom is blowing in from Poland. The Polish exchange students at our university are asking for our support. Russian troops are surrounding Warsaw, but the Polish army is also encircling the Russians. The city of Poznan is also free, but surrounded. Poland is showing the way and is asking for our solidarity. We will not let them down! We, the students of Szeged, have decided to follow the Poles in establishing our independent student organization, the MEFESZ. Please join us. Please do not believe the lies. Please form your own MEFESZ!"

At that point he seemed confused. His voice faltered. And then, haltingly, without a tune, he started to mumble the words of our forbidden hymn, the hymn most hated by the Communists: our national anthem. This anthem had not been heard in public for nearly a decade; one could sing it only in church, after the mass. This anthem that stood for the things the Communists most despised: God, country, and liberty. The anthem that we call our national prayer, the anthem that a Hungarian can sing only while standing at attention.

The great chandelier of the aula trembled and the windows shook as we sang our hearts out. As we finished we were all weeping. And during those couple of minutes of singing, a miracle occurred in that great hall. We were not the same people we had been a few minutes earlier. We, these tearful kids still standing at attention in that great hall, we had been reborn. We had stopped being scared. And therefore we were free! . . .

Discussion Questions

1. Why do you think the microphone had such central importance to this event?

2. What does this passage reveal about the norms of everyday life under Soviet communism?

3. How did Lipták's sense of freedom and confidence challenge the communist mentality?

4. Although this protest occurred in the presence of armed guards, not a shot was fired. Why do you think the guards refrained from using their weapons? What does this suggest about the power of words over weaponry?

COMPARATIVE QUESTIONS

1. How does the Cominform's vision of communism in the abstract compare with Béla Lipták's view of communism in practice?

2. Based on the Cominform declaration and National Security Council paper, what similarities do you see between Soviet and U.S. cold war attitudes and corresponding policies?

3. How would you compare the struggles of Ho Chi Minh, Simone de Beauvoir, and Béla Lipták against rigid power structures during the postwar era?

4. How does a deep sense of anxiety permeate the documents? What was the source of such anxiety, and where does it surface in the documents?

Postindustrial Society and the End of the Cold War Order, 1965–1989

The 1960s and 1970s were filled with turmoil fueled by feelings of both optimism and despair. During these years, millions of people took to the streets to challenge cold war politics and society. As the first document illustrates, for a few brief months in 1968, people in Czechoslovakia challenged Soviet communism and implemented a liberal government. A wave of public demonstrations swept across Europe and into the United States, where students protested against the war in Vietnam and for a more open political discourse. The second document captures some of their voices while the third — a photograph of Vietnamese children burned by napalm, which appeared in newspapers worldwide — puts human faces on the tragedy of war. At the same time, new threats to world stability emerged, as the fourth and fifth documents illustrate. In 1973, Arab countries attacked Israel and united to restrict the West's access to crude oil. The growing threat of terrorism in the major Western nations posed additional challenges. No one could have foreseen that the political landscape would dramatically shift in the late 1980s when the Soviet Empire disintegrated. The final document pulls back the curtain on this drama, revealing how government-sponsored state reforms set the stage not for brutal repression, as they had in Prague twenty years earlier, but rather for the end of the cold war.

1.
Prague Spring
Josef Smrkovský, *What Lies Ahead* (February 9, 1968)

In the immediate aftermath of World War II, the Soviet Union created a buffer of satellite states in eastern Europe, including Czechoslovakia. By 1957, when the pres-

idency there passed to Antonín Novotný (1904–1975), a politician committed to communist unity with the Soviet Union, Czechoslovakia had become an authoritarian state with collectivized property and suppressed civil liberties. However, a group led by Josef Smrkovský (1911–1974) and Alexander Dubcek (1921–1992) calling for more political and social openness secretly gathered strength in the highest ranks of the Czechoslovakian Communist Party. In January 1968, Dubcek succeeded Novotný as the head of the party, and he initiated a broad range of reforms, including free speech, an independent press, the right to assemble, and religious freedom. The following newspaper article excerpt, written by Smrkovský a month after Dubcek gained power, became the new government's most important manifesto. In it, Smrkovský emphasized a break with the "old" party, while calling for all the people of Czechoslovakia to build a "new," liberal Communist party. The reforms were not to last. In August 1968, Soviet dominance returned after Soviet and Warsaw Pact troops invaded Czechoslovakia, killed more than one hundred people, and arrested Dubcek and his allies.

On the Conclusions of the January Plenum of the CPCz CC[1]

The questions that the Central Committee of the party considered and resolved in December and January have set the entire party in motion, and the public at large has been paying great attention to them. This is so even though we failed to ensure the prompt and sufficient release of information. We must put this right, and that is precisely what we are doing, since there must be no discrepancy between our statements of Leninist principles and democratic traditions, on the one hand, and our future practical activities, on the other.

We can already say that in general the last Central Committee session has met with a favorable response in politically active sections of society. As more information has become available, discussions have been gaining momentum, and this in turn has generated greater enthusiasm for political activity. Yet even sincere persons who in the past have often been disappointed still show signs of skepticism. Old practices are still embedded in the activities of many of our organs and in the minds of people working in them. This creates doubts and insecurity. People are demanding guarantees. . . .

A Common Republic

Still, the common interest in truly maintaining the republic's internal unity demands that we rely on proven traditions, stemming from the joint anti-fascist liberation struggle, and that we come to grips with the issue of our relations in the interest of a modern socialist community. . . . For the first time in the his-

---

From Jaromir Navrátil, ed., *The Prague Spring 1968: A National Security Archive Documents Reader* (New York: Central European Press, 1998), 45–50.

[1]The Central Committee of the Czechoslovakian Communist Party.

tory of the CPCz, a Slovak communist has been placed at the helm of the party. Cde. Dubcek has become first secretary as an honest and experienced communist. At the CPCz CC session it was not at all a question of a "power seizure by the Slovaks" as we sometimes hear because of a lack of information in Czech circles.

Confidence in the Intelligentsia

By the same token, no one has threatened the working-class nature of the party. Those who spoke in the discussion could not be divided into intellectuals and workers, as is claimed erroneously in certain quarters. The open and passionate debate included intellectuals as well as workers and peasants, who were motivated by the same sincere concern for the cause of the republic, the interests of the people, and the improvement and consolidation of socialism. As a workers' official, which I consider myself to be, this is something I wish to emphasize. . . . The present era of the scientific-technical revolution — in which, unfortunately, we are badly lagging behind — demands more than ever that the creative forces of the working class, the peasantry, and the intelligentsia combine their efforts. . . .

Even further from the truth is the suggestion that what happened at the recent sessions of the CPCz CC was no more than a personal quarrel and a rotation of individuals. Of course, no one finds it easy to set aside his personal biases, not even at sessions of the party's Central Committee. Nevertheless, the personnel changes were in fact motivated by considerations that are of far greater urgency and importance to the party: the imperative to remove the obstacles that for some time have been obstructing the party's progressive efforts, and the need to remove everything . . . that inhibits the activation of all healthy forces in the party and among the people. . . . It is also essential to eliminate everything that has been distorting socialism, damaging people's spirits, causing pain, and depriving people of their faith and enthusiasm. This means we must do whatever is necessary to rehabilitate communists and other citizens who were unjustly sentenced in political trials so that we, as communists, can look ourselves in the face without shame. . . .

The CC session attempted to find the cause of the passivity and indifference in our country, things which we can no longer conceal. There is a conviction growing that everything we have achieved in transforming the structure of the society will facilitate — indeed will absolutely necessitate — a basic change of course. Such a change must be aimed at the democratization of the party and the society as a whole, and must be brought about consistently and honestly; it also must be backed by realistic guarantees that are understood by the majority to ensure that it will not be undermined by hedging and reservations. . . .

. . . What, then, lies ahead? We shall find no ready-made solutions. It is up to us, both Czechs and Slovaks, to launch out courageously into unexplored territory and search for a Czechoslovak road to socialism. . . .

The Example of the Central Committee

The first task is to inform the party, the whole party, of the content of the discussion at the CC session. . . . Scope must be given to a sincere and frank exchange of views from top to bottom, with priority to be given to the cogency of the arguments rather than to the power of the voice or the office. Priority also will be given to action instead of to indifference and passive submission. All truly progressive and responsible trends must be given a chance, and their chance must be given boldly and judiciously, sooner rather than later.

No mistake would be greater than to start carrying out these tasks on the basis of obsolete procedures, in the form of a one-off campaign that would, as usual, pay lip-service and then wither and die a few months later. . . .

The whole set of tasks and problems that are accumulating today before us can best be characterized as a steady process of democratization within both the party and the state. This process is the main precondition for a truly mature and thus voluntary form of discipline, without which the party would lose its capacity to act. Although we must cure and revive the whole party organism, we cannot do so through some "back-door" method. Nor can we compensate by relying on even the most hard-working apparatus. The entire party and each of its members must be convinced that the party as a whole is responsible not only for the implementation of tasks, but also for their conceptualization — that is, for the formulation of party policy, in which each communist must participate so that they can then regard it as their very own.

No doubt, we must "clear the table" — a phrase one often hears among comrades nowadays — but this must be done peacefully and in a businesslike manner so that we can prudently return to our former work and can reaffirm and develop whatever has been successful in the past, while rectifying shortcomings and mistakes in a just and sincere manner. Let us give to the past what it deserves — truth, purity, and justice. Let us do this without further delay and without scandals and recriminations, and let us do it consistently so we can then fully concentrate on what has always been the main interest of all communists: the future. . . .

The Position of the Party

. . . Let us not have any illusions. Nothing will happen on its own, without a struggle, or without some effort. Nothing will fall into our laps, and no one should expect charitable donations. There must be a sense of responsibility both "at the top" and "at the bottom."

People have emerged from various quarters who talk about a shake-up and turbulence; more such people will emerge, and the talk will continue. This eventful session, where people spoke frankly, openly, courageously, critically, and self-critically, may appear turbulent to some. But there are different types of turbulence. I think it will be a good thing if the December and January plenary sessions bring a real shake-up — a shake-up that is beneficial in releasing and re- viving new and fresh forces that can move our society and our socialist republic forward into a new phase. All this is fully within the power of the party and within the power of our 1.5 million communists, who can count on the total help and support of broad masses of the population who want the same things that we do.

Discussion Questions

1. Why do you think Smrkovský devoted so much of his newspaper article to dis- pelling the skepticism, doubt, and insecurity of his readers?

2. How did the practices of the Czechoslovakian Communist Party compare to the new proposals?

3. How do you think this article was received when it was first published? What as- pects do you think were most controversial then, and what aspects seem most revolutionary to you today?

2.

A Revolutionary Time

Student Voices of Protest (1968)

College campuses were hotbeds of social activism during the 1960s, and they exploded into action with unprecedented force in the spring of 1968. The year was beset with tragedies, from the mounting number of casualties in the Vietnam War to the assassi- nation of American civil rights leader Martin Luther King Jr. and presidential candi- date Robert F. Kennedy. Students from New York to Paris to Berlin rose up in protest, particularly over racial and antiwar issues. They demonstrated, occupied buildings, shut down classes, and went on strike. The following excerpts bring these students to life in their own words, which convey not only frustration and despair but also a de- sire to bring about lasting change.

My most vivid memory of May '68? The new-found ability for everyone to *speak*— to speak of anything with anyone. In that month of talking during May you learnt more than in the whole of your five years of studying. It was really another world — a dream world perhaps — but that's what I'll always remember: the need and the right for everyone to speak. — René Bourrigaud, student at the École Supérieure d'Agriculture, Angers, France

People were learning through doing things themselves, learning self-confidence. It was magic, there were all these kids from nice middle-class homes who'd never

---

From Ronald Fraser et al., *1968: A Student Generation in Revolt* (New York: Pantheon Books, 1988), 9–12.

done or said anything and were now suddenly speaking. It was democracy of the public space in the market place, a discourse where nobody was privileged. If anything encapsulated what we were trying to do and why, it was that. . . . — Pete Latarche, leader of the university occupation at Hull, England, 1968

It's a moment I shall never forget. Suddenly, spontaneously, barricades were being thrown up in the streets. People were building up the cobblestones because they wanted — many of them for the first time — to throw themselves into a collective, spontaneous activity. People were releasing all their repressed feelings, expressing them in a festive spirit. Thousands felt the need to communicate with each other, to love one another. That night has forever made me optimistic about history. Having lived through it, I can't ever say, "It will never happen." . . . — Dany Cohn-Bendit, student leader at Nanterre University, on the night of the Paris barricades, 10/11 May 1968

The unthinkable happened! Everything I had ever dreamt of since childhood, knowing that it would never happen, now began to become real. People were saying, fuck hierarchy, authority, this society with its cold rational elitist logic! Fuck all the petty bosses and the mandarins at the top! Fuck this immutable society that refuses to consider the misery, poverty, inequality and injustice it creates, that divides people according to their origins and skills! Suddenly, the French were showing they understood that they had to refuse the state's authority because it was malevolent, evil, just as I'd always thought as a child. Suddenly they realized that they had to find a new sort of solidarity. And it was happening in front of my eyes. That was what May '68 meant to me! . . . — Nelly Finkielsztejn, student at Nanterre University, Paris

My world had been very staid, very traditional, very frightened, very middle-class and respectable. And here I was doing these things that six months before I would have thought were just horrible. But I was in the midst of an enormous tide of people. There was so much constant collective reaffirmation of it. The ecstasy was stepping out of time, out of traditional personal time. The usual rules of the game in capitalist society had been set aside. It was phenomenally liberating. . . . At the same time it was a political struggle. It wasn't just Columbia. There *was* a fucking war on in Vietnam, and the civil rights movement. These were profound forces that transcend that moment. 1968 just cracked the universe open for me. And the fact of getting involved meant that never again was I going to look at something outside with the kind of reflex condemnation or fear. Yes, it was the making of me — or the unmaking. — Mike Wallace, occupation of Columbia University, New York, April 1968

We'd been brought up to believe in our hearts that America fought on the side of justice. The Second World War was very much ingrained in us, my father had volunteered. So, along with the absolute horror of the war in Vietnam, there was also a feeling of personal betrayal. I remember crying by myself late at night in my room listening to the reports of the war, the first reports of the bombing. Vietnam was the catalyst. . . . — John Levin, student leader at San Francisco State College

I was outraged, what shocked me most was that a highly developed country, the super-modern American army, should fall on these Vietnamese peasants — fall on them like the conquistadores on South America, or the white settlers on the North American Indians. In my mind's eye, I always saw those bull-necked fat pigs — like in Georg Grosz's pictures — attacking the small, child-like Vietnamese. — Michael von Engelhardt, German student

The resistance of the Vietnamese people showed that it could be done — a fight back was possible. If poor peasants could do it well why not people in Western Europe? That was the importance of Vietnam, it destroyed the myth that we just had to hold on to what we had because the whole world could be blown up if the Americans were "provoked." The Vietnamese showed that if you were attacked you fought back, and then it depended on the internal balance of power whether you won or not. . . . — Tariq Ali, a British Vietnam Solidarity Campaign leader

So we started to be political in a totally new way, making the connection between our student condition and the larger international issues. A low mark in mathematics could become the focal point of an occupation by students who linked the professor's arbitrary and authoritarian behavior to the wider issues, like Vietnam. Acting on your immediate problems made you understand better the bigger issues. If it hadn't been for that, perhaps the latter would have remained alien, you'd have said "OK, but what can *I* do?" — Agnese Gatti, student at Trento Institute of Social Sciences, Italy

Creating a confrontation with the university administration you could significantly expose the interlocking network of imperialism as it was played out on the campuses. You could prove that they were working hand-in-hand with the military and the CIA, and that ultimately, when you pushed them, they would call upon all the oppressive apparatus to defend their position from their own students. . . . — Jeff Jones, Students for a Democratic Society (SDS), New York regional organizer

Everybody was terribly young and didn't know what was going on. One had a sort of megalomaniac attitude that by sheer protest and revolt things would be changed. It was true of the music, of the hallucinogenics, of politics, it was true across the board — people threw themselves into activity without experience. The desire to do something became tremendously intense and the capacity to do it diminished by the very way one was rejecting the procedures by which things could be done. It led to all sorts of crazy ideas. — Anthony Barnett, sociology student, Leicester University, England

DISCUSSION QUESTIONS

1. What were some of the students' principal targets for criticism, and why?

2. In what ways did the events of 1968 personally transform some of these students?

3. Some historians argue that the student protests of 1968 made governments less inviolable and sacred. What evidence can you find here to support this assertion?

3.
Children Fleeing from a Napalm Attack in South Vietnam
Nick Ut, *Photograph* (June 8, 1972)

Although the cold war dominated the European landscape during the 1950s and 1960s, it also loomed large in Asia. Responding to years of resistance against French colonial rule led by the founder of the Indochinese Communist Party, Ho Chi Minh (1890– 1969), the Geneva Convention divided Vietnam into North and South in 1954. Ho Chi Minh and his followers were ordered to retreat to the North. U.S. leaders feared that the communist presence there would spread elsewhere in the region, and gradually their commitment to a non-Communist South Vietnam escalated to all-out war. By 1966, the United States had more than a half million soldiers in South Vietnam. One of the most compelling images of the Vietnam War is that of children running

AP IMAGES/Nick Ut

down a dusty road, screaming in terror and pain after a napalm attack on their vil-
lage. The photograph, taken by Associated Press photographer Nick Ut, appeared on the
front pages of newspapers around the world and helped turn public opinion against the
war. Although South Vietnamese aircraft executed the attack, it had been ordered by
the U.S. Army — a fact that shocked much of the American public. In the years fol-
lowing its publication, the North Vietnamese government used the photograph as ev-
idence of American atrocities.

Discussion Questions

1. Why do you think this image had such a powerful impact on the public at the time?

2. What does the image of the young girl in the center of the photograph, with her clothes having been burned off and her skin on fire, reveal about the technology of war and its human costs?

3. How might the photograph's effect on U.S. public opinion have been different had the perpetrators of the napalm attack been the North Vietnamese army rather than the South Vietnamese and the Americans?

4. What do you think the political impact of this photograph was in North Vietnam after its publication?

4.
The Rising Power of OPEC

U.S. Embassy, Saudi Arabia, *Saudi Ban on Oil Shipments to the United States* (October 23, 1973)

In a show of pan-Arabian unity and nationalism, military forces from Egypt and Syria invaded Israel on October 6, 1973. The United States quickly offered extensive financial aid to Israel. As punishment for U.S. support of Israel, the Organization of the Petroleum Exporting Countries (OPEC) banned its members from exporting oil to the United States and raised the price of oil for the U.S. allies in western Europe. Overnight, the price of a barrel rose from $3 to $5.11, and by January 1974, it had risen to $11.65, resulting in widespread fuel shortages across the West. Infused with Arab nationalism, the actions of OPEC shocked citizens in Europe and the United States, who were not accustomed to being at the mercy of nations they once domi-nated. In this confidential cable, which was only declassified in September 2003, an unidentified writer from the U.S. Embassy in Saudi Arabia offers an inside view of the Saudis' strategy in their decision to participate in the OPEC ban on exporting oil to the United States.

From U.S. Embassy in Saudi Arabia, Cable 4663 to U.S. State Department, "Saudi Ban on Oil Shipments to U.S.," 23 October 1973 (Washington, D.C.: National Security Archive).

23 OCTOBER 1973
FROM: AMERICAN EMBASSY IN SAUDI ARABIA
TO: THE SECRETARY OF STATE, WASHINGTON D.C.
SUBJECT: SAUDI BAN ON OIL SHIPMENTS TO U.S.

SUMMARY: SAUDI DECISION TO CUT OFF OIL SHIPMENTS TO U.S. ATTRIB-
UTABLE TO KING'S OWN DECISION: KING ANGRY AT ANNOUNCEMENT
OF LARGE U.S. MILITARY GRANT PROGRAMS TO ISRAEL AND PROBABLY
FELT THAT ANY LESSER RESPONSE WOULD LEAVE SAUDI ARABIA UN-
COMFORTABLY ISOLATED IN ARAB WORLD. U.S. MISSION CONTACTS WITH
HIGH-LEVEL SAG [the Government of Saudi Arabia] OFFICIALS, HOWEVER, IN-
DICATE SAG WISHES TO MINIMIZE DAMAGE THAT PRESENT CRISIS MAY
DO TO U.S.-SAG RELATIONS. JOINT U.S.-USSR RESOLUTION IN SECURITY
COUNCIL, POTENTIALLY A RADICALLY POSITIVE STEP, BUT IF IT DOES NOT
SUCCEED, SAG MAY FEEL COMPELLED TO INCREASE PRESSURE ON U.S. IN-
TERESTS IN MILITARY, COMMERCIAL, ENERGY AND FINANCIAL AREAS.
EMBASSY IS STRESSING WITH SAG NEED THAT CHANNELS OF COMMUNI-
CATION REMAIN OPEN, AND THAT EACH SIDE GIVE [each] OTHER MAXI-
MUM ADVANCE NOTICE OF ANY MEASURES IT IS CONTEMPLATING. END
SUMMARY.

1. THERE IS LITTLE DOUBT THAT SAG DECISION TO BAN PETROLEUM
   EXPORTS TO U.S. STEMMED FROM KING FAISAL HIMSELF. DISCUSSION
   BETWEEN HIGH-RANKING SAG OFFICIALS AND AMBASSADOR IN 24
   HOURS PREVIOUS HAD NOT INDICATED SAG ON VERGE OF TAKING
   SUCH BIG STEP.

2. SOURCES IN ROYAL DIWAN OCT 21 HAVE CONFIRMED TO EMBASSY
   THAT DECISION [was] TAKEN BY KING, AND WAS PRINCIPALLY MOTI-
   VATED BY U.S. PROPOSAL TO PROVIDE ISRAEL WITH 2.2 MILLION DOL-
   LARS OF GRANT [money for] MILITARY AID. WAS TOLD BY CHIEF OF
   ROYAL DIWAN, AHMAD ABDUL WAHAB (A WELL-ADJUSTED PRO-
   AMERICAN FIGURE) THAT KING WAS AS FURIOUS AS HE HAD EVER
   SEEN HIM AND THAT HE TOOK PARTICULAR UMBRAGE AT WHAT HE
   CONSIDERED TO BE DIFFERENCE BETWEEN REASSURING TONE OF
   VARIOUS COMMUNICATIONS HE HAD RECEIVED FROM USG [the United
   States Government] AND U.S. ANNOUNCEMENT OF "INCREDIBLE"
   AMOUNT OF AID TO GOI [the Government of Israel]. KING'S SUBSEQUENT
   CALL FOR JIHAD CAN ALSO BE ASCRIBED TO KING'S DISPLEASURE.
   KING'S MOOD EMPHATICALLY REFLECTED ALSO BY ABLE, NATIONAL-
   IST MINISTER HISHAM NAZER, HEAD OF CENTRAL PLANNING OR-
   GANIZATION.

3. WE SHOULD NOT, HOWEVER, OVERSTRESS THE CAUSATIVE EFFECT OF
   PURE EMOTION IN KING'S DECISION TO CUT BACK OIL SHIPMENTS TO

U.S. A NUMBER OF ARAB COUNTRIES HAD ALREADY TAKEN STEP OF BANNING SUCH SHIPMENTS, AND [Sheikh Zaki] YAMANI [the official in charge of Saudi oil policy in 1973] HAD INFORMED AMBASSADOR THAT OTHERS WOULD PROBABLY FOLLOW. AS IMPACT OF U.S. AID DECISION MADE ITSELF FELT IN ARAB WORLD, KING MAY HAVE FELT THAT SAG WOULD OCCUPY EXPOSED SALIENT IF IT — ALONE AMONG ARAB OIL PRODUCERS — CONTINUED TO PROVIDE OIL TO U.S.

4. EMBASSY CONTACTS ELSEWHERE IN SAG, MOREOVER, TEND TO CONFIRM OUR ASSESSMENT THAT SAG WISHES [to] MINIMIZE DAMAGE THAT PRESENT CRISIS COULD CAUSE TO U.S.-SAUDI RELATIONS. . . . DURING MEETING OCT 21 BETWEEN CHIEF OF U.S. MILITARY TRAINING MISSION (USMTM), GENERAL HILL, DEPUTY MUDA, AND KING'S BROTHER PRINCE TURKI, PRINCE STATED "WE HAVE HAD TO TAKE CERTAIN POLITICAL DECISIONS DURING THE WAR JUST AS YOU HAVE, BUT THAT MUST BE KEPT ENTIRELY SEPARATE FROM RELATIONSHIPS BETWEEN MUDA AND USMTM." PRINCE IN SOMBER MOOD, BUT WAS AT ALL TIMES COURTEOUS AND FRIENDLY TO GENERAL HILL AND HIS STAFF. . . .

6. SAG ACTION COULD ALSO DELIVER A SETBACK TO IMPORTANT U.S. COMMERCIAL AND MILITARY SALES: SAG HAS GROWN TO BE ONE OF LARGEST MARKETS FOR AMERICAN PRODUCTS . . . WITH SALES RUNNING AT MORE THAN A THIRD OF A BILLION DOLLARS THIS YEAR. OUR MILITARY SALES PROGRAMS MOREOVER HAVE . . . IN THE PAST THREE YEARS EXCEEDED 500 MILLION DOLLARS, AND THERE ARE GOOD PROSPECTS FOR CASH SALES OF A SIMILAR ORDER TO BE CONCLUDED WITHIN THE NEXT TWO YEARS. WE SHOULD REMEMBER THAT EUROPE, PARTICULARLY FRENCH AND BRITISH SOURCES, ARE MORE THAN PREPARED TO PICK UP THE FALLOUT FROM THE AMERICAN DILEMMA IN THE MIDDLE EAST CONFLICT.

7. IN THE MEANTIME, AMBASSADOR HAS PASSED WORD TO CHIEF OF ROYAL DIWAN THAT IT IS ESSENTIAL FOR CHANNELS OF COMMUNICATION BETWEEN HIM AND SAG TO REMAIN OPEN AT ALL TIMES. . . .

8. FINALLY, WITH REGARD TO SAUDI ACTIONS AGAINST U.S. OIL AND OTHER INTERESTS, WE SHOULD AVOID ACRIMONIOUS COMMENTS, SINCE THESE TEND TO KEEP AN UNHELPFUL DIALOGUE GOING.

Discussion Questions

1. What do you think the writer's main concern was in sending this cable to the U.S. State Department?

2. How would you characterize the writer's attitude toward Saudi Arabian government officials?

3. How were European countries directly affected by U.S. policies toward Saudi Arabia and other OPEC countries? Where do you see direct references to this in the telegram?

5.
Facing Terrorism

Jacques Chirac, *New French Antiterrorist Laws*
(September 14, 1986)

Along with the energy crisis, the rise of terrorism in the 1970s and 1980s posed a serious challenge to Western governments. Although there is disagreement as to the precise definition of "terrorism," at the most basic level it involves the premeditated use of violence for political ends. Civilian populations have often born the brunt of terrorist attacks, as was brutally apparent in France in September 1986. In the span of eight days, a number of bombs exploded in Paris stores, restaurants, and public buildings, killing at least ten people and wounding scores more. The principal suspects were members of a group with Syrian links, the Lebanese Armed Revolutionary Faction (FARL), whose leader was imprisoned in France. It appears that the group hoped the bombings would secure his release. In response to the violence, French prime minister Jacques Chirac implemented a series of antiterrorism measures, which he presented to the French people on September 14 in a televised statement, excerpted here.

Since our election and the formation of this government we have been working on a series of bills that are now ready. The laws on security and particularly on terrorism that were voted on during the last session were promulgated a few days ago according to the democratic legislative process for passing laws. We will implement their provisions immediately and with the greatest authority. What do these laws provide for? First of all, improvement of prevention by extension of police custody, general identity checks, and searches on premises.

On the question of identity checks I ask every one of our citizens to understand that, in the current situation, the constraint that these controls represent should be accepted with, so to speak, good humor. It is necessary for everyone's security.

These laws also centralize investigations and legal proceedings in Paris, in the hands of specialists, in order to be more effective in the prosecution of those who are implicated of direct or indirect involvement in terrorist acts.

From Bruce Maxwell, *Terrorism: A Documentary History* (Washington, D.C.: CQ Press, 2003), 85–87.

The second set of decisions we have taken will naturally aggravate a certain number of our foreign friends visiting France. We have in effect decided to require a mandatory visa for all foreigners entering France, regardless of their origin, with the exception, of course, of the European Community and Switzerland.

But for all others, no matter what their origin, the North or the South, Asia or Africa, from tomorrow on visas will be required, albeit with a few days' delay, for technical reasons, before actual implementation begins. The visas will be issued by our consulates around the world and will enable us to prohibit entry into France to all sorts of people who appear at the borders and enter the territory with passports which, as everyone knows, are all too often irregularly issued, or are forgeries that we cannot verify.

I ask all our foreign friends to understand that, in the crisis situation in which we find ourselves, this measure is necessary. Unfortunately it is likely to provoke some problems when enforced, such as delays in airports or at points of entry into France, but these are inevitable incidents in the implementation of this type of measure.

My next point concerns checks and, where necessary, expulsion. Everyone knows that the police have an eye on a certain number of people whom they suspect, but cannot accuse, of belonging to what I would call the terrorist organizations' sphere of influence. We have decided to strengthen considerably checks on and surveillance of all those active in the terrorist movements' sphere of influence, hence the series of arrests which you have probably heard about in the last few days and which will result in expulsion — and which has in the last two days resulted in the expulsion of persons whose presence in France we consider a danger to the public order. That has begun, will continue and be carried out with the greatest determination and the greatest firmness.

Finally, there is the problem of security in public places. As you saw earlier, reports have just come in, and will perhaps be corrected since this occurred virtually as we were coming into the studio, of a dubious package apparently, I say apparently being discovered in the Renault Pub, a place where there are a lot of people, and being taken down into the basement, where it unfortunately exploded, wounding three policemen: that clearly illustrates the vulnerability of public places. They must have proper security. I am mayor of Paris, I see what happens in the close vicinity of my City Hall. Everyone who enters the Bazar de l'Hotel de Ville [a large department store] with a package, even a small one, has to open it. I tell you that this has not caused the slightest problem nor created the slightest incident in the last three or four years. And this has made the Bazar de l'Hotel de Ville a very safe place. Other stores, like the Galeries Lafayette and others as well, do the same thing. I want private places frequented by the public to enforce those security measures, which are a very considerable deterrent.

There you have a certain number of measures, those that can be announced. I tell you right away that there are others, but these others are the sole responsibility of the public authorities and, because of their nature, are not being publicized and I shall not answer questions or comment on them. However, they are also being taken in the context of this calm, firm fight against this veritable scourge of modern times that is terrorism.

In conclusion, I shall say that everyone must feel he or she has a part to play in these matters. Everyone's safety is at stake. Terrorism is, by definition, blind and spares no one, not you, me or anyone. . . .

I would like everyone to be certain that the day, and it will inevitably come, there's no doubt about that, when we catch a terrorist in the act, he will talk and those manipulating him must clearly realize that they will receive draconian retribution, that we shall be pitiless, regardless of the consequences. They must realize that.

DISCUSSION QUESTIONS

1. How does Chirac define terrorism and the dangers it poses to the public?

2. What specific measures did he propose to counter these dangers?

3. Do you see any tension in these measures between maintaining security and protecting individual rights? What does this suggest about the particular threat terrorism poses to democratic societies?

6.
Debating Change in the Soviet Union
Glasnost *and the Soviet Press* (1988)

When Mikhail Gorbachev (b. 1931) became the general secretary of the Soviet Communist Party in 1985, the nation's economy was in ruins, and people struggled to meet even their most basic needs. Gorbachev implemented revolutionary policies of economic restructuring (perestroika) *and "openness"* (glasnost) *to confront the crisis. The two articles excerpted here illuminate the crucial role of the Soviet press in this process as a forum for public debate. Never before had Soviet citizens experienced such freedom of speech and expression. Written by Nina Andreyeva, the first article appeared as a letter to the editor on the front page of the prestigious newspaper* Sovetskaya Rossiya *in March 1988. Politically conservative, Andreyeva attacked Gorbachev's reforms as a violation of socialist ideology. Gorbachev and his supporters countered her assault in an article of their own, published three weeks later in* Pravda, *defending* glasnost *and* perestroika *as the path to a better future.*

Polemics: I Cannot Waive Principles

Nina Andreyeva

I decided to write this letter after lengthy deliberation. I am a chemist, and I lecture at Leningrad's Lensovet Technology Institute. Like many others, I also look after a student group. Students nowadays, following the period of social apathy and intellectual dependence, are gradually becoming charged with the energy of

From Isaac J. Tarasulo, ed., *Gorbachev and Glasnost: Viewpoints from the Soviet Press* (Wilmington: SR Books, 1989), 277–78, 281–85, 290–95, 299–302.

revolutionary changes. Naturally, discussions develop about the ways of restructuring and its economic and ideological aspects. *Glasnost*, openness, the disappearance of zones where criticism is taboo, and the emotional heat of mass consciousness (especially among young people) often result in the raising of problems that are, to a greater or lesser extent, "prompted" either by Western radio voices or by those of our compatriots who are shaky in their conceptions of the essence of socialism. And what a variety of topics that are being discussed! A multiparty system, freedom of religious propaganda, emigration to live abroad, the right to broad discussion of sexual problems in the press, the need to decentralize the leadership of culture, abolition of compulsory military service. There are particularly numerous arguments among students about the country's past. . . .

In the numerous discussions now taking place on literally all questions of the social sciences, as a college lecturer I am primarily interested in the questions that have a direct effect on young people's ideological and political education, their moral health, and their social optimism. Conversing with students and deliberating with them on controversial problems, I cannot help concluding that our country has accumulated quite a few anomalies and one-sided interpretations that clearly need to be corrected. I would like to dwell on some of them in particular.

Take, for example the question of Joseph Stalin's place in our country's history. The whole obsession with critical attacks is linked with his name, and in my opinion this obsession centers not so much on the historical individual himself as on the entire highly complex epoch of transition, an epoch linked with unprecedented feats by a whole generation of Soviet people who are today gradually withdrawing from active participation in political and social work. The industrialization, collectivization, and cultural revolution which brought our country to the ranks of the great world powers are being forcibly squeezed into the "personality cult" formula. All of this is being questioned. Matters have gone so far that persistent demands for "repentance" are being made of "Stalinists" (and this category can be taken to include anyone you like). There is rapturous praise for novels and movies that lynch the epoch of "storms and onslaught," which is presented as a "tragedy of the peoples." . . .

I support the party's call to uphold the honor and dignity of the trailblazers of socialism. I think that these are the party-class positions from which we must assess the historical role of all leaders of the party and the country, including Stalin. In this case, matters cannot be reduced to their "court" aspect or to abstract moralizing by persons far removed both from those stormy times and from the people who had to live and work in those times, and to work in such a fashion as to still be an inspiring example for us today. . . .

I think that, no matter how controversial and complex a figure in Soviet history Stalin may be, his genuine role in the building and defense of socialism will sooner or later be given an objective and unambiguous assessment. Of course, unambiguous does not mean an assessment that is one-sided, that whitewashes, or that eclectically sums up contradictory phenomena making it possible subjectively (albeit with slight reservations) "to forgive or not forgive," "to reject or retain." Unambiguous means primarily a specific historical assessment detached from short-term considerations which would demonstrate — according to historical results! — the dialectics of the correlation between the individual's actions and the basic laws governing society's development. In our country these laws were also linked with the answer to the question "Who will defeat whom?" in its domestic as well as international aspects. If we are to adhere to the Marxist-Leninist methodology of historical analysis then, in Mikhail Gorbachev's words, we must primarily and vividly show how the millions of people lived, how they worked, and what they believed in, as well as the coupling of victories and failures, discoveries and errors, the bright and the tragic, the revolutionary enthusiasm of the masses and the violations of socialist legality and even crimes at times. . . .

It seems to me that the question of the role and position of socialist ideology is extremely acute today. The authors of timeserving articles circulating under the guise of moral and spiritual "cleansing" erode the dividing lines and criteria of scientific ideology, manipulate glasnost, and foster nonsocialist pluralism, which applies the brakes on perestroika in the public conscience. This has a particularly painful effect on young people which, I repeat, is clearly sensed by us, the college lecturers, schoolteachers, and all who have to deal with young people's problems. As Mikhail Gorbachev said at the CPSU Central Committee February plenum, "our actions in the spiritual sphere — and maybe primarily and precisely there — must be guided by our Marxist-Leninist principles. Principles comrades, must not be compromised on any pretext whatever."

This is what we stand for now, and this is what we will continue to stand for. Principles were not given to us as a gift, we have fought for them at crucial turning points in the fatherland's history.

Principles of Perestroika: The Revolutionary Nature of Thinking and Acting

Pravda Editorial

The CPSU Central Committee February plenum solidified the party's new tasks in restructuring all spheres of life at the present stage. The plenum speech of Mikhail Gorbachev, general secretary of the CPSU Central Committee ("Revolutionary Perestroika Requires Ideology of Renewal") made a clear analysis of today's problems and set forth a program of ideological support for perestroika. People want to be better aware of the nature of the changes that have begun in society, to see the essence and significance of the proposed solutions, and to know what is meant by the new quality of society we want to achieve. The struggle for perestroika is being waged both in production and in the spiritual sphere. And even though this struggle does not take the form of class antagonisms, it is proceeding sharply. The emergence of something new always excites attitudes toward and judgments about the new thing.

The debate itself and its nature and thrust attest to the democratization of our society. The diversity of judgments, assessments, and positions is one of the most important signs of the times and attests to the socialist pluralism of opinions which really exists now.

But it is impossible not to notice one very specific dimension of this debate. It occasionally declares itself not in a desire to interpret what is happening and to investigate it nor in a wish to advance the cause but, on the contrary, in attempts to slow it down by shouting the usual incantations: "They are betraying ideals!" "Abandoning principles!" "Undermining foundations!" . . .

The long article "I Cannot Waive Principles" [pp. 277–79] that appeared in the newspaper *Sovetskaya Rossiya* on March 13 was a reflection of such feelings. . . .

Whether the author wanted it or not, primarily the article artificially sets off certain categories of Soviet people against one another. And this at precisely the moment when the unity of creative forces, despite all the shades of opinion, is more necessary than ever and when such unity is the prime requirement of perestroika and an absolute necessity simply for normal life, work, and the constructive renewal of society. Herein resides the fundamental feature of perestroika, which is designed to unite the maximum number of like-minded people in the struggle against phenomena impeding our life. Precisely and principally against all of these phenomena, not only or simply against certain incorrigible proponents of bureaucracy, corruption, abuse, and so forth.

In addition, the article is unconstructive. In an extensive, pretentiously titled article essentially no space was found to work out a single problem of perestroika. Whatever it discussed — glasnost, openness, the disappearance of areas free from criticism, youth — these processes and perestroika itself were linked only with difficulties and adverse consequences. . . .

There are, in point of fact, two basic theses running throughout the article: Why all of this perestroika, and haven't we gone too far with democratization and glasnost? The article urges us to amend and adjust perestroika; otherwise, it is alleged, "people in authority" will have to rescue socialism.

It is evident that not everyone has realized clearly yet the dramatic nature of the situation the country found itself in by April 1985, a situation which today we rightfully describe as precrisis. It is evident that not everyone is fully aware yet that administrative edict methods are totally obsolete. It is time that anyone who still places hopes in these methods or in their modification understands that all of this has already been tried, tried repeatedly, and it has failed to produce the desired results. Any ideas about the simplicity and effectiveness of these methods are nothing but illusions without any historical justification.

So, how is socialism to be "saved" today?

Should authoritarian methods, the practice of blind obedience, and the stifling of initiative be retained? Should we retain the system in which bureaucratism, lack of control, corruption, bribery, and petty bourgeois degeneration flourished lavishly?

Or should we revert to Leninist principles, whose essence is democratism, social justice, economic accountability, and respect for the individual's honor, life, and dignity? Do we have the right, in the face of the real difficulties and unsatisfied needs of the people, to adhere to the same old approaches that prevailed in the 1930s and 1940s? Has not the time come to clearly differentiate between the essence of socialism and the historically restricted forms of its implementation?

Has not the time come for a scientifically critical investigation of our history, primarily in order to change the world in which we live and to learn harsh lessons for the future?

Almost half of the article is devoted to an assessment of our distant and recent history. The last few years have provided graphic proof of the growing interest in the past shown by the broadest strata of the population. The principles of scientific historicism and truth are increasingly the basis on which the people's historical awareness is taking shape. At the same time, there are instances of people playing on the idea of patriotism. Those who loudly scream about alleged "internal threats" to socialism, those who join certain political extremists and look everywhere for internal enemies, "counterrevolutionary nations," and so on, those are not patriots. The patriots are those who act in the country's interests and for the people's benefit, without fearing any difficulties. We do not need contemplative or verbal patriotism, we need creative patriotism. Not nostalgic and backward-looking patriotism, but the patriotism of socialist transformations. Patriotism based not only on love for the area of your birth, but also imbued with pride in the accomplishments of the great motherland of socialism.

Past experience is vitally necessary for the present, for solving the tasks of perestroika. Life's demand — "More socialism!" — makes it incumbent upon us to investigate what we did yesterday and how we did it, what has to be rejected and what has to be retained. Which principles and values ought to be considered really socialist? And if today we are taking a critical look at our history, we are doing so only because we want a better and more complete idea of our path into the future. . . .

The best teacher of perestroika — the one to whom we should constantly listen — is life, and life is dialectical. We should constantly remember the words of [Friedrich] Engels to the effect that nothing has been unconditionally established once and for all as sacrosanct. It is this continual motion and the constant renewal of nature, society, and our thinking that is the point of departure for and the initial, most cardinal principle in our thinking.

Let us return to the question: What has been done already? How are the party's course and the decisions of the 27th Party Congress and Central Committee plenums being implemented? What positive changes are taking place in people's lives?

We have really got down to tackling the most pressing, highest priority problems: housing, food, and the supply of goods and services to the population. A turn toward accelerated development of the social sphere has begun. Concrete decisions about restructuring education and health care have been adopted. Radical economic reform, our main lever for implementing large-scale transformations, is being put into practice. "That is the main political result of the last three years," M. Gorbachev said at the 4th All-Union Congress of *kolkhoz* members.

The voice of the intelligentsia and of all the working people has begun to make itself heard powerfully and strongly in society's spiritual life. This is one of the first gains accomplished by perestroika. Democratism is impossible without freedom of thought and speech, without the open, broad clash of opinions, without keeping a critical eye on our life. . . .

There are no prohibited topics today. Journals, publishing houses, and studios decide for themselves what to publish. But the appearance of the article "I Cannot Waive Principles" is part of an attempt little by little to revise party decisions. It has been said repeatedly at meetings in the party Central Committee that the Soviet press is not a private concern, that Communists writing for the press and editors should have a sense of responsibility for articles and publications. In this case the newspaper *Sovetskaya Rossiya*, which, let us be frank, has done much for perestroika, departed from this principle.

Debates, discussions, and polemics are, of course, necessary. They lie in store for us in our future, too. There are also many pitfalls in store for us, traps laid by the past. We must all work together to clear these traps from our path. We need disputes that help to advance perestroika and lead to the consolidation of forces, to cohesion around perestroika, and not to disunity. . . .

More light. More initiative. More responsibility. A more rapid mastery of the full profundity of the Marxist-Leninist concept of perestroika, of the new political thinking. We can and must revive the Leninist practice of the socialist society — the most humane, the most just. We will firmly and steadily follow the revolutionary principles of perestroika: more glasnost, more democracy, more socialism.

Discussion Questions

1. Why is Andreyeva so critical of Gorbachev's reforms?
2. What arguments do Gorbachev's supporters use to counter her criticisms?
3. According to the *Pravda* article, what are the fundamental features of glasnost and perestroika?
4. In what ways do these two articles reflect different understandings of Soviet history and its role in shaping the country's future?

Comparative Questions

1. Based on the first two documents, how did the events of the 1960s turn Western society upside down, and why?
2. How do the second, third, fourth, and fifth documents represent a broader debate concerning Western political values and global dominance?
3. How did disagreements over ideology and generational conflict drive the protests of the 1960s and 1970s?
4. What similarities do you see between the message and the medium of the Prague manifesto and those of Gorbachev two decades later? Why did Smrkovský's reforms fail and Gorbachev's succeed?

The New Globalism: Opportunities and Dilemmas, 1989 TO THE PRESENT

After decades of superpower rivalry, the cold war came to a halt in the 1990s when the Soviet Empire disintegrated, ushering in a new age of global challenges and opportunities. New countries emerged from the Soviet shadow to declare their independence, which radically changed the political map of eastern Europe. However, the transition from one party rule to democracy was fraught with difficulties. The first document shows the brutal consequences of the end of communism for people living in the former Yugoslavia while the second document, a political cartoon, lampoons European leaders who sought to redefine Europe's role in a post–cold war era. The third document reveals that, as European governments moved beyond the nation-state, so too did supranational organizations committed to addressing pressing social issues around the globe. The fourth and fifth documents spotlight political and economic changes in Africa and Asia as new forces emerged to rival those of the West and its imperial past. With the boundaries between peoples and cultures becoming more fluid and diverse, the final document warns that new conflicts may arise from using rigid frameworks to define civilizations in the global age.

1.
Ethnic Cleansing

The Diary of Zlata Filipović (October 6, 1991–June 29, 1992)

The end of communist rule in the multiethnic state of Yugoslavia unleashed turmoil and violence unseen in Europe since World War II. Following the rise to power of nationalist leaders during the 1980s, the country fell into chaos when four of the six republics declared independence beginning in 1991. Serbian president Slobodan Milosevic opposed the independence movements and supported the military efforts of Serb nationals in the breakaway republics of Bosnia and Croatia. One of the deadliest conflicts occurred in a three-way war in Bosnia among Serb, Croat, and Muslim factions. Beginning in 1992, the Bosnian capital of Sarajevo was the focus of a four-year siege by Serb forces in which 12,000 people were killed, including 1,600 children. Zlata Filipović was eleven years old when fighting broke out in Sarajevo. The following entries recorded in her diary during that time provide a child's perspective of life in a war-torn city. In 1993, Zlata and her family were allowed to leave Sarajevo for Paris after the publication of her diary gained her worldwide attention.

Sunday, October 6, 1991

I'm watching the American Top 20 on MTV. I don't remember a thing, who's in what place.

I feel great because I've just eaten a "Four Seasons" PIZZA with ham, cheese, ketchup and mushrooms. It was yummy. Daddy bought it for me at Galija's (the pizzeria around the corner). Maybe that's why I didn't remember who took what place — I was too busy enjoying my pizza.

I've finished studying and tomorrow I can go to school BRAVELY, without being afraid of getting a bad grade. I deserve a good grade because I studied all weekend and I didn't even go out to play with my friends in the park. The weather is nice and we usually play "monkey in the middle," talk and go for walks. Basically, we have fun.

Wednesday, October 23, 1991

There's a real war going on in Dubrovnik. It's being badly shelled. People are in shelters, they have no water, no electricity, the phones aren't working. We see horrible pictures on TV. Mommy and Daddy are worried. Is it possible that such a beautiful town is being destroyed? Mommy and Daddy are especially fond of it. It was there, in the Ducal Palace, that they picked up a quill and wrote "YES" to spending the rest of their lives together. Mommy says it's the most beautiful town in the world and it mustn't be destroyed!!!

We're worried about Srdjan (my parents' best friend who lives and works in Dubrovnik, but his family is still in Sarajevo) and his parents. How are they coping with everything that's happening over there? Are they alive? We're trying to talk to him with the help of a ham radio, but it's not working. Bokica (Srdjan's wife) is miserable. Every attempt to get some news ends in failure. Dubrovnik[1] is cut off from the rest of the world.

From Zlata Filipović, *Zlata's Diary: A Child's Life in Sarajevo*, trans. Christina Pribichevich-Zorić (New York: Penguin, 1995), 3, 6, 7, 9–11, 18, 26–35, 41–43, 46–48, 51–58, 65–66.

[1]Croation city on Dalmation coast less than 80 miles from Sarajevo.

Thursday, November 14, 1991

Daddy isn't going to the reserves anymore. Hooray!!! . . . Now we'll be able to go to Jahorina and Crnotina on weekends. But, gasoline has been a problem lately. Daddy often spends hours waiting in the line for gasoline, he goes outside of town to get it, and often comes home without getting the job done.

Together with Bokica we sent a package to Srdjan. We learned through the ham radio that they have nothing to eat. They have no water, Srdjan swapped a bottle of whisky for five liters of water. Eggs, apples, potatoes — the people of Dubrovnik can only dream about them.

War in Croatia, war in Dubrovnik, some reservists in Herzegovina. Mommy and Daddy keep watching the news on TV. They're worried. Mommy often cries looking at the terrible pictures on TV. They talk mostly politics with their friends. What is politics? I haven't got a clue. And I'm not really interested. I just finished watching *Midnight Caller* on TV.

Thursday, December 19, 1991

Sarajevo has launched an appeal (on TV) called "Sarajevo Helps the Children of Dubrovnik." In Srdjan's parcel we put a nice New Year's present for him to give to some child in Dubrovnik. We made up a package of sweets, chocolates, vitamins, a doll, some books, pencils, notebooks — whatever we could manage, hoping to bring happiness to some innocent child who has been stopped by the war from going to school, playing, eating what he wants and enjoying his childhood. It's a nice little package. I hope it makes whoever gets it happy. That's the idea. I also wrote a New Year's card saying I hoped the war in Dubrovnik would end soon.

Thursday, March 5, 1992

Oh, God! Things are heating up in Sarajevo. On Sunday (March 1), a small group of armed civilians (as they say on TV) killed a Serbian wedding guest and wounded the priest. On March 2 (Monday) the whole city was full of barricades. There were "1,000" barricades. We didn't even have bread. At 6:00 people got fed up and went out into the streets. The procession set out from the cathedral. It went past the parliament building and made its way through the entire city. Several people were wounded at the Marshal Tito army barracks. People sang and cried "Bosnia, Bosnia," "Sarajevo, Sarajevo," "We'll live together" and "Come outside." Zdravko Grebo[2] said on the radio that history was in the making.

At about 8:00 we heard the bell of a streetcar. The first streetcar had passed through town and life got back to normal. People poured out into the streets hoping that nothing like that would ever happen again. We joined the peace procession. When we got home we had a quiet night's sleep. The next day everything was the same as before. Classes, music school . . . But in the evening, the news came that 3,000 Chetniks [Serbian nationalists] were coming from Pale [resort outside of

---

[2]President of the Soros Foundation in Sarajevo and editor-in-chief of ZID, the independent radio station.

Sarajevo] to attack Sarajevo, and first, Baščaršija [the old part of town]. Melica said that new barricades had been put up in front of her house and that they wouldn't be sleeping at home tonight. They went to Uncle Nedjad's place. Later there was a real fight on YUTEL TV. Radovan Karadžič [Bosnian Serb leader] and Alija Izetbegovič [president of Bosnia-Herzegovina] phoned in and started arguing. Then Goran Milič[3] got angry and made them agree to meet with some General Kukanjac.[4] Milič is great!!! Bravo!

On March 4 (Wednesday) the barricades were removed, the "kids" [a popular term for politicians] had come to some agreement. Great?!

That day our art teacher brought in a picture for our class-mistress (for March 8, Women's Day). We gave her the present, but she told us to go home. Something was wrong again! There was a panic. The girls started screaming and the boys quietly blinked their eyes. Daddy came home from work early that day too. But everything turned out OK. It's all too much!

Monday, March 30, 1992

Hey, Diary! You know what I think? Since Anne Frank called her diary Kitty, maybe I could give you a name too. What about:

ASFALTINA   PIDŽEAMETA
ŠEFIKA   HIKMETA
ŠEVALA   MIMMY

or something else???

I'm thinking, thinking . . .

I've decided! I'm going to call you

MIMMY

All right, then, let's start.

Dear Mimmy,

It's almost half-term. We're all studying for our tests. Tomorrow we're supposed to go to a classical music concert at the Skenderija Hall. Our teacher says we shouldn't go because there will be 10,000 people, pardon me, children, there, and somebody might take us as hostages or plant a bomb in the concert hall. Mommy says I shouldn't go. So I won't.

Hey! You know who won the Yugovision Song Contest?! EXTRA NENA!!!???

I'm afraid to say this next thing. Melica says she heard at the hairdresser's that on Saturday, April 4, 1992, there's going to be BOOM — BOOM, BANG — BANG, CRASH Sarajevo. Translation: they're going to bomb Sarajevo.

Love,

Zlata

---

[3]A well-known newscaster on television; one of the founders of the YUTEL television station before the war.

[4]General of the then Yugoslav Army, who was in Sarajevo when the war broke out.

Sunday, April 5, 1992

Dear Mimmy,

I'm trying to concentrate so I can do my homework (reading), but I simply can't. Something is going on in town. You can hear gunfire from the hills. Columns of people are spreading out from Dobrinja. They're trying to stop something, but they themselves don't know what. You can simply feel that something is coming, something very bad. On TV I see people in front of the B-H parliament building. The radio keeps playing the same song: "Sarajevo, My Love." That's all very nice, but my stomach is still in knots and I can't concentrate on my homework anymore.

Mimmy, I'm afraid of WAR!!!

Zlata

Thursday, April 9, 1992

Dear Mimmy,

I'm not going to school. All the schools in Sarajevo are closed. There's danger hiding in these hills above Sarajevo. But I think things are slowly calming down. The heavy shelling and explosions have stopped. There's occasional gunfire, but it quickly falls silent. Mommy and Daddy aren't going to work. They're buying food in huge quantities. Just in case, I guess. God forbid!

Still, it's very tense. Mommy is beside herself, Daddy tries to calm her down. Mommy has long conversations on the phone. She calls, other people call, the phone is in constant use.

Zlata

Tuesday, April 14, 1992

Dear Mimmy,

People are leaving Sarajevo. The airport, train and bus stations are packed. I saw sad pictures on TV of people parting. Families, friends separating. Some are leaving, others staying. It's so sad. Why? These people and children aren't guilty of anything. Keka and Braco came early this morning. They're in the kitchen with Mommy and Daddy, whispering. Keka and Mommy are crying. I don't think they know what to do — whether to stay or to go. Neither way is good.

Zlata

Saturday, May 2, 1992

Dear Mimmy,

Today was truly, absolutely the worst day ever in Sarajevo. The shooting started around noon. Mommy and I moved into the hall. Daddy was in his office, under our apartment, at the time. We told him on the intercom to run quickly to the downstairs lobby where we'd meet him. We brought Cicko [Zlata's canary] with us. The gunfire was getting worse, and we couldn't get over the wall to the Bobars', so we ran down to our own cellar.

The cellar is ugly, dark, smelly. Mommy, who's terrified of mice, had two fears to cope with. The three of us were in the same corner as the other day. We listened to the pounding shells, the shooting, the thundering noise overhead. We even heard planes. At one moment I realized that this awful cellar was the only place that could save our lives. Suddenly, it started to look almost warm and nice. It was the only way we could defend ourselves against all this terrible shooting. We heard glass shattering in our street. Horrible. I put my fingers in my ears to block out the terrible sounds. I was worried about Cicko. We had left him behind in the lobby. Would he catch cold there? Would something hit him? I was terribly hungry and thirsty. We had left our half-cooked lunch in the kitchen.

When the shooting died down a bit, Daddy ran over to our apartment and brought us back some sandwiches. He said he could smell something burning and that the phones weren't working. He brought our TV set down to the cellar. That's when we learned that the main post office (near us) was on fire and that they had kidnapped our President. At around 8:00 we went back up to our apartment. Almost every window in our street was broken. Ours were all right, thank God. I saw the post office in flames. A terrible sight. The fire-fighters battled with the raging fire. Daddy took a few photos of the post office being devoured by the flames. He said they wouldn't come out because I had been fiddling with something on the camera. I was sorry. The whole apartment smelled of the burning fire. God, and I used to pass by there every day. It had just been done up. It was huge and beautiful, and now it was being swallowed up by the flames. It was disappearing. That's what this neighborhood of mine looks like, my Mimmy. I wonder what it's like in other parts of town? I heard on the radio that it was awful around the Eternal Flame. The place is knee-deep in glass. We're worried about Grandma and Granddad. They live there. Tomorrow, if we can go out, we'll see how they are. A terrible day.

This has been the worst, most awful day in my eleven-year-old life. I hope it will be the only one. Mommy and Daddy are very edgy. I have to go to bed.
Ciao!
Zlata

Wednesday, May 13, 1992

Dear Mimmy,
Life goes on. The past is cruel, and that's exactly why we should forget it.

The present is cruel too and I can't forget it. There's no joking with war. My present reality is the cellar, fear, shells, fire.

Terrible shooting broke out the night before last. We were afraid that we might be hit by shrapnel or a bullet, so we ran over to the Bobars'. We spent all of that night, the next day and the next night in the cellar and in Nedo's apartment. (Nedo is a refugee from Grbavica. He left his parents and came here to his sister's empty apartment.) We saw terrible scenes on TV. The town in ruins, burning, people and children being killed. It's unbelievable.

The phones aren't working, we haven't been able to find out anything about Grandma and Granddad, Melica, how people in other parts of town are doing. On TV we saw the place where Mommy works, Vodoprivreda, all in flames. It's on the aggressor's side of town (Grbavica). Mommy cried. She's depressed. All her years of work and effort — up in flames. It's really horrible. All around Vodoprivreda there were cars burning, people dying, and nobody could help them. God, why is this happening?

I'M SO MAD I WANT TO SCREAM AND BREAK EVERYTHING!

Your Zlata

Sunday, May 17, 1992

Dear Mimmy,

It's now definite: there's no more school. The war has interrupted our lessons, closed down the schools, sent children to cellars instead of classrooms. They'll give us the grades we got at the end of last term. So I'll get a report card saying I've finished fifth grade.

Ciao!

Zlata

Saturday, May 23, 1992

Dear Mimmy,

I'm not writing to you about me anymore. I'm writing to you about war, death, injuries, shells, sadness and sorrow. Almost all my friends have left. Even if they were here, who knows whether we'd be able to see one another. The phones aren't working, we couldn't even talk to one another. Vanja and Andrej have gone to join Srdjan in Dubrovnik. The war has stopped there. They're lucky. I was so unhappy because of that war in Dubrovnik. I never dreamed it would move to Sarajevo.

Wednesday, May 27, 1992

Dear Mimmy,

SLAUGHTER! MASSACRE! HORROR! CRIME! BLOOD! SCREAMS! TEARS! DESPAIR!

That's what Vaso Miškin Street looks like today. Two shells exploded in the street and one in the market. Mommy was nearby at the time. She ran to Grandma and Granddad's. Daddy and I were beside ourselves because she hadn't come home. I saw some of it on TV but I still can't believe what I actually saw. It's unbelievable. I've got a lump in my throat and a knot in my tummy. HORRIBLE. They're taking the wounded to the hospital. It's a madhouse. We kept going to the window hoping to see Mommy, but she wasn't back. They released a list of the dead and wounded. Daddy and I were tearing our hair out. We didn't know what had happened to her. Was she alive? At 4:00, Daddy decided to go and check the hospital. He got dressed, and I got ready to go to the Bobars', so as not to stay at home alone. I looked out the window one more time and . . . I SAW MOMMY RUNNING ACROSS THE BRIDGE. As she came into the house she started shaking and crying. Through her tears she told us how she had seen dismembered bodies. All the neighbors came because they had been afraid for her. Thank God, Mommy is with us. Thank God.

A HORRIBLE DAY. UNFORGETTABLE.

HORRIBLE! HORRIBLE!

Your Zlata

Saturday, May 30, 1992

Dear Mimmy,

The City Maternity Hospital has burned down. I was born there. Hundreds of thousands of new babies, new residents of Sarajevo, won't have the luck to be born in this maternity hospital now. It was new. The fire devoured everything. The mothers and babies were saved. When the fire broke out two women were giving birth. The babies are alive. God, people get killed here, they die here, they disappear, things go up in flames here, and out of the flames, new lives are born.

Your Zlata

Friday, June 5, 1992

Dear Mimmy,

There's been no electricity for quite some time and we keep thinking about the food in the freezer. There's not much left as it is. It would be a pity for all of it to go bad. There's meat and vegetables and fruit. How can we save it?

Daddy found an old wood-burning stove in the attic. It's so old it looks funny. In the cellar we found some wood, put the stove outside in the yard, lit it and are trying to save the food from the refrigerator. We cooked everything, and joining forces with the Bobars, enjoyed ourselves. There was veal and chicken, squid, cherry strudel, meat and potato pies. All sorts of things. It's a pity, though, that we had to eat everything so quickly. We even overate. WE HAD A MEAT STROKE.

We washed down our refrigerators and freezers. Who knows when we'll be able to cook like this again. Food is becoming a big problem in Sarajevo. There's nothing to buy, and even cigarettes and coffee are becoming a problem for grown-ups. The last reserves are being used up. God, are we going to go hungry to boot???

Zlata

Monday, June 29, 1992

Dear Mimmy,

BOREDOM!!! SHOOTING!!! SHELLING!!! PEOPLE BEING KILLED!!! DESPAIR!!! HUNGER!!! MISERY!!! FEAR!!!

That's my life! The life of an innocent eleven-year-old schoolgirl!! A schoolgirl without a school, without the fun and excitement of school. A child without games, without friends, without the sun, without birds, without nature, without fruit, without chocolate or sweets, with just a little powdered milk. In short, a child without a childhood. A wartime child. I now realize that I am really living through a war, I am witnessing an ugly, disgusting war. I and thousands of other children in this town that is being destroyed, that is crying, weeping, seeking help, but getting none. God, will this ever stop, will I ever be a schoolgirl again, will I ever enjoy my childhood again? I once heard that childhood is the most wonderful time of your life. And it is. I loved it, and now an ugly war is taking it all away from me. Why? I feel sad. I feel like crying. I am crying.

Your Zlata

DISCUSSION QUESTIONS

1. How are children and their communities affected by war? How does war inter-fere with daily activities?

2. How does Zlata's tone shift from the earlier entries about the war approaching her city to the later sections describing the siege of Sarajevo?

3. How much do you think Zlata understood about what she calls the "politics" that caused the war?

4. What does Zlata's account reveal about the nature of warfare at the end of the twentieth century?

2.
Critiquing the European Union

Leif Zetterling, *Klasskamrater (Classmates) Cartoon*
(January 22, 2001)

At the turn of the twenty-first century, when the European Union was gaining strength as a supranational entity that united much of the European continent, it also faced the challenge of amalgamating many diverse countries, cultures, and political traditions

From Leif Zetterling. Courtesy of Leif Zetterling; From The Professional Cartoonist Index: http://cagle.slate.msn.com.

*into a viable, united body. Although the use of a common currency had been antici-
pated in 1992 when the European Union decided to adopt the economic and monetary union, enthusiasm for the euro flagged in some member states as the 2002
deadline for its adoption approached. Other thorny debates ensued whenever the
question of enlarging the European Union arose, or when smaller member states
sensed that their voices were being drowned out by those of the larger, more dominant
members. In this political cartoon, Swedish illustrator Leif Zetterling depicts the
European Union as a classroom and its national leaders as children. A description of
the classmates follows below. Their political positions were current as of 2001; many
have since left office.*

The "classmates," from left to right, are Giuliano Amato, prime minister of Italy; Paavo
Lipponen, prime minister of Finland (on the floor); Jean-Claude Juncker, prime minister of Luxembourg (balancing something on his nose); Wim Kok, prime
minister of the Netherlands (on the floor in striped trousers); Göran Persson, prime
minister of Sweden (the largest figure, sitting on the teacher's desk); Gerhard
Schröder, chancellor of Germany (holding airplane); José Maria Aznar, prime
minister of Spain (in track suit); Poul Nyrup Rasmussen, prime minister of Den-
mark (holding paper airplane); Jacques Chirac, president of France (with wine
glass); Bertie Ahern, prime minister of Ireland (behind Chirac, also with wine
glass); Anna Lindh, Swedish minister of foreign affairs (at the chalkboard). (During the Swedish presidency of the European Union (EU), when this cartoon was
drawn, Lindh was the chairman for the Council of the European Union. A vocal
advocate for Sweden's adoption of the euro, she was brutally assassinated on
September 10, 2003, a few days before the Swedes were to vote on the euro.)
The rest are Guy Verhofstadt, prime minister of Belgium (in front row with
hand raised); Antonio Guterres, prime minister of Portugal; Tony Blair, prime
minister of the United Kingdom (holding a baby); and Romano Prodi, former
prime minister of Italy, now president of the European Commission (in the
doorway).

At the left, the countries excluded from the "classroom," from left to right, are
Romania or Turkey — the flag is partially obscured and therefore hard to identify
(Romania was admitted to the EU in 2007 while negotiations for Turkey's entry
are still under way); Estonia (became a member in 2004); Malta (became a member in 2004); and Bulgaria, Solvenia, or Slovakia (difficult to tell which country is
intended here). Slovenia and Slovakia became member states in 2004. Bulgaria was
admitted in 2007, bringing the total EU membership to twenty-seven.

DISCUSSION QUESTIONS

1. What does this cartoon tell you about Leif Zetterling's opinion of the European
   Union and its leaders?

2. Why do you suppose Zetterling chose to use a classroom setting? What meaning
   does the setting add to the illustration?

3. Of the ideals listed on the classroom's chalkboard, why do you suppose "Equality" and "Euro" are crossed out? Why were the other words left untouched?

4. What is the advantage of studying a period of time through its political cartoons? What are the challenges a historian faces when trying to understand a cartoon created in a different time period than his or her own?

3.
Doctors Without Borders

Joelle Tanguy and Fiona Terry,
On Humanitarian Responsibility (December 12, 1999)

On December 10, 1999, Médicins San Frontières (MSF — also known in English as "Doctors Without Borders") was awarded the Nobel Peace Prize "in recognition of the organization's pioneering humanitarian work on several continents." Headquartered in Geneva, Switzerland, its stated mission is twofold: "Providing medical aid wherever needed, regardless of race, religion, politics, or sex, and raising awareness of the people we help." Founded in 1971 by a group of French doctors and journalists in the wake of a famine in Biafra, Nigeria, MSF has grown to include more than 3,000 physicians, nurses, and journalists who volunteer their time each year. Although MSF provides services similar to those offered by the International Red Cross or Oxfam International, organizations that remain politically neutral no matter what the circumstances, MSF publicly criticizes governments or other international organizations if their policies compromise the welfare of victims. In 1995, for example, MSF called for military intervention to stop the genocide in Rwanda, something an avowedly neutral organization would never have done. The following article, written by two MSF leaders and posted on the MSF Web site, restates its position on humanitarian responsibility.

What Doctors Without Borders/Médecins Sans Frontières (MSF) stands for, in the community of humanitarian actors, is a humanitarianism concerned with advocating against injustice and indifference, and with asserting basic rights and quality of assistance for vulnerable populations.

On Neutrality and Impartiality

MSF, from the outset, chose to step away from the classical Red Cross approach of a "silent neutrality" and sought to put the interest of victims ahead of sovereignty considerations. MSF's determination to speak in public when faced with mass

Joelle Tanguy and Fiona Terry, "On Humanitarian Responsibility," December 12, 1999. Adapted from their article originally published in *Ethics & International Affairs*, 13, (1999) by the Carnegie Council on Ethics and International Affairs; http://www.cceia.org.

violations of human rights, including forced displacement or forced repatriation, war crimes, crimes against humanity, and genocide, is a defining principle of the organization.

This aversion to silence stemmed from the post-Holocaust debate in Europe, influencing the intellectual generation that presided over the birth of the "Sans Frontières" movement. Often the sole witnesses to violations, MSF volunteers consider themselves accountable to international civil society and humanitarian principles, rather than to governmental or multilateral financial backers of aid. As a consequence, MSF's testimony ("*temoignage*") is raised in public rather than in closed diplomatic circles.

Far from rejecting the principle of impartiality, MSF adopted as a fundamental principle of its operations the provision of aid in proportion to need and without discrimination — the very tenants of impartiality. And since true impartiality requires operational independence from economic and political pressures, MSF has also inscribed independence — and financial independence — as a key principle and operational reality, with the majority of its funds raised from individual private donors throughout the world.

MSF has not abandoned or rejected the principle of neutrality either, defined as "not taking sides with warring parties." While it worked on the U.S.-backed side of the Afghanistan conflict and in refugee camps inhabited by asylum seekers fleeing totalitarian systems, MSF was actually one of only a handful of aid organizations which worked in both the Salvadoran (left-wing guerrilla) and Nicaraguan (Contra) controlled refugee camps in Honduras, recognizing that victims occur on both sides of a conflict, regardless of the "goodness" of the political ideology espoused by either side.

And in the mid 1980s, MSF was simultaneously expelled from Ethiopia by Soviet-backed Mengistu and from Guatemala by a US-backed government eager to send away potential witnesses to the violence. Rather than "siding" with one or other party to the conflict, MSF has, at times, judged that the victims are more in need on one side than another, and designed its missions based on the "proportionality" principle embedded in impartiality.

Faced with massive human rights violations, misuse of humanitarian assistance, or a totalitarian regime, MSF may exclude working with one party to the conflict, as was the case with the Khmer Rouge in the Thai border camps. But this position is less an expression of political preference than a determination to claim and operate within humanitarian space. Such "humanitarian space" entails the ability to independently assess the needs of the population; retain unhindered access to the population; conduct, monitor, and evaluate the distribution of aid commodities; and obtain security guarantees for local and expatriate aid personnel.

Thus if neutrality is defined as remaining silent, even when confronted with grave breeches of fundamental humanitarian principles, MSF is not neutral. However, as long as neutrality is defined as "not taking sides with warring parties," MSF upholds a spirit of neutrality throughout its operations.

On Humanitarianism and Politics

MSF volunteers bear witness to the situation of populations in danger they assist. This "temoignage" seeks to combat indifference to the plight of populations and to signal the need for local and international responsibility to uphold basic humanitarian and human rights principles.

Most "humanitarian crises" are fundamentally political crises with humanitarian consequences. All the ambiguities of intervention lie in this essential link. Humanitarian agencies are caught between governments seeking an alibi for their political inaction, and media tending to focus on human tragedy rather than its political roots. Refusing to act as a relief-service provider contracted by state or multilateral financial backers, MSF seeks instead to be both a humanitarian actor and an agent of change: to do so often requires highlighting the political responsibilities of the local and international community.

On Aid Fuelling War

Humanitarian intervention can also fuel the crises it seeks to alleviate, and all the more so since the number of NGOs and their funding multiplied in the 1990s. Aid can be taxed, hijacked, looted, racketeered. Interventions can be manipulated to build internal or international legitimacy, to freeze military gains, to sustain ethnic cleansing, to enforce population displacement, to support famine policies.

When confronted with the dilemma of fuelling a war economy or sustaining political or military strategies, MSF strives for a lucid and responsible approach that might involve minimalist programming or even abstention, but remains essentially concerned with preserving humanitarian space. Every situation requires careful analysis.

Hence once the emergency needs of the population have been met, MSF has reduced or even withdrawn when humanitarian aid had a strong chance of prolonging the war. This was the case in the Rwandan refugee camps in Zaire and Tanzania, from which MSF withdrew in late 1994.

On Contemporary Crises

There's never been a "golden age" of humanitarianism. Humanitarian aid has always been fraught with tremendous political and ethical controversies. In our experience, while it is clear that the context has changed, aid organizations have always been faced with these types of intractable dilemmas.

The dominant discourse on contemporary crises frequently invokes a "new complexity," characterized by "an increased disregard for humanitarian law," "direct targeting of civilians," and "the protracted nature" of conflict. We challenge the notion that this "new complexity" derives from a tendency towards increased barbarity. Two instances of genocide fifty years apart, two famines, in Mao's China and in today's Sudan, illustrate this well. Aspects of conflict have changed with the end of the Cold War: the fragmentation of armed movements, in particular, increases the difficulties of identifying reliable interlocutors, and the distinctions between state and non-state, private and public, political and business initiatives are increasingly blurred.

But rather than a causal emphasis, the "complexity" associated with contemporary crises better reflects the response of the multiplicity of actors present in the heart of conflicts. The increasingly blurred distinction among these actors has led to a confusion of roles and increased manipulation and misuse of aid. Humanitarian aid, once a tool of states to promote foreign policy objectives, has become a tool with which to avoid foreign policy engagement. And aid organizations, although lamenting the "humanitarian alibi," are lined up to receive more government funding.

On Broadening the Humanitarian Mandate

Far from aiming to resolve conflicts or even calling for an end to war, MSF's political humanitarianism is concerned with advocating against injustice and indifference, and with asserting basic rights and quality of assistance for vulnerable populations.

DISCUSSION QUESTIONS

1. What are the main differences between what Tanguy and Terry describe as "silent neutrality" and the impartiality practiced by MSF?

2. According to Tanguy and Terry, how have the challenges posed to humanitarian aid organizations changed in recent years? Which challenges remain the same?

3. Imagine you are an official from the International Red Cross. What aspects of Tanguy and Terry's philosophy might you disagree with, and why?

4.
An End to Apartheid

The African National Congress, *Introductory Statement to the Truth and Reconciliation Commission* (August 19, 1996)

In 1995 Nelson Mandela, the first postapartheid president of South Africa, appointed the Truth and Reconciliation Commission (TRC) to help his country make the transition from an oppressive apartheid regime to a democratic multiracial state. The TRC was charged with establishing "as complete a picture as possible of the nature, causes, and extent of gross violations of human rights" committed in South Africa between 1960 and 1994. The commission spent two and a half years evaluating more than

---

From African National Congress's Web site: www.anc.org.za/ancdocs/misc/trctoc. html.

21,000 statements from apartheid victims and perpetrators, and subpoenaed hundreds more, to learn the full extent of the crimes that took place. The TRC's charge was to investigate the crimes in a way that would promote national unity and reconciliation rather than continued bitterness and hatred. The TRC offered amnesty from prosecution for perpetrators who testified about past crimes and provided restitution to victims. In this excerpt, the African National Congress (ANC), a political organization that had lobbied against apartheid since 1912, introduces its statement to the TRC by outlining the need for national reconciliation and the protection of human rights.

Introduction

As part of the process of the transformation of our country, the ANC had to consider its approach to the difficult but critically important question of what the new South Africa should do with those among our citizens who were involved in gross human rights violations during the struggle for our emancipation.

The choices we had to make can be stated in a simple and straightforward manner.

We could have decided to hold our own Nuremberg Trials.

We could have decided that all that should be done should be to forgive everything that has happened in the past.

We, however, reached the conclusion that neither of these would be the correct decision to take.

In considering the correctness or otherwise of this conclusion, the point needs to be borne in mind that we are in transition from an apartheid to a democratic society.

This is not a single event but a protracted process.

What this speaks to is an unjust cause on one side and a just cause on the other.

Inherent to the system of white minority domination, in this and all other countries where it occurred, was the philosophy and practice of the use of force to ensure the perpetuation of the system.

Force and violence by the dominant against the dominated, the contraposition of power to powerlessness, the attribution of mystical possibilities of retribution to the governors who can visit their wrath on the third and fourth generations of those who hate them, the suspension of all social norms, to enable the state and servants of the state to resort to the unbridled use of violence — all this, and more besides, sustains the continuity of colonial rule.

To maintain its internal integrity, coherence and rationale, this system could not but integrate in its world vision the concept of humans with a right to govern and sub-humans privileged to be governed.

Among other things, this paradigm allows those who enjoy the right to govern the ethical framework which permits them to use maximum force against any sub-human who would dare question his or her duty to accept the sacred obligation to respect the need to be governed.

The simultaneous and interdependent legitimization of the two inherently anti-human concepts of racial superiority and the colonial state as the concentrated expression of the unlimited right to the use of force, of necessity and according to the inherent logic of the system of apartheid, produced the gross violations of human rights by the apartheid state which are the subject of part of the work of the Truth and Reconciliation Commission.

It was as a result of the correct understanding of the nature of the system of apartheid that the United Nations characterized the system itself, and not merely its logical results, as a Crime Against Humanity.

With regard to the narrower context within which the TRC is considering this matter, the theoretical foundation of the enquiry would be the matter we have referred to, the legitimization of the use of force in general but especially against those who would dare challenge the system.

This has two consequences.

One of these is the elevation of the state organs of repression above all other state structures, their exemption from all norms of common law consistent with limitations on the use of force, the conferring of powers on individuals to mete out violence as they deem fit and the consequent brutalization of such individuals so that the perpetration of violence becomes their second nature.

The second of these consequences is the demonizing by the state of those it seeks to destroy and against whom therefore, it permits the maximum use of force. . . .

National Reconciliation

The most important issue in this regard is that the grief of particular individuals, important as it is to the affected individuals and the nation, is relevant also to the extent that it contributes to the achievement of the larger goal of national reconciliation.

National reconciliation will only have meaning if it addresses the historic conflict in our country between black and white.

Through centuries of this conflict, the names of the players have changed continuously, regardless of their color and the causes they served.

What never changed was the character of the conflict, which was between the white colonizing forces and a black liberation movement, based on a social system which elevated the white at the expense of the black.

National reconciliation has to be between black and white.

Without transformation to end the disparities of privilege and deprivation which are the legacy we have inherited from our colonial and apartheid past, but which continue to define the present, national reconciliation is impossible.

Whichever way the TRC interprets its mandate, it cannot avoid the conclusion that the ghost that needs to be laid to rest is — the ending of the domination of the black by the white, in all spheres of social existence.

If our society does not achieve this, racial conflict will continue. The goal of national reconciliation will not be achieved.

Clearly, this objective cannot be achieved by the TRC alone.

It also emphasizes the obligation that rests on the Commission to make its own recommendations as to what the larger and varied society from which it is drawn might do, to contribute to the realization of the goal of national reconciliation.

Protection from Gross Violations of Human Rights

Systematic violations of human rights are a manifestation of a social system, rather than the exceptional faults of particular individuals.

To ensure that our country and people are never again exposed to such systematic violations of human rights as occurred under apartheid, it is necessary that we construct a constitutional, political, and socioeconomic order which inherently protects human rights, and has the means to defend itself against any tendency to limit or violate those rights.

The mandate for the construction of such a system of course rests with bodies other than the TRC. As a movement, we are convinced that these institutions are carrying out their mandate.

But we also believe that the TRC has an important role to play in helping to ensure that the specialized institutions established by the apartheid regime to carry out a campaign of repression are completely dismantled.

We refer here not to normal state organs, such as the police, the Defense Force, and the intelligence services, but to other clandestine structures established under the National Security Management System, some of which continue to operate as part of the "third force."

The exposure and destruction of these structures is important to ensure that they are stopped from actually or potentially engaging in any acts of destabilization.

This is particularly important in light of the fact that persons who belong to these structures have been trained and motivated as anti-democratic operatives and, in many instances, will not have changed their ideological colors.

It is also important that the nation as a whole should be familiar with this machinery as part of the process of raising the level of national vigilance so that it is difficult for any government in [the] future to create similar structures for use against the people of our country. . . .

Conclusion

The ANC is committed to doing everything in its power to help the TRC and the nation to know as much as is possible about the events of the period the TRC is mandated to investigate.

We believe that the TRC should conclude its work as quickly as possible so that we do indeed let bygones be bygones and allow the nation to forgive a past it nevertheless dare not forget.

DISCUSSION QUESTIONS

1. What do you make of the ANC's emphasis on institutions and ethics rather than individuals? Why do you suppose the ANC concerned itself mainly with these larger structures?

2. What was the ANC's main objective in making this statement to the TRC? What did they hope to achieve through the TRC?

3. What is the advantage in the TRC's granting amnesty to those who agree to tell everything they know about crimes that they or people they knew committed under apartheid? What is the disadvantage of granting amnesty to these persons?

4. At the beginning of this document, the ANC mentions that South Africans could have used a Nuremberg Trial-style system to uncover the truth about crimes committed under apartheid. Why do you think they opted for the TRC-style of investigation, which focused on reconciliation instead of punishment?

5.
China in the Global Age

Chinese Olympic Committee, *Announcements on Preparations for the 2008 Summer Olympic Games* (2004–2007)

In the 1990s, China emerged as a major player in the global economy. To highlight its growing importance on the world stage, Beijing lobbied hard for the honor of hosting the 2000 Summer Olympic Games. When Sydney, Australia, was chosen instead, Beijing tried again, this time with success. On July 13, 2001, the International Olympic Committee (IOC) chose the city to host the 2008 summer Olympic games. Many nations urged the IOC to reconsider its choice, given China's record on human and civil rights, and the European Parliament even drafted a formal complaint, urging the IOC to "reconsider Beijing's candidacy when the authorities of the People's Republic of China have made a fundamental change in their policy on human rights, and the promotion of democracy and the rule of law." Chinese officials took the IOC's decision as an endorsement of progress China had made, both economically and politically. Vice Premier Li Lan-Qing proudly declared, "The winning of the 2008 Olympic bid is an example of the international recognition of China's social stability, economic progress, and the healthy life of the Chinese people." In the years and months leading up to the Olympic Games, the Beijing Organizing Committee for the Games of the XXIX Olympiad (BOCOG) posted regular updates about its Olympic preparations on its Web site. These statements, which were widely distributed in the international press, show a country at pains to prove that it is, once and for all, ready to host the world.

Official: Beijing Olympic Projects Should Be Corruption-Free

BEIJING, Jan. 9, 2004 — A top official from the Ministry of Supervision on Thursday urged the Beijing municipal government to strengthen supervision over Olympic venue construction to avoid corruption.

"Projects for the 2008 Beijing Olympic Games should be projects 'in the sun'," said deputy Minister Huang Shuxian at a meeting with local officials and operators of the four venues under construction.

From Chinese Olympic Committee, http://en.olympic.cn/

He made the remarks after an inspection tour of the construction site of the National Stadium and the National Swimming Center in north Beijing.

Huang, also director of the Supervision Commission for the 2008 Games, praised supervision efforts made by the municipal government as construction of the first batch of Olympic venues has got [*sic*] underway smoothly.

"It is a good beginning," he said.

The Beijing Municipal Bureau of Auditing has finished comprehensive auditing reports over public bidding of five Olympic projects including the National Stadium, the Olympic Village and the Wukesong Cultural and Sports Center and is ready to submit them to the supervision commission, said Yang Xiaochao, the bureau director.

Venue construction will be in full swing this year as 11 gymnasiums and their accessory facilities are expected to break ground.

"All of the project spending is required to strictly adhere to the authorized budget," said Zhou Yuzhen, vice-director of the Beijing Municipal Bureau of Supervision.

Every project is required to receive independent auditing and supervision from authorities in the process of bidding and construction, he added.

Zhou, also a member of the Beijing Municipal Olympic Venue Construction Supervision Leading Group established last month, said a supervision information network to oversee Olympic venue construction will be completed by April this year.

A total of 35 venues will be used during the 2008 Olympics, including 30 in Beijing and five in Qingdao, Qinhuangdao, Shenyang, Tianjin, and Shanghai. Beijing has vowed to complete the construction of Olympic venues by the end of 2006.

Beijing to Further Promote Civility

BEIJING, Feb. 20, 2006 — The Beijing Municipality will further improve civility of citizens in an effort to create a more favorable environment for the Beijing Olympic Games.

Although the citywide campaign is to be officially launched next month, some projects for the purpose have already been put on the agenda, according to a press conference held yesterday on the occasion of 900 day countdown to the Games to be held from August 8–24, 2008.

The education department has prepared to release a reader to popularize civility and courtesy, with an aim to cover some 4.3 million families.

Meanwhile, the public are encouraged to take part in selecting Top Ten Model Persons of Social Ethics. In public places such as squares, airports, train stations and key sports venues, model sectors of public civility are to be set up. . . .

Civility at transport stations is also a key point to be emphasized. Some of the bus stops in Beijing have already seen orderly queuing. To make this an overwhelming routine, the city will dispatch more supervisors to more bus stops and will extend the activity from the city to outskirts.

In 2006, Beijing will embark on an all-round campaign to get rid of "villages in the center of the city" and other illegal buildings and outdoor advertisement boards. The departments concerned will take harsh measures against spitting and littering in public places and will deploy more trash cans and spit bags.

Capital Takes Steps to Rein in Pollution

BEIJING, March 17, 2006 — Beijing will introduce vehicle-exhaust monitoring devices in a bid to tackle the pollution that continues to plague the city.

The new move is designed to strengthen controls on harmful emissions from the capital's 2.6 million vehicles, which are believed to contribute to around half of the city's ozone pollution, according to the Beijing Municipal Bureau of Environmental Protection.

Bureau official Wang Dawei said that ozone pollution, which has plagued many cities in developed countries since the 1950s, has recently become an increasingly grave problem in the Chinese capital due to the explosion in the number of cars. . . .

He warned that this pollution could pose a major problem during the 2008 Beijing Olympics, as the strong summer sunshine would accelerate the formation of photochemical smog, which may damage health.

Besides placing monitoring devices on roads, the city is considering offering financial assistance to private owners of cars which produce heavy fume [sic] to purchase new cars whose exhaust-gas emissions meet the upgraded standards introduced in late 2005, said Pei Chenghu, the bureau's deputy director.

Meanwhile, around 8,000 of the city's old taxis and 2,000 buses will be required to have new technology installed that helps cut their emissions. It is estimated that emissions from one old car are the same as from 14 new cars that meet the new standard.

Apart from vehicles, the city will also take steps this year to curb heavy pollution from around 200 plants in the power, petrochemical, steel and sewage treatment sectors. All of these plants, which account for 80 percent of the city's total industrial pollution, will be equipped by the end of this year with real-time monitors on their gas and water discharges. Pei warned that the operation of those plants that exceed the discharge standards will be suspended or they may even be closed.

These moves are part of a raft of measures that the city's authorities have taken this year to tackle pollution. Other steps include stricter supervision of construction sites and the expanded use of low-sulphur coal.

This year, the city has pledged that at least 238 days should meet good or excellent air quality standards.

Beijing Able to Treat 90 Percent of Sewage

BEIJING, Feb. 5, 2007 — The nine sewage treatment plants in Beijing's urban area treated 780 million cubic meters of waste water, or 90 percent of Beijing's total in 2006, meeting its water purification target for the Beijing Olympic Games ahead of time, the Venue and Environment Department of the Beijing Organizing Committee for the Games of the XXIX Olympiad (BOCOG) said Monday.

The city's sewage disposal capacity of 2.914 million tons per day has now exceeded the objective of 2.68 million tons per day set in its bid to host the Olympic Games, the department quoted the Beijing Water Drainage Group as saying.

During the 2001–2006 period, the group built a total of 14 sewage treatment plants with a combined daily capacity of 1.834 million tons, in addition to the capacity of 1.08 million tons of the three plants built before 2001. The total capacity has now outstripped the Olympic bid target of 2.68 million tons per day, the group said. The group is striving to reuse 50 percent of the treated water in 2007, a target for the Olympic Games.

Beijingers Urged to Queue on Monthly "Queuing Day"

BEIJING, Feb. 11, 2007 — The girl carefully pasted the card with her signature on an exhibiting board. On the card, the four-year-old Liang Miaozhu vowed to queue in the public and respect order.

Liang, accompanied by her mom, is among hundreds of Beijing citizens who participated on Sunday in activities in Beijing's busy Wangfujing Street to promote the city's first "queuing day."

The 11th day of every month is chosen as the promotion day for queuing up as part of a drive to improve the city's image before next year's Olympics, according to Zhang Huiguang, director of Beijing's Capital Ethic Development Office earlier this month.

The number 11 resembles two queuing persons, according to Zhang. "That means that even if there are only two people, they should wait in line," she said.

People expressed their support for the move. "The Beijing Olympic Games is drawing near, but bad behaviors still exist in the city," said 63-year-old Liu Chun'e, "we should display to our foreign guests the courtesy of Chinese people."

Although netizens voiced their doubt on the Internet and large numbers of bus passengers made it difficult to keep order, Zhang noted that it was important to create an environment where the wrongdoing was a shame. "The Chinese people don't like to lose face," she said.

Before the Olympics, the city is also determined to eradicate bad habits like spitting in the public and littering.

Beijing Getting Rid of Badly Translated Signs

BEIJING, Feb. 27, 2007 — Work has begun to ensure all of Beijing's signs are grammatically correct and free of "Chinglis" by the end of 2007, before hordes of foreign visitors arriving [*sic*] in town for the 2008 Summer Olympics, yesterday's China Youth Daily reported.

"We have worked out 4,624 pieces of standard English translations to substitute the Chinglish ones on signs around the city," said Lu Jinlan, head of the organizing committee of the Beijing Speaks Foreign Languages Program (BSFLP). The committee plans to focus on improving English menus after the English translations of signs are all corrected.

Lu admitted that the committee faced many difficulties in consigning Chinglish to history, particularly in correcting the English translations used by private businesses.

For years, foreigners in China have delighted in the loopy English translations that appear on the nation's signs. They range from the offensive — "Deformed Man," outside toilets for the handicapped — to the sublime — "Show Mercy to the Slender Grass," on park lawns.

Ten teams of linguistic monitors have patrolled the city's parks, museums, subway stations, and other public places searching for gaffes to fix.

The city has replaced thousands of road signs that carried bewildering admonitions such as: "To take notice of safe: The slippery are very crafty." (Translation: Be careful, road slippery.) Replacing signs is expected to cost the city a substantial amount of money.

The sign initiative is the latest of a campaign to improve English translations in public. The BSFLP is headed by Chen Lin, an elderly language professor who acts as its language police chief.

"We want everything to be correct. Grammar, words, culture, everything," says Professor Chen. "Beijing will have thousands of visitors coming. We don't want anyone laughing at us."

DISCUSSION QUESTIONS

1. What might the International Olympic Committee's main concerns about Beijing's infrastructure and conditions be, judging from the announcements made by the Chinese Olympic Committee?

2. Given the changes that Beijing is trying to make, what attitudes or behaviors does the Chinese Olympic Committee find most embarrassing about current Chinese society?

3. Although these announcements were public, aimed at attracting world attention, some of the language used is still opaque. What, for example, might the phrase "villages in the center of the city" refer to in the statement on civic cleanup?

6.
The Post-9/11 Era

Amartya Sen, *A World Not Neatly Divided* (November 23, 2001)

Following the September 11, 2001, terrorist attacks on the United States, some academics, politicians, and journalists framed the event as a "clash of civilizations" between Western democracy and radical Islam. They predicted that this "clash" would launch a new phase in world politics that would be dominated by cultural conflict.

From Amartya Sen, "A World Not Neatly Divided," *New York Times* editorial, November 23, 2001, A39.

Others anticipated that this conflict would replace the cold war as the framework for international relations and domestic politics. In this New York Times *editorial published shortly after the United States attacked Taliban targets in Afghanistan, Nobel Prize-winning economist Amartya Sen warned that segmenting people into separate camps, such as "the Islamic world" and "the Western world," is a simplistic — and potentially dangerous — view that ignores the diversity of the world's people.*

When people talk about clashing civilizations, as so many politicians and academics do now, they can sometimes miss the central issue. The inadequacy of this thesis begins well before we get to the question of whether civilizations must clash. The basic weakness of the theory lies in its program of categorizing people of the world according to a unique, allegedly commanding system of classification. This is problematic because civilizational categories are crude and inconsistent and also because there are other ways of seeing people (linked to politics, language, literature, class, occupation, or other affiliations).

The befuddling influence of a singular classification also traps those who dispute the thesis of a clash: To talk about "the Islamic world" or "the Western world" is already to adopt an impoverished vision of humanity as unalterably divided. In fact, civilizations are hard to partition in this way, given the diversities within each society as well as the linkages among different countries and cultures. For example, describing India as a "Hindu civilization" misses the fact that India has more Muslims than any other country except Indonesia and possibly Pakistan. It is futile to try to understand Indian art, literature, music, food, or politics without seeing the extensive interactions across barriers of religious communities. These include Hindus and Muslims, Buddhists, Jains, Sikhs, Parsees, Christians (who have been in India since at least the fourth century, well before England's conversion to Christianity), Jews (present since the fall of Jerusalem), and even atheists and agnostics. Sanskrit has a larger atheistic literature than exists in any other classical language. Speaking of India as a Hindu civilization may be comforting to the Hindu fundamentalist, but it is an odd reading of India.

A similar coarseness can be seen in the other categories invoked, like "the Islamic world." Consider Akbar and Aurangzeb, two Muslim emperors of the Mogul dynasty in India. Aurangzeb tried hard to convert Hindus into Muslims and instituted various policies in that direction, of which taxing the non-Muslims was only one example. In contrast, Akbar reveled in his multiethnic court and pluralist laws, and issued official proclamations insisting that no one "should be interfered with on account of religion" and that "anyone is to be allowed to go over to a religion that pleases him."

If a homogeneous view of Islam were to be taken, then only one of these emperors could count as a true Muslim. The Islamic fundamentalist would have no time for Akbar; prime minister Tony Blair, given his insistence that tolerance is a defining characteristic of Islam, would have to consider excommunicating Aurangzeb. I expect both Akbar and Aurangzeb would protest, and so would I. A similar crudity is present in the characterization of what is called "Western civilization." Tolerance and individual freedom have certainly been present in European history. But there is no dearth of diversity here, either. When Akbar was making his pronouncements on religious tolerance in Agra, in the 1590s, the Inquisitions were still going on; in 1600, Giordano Bruno was burned at the stake, for heresy, in Campo dei Fiori in Rome.

Dividing the world into discrete civilizations is not just crude. It propels us into the absurd belief that this partitioning is natural and necessary and must overwhelm all other ways of identifying people. That imperious view goes not only against the sentiment that "we human beings are all much the same," but also against the more plausible understanding that we are diversely different. For example, Bangladesh's split from Pakistan was not connected with religion, but with language and politics.

Each of us has many features in our self-conception. Our religion, important as it may be, cannot be an all-engulfing identity. Even a shared poverty can be a source of solidarity across the borders. The kind of division highlighted by, say, the so-called "antiglobalization" protesters — whose movement is, incidentally, one of the most globalized in the world — tries to unite the underdogs of the world economy and goes firmly against religious, national, or "civilizational" lines of division.

The main hope of harmony lies not in any imagined uniformity, but in the plurality of our identities, which cut across each other and work against sharp divisions into impenetrable civilizational camps. Political leaders who think and act in terms of sectioning off humanity into various "worlds" stand to make the world more flammable — even when their intentions are very different. They also end up, in the case of civilizations defined by religion, lending authority to religious leaders seen as spokesmen for their "worlds." In the process, other voices are muffled and other concerns silenced. The robbing of our plural identities not only reduces us; it impoverishes the world.

Discussion Questions

1. Why does Sen object to dividing the world into separate civilizations? What problems does such classification present?

2. What does Sen mean by our "plural identities"?

3. What are the particular dangers of defining separate worlds according to religion?

4. What present-day examples might support Sen's concern about defining civilizations solely along religious lines?

Comparative Questions

1. How are Zlata Filipović's experiences and those of MSF volunteers reflected in Amartya Sen's warning against dividing the world into discrete civilizations?

2. What are the similarities between the end of communism in eastern Europe (Chapter 28) and the end of apartheid in South Africa? What are the differences?

3. What comparisons can be made between the European Union's expansion and China's preparations for the 2008 Summer Olympic Games? In what ways do they reflect each region's efforts to redefine its role in the twenty-first century?

4. Compare Amartya Sen's vision of finding harmony in the "plurality of our identities" to the Truth and Reconciliation Committee's goals for attaining national unity and reconciliation in South Africa.

Acknowledgments *(continued from p. iv)*

Chapter 14
Defending Native Humanity: Bartolomé de Las Cases, *In Defense of the Indians*, c. 1548–1550. From *In Defense of the Indians* (pp. 41–46), translated by Stafford Poole. Copyright © 1974 by Northern Illinois University Press. Used with permission of Northern Illinois University Press.

Reforming Christianity: John Calvin, *Articles Concerning Predestination* and *The Necessity of Reforming the Church*, c. 1560 and 1543. From Calvin: *Theological Treatises*, vol. 22 (pp. 188–91), translated by The Rev. J. K. S. Reid. Copyright © 1954 by The Westminster Press. Reprinted by permission of Westminster John Know Press.

Responding to Reformation: Saint Ignatius of Loyola, *A New Kind of Catholicism*, 1546, 1549, 1553. From *Saint Ignatius of Loyola, Personal Writings: Reminiscences, Spiritual Diary, Select Letters, Including the Text of the Spiritual Exercises* (pp. 165–66, 230, 233–34, 257, 259, 262–63), edited and translated by Joseph A. Munitiz and Philip Endean (Penguin Classics, 1996). Copyright © 1996 by Joseph A. Munitiz and Philip Endean. Reprinted by permission of Penguin Books, Ltd. (UK).

Chapter 15
Legislating Tolerance: Henry IV, *Edict of Nantes*, 1598. From English text of "The Edict" as in Edmund Everard, *The Great Pressures and Grievances of the Protestants in France*, London 1681, appendix 4, in *The Assassinations of Henry IV*, translated by Joan Spencer. Copyright © 1964 Editions Gallimard, Paris. Reprinted by permission on Editions Gallimard.

Barbarians All: Michel de Montaigne, *Of Cannibals*, 1580s. From *Selected Essays of Montaigne* (pp. 74, 77–79, 82–84), by Michel de Montaigne, translated by C. Cotton, W. C. Hazlit, edited by Blanchard Bates. Copyright © 1949 by Random House, Inc. Used by permission of Random House, Inc. For on-line information about other Random House, Inc. books and authors, see the Internet website @ www.randomhouse.com.

The Scientific Challenge: Galileo, *Letter to the Grand Duchess Christina*, 1615. From *Discoveries and Opinions of Galileo* (pp. 175–86), by Galileo Galilei, translated by Stillman Drake. Copyright © 1957 by Stillman Drake. Used by permission of Doubleday, a division of Random House, Inc.

The Persecution of Witches: *The Trail of Suzanne Gaudry*, 1652. From *Witchcraft in Europe, 1100–1700: A Documentary History* (pp. 266–75), edited by Alan C. Kors and Edward Peters. Copyright © 1972 by University of Pennsylvania Press. Reprinted by permission of the University of Pennsylvania Press.

Chapter 16
Civil War and Social Contract: Thomas Hobbes, *Leviathan*, 1651. From www.uoregon.edu/renascenceditions (p.d.)

The Consent of the Governed: John Locke, *The Second Treatise of Government*, 1690. From www.ilt.columbia.edu/academic/digitexts/locke (p.d.).

Opposing Serfdom: Ludwig Fabritius, *The Revolt of Stenka Razin*, 1670. From *Russia under Western Eyes*, 1517–1825 (pp. 120–23), edited by Anthony Glenn Cross. Published by St. Martin's Press (1971).

Chapter 17
A "Sober and Wholesome Drink": *A Brief Description of the Excellent Vertues of That Sober and Wholesome Drink, Called Coffee*, 1674. *Eighteenth-Century Coffee-House Culture*, vol. 1,

Restoration Satire (pp. 129), edited by Markman Ellis. Copyright © 2006. Reproduced from *Eighteenth-Century Coffee-House Culture* with the permission of Pickering & Chatto Publishers.

In Defense of Miliary Action: Tsar Peter I, *Letter to His Son, Alexei*, October 11, 1715 and *Alexei's Response*, October 31, 1715. From "Correspondence between Peter and Alexis, 1715–1717" in *A Source Book for Russian History from Early Times to 1917*, vol. II (pp. 338–39), edited by George Vernadsky. Copyright © 1972 by Yale University Press. Reprinted by permission of Yale University Press.

Questioning Women's Submission: Mary Astell, *Reflections upon Marriage*, 1706. From *The First English Feminist: Reflections Upon Marriage and Other Writings* (pp. 69–76), edited and introduced by Bridget Hill. Copyright © 1986 by St. Martin's Press. Reprinted by permission of St. Martin's Press.

Chapter 18

An Enchanted Worker: Jacques-Louis Ménétra, *Journal of My Life*, 1764–1802. Excerpt from *Journal of My Life* (pp. 129–30), introduction by Daniel Roche and translated by Arthur Goldhammer. Copyright © 1986 by Columbia University Press. Reprinted by permission of Columbia University Press.

Reforming Law: Cesare Beccaria, *On Crimes and Punishments*, 1764. From *On Crimes and Punishments and Other Writings* (pp. 39–44), edited by Richard Bellamy. Copyright © 1995 by Cambridge University Press. Reprinted with the permission of Cambridge University Press.

Enlightened Monarchy: Frederick II, *Political Testament*, 1752. From *Europe in Review*, edited by George L. Mosse, Rondo E. Cameron, Henry Bertram Hill and Michael B. Petrovich. Copyright © 1957, Rand McNally and Company, pp. 111–12.

Chapter 19

Defining the Nation: Abbé Sieyès, *What Is the Third Estate?*, 1789. From *The French Revolution and Human Rights: A Brief Documentary History* (pp. 65–70), edited and translated by Lynn Hunt. Copyright © 1996 by Lynn Hunt. Reprinted by permission of Bedford/St. Martin's.

Defending Terror: Maximilien Robespierre, *Report on the Principles of Political Morality*, 1794. From *The Ninth of Thermidor: The Fall of Robespierre* (pp. 33–36, 38–39), edited by Richrd Bienvenu. Copyright © 1968 by Oxford University Press. Reprinted by permission of Oxford University Press.

Dissent on Trial: Olympe de Gouges, *Letters on the Trial*, 1793. From *Women in Revolutionary Paris, 1789–1795: Selected Documents Translated With Notes and Commentary* (pp. 103–04, 169–72), translated with notes and commentary by Darline Gay Levy, Harriet Branson Applewhite and Mary Durham Johnson. Copyright © 1979 by the Board of Trustees of the University of Illinois. Used by permission of the editors and the University of Illinois Press.

Liberty for All?: Françoise Dominique Toussaint L'Ouverture, *Revolution in the Colonies*, 1794–1795. From *Toussaint L'Ouverture à Travers sa Correspondance* (1794–1798) by Gérard M. Lauent (pp. 103–04, 169–72), (Madrid, 1953), translated by Katharine J. Lualdi.

Chapter 20

Napoleon in Egypt: *The Chronicle of Abd al-Rahman al-Jabartî*. From *Napoleon in Egypt: Al Jabartî's Chronicle of the French Occupation*, 1798 (pp. 24–33), by Markus Wiener and translated by Shmuel Moreh. Copyright © 1993. Reprinted by permission of Brill.

The Conservative Order: Prince Klemens von Metternich, *Results of the Congress at Laybach*, 1821. From *Memoirs of Prince Metternich*, vol. 3, 1815–1829 (pp. 535–39), edited by Richard Metternich and translated by Mrs. Alexander Napier. Copyright © 1970 by Howard Fertig Publishing, Inc., reprint of 1881 edition. (p.d.)

Challenge to Autocracy: Peter Kakhovsky, *The Decembrist Insurrection in Russia*, 1825. From *The First Russian Revolution, 1825* (pp. 274–77), edited by Anatole G. Mazour. Copyright © 1937 by the Board of the Leland Stanford Junior University. Renewed 1964 by Anatole Mazour. Used with permission of Stanford University. www.sup.org. All rights reserved.

The Romatic Imagination: John Keats, *Letter to Benjamin Bailey*, 1817. Reprinted by permission of the publisher from *The Letters of John Keats, 1814–1821*, vol. 1 (pp. 184–85), edited by Hyder Edward Rollins, Cambridge, Mass.: Harvard University Press. Copyright © 1958 by the President and Fellows of Harvard College. Reprinted by permission of Harvard University Press.

Chapter 21

Establishing New Work Habits: *Factory Rules in Berlin*, 1844. From *Documents of European Economic History*: vol. I: *The Process of Industrialization 1750–1870* (pp. 534–36), by Sidney Pollard and C. Holmes. Copyright © 1968 by St. Martin's Press, Inc. Reprinted by permission of St. Martin's Press, Inc.

What is the Proletariat?: Friedrich Engels, *Draft of a Communist Confession of Faith*, 1847. From Karl Marx and Frederick Engels, *Collected Works*. Copyright © 1975, Vol 6, 96–103. Reprinted by permission of International Publishers Company, NY.

The Poetry of Freedom: Sándor Petofi, "*National Song*" of Hungary, 1848. From *Russia, Austria-Hungary, The Balkan States and Turkey: The World's Story. A History of the World in Story, Song, and Art*, vol. VI, edited by Eva March Tappan. Published by Houghton Mifflin, Boston: 1914, pp. 408–10. (p.d.)

Imperialism and Opium: Commissioner Lin, *Letter to Queen Victoria*, 1839. From *Modern Asia and Africa*, (pp. 113–18), edited by William H. McNeill and Mitsuko Iriye. Copyright © 1971 by William H. McNeill and Mitsuko Iriye, eds., pp. 113–18. Published by Oxford University Press (1971).

Chapter 22

Fighting for Italian Nationalism: Camillo di Cavour, *Letter to King Victor Emmanuel*, July 24, 1858. From *The Making of Italy, 1796–1870* (pp. 238–42), edited by Denis Mack Smith. Copyright 1968 by Harper & Row.

Realpolitik and Otto von Bismarck: Rudolf von Ihering, *Two Letters*, 1866. From *Germany in the Age of Bismarck* (pp. 110–13), by Walter Michael Simon. Copyright © 1968 by Walter Michael Simon. Reprinted by permission of Taylor and Francis, Books, U.K.

Social Evolution: Walter Bagehot, *Physics and Politics*, 1872. From *Physics and Politics* (pp. 41–44, 49), edited with an introduction by Roger Kimball. Copyright © 1873 by D. Appleton and Co., 1999 by Ivan R. Dee, Publisher. (p.d.)

Chapter 23

Defending Conquest: Jules Ferry, *Speech before the French National Assemby*, 1883. From *Modern Imperialism: Western Overseas Expansion and Its Aftermath, 1776–1965* (pp. 69–74), edited by Ralph A. Austin. Copyright © 1969 by D. C. Heath, Reprinted by permission of R.A. Austin.

The Advance of Unionism: Margaret Bondfield, *A Life's Work*, 1948. Extract from "The Shop Girl" in *A Life's Work* (pp. 27–29, 36). Copyright © 1948 by the Hutchinson & Co., Ltd. Reprinted by permission of The Random House Group Ltd.

Artistic Expression: Edgar Degas, *Notebooks*, 1863–1884. From *Impressionism and Post-Impressionism*, 1874–1904, edited by Linda Nochlin. Published by Prentice-Hall (1966): 61–63. Reprinted by permission of the author.

Chapter 24

"God Is Dead": Friedrich Nietzsche, *The Gay Science*, 1882. From *The Gay Science— With a Prelude in Rhymes and an Appendix of Songs* by Friedrich Nietzsche, pp. 163–64, 180–82, 228–29, 273–74. Copyright © 1974. Used with permission of Random House, Inc.

The Dreyfus Affair: Emile Zola, *"J'accuse!"* January 13, 1898. Excerpted from *The Dreyfus Affair, "J'Accuse" and Other Writings* by Alain Pagen, ed. Translation by Eleanor Levieux. Copyright © 1996. pp. 43–47, 50–53. Reprinted by permission of Yale University Press.

Rising Up against Western Imperialism: The I-ho-ch'uan (Boxers), *The Boxers Demand Death for All "Foreign Devils,"* 1900. From *The Imperialism Reader: Documents and Readings on Modern Expansionism* by Louis L. Snyder, ed. Published by Van Norstrand (1962), pp. 322–23.

Tapping the Human Psche: Sigmund Freud, *The Interpretation of Deams*, 1990. From *The Basic Writings of Sigmund Freud* translated and edited by A. A. Brill. By Permission.

Chapter 25.

The Horrors of War: Siegfried Sasson, "Counter-Attack," From *Collected Poems of Siegfried Sasson* by Siegfried Sasson. Copyright © 1918, 1920 by E. P. Dutton. Copyright © 1936, 1946, 1947, 1948 by Siegfried Sasson. Used by permission of Viking Penguin, a divison of Penguin Group (USA) Inc. Copyright Siegfried Sassoon by kind permission of the Estate of George Sassoon.

Mobilizing for Total War: L. Doriat, *Women on the Home Front*, 1917. Excerpt from *Lines of Fire: Women Writers of World War I* by Margaret R. Higonnet, editor, pp. 129–31. Copyright © 1999 Margaret R. Higonnet. Reprinted by permission of Sanford J. Greenberger, Inc.

Revolutionary Marxism Defended: Vladimir Ilyich Lenin, *Letter to Nikolai Aleksandrovich Rozhkov*, January 29, 1919. From *The Unknown Lenin: From the Secret Archive* by Richard Pipes, editor, pp. 62–63. Copyright © 1999 Yale University Press. Reprinted by permission of the publisher.

Estalishing Fascism in Italy: Benito Mussolini, *The Doctrine of Fascism*, 1932. From "Fundamental Ideas" in *The Social and Political Doctrines of Contemporary Europe*, edited and translated by Michael Oakeshott. Copyright © 1947, pp. 164–79. Reprinted with permission of Cambridge University Press.

A New Form of Anti-Semitism: Adolf Hitler, *Mein Kampf*, 1925. From *Mein Kampf*, translated by Ralph Manheim. Copyright © 1999, pp. 290, 300, 303, 326, 643, 646, 649, 652–53. Reprinted by permission of Houghton Mifflin Copmany. All rights reserved.

Chapter 26.

Socialist Nationalism: Joseph Goebbels, *Nazi Propaganda Pamphlet*, 1930. From *Documents of German History*, edited by Louis L. Snyder, pp. 414–16. Copyright © 1958 by Rutgers, the State University. Reprinted by permission of Rutgers University Press.

The Spanish Civil War: Isadora Dolores Ibárruri Gómez, *La Pasionaria's Farewell Address*, November 1, 1938. From Online Journal and Multimedia Companion to Cary Nelson, editor *Anthology of Modern American Poetry*. www.english.uiuc.edu. Reprinted with permission.

The Final Solution: Sam Bankhalter and Hinda Kibort, *Memories of the Holocaust*, 1938–1945. From *Witnesses to the Holocaust: An Oral History* by Rhoda G. Lewin. Copyright © 1990 Twayne Publishers. Reprinted with the permission of the Gale Group, a division of Thomson Learning: www.thomsonrights.com. Fax 800-730-2215.

Atomic Catastrophe: Michihiko Hachiya, *Hiroshima Diary*, August 7, 1945. Excerpt from *Hiroshima Diary: The Journal of a Japanese Physician, August 6-September 30, 1945* by Michihiko Hachiya, translated and edited by Warner Wells, M.D. Copyright © 1955 by the University of North Carolina Press. Renewed 1983 by Warner Wells. Foreword by John W. Dower. © 1995 by the University of North Carolina Press. Used by permission of the publisher.

Chapter 27

Throwing Off Colonialism: Ho Chi Minh, *Declaration of Independence of the Republic of Vietnam*, 1945. From *Conflict in Indo-China and International Repercussions: A Documentary History, 1945–1955* by Allan B. Cole, ed, pp. 20–21. Copyright © 1956. Used by permission of Cornell University Press.

The Condition of Modern Women: Simone de Beauvoir, *The Second Sex*, 1949. From *The Second Sex*, edited and translated by H.M. Parshley. Copyright © 1952 and renewed 1980 by Alfred A. Knopf, a division of Random House, Inc. Used with permission of Alfred A. Knopf, a division of Random House, Inc.

The Hungarian Uprising: Béla Lipták, *Birth of MEFESZ*, 1956. From *A Testament of Revolution* by Béla Lipták, pp. 25–29. Copyright © 2001. Reprinted by permission of Texas A&M University Press.

Chapter 28

Prague Spring: Josef Smrkovský, *What Lies Ahead*, February 9, 1968. From *The Prague Spring 1968: A National Security Archive Documents Reader* by Jaromir Navratil, editor, pp. 45–50. Copyright © 1998. Reprinted by permission of The Central European Press.

A Revolutionary Time: *Student Voices of Protest*, 1968. From *A Student Generation in Revolt* by Ronald Fraser et al. Copyright © 1988 by Ronald Fraser, pp. 9–12. Reprinted by permission of Pantheon Books, a division of Random House, Inc. and courtesy of Darhansoff, Verrill, Feldman Literary Agents.

Facing Terrorism: Jacques Chirac, *New French Antiterrorist Laws*, September 14, 1986. From *A Documentary History* by Bruce Maxwell. In *CQ Press*, 2003: 85–87. Copyright © 2003 CQ Press, Inc. Reprinted by permission of the publisher.

Debating Change in the Soviet Union: Glasnost *and the Soviet Press*, 1988. From *Gorbachev and Glasnost: Viewpoints from the Soviet Press* by Isaac J. Tarasulo, editor. Copyright © 1989 by Scholarly Resources, Inc. Published by Rowman & Littlefield Publishers, Incorporated. Reproduced with permission of Scholarly Resources, Inc. in the format Textbook via Copyright Clearance Center.

Chapter 29

Ethnic Cleansing: *The Diary of Zlata Filipović*, October 6, 1991–June 29, 1992. From *Zlata's Diary: A Child's Life in Sarajevo* translated by Christina Pribichevich-Zoric. Copyright © 1994 Editions Robert Laffont/Fixot, pp. 3, 6, 7, 9–11, 18, 26–35, 41–43, 46–48, 51–58, 65–66. Used by permission of Viking Penguin, a division of Penguin Group (USA) Inc.

Doctors Without Borders: Joelle Tanguy and Fiona Terry, *On Humanitarian Responsibility*, December 12, 1999. Adapted from their article originally published in *Ethics & International Affairs*, vol. 13, 1999. Published by the Carnegie Council on Ethics and International Affairs. www.ccceia.org. Reprinted by permission of Blackwell Publishing Ltd.

An End to Apartheid: African National Congress, *Introductory Statement to the Truth and Reconciliation Commission*, August 19, 1996. From African National Congress's Web site: www.anc.org.

China in the Global Age: Chinese Olympic Committee: *Announcements on Preparations for the 2008 Summer Olympic Games*, 2004–2007.Beijing Organizing Committee for the Games of the XXIX Olympiad. Chinese Olympic Committee.

The Post- 9/11 Era: Amartya Sen, *A World Not Neatly Divided*, November 23, 2001. From *The New York Times* editorial page, A39. Copyright © 2001 by The New York Times Company. Reprinted with permission.